RESEARCH IN ORGANIZATIONAL BEHAVIOR

Volume 4 • 1982

RESEARCH IN ORGANIZATIONAL BEHAVIOR

An Annual Series of Analytical Essays and Critical Reviews

Editors: **BARRY M. STAW**
School of Business Administration
University of California, Berkeley

L. L. CUMMINGS
Kellogg Graduate School of Management
Northwestern University

VOLUME 4 • 1982

 JAI PRESS INC.

Greenwich, Connecticut   *London, England*

CONTENTS

LIST OF CONTRIBUTORS

Howard Aldrich

New York School of Labor
and Industrial Relations
Cornell University

John Bigelow

School of Business
Oregon State University

John Freeman

School of Business Administration
University of California,
Berkeley

David W. Gerbing

Department of Psychology
Baylor University

John E. Hunter

Department of Psychology
Michigan State University

Gary Johns

Faculty of Commerce and
Administration, Concordia
University

Marshall W. Meyer

Department of Sociology
University of California,
Riverside

Susan Mueller

New York School of Labor
and Industrial Relations
Cornell University

Nigel Nicholson

MRC Social and
Applied Psychology Unit
University of Sheffield

William Notz

Faculty of Administrative
Studies, University of Manitoba

Paul Salipante

School of Management
Case Western Reserve University

George Strauss

Institute of Industrial Relations
University of California,
Berkeley

EDITORIAL STATEMENT

This volume of *Research in Organizational Behavior* spans recent developments in several areas of the field. The chapters represented here could be categorized as macro, micro and methodological; they could also be grouped by whether they are addressing a new problem for the field or recasting an older issue in a new way.

The volume begins with two essays which address the question of why organizations possess the form and structure they do. Both of these papers take a dramatic turn from the traditional literature on structure by using a social-evolutionary model of organizations. John Freeman shows how natural selection processes affect the distribution of organizational characteristics over time via the entry and exit of firms from an industry. Howard Aldrich then shows how organizational forms are the evolutionary product of social, political and economic forces, and how changes in these factors provide selection criteria which, in turn, affect the distribution of organizational characteristics.

The next three chapters focus on some well-established questions in organizational research, but they do so by reconceptualizing the variables involved. Marshall Meyer traces the history of debate on bureaucratic versus profit forms of organization, concentrating on the efficiency, growth and control of these alternative systems. Gary Johns and Nigel Nicholson examine the whole question of what absenteeism is, and, by specifying a series of new propositions, they virtually re-open the subject for fresh research. Finally, George Strauss takes the reader on a world-wide tour of recent research on worker participation, providing many thought-provoking questions about the way we use the construct of participation as well as the way we research the issue

The volume closes with two chapters on the methodology of organizational research. Jack Hunter and David Gerbing provide a broad summary and critique of current measurement and theory construction techniques. They outline improvements in a measurement model using confirmatory factor analysis and causal modeling using path-analytic methods. The final chapter by Paul Salipante, William Notz and John Bigelow proposes a new method of gathering and presenting research findings in literature reviews. By classifying research findings in a matrix of design strengths and weaknesses, we may be better able to isolate research blind-spots as well as to assess better our confidence in cumulative results.

We believe this volume fits well the series' original aim of taking the field in new directions and of reformulating older research issues. The chapters were written by an invited group of scholars who wished to develop their ideas in a more complete way than is typically available in the journals. The utility and impact of these essays will, as with previous volumes in the series, be determined by the reactions of our present and future colleagues.

Barry M. Staw
Berkeley, California

L. L. Cummings
Evanston, Illinois

ORGANIZATIONAL LIFE CYCLES AND NATURAL SELECTION PROCESSES

John Freeman

ABSTRACT

"Life cycles processes" and "natural selection processes" are defined. Arguments are advanced that are intended to establish that assumptions about the workings of one kind of process are usually presumed in the analysis of the other. The role of organizational innovation in the two kinds of processes is considered and the relationship of both to "political economy" approaches for studying organizations is analyzed.

Research in Organizational Behavior, Vol. 4, pages 1–32
Copyright © 1982 by JAI Press Inc.
All rights of reproduction in any form reserved.
ISBN: 0-89232-147-4

INTRODUCTION

In this article we consider the intimate relationship between natural selection processes manifested by organizational populations and organizational life cycles. The thesis of this article is that knowledge of the former is generally presumed for analysis of the latter. By "life cycle process" we mean the patterns over time through which new organizations come into being, change, and disappear. "Natural selection" refers to the differential reproduction and survival of organizations depending on relative competitive advantages.

We explore the relationship between these two processes first by considering the logic of natural selection. It is quite different from the usual mode of social science theorizing. Because this logic is different, many methodological problems arise that are not ordinarily the subject of attention and consequently have not been solved during the course of previous empirical research. Next, we consider how new organizational forms are developed. It seems useful to distinguish between creating a new form of organization and copying an already-existing form. The latter issue is important, however, because it represents one side of the root issue in studying population dynamics—*net mortality,* which is the relative number of deaths and births.

In considering the relationship between the two forms of organizational birth—creating new forms and copying existing forms—we are led to an examination of entrepreneurship and the employment relationship. Entrepreneurs rarely begin without extensive experience in similar kinds of organizational activity. Consequently, the decision to leave one's current organization and to start another is in part a question of the structure, operating procedures, and incentives employed by the current employer. This suggests that it may prove fruitful to consider entrepreneurship as an *organizationally generated* phenomenon, not simply as a mode of behaving based on psychological predispositions.

The last two issues we consider are density dependence and the relationship between natural selection processes and the political economy of organizations. Density dependent selection refers to the competitive relationships between organizational populations as the numbers of organizations expand in a finite resource space. These competitive relationships are reflected in the various devices that individual organizations employ to manage their environments. It is argued that such theories of resource distribution and structure of individual organizations supply a view of organizations that, far from being an alternative to natural selection models, is a complement. The differences lie more in where one's attention is focused than in how one sees organizations as operating. In principle there is no reason why one cannot freely shift from one kind of analysis to the other.

NATURAL SELECTION LOGIC

Two important conceptual properties of natural selection processes should be noted straight away. First, natural selection presumes a population logic. Although selection always involves things that happen to individuals, the effort is directed toward understanding the range of variation in morphological characteristics as displayed in some population or set of populations. Just as biological ecologists do not often concern themselves with the behavior of individual organisms (the province of animal ethologists for the most part), organizational ecologists do not concern themselves with individual firms.

The second conceptual property of natural selection theories is that they are dynamic. One explains the pattern of variation observable at one point in time through reference to a theory that considers the time path of some set of variables. Viewing organizations this way will prove fruitful to the extent that equilibrium assumptions are unrealistic. The usual way of studying organizational structures is to presume that at any given point in time the structure is in tune with its environment. Shocks to the organizational system introduced by technological or environmental changes have worked themselves out so that their causal effects have already been manifested. A static form of analysis is therefore appropriate. The dynamic quality of natural selection theories focuses attention on the speed with which various processes occur and the lag structures that result.[1]

Because most organizational theory assumes such equilibria, researchers have not been led to study organizations over time. It is rare to see empirical studies of change processes at all. Birth and death of organizations is not commonly studied in detail. Consequently not much attention has been given to the obvious fact that the different indicators of organizational life do not occur simultaneously. "Brain death" and "heart death" have obvious parallels in organizations. Similarly, the founding process is not an instantaneous event. It is actually a series of events such as signing partnership papers, leasing space, hiring employees, organizing them and turning out (and shipping) the first product.

There are parallels at the population level. It is common for people not intimately involved in selection modeling to view the "survival of the fittest" as being concerned entirely with differential rates of mortality. In fact, the issue is *net* mortality: deaths relative to births. In an earlier article (Hannan and Freeman, 1977), emphasis was placed on differential rates of mortality because the failure of organizations as a source of variation had been almost completely ignored.

Most organizations theorists assume that survival is not problematic. For example, Starbuck (1965, p. 464), in commenting on some assertions by Barnard on the importance of efficiency, argued as follows:

> The problem with a statement like Barnard's is that it implies that survival is difficult, and hence that a relatively high level of efficiency is required. This can soon lead to a "survival of the fittest" point of view. The fact of the matter is that nearly all organizations, nearly all of the time, find survival easy.

It is, of course, an empirical question whether most organizations find survival easy or whether failure is a likely prospect. If survival is "easy" we would expect to find most firms surviving most of the time. Although there is not a large amount of empirical research on the subject, it is generally assumed that large organizations fail less often than small organizations. If we define "birth" as appearance in a population defined as firms with 500 or more employees in a particular industry, and "death" the movement out of that population, we can see that even large populations are quite volatile.

The first thing to notice in Table 1. is that the proportion of all business firms with at least 500 employees is quite small: less than 1 percent of the total in 1972. Of the total 5238 large firms in 1967, 17.8 percent or some 932 disappear in the ensuing 5 years. These firms are replaced and their number is augmented by 258. It is true that some of these "births" are movements over the 500-employee boundary (i.e., growth). It is also true that acquisitions are counted as disappearances in this table. It is difficult to see, however, that survival is easy when the numbers of appearances and disappearances in the population over 5 years sum to half the population size at the beginning of the period (i.e., VOL = .549 for the full population).

Aldrich (1979, pp. 36–37) provides data on new and discontinued businesses not subject to the size limitations in Table 1. He shows that between 1940 and 1962 some 3,390,000 new firms were created in the United States, and some 2,847,000 firms were discontinued. When we divide these figures by 22, to get the yearly average, and divide again by 5,000,000 (the approximate number of firms in 1972 from Table 1), we obtain an approximation of the yearly VOL index: .057. This means that for every 100 firms in existence at the beginning of each year, slightly fewer than three disappear, and slightly more than three are founded. So whereas 3.1 percent of the large firms in Table 1 fail in the 5-year period covered by the table, a similar number fail *yearly* when all firms are considered.

The assertion that smaller and younger organizations experience more volatile demographics is supported in studies by Wedervang (1965) and Churchill (1955) on Norwegian and United States firms. Wedervang (1965, p. 175) found that disentangling the effects of age and size was difficult but that age had more pronounced effects. Work under way by the author and his colleagues on labor unions, semiconductor firms, and

Table 1. The Demography of Large Firms: 1967–1972[a]

	1967	1972								
	No. Firms >500	% Survive	% Acquired Same Ind.	Other Ind.	% Out of Bus.	Mort.	Birth	Vol[b]	No. Firms >500	Firms Any Size
Minerals	88	79.6	6.8	12.5	1.1	9.2	27	.411	81	18,199
Construction	298	85.2	2.0	6.4	6.4	44.1	159	.682	359	893,933
Wholesale	177	82.5	2.2	13.0	2.3	31.0	135	.938	234	328,535
Retail	709	84.0	5.6	7.9	2.4	113.4	329	.624	861	1,845,307
Service	460	84.2	4.8	6.3	4.7	72.7	229	.656	555	1,675,717
Manufacturing	3506	81.3	5.8	9.9	2.9	655.6	1066	.491	3406	265,052
All	5238	82.2	5.4	9.3	3.1	932.4	1945	.549	5496	5,026,743

[a] Sources: U.S. Bureau of the Census, 1972 ENTERPRISE STATISTICS "General Report on Industrial Organization," (ES72-1). Sept., 1972. Table 5. "Company Statistics by Employment Class Size: 1972" (pp. 142–213) and Table 9. "Changes in Classification Status of Large Companies Between 1967 and 1972" (pp. 316–324).

[b] VOL is an index of volatility that equals births plus deaths divided by 1967 number of firms with more than 500 employees.

restaurants in the United States shows similar results. Wedervang also found that differences between sole proprietorships, partnerships, and corporations (which he called "companies") were small. Finally, he found pronounced effects of the business cycle; and, most interestingly, he found that booms and busts had stronger effects on failure rates than on entry rates.

Comparing the United States and Norway, Wedervang (1965, pp. 172–173) presented the statistics given in Table 2. The high rates overall, and the particularly high rates among U.S. firms in the first rate beg explanation. Such explanation is not readily forthcoming from organization theory.

Work by Meyer (1980) shows that rates of reorganization among government agencies are higher than one would expect from assertions such as Starbuck's. Because local government units seldom actually disband, reorganization is probably as close as we can come to a comparable phenomenon. For Chicago, Detroit, and Philadelphia, department and sections of city government were studied over a period of 85 years. Yearly rates of formation and dissolution for divisions range from 6 to 10 percent, and for sections of divisions, from 13 to 24 percent. Again, the point here is that organizations fail at rates that are too high to support the contention that survival is easy.

In arguing that population ecology cannot be used to explain everything, Aldrich and Pfeffer (1976) agree that this approach is useful mainly for studying small and young organizations. Scott (1981, pp. 203–205) makes a similar assertion. Although one would be foolish to argue that any one way of studying organizations is optimal for every purpose, limiting this approach to the study of small and young organizations is unnecessary. Long-living organizations, like long-living organisms, can be studied with a natural selection logic to good effect if the number of organizations or the time span of the study is expanded.

An additional observation along these lines is rooted in Stinchcombe's (1965) paper: given some nonnegligible level of inertia, conditions prevalent at the time of founding leave their stamp on the organization throughout its life. In the extreme, when inertia is very high, current

Table 2. Failure Rates of Business Firms in the United States
and Norway

	United States	Norway
Yearly failures in first 3 years	17.7%	6.5 %
Yearly failures between 4 and 7 years	8.0%	5.75%

technological and environmental conditions have nothing to do with explaining the current structure. Rather, one must look to those characteristics at the time of founding, when the organization was smaller than it likely is today. Simple causal theories assume variations in independent variables are followed in more or less short order by variations in dependent variables. Long lags between the two lead to chicken and egg problems. Selection theories pose particularly difficult problems of this kind.

Explanation of organizational variability through selection logic is confusing to some because the usual logic is turned on its head. Suppose we were studying the populations of men's liberal arts colleges and women's liberal arts colleges during the 1960s and 1970s. We would see that the women's colleges were dying at a much more rapid rate than the men's colleges. The question that comes immediately to mind is why do the men's schools compete successfully, whereas the women's schools do not? A difference of some importance is the fact that men's colleges are more likely to be endowed than are women's colleges. But organizations researchers are not often simply interested in the effects of endowment size on the probability of failure. One would more likely be interested in what it is about the environment that makes endowment size important. That is, in what environmental circumstances is endowment important? An answer is that when other sources of funding are tight, endowment becomes particularly important. In the 1960s and 1970s, then, when funding became increasingly hard to come by, men's colleges out-competed women's colleges because they were more likely to be heavily endowed.

Obviously, it is always better to have a large endowment than a small one. And just as obviously, when times are difficult more organizations of all kinds will fail than when the funding environment is munificent. It is the combination of the two that is most interesting for its effect on the mix of colleges observed in the early 1980s. The question, then, is why are there so many more men's schools around than women's schools?

To see how such explanations work in biology, consider the following example (taken from Pianka, 1978, p. 216). It shows how selection logic works in a biological research setting (Table 3).

In an elegant series of experiments, Kettlewell made reciprocal transfers of pale moths from a nonpolluted woods with melanic moths from a polluted area. These moths, along with resident moths occurring at each locality, were marked with a tiny inconspicuous paint spot beneath their wings, and attempts were made to recapture them on later days. As expected, pale moths had lower survivorship in the polluted woods and melanic moths had lower survivorship in clean, lichen-covered forests. Moreover, Kettlewell actually observed foraging birds catching mismatched moths!

Table 3. Numbers of Typical and Melanic Marked Moths
(*Biston betularia*) Released and Recaptured in a Polluted Woods near
Birmingham and an Unpolluted Woods near Dorset

	Polluted Woods	Nonpolluted Woods	Total
Numbers of Marked Moths Released			
Typical	64	496	560
Melanic	154	473	627
Total	218	969	1187
Number Recaptured			
Typical	16 (25%)	62 (12.5%)	78 (14%)
Melanic	82 (53%)	30 (6.34%)	112 (18%)
Total	98 (45%)	92 (9.5%)	190 (32%)

The general purpose of this research is to explain the patterns of coloration one observes among moths in particular and animals in general. The explanation lies in the ability of the moth to avoid predation by camouflage. Notice that the "main effects" of coloration and presence/absence of pollution are quite strong but irrelevant. It is the difference in the differences of proportion surviving on which the crucial inference is based, the *interaction effect.*

The rate of founding or failure over time is properly interpreted relative to the rates of comparable organizational forms. The context is the rarity or commonness of the trait being selected for or against. A failure rate of only 1 or 2 percent per year can have a profound effect on the pattern of variation if those failures are concentrated in a particular subpopulation. For example, we might have three forms: A, B, and C. Suppose they start out as equally common. About 2 percent of the organizations fail each year, and all of these are of type C. Because the C form is not doing well, no new ones are started. At the end of 10 years, the distribution would be approximately 43, 43, and 13 percent for A, B, and C, respectively. Aside from the obviously important impact the process has on the distribution, even with a small yearly rate of failure and replacement, the significance of a particular pattern should be interpreted in theoretical context. Perhaps these are business firms owned by ethnic minorities. Perhaps they are research universities. Depending on the question being asked, a modest shift in the distribution may be highly informative.

Up to this point our argument has stressed the interaction effects between environmental characteristics and organizational characteristics as they jointly affect the probability of survival of organizations. It should be clear, however, that selection logic can explain variation in organizational characteristics that do not themselves have survival implications: For example, family firms derive part of their competitive advantage in small business from the flexible, cheap, and reliable labor supply provided by family structure. Mobility patterns for family and nonfamily members are likely to be quite different. Nonfamily employees may find promotion above a certain level to be impossible. This might have survival implications under some circumstances, but whether it does or does not, we would expect a correlation between the incidence of blocked mobility and family form of ownership. In environments where family firms are at a competitive advantage, we would expect to see more of them and, in consequence, more blocked mobility across the population of organizations.

In general, then, researchers who build selection models study the covariation of a large number of organizational features, some of which have direct and obvious survival advantages or disadvantages in specific environments. Others have derivative survival implications in that they support or make possible the characteristics of primary interest. Finally, some have no survival implications at all or have implications that are so remote as to be irrelevant from the point of view of survival. They are carried along as excess baggage by the variables relevant to survival. For many researchers, however, survival of organizations or their failure to survive is uninteresting. Variables such as the level of blocked mobility may be the important substantive issue to be explained.

The bag of variables that covary as a result of differential net mortality is what we call an *organizational form*. We turn now to the development of new forms and then to their diffusion through population expansion, which we term "proliferation" (Brittain and Freeman, 1980).

INNOVATION: THE DEVELOPMENT OF NEW FORMS

Probably the most important difference between natural selection approaches to the study of organizations and approaches featuring gradual adaptation, such as suggested by contingency theory, is that natural selection presumes that one can identify *populations* of organizations whose demographics can be studied. This requires a rule for including or excluding organizations and a theoretical rationale for the use of that rule. In other words, a species analog must be developed. Researchers may find such an analog to be more or less permanently useful, or they may construct new ones for each research issue.

Just as we need a rule to define the spatial boundaries of organizational populations, we need a boundary in time. We have to construct a rule to tell us when an organization has left the population. The reader no doubt was provoked to such considerations by the discussion of Table 1 in which movement over a size boundary was the rule employed. The problem with such a rule is that it appears to be an arbitrary point on a continuum of change.

If population thinking is going to tell us things we would not discover by studying individual organizations, organizational change must have some discontinuous properties. Suppose all organizations are gradually adjusting to their environments all the time. Churches gradually transform themselves into gas stations and universities modify their operations, dropping departments and adding foundaries so that they slowly turn themselves into steel mills. One would probably have to look very hard to see anything that could unambiguously be called a "church" or a "university." If organizations are very plastic and change in the continuous manner just described, categorizing them in a meaningful way will prove difficult because they will tend to drop out of the categories. However, they must change very slowly indeed if one is to develop sets of categories that are themselves generally and permanently useful. The assumption under which this article is written is that most organizations are somewhat plastic, but that their level of plasticity falls somewhere between the very high level that would preclude meaningful ecological analysis and the very low level that would make useful large scale permanent classificatory schemes like those employed by biologists.

There are two general methods for developing an operational definition of an organizational form (McKelvey, 1980). First, one can pursue a *naturalist* strategy and develop classification schemes based upon the organizations one encounters, focusing one's attention on the characteristics that one's theory suggests might prove most fundamental. Note that people routinely categorize organizations. For the layman, it is about as easy to distinguish a horse from a llama as it is to distinguish a Catholic church from a synagogue. One can also use data reduction techniques such as cluster analysis to determine which characteirstics seem to covary in typologically interesting ways. This *numerical* method offers the advantage of uncovering patterns in the data that would not be obvious to the naturalist. Its use entails a number of disadvantages. The first stems from the fact that the categories constructed by use of such methods serve as the bases for analysis of substantive data. The researcher may be seriously misled by nonrandom measurement and sampling error. A second disadvantage is the risk that independent variables will be used to define types, thereby precluding their later analytical use. Finally, numerical techniques threaten to make even more remote an already abstract style of research. The naturalist method would usually require field research or the use of less systematic techniques in advance of gathering demographic data.

Complexities introduced by continuous change over time plague biological ecology almost as much as they threaten organizational ecology. Stanley (1979) describes species that emerge over time in gradual ways as "chronospecies" and admits that decisions about when to declare the existance of a new species are necessarily arbitrary.

Because sexual reproduction has no obvious parallel among organizations, it is important to ask how structural innovation occurs, given some level of inertia that makes plasticity less than perfect. Brittain and Freeman (1980) began work on this subject in a study of the semiconductor industry. They found that the rapid rate of technical innovation in that industry provided part of this question's answer.

Economists who study technical innovation usually view the level of effort devoted to research and development as a managerial decision to be evaluated in terms of rate of return (Mansfield, 1968). Brittain and Freeman gained a different impression of semiconductor firms. As the technology developed, most management people knew very well that the next advance was likely to be. Rather than deciding whether or not to invest in research, executives in these firms seemed to view themselves as participants in a race. Failure to keep up meant the firm's failure. The point is that once started, the technology develops as a flower unfolds. The process transcends the actions of any one individual or any one firm.

At the same time that the technology was developing, the market for transistors, integrated circuits, and other semiconductor devices exploded. Sales grew from nothing to five billion dollars in 30 years. One might ask why the established electrical equipment companies allowed this to happen without taking over the business. Why did they let Texas Instruments, Fairchild, and later, National Semiconductor, Intel, and the others take hold? The answer lies in the speed with which the market grew—astonishing virtually all involved, in the very high risks associated with the early technology, and in the inertia characterizing the large firms dominating the electrical equipment industry. Transistors were originally produced in ways that tied the production process to the product. When a new product was developed or an old one became obsolete, the investment in equipment was lost as well (Brittain and Freeman, 1980). Early efforts to enter the business by such firms as RCA and General Electric foundered because the transistor group was usually housed in the vacuum tube department or division. Vacuum tube production was very well understood and productive efficiency was the key to manufacturing success. Consequently, the volatile and risky semiconductor venture received scant encouragement in many of these established firms. The industry's experience mirrors the observations of Burns and Stalker (1961) on Scottish and English plastics and electronics firms.

An example of risk that was taken closely to heart by many managers

in the industry was Philco's effort in developing a new device, along
with the production facility it required. This effort involved the investment of millions of dollars. Six months after introducing their new device,
a better one was introduced by a competitor and the investment was
lost. Shortly afterward Philco was absorbed by Ford Motor Company.

After encountering similar experiences, many of the established electrical equipment companies chose to retire from the business, awaiting
the slowdown in technical change that was bound to come. However,
the rate of market growth and the consequent growth of many semiconductor firms made subsequent entrance difficult. In 1961, Fairchild
introduced the planar process, which permitted the continued use of
production equipment as successively more sophisticated devices were
developed. At this point the business became less risky and the growing
population received an infusion of capital that allowed its development
into a large and internally diverse set of organizational forms.

The natural history of the industry has stretched over a scant 30 years.
Many individuals have experienced this natural history and have been
able to translate that history into a flow of personal opportunities. So
as the technology developed and the market grew, individual firms were
founded, prospered, and failed. The population of those firms grew
enormously, and the forms that could be discerned in that general population elaborated as well. Firms founded their own semiconductor divisions or bought out existing firms. Many of these divisions sold only
to the parent firm and thus became "captive producers." As the inven-
tory of devices developed, firms found that the research and development
effort required to be first was often inconsistent with the allocation of
effort to produce efficiently. As the industry matured, then, the usual
economist's view became more accurate. Temporary monopolies generated by "first mover advantages" led to specialized producers whose
forte was state-of-the-art design, producers who competed on the basis
of price in well-established markets, and other forms as well.

Each form can be described in terms of the characteristics of its resource base. What part of the spectrum of labor do firms of the kind in
question use? Do they use all of the raw materials available to semiconductor firms or only some of them? Do the firms in question operate
in narrowly local environments or on a world-wide basis? All of these
questions indicate that the combinations of resources used are characteristics of the form and can be expected to exhibit the discontinuous
distributions that go with the definition of forms. These characteristics
are fundamental to ecological analysis. Taken together, they define the
niche that characterizes an organizational form.

Niches change over the course of an industry's development. This is
what natural history is all about. It may be less apparent that they change

over the course of an individual organization's life as well. Such observations, in fact, underlie Starbuck's (1965) well-known comparison of models of growth and development.

Cell-Division Models

Models of this sort presume growth rates to be independent of contemporaneous size. Examples are Haire's (1959) "square-cube law" and the work of Simon and Bonini (1958) and Ijiri and Simon (1964) based on "Gibrat's Law," the Law of Proportionate Growth. This model is more of a description than an explanatory device. Starbuck is probably correct in doubting its validity for small firms, perhaps even for other than the largest of a class of organizations. Simon and his associates only studied such large organizations. It seems clear that what are called niche characteristics here are presumed constant over the typical firm's life cycle.

Metamorphosis Models

Such views of organization stress change in stages, usually because greatest theoretical attention is devoted to high-level policy decisions. The coincidence of people with policies and policy changes gives them their discontinuous flavor. The importance of such models for current purposes is that they suggest that as organizations grow, they change so dramatically and discontinuously that it might be useful to view the later version as an example of a different form. This is to say that one of the ways in which failure occurs is through metamorphic change of an organization. Whereas many such changes may be adaptive, it should be clear that population models and adaptation models do not exactly coincide under such circumstances. The population models presume that similar metamorphic changes occur at a roughly similar point in an organization's life history. The focus is still on the population. Furthermore, such metamorphic changes may be maladaptive. Metamorphic change may be the last, desperate act of a failing organization. Such acts of desperation are as likely to bring on the end sooner as they are to stave it off.

Will-o'-the-Wisp Models

This might be called opportunistic growth. The most prominent examples are microeconomic: Penrose's (1959) theory of the firm and Williamson's (1975) theory of market and organizational failures. In both, the central question is what limits the growth potential of firms? Penrose's answer is that the availability of managerial talent is the primary limiting factor. Williamson argues that the pattern of transaction costs within and between firms determines if it is less costly to coordinate production within the boundaries of an organization, or through market mechanisms. In particular, limits of rational decision making, information costs, and the disjuncture between the preferences of individuals and the firms of which they are members impose transactional cost advantages to one or the other.

The importance of such models for the purpose at hand is that they provide a rationale for differences among organizations. By determining the degree to which honing of internal procedures to increase efficiency is traded off against opportunistic growth, they suggest different circumstances under which one strategy will prevail over the other.

Decision-Process Models

These models are not really models of growth, but represent descriptions of the decision processes used by individuals in provoking or retarding growth. As such, they are psychological. They are most relevant in providing assumptions about how individual firms forage over their resource bases.

It may very well be that rather than having one niche, a regular progression of niches is characteristic of a form, so that the population at any given moment, comprising organizations at various life cycle stages, will be adapted to different niches. Additionally, there may be generally observable niche evolution. Young organizations, for instance, rarely have the slack that would be required to perform Thompson's (1967, p. 20) insulating structural adaptations. They frequently deal with a labor market environment in which their own uniqueness works against their ability to attract and hold people with relevant experience. New organizations of an old type still have this problem, but to a lesser degree because the experience of people who have previously worked in similar organizations is relevant to them. Older, larger organizations have often grown to the point where they can dominate their environments rather than adjust to them. But such short-run success at dealing with the material environment inevitably generates legitimacy challenges. If General Motors does not have to play by the same rules as smaller and younger corporations, it seems natural for critics to attack the firm's moral position.

While it is clearly premature to make generalizations about such evolutionary trends of niches, it does seem clear that small new organizations are most constrained by a labor market that encourages experienced people to go to older established organizations. Experienced people are likely to have versatile, general skills. Young and small firms are likely to have a simple division of labor; thus requiring people with general skills. Such a paradox suggests a continuing competitive disadvantage imposed by the labor market.

Organizations that have survived the early years can attract more experienced and better-trained participants. The labor market is less problematic for this group. They are, however, vulnerable in the financial and product markets. In particular, they are likely targets of takeover attempts as their success removes many of the apparent uncertainties that made them unattractive previously. Whereas the owners may be happy about a lucrative offer, the consequence from a survival point of view is the same. The original form becomes less numerous.

Very large and mature organizations face legal and political environments that reflect the legitimacy issues raised earlier. Government antitrust regulation, product liability suits, and other forms of legal and regulatory limitation plague them and occasion moralistic outcries. Their managements claim that they should be treated as if they still faced the environments that operated when they were newer. Such moralistic reaction properly should be viewed as epiphenomenal, that is, as an expression of the changed environments that are built into the forms associated with "big business."

Management, then, figures in this mode of analysis as a resource that some kinds of organizations have difficulty obtaining but that others have in superabundance. Business schools train people to work for large, mature corporations. Recruiters from smaller and newer firms have a difficult time competing for such management trainees. Second, management varies as part of the form. Characteristics of the managers themselves, such as their age, sex, ethnicity, training, and personal style, vary with the kind of firm.

The limitations on adaptability and innovation imposed by decisions made early in an organizatonion's life cycle were evident in Burns and Stalker's *The Management of Innovation* (1961), one of the central studies in the organization and innovation literature. In general, this line of theory stresses the trade-off between discipline and creativity. Organizations that operate in uncertain environments or with highly changeable or poorly understood technologies have more team-oriented structures.[2] Burns and Stalker described a series of case studies in which organizations attempt to evolve in the "organic" team-oriented direction. They all fail. It seems likely, then, that such structures are born and not made. How then do organizations that are not set up to deal with innovation bring it about? Given the inertial tendencies described so well by Burns and Stalker and the likelihood that change-oriented, risk-taking managers either will be not hired at all, socialized into a more conformist style if they are hired, or gotten rid of, firms often purchase innovation in the form of preexisting firms that have survived the early selection pressures and gained a reputation for innovativeness. To the degree that the newly acquired firm is to be integrated into the parent firm's structure, the internal pressures spill over into the new firm.

PROLIFERATION: THE EXPANSION OF ORGANIZATIONAL FORMS THROUGH POPULATION GROWTH

Organizational theory has little to say about the conditions under which organizations are set up. Scant attention has been given to the issue of deciding when they begin and end (Freeman, 1978, 1980). Hirschman's (1970) analysis is one of the few studies of the process of failure. Entrepreneurship is most often studied as a psychological phenomenon. The founding of organizations is to be explained through reference to the level of risk-aversion or need for achievement of individuals. The problem with such an approach is that it ignores the obvious fact that the kind of organization any particular person might found is not randomly distributed across the population of potential founders. People who start Catholic convents do not do so after toying with the notion of beginning cement plants, advertising agencies, or universities. Furthermore, it seems safe to speculate that there are aggressive people aplenty with experience in most kinds of organizations. So if we wish to explain an upsurge in the founding of convents, individual aggressiveness seems unpromising as a place to start. People inclined to take risks (if such inclinations are truly personality factors), are stimulated to take action by factors such as the availability of new technologies, venture capital, and unexploited markets. In short, the opportunities that risk-takers seek are also assumed by psychological theorists to be randomly distributed over time. Finally, information about such opportunities is not equally available to all. One's current organizational position may prove to be the most valuable asset of all. Such a position may allow one to know what technical breakthroughs are likely to occur next, where unexploited markets are to be found, and the contacts through which venture capital may be secured.

If we are to study the factors that systematically encourage or discourage the founding of new organizations, we may begin with the characteristics of the broader society that facilitate organizing (Stinchcombe, 1965, p. 150). In broad historical terms, the wave of organization building that was part of the industrial revolution occurred because of rising literacy rates, urbanization, and the spread of the money economy. Organizational experience makes organization founding easier. The process feeds upon itself. Finally, political revolution creates turmoil in the organizational base of society, opening new niches and making new forms of organization viable. In a world in which old organizational forms no longer seem to work, new and apparently successful ones are quickly copied.

We can see organizations as concentrations of resources such as money, energy, human activity, and information. The mechanisms by which such resources are accumulated vary over time as well as over space. The concentrations that urban places represent in space occur in time as members of the social elite develop means for concentrating resources through organization. In particular, social institutions such as the limited liability joint stock corporation developed and then served as the basis for waves of organizing (Stinchcombe, 1965; Aldrich, 1979).

The rationale for expecting such waves is rooted in some features of organizational life cycles. First, established organizations have substantial competitive advantages over newly founded organizations. Organizations of a new form are at a particular competitive disadvantage; Stinchcombe called this the "liability of newness" (1965, pp. 148–150). When new organizations are formed one would expect a shaking-out period in which people learn their roles. If the organization is of a new type, the formal structure will have to be designed during this period. People will develop their roles as they grope along. The more completely original the new organization, the less likely it is that there will be veterans whose experience can be used for socialization of new entrants. In addition, new organizations have problems establishing relationships with resource suppliers. Business firms need to convince workers that they will be paid. They need to convince landlords that they will pay the rent. And suppliers of raw materials and equipment must deliver as well. In all of these ways, the new organization needs credit, and that credit is more difficult to obtain the more unusual the organization is. On the other hand, if the new organization is an identical copy of others, it has no competitive advantage. If the markets in which the new organization sells its services are expanding, exact copying may suffice. In a stagnant market or in a market that is shrinking, there is a strong tendency for new organizations to balance difference (required to attract resources) and similarity (required to establish credibility).

Hannan and Freeman (1974, 1977) developed Stinchcombe's ideas about waves of organizing by pointing out a number of reasons for expecting organizational inertia. Existing organizations derive their competitive advantages from the stability of their internal social relationships and on the basis of their relationships with other organizations. This often leads to the development of ideologies and traditions that at once legitimate the status quo and dampen innovative tendencies. In addition, basic changes in product, technology, and organizational structure threaten to upset patterns of accommodation that were often quite expensive to develop. "Sunk costs" in equipment, facilities, and product designs are matched by allocations of resources to activities and structures within the organization that are no less constraining. In essence, the travail that characterizes the period of founding is avoided later by reliance on established methods and established structures.

Again, consider an example from the semiconductor industry. In Figure 1, entries and exits to the "discrete" product semiconductor technology are presented. Firms that begin to produce a particular device or stop producing that device were coded as "entries" or "exits." The data cover the years 1951 to 1965. These devices constituted the bulk of the semiconductor industry prior to the introduction of integrated circuits in 1961. The pattern is clear. Exits lag entries by approximately 2 years.

Figure 1.   Entries and Exits of Firms Producing Diodes and
Transistors

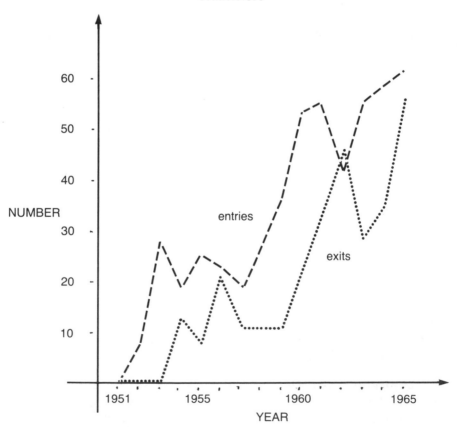

Keep in mind that this was a period of enormous market growth. It is not the case that there was only a fixed amount of business to go around. Neither is it true that there is some technologically based minimum or maximum firm size. The range of size in any given year is substantial.

Organizational founding, then, is not free-flowing innovation any more than strategic choice is an everyday occurrence. Organizations can be expected to minimize the survival-threatening risks associated with birth by copying other organizations in most ways. *Imitation* is thus one of the ways in which proliferation occurs. If a new organization innovates in a successful way, the new form it represents spreads until it reaches some limit imposed by the level of resources and the numbers of competitors. Imitation is fostered by having an individual in the new organization familiar with the structures, technologies, and methods used by the previously existing organization. This means that the movement of *people* is an important mechanism through which proliferation occurs.

A similar way in which proliferation occurs is through *schism*. Organizations sometimes break up, as when apostate sects split off from churches or when corporations "spin off" subsidiaries. Sometimes a venture proves to be inconsistent with the rest of the organization and is sold off. Schisms are important because the newly independent organization starts with many of the liabilities of newness ameliorated.

What is it about some organizations that causes them to serve as the spawning grounds for imitators? One can examine this question by considering the opportunity structure within the organization as compared with the environment. This opportunity structure consists of *positions* that associate various levels of reward and contributions, *structures* within which those positions are located, and *information* that describes the structures and positions both within existing firms and elsewhere.

If we begin with the assumptions that resources are constantly being dispersed and concentrated in society and that organizations are instruments for fixing what would otherwise be temporary concentrations, *opportunities* can be defined as circumstances in which the resource concentrations have not yet been matched by organizational structures. The entrepreneurial act, then, involves locating those concentrations and building a structure of social relationships—an organization—that will fix them in space and time, perhaps for only a short period. Such a view places more emphasis on the historical forces that generate concentrations of resources than on the individual entrepreneur. The auto industry would have occurred whether or not Henry Ford had ever been born. The same can be said for Rockefeller and the petroleum industry.

People become entrepreneurs when they create these organizational structures. They do so on the basis of information about currently accumulating concentrations of money, labor, energy, and the like. This information is not, of course, randomly distributed in the society. Current organizational position is frequently the greatest single advantage an individual can have in knowing where such concentrations are likely to emerge. University professors in fields such as chemistry, physics, engineering, and business administration often know about such opportunities because their university work involves them in communications networks. Information from diverse sources to which they thereby gain access points the way in a frequently disjointed fashion. The same can be said for engineers and other technically sophisticated people in private firms. If resources are being concentrated through technical innovation, people in research and development are often the first to know it. They are likely to know what is happening in their own firms but also in the other firms in the industry. When changes in buying patterns create demand that is unfilled, marketing executives have a similar advantage. So access to information is in many respects an organizational phenomenon.

If organizational position serves as the basis for gaining the information necessary to start new organizations, why do some firms produce many entrepreneurs while others produce few? Firms offer internal opportunities that correspond in many ways to opportunities outside. That is, they concentrate organizational resources in ways that offer managerially interesting and rewarding occasions for organizing. They offer risk, and choice, in patterned ways.

People's willingness to take risks probably varies in systematic ways over their lives. Opportunities generated from inside the organization and opportunities generated from outside of it do not necessarily occur at the same time in a person's life/career. Younger people, who are without family responsibilities, financial commitments, and outside interests tying them to the local area, are probably more receptive to opportunities than those same people would be 20 years hence. But organizational position represents more than access to information. It also represents experience, which is an important basis for credibility among outsiders. All of these advantages accruing to position are more substantial the higher the position in the organization's hierarchy.

Because higher level positions are likely to be filled by older people, age is associated with organization-based entrepreneurial advantages as well. Considering both of these arguments together, one might expect to see an inverted U-shaped function relating age to the probability of entrepreneurial activity. As Pfeffer (1979) points out, the age distribution observable at any given point in time is a function of previous organizational growth, the circumstances under which it was founded, its promotion and retirement practices, and the hiring practices regarding training and experience. So life cycle characteristics of individual organizations, rooted in the circumstances under which its form was originated, affect its tendencies to generate entrepreneurs, and the relative probabilities that various people will engage in entrepreneurial activity.

Finally, competition is not viewed as an implicit property of a structure by ecologists as it seems to be by economists. It is a process to be studied and occurs at the level of species–populations rather than at the level of individual organisms. Where economists are primarily concerned with the pricing behavior of various members of a single industry (for example, each of several steel mills), ecologists are more typically concerned with the implication of more or less numerous competing species for the population dynamics of some other species. Competition among individual starlings, for example, is not completely ignored to be sure, but it generally seems less interesting than competition between starlings and grackles. Organizational ecologists are not concerned with market behavior to the exclusion of other resource distribution systems. Resources of interest are not even necessarily material resources. Collins (1980) examines the rise and fall of European universities in response to political crises in the societies of which they are a part. It is their role in extending the state's political culture that seems pivotal to Collins. Similarly, Carroll and Delacriox (1981) find that newspaper populations are frequently as sensitive to events in the polity as to purely economic issues. Coups have enormous effects on such organizational populations. Put differently, newspapers born in a year of political turmoil have shorter life expectancies than those born in years of political stability. Demand in the economic sense remains more or less stable during periods of enormous turbulence in the organizational populations.

DENSITY DEPENDENCE

Selection may operate in such a way that the proportion of organizations affected increases with population size. This is called *density-dependent* selection. The effect is usually negative with regard to foundings and positive with regard to failures. Density dependence is important because it generates homeostatic processes in populations; that is, it generates equilibrium levels toward which population sizes adjust, usually at decelerating rates.

One of the common devices for modeling such processes is with logistic growth equations, or more specifically, with a family of such equations based on the following

$$\frac{dN}{dt} = rN\left(\frac{K - N}{K}\right)$$

where K is the carrying capacity of the population

N is the population size

r is the intrinsic rate of population growth.

If we consider the proliferation of an organizational population, it seems reasonable to argue that the process should begin with some organizational innovation. At first the viability of the new kind of organization is subject to doubt. Over time it begins to attract imitators. It also internally generates an increasing number of people each of whom is sufficiently experienced to run an organization like it. The number of organizations grows, and each of the imitators serves as an example and a training ground for still more imitators. Finally, the size of the population levels off as resources per organization fall to minimum levels required for individual viability. The market for goods or services produced is saturated. The labor market is exhausted. Or the physical space becomes so dear that further additions are impossible. At this point the *carrying capacity* is approached and the population growth rate approaches zero.

This model is deficient in at least three ways. First, it does not consider the effects of competing organizational forms. Fortunately, an extension exists and uses simultaneous equations (one for each population) to represent competitive interactions—the so-called Lotka-Volterra equations (see Hannan and Freeman, 1977). The second problem is that the model does not take into account variations in carrying capacities. For example, if the resource gradient limiting population size is demand for product, an expanding market allows for a continuously growing population. The third problem is that the model does not consider organizational growth or decline. An alternative to population expansion is the expansion of a single organization. We will examine this problem in the paragraphs that follow.

If it is true that growth is likely to be metamorphic, then the form changes as organizations grow. There may be small, medium, and large versions of the basic form, each of which has a distinctive mode of organizing. Mass producers of automobiles compare with custom auto producers in this way. Such views were common among organizational theorists in their initial attempts to understand structure (Haire, 1959; Caplow, 1957).

Alternatively, organizations may grow symmetrically. If they could grow without limit and keep the same basic mode of organizing, the appearance of new entrants to the population would depend on the growth capability of the originator. If that organization is incapable of growing as fast as the resource base, the niche is not completely filled and other similar organizations spring up. The new organization may also compete successfully if they are specialized to part of the resource gradient used by the original organization but inefficiently exploited by it.

It seems to be generally true in nature that species trading on efficient exploitation of a resource will compete successfully against species that trade on quick exploitation of that resource. If a new habitat opens up, the species set up to quickly capture that resource through population growth have a temporary advantage and do quite well. Such species are called "*r*-strategists" after the coefficient *r* in the logistic growth equation presented earlier. *r* represents the intrinsic rate of population growth. Other species, which trade on efficient exploitation of the crucial resources are called "*K*-strategists," where the coefficient *K* refers to the carrying capacity (defined as the maximum size of the population at equilibrium). With a stable resource base, *K*-strategists compete successfully against *r*-strategists, forcing them out of the habitat. Brittain and Freeman (1980) discuss this at length. The issue, of course, is stability. When the resources in question are available variably over time or in patches over space, *r*-strategists may do quite well in the face of competition from *K*-strategists.

We expect to find diversity of organizational forms, then, either because growth leads to change of form (metamorphic development) or because single organizations have difficulty growing fast enough and simultaneously being efficient enough to prevent the appearance of competing forms of organizations. Only when the resource base is stable or growing slowly do we expect to see a single organization innovating and then maintaining dominance in any but the smallest resource environments.

INDIVIDUAL CHOICE AND OPTIMIZATION

Natural selection approaches to the study of organizations (focusing as they do on populations of organizations) seem to leave no role for individual choice. Managers' wants, skills, and ambitions do not figure prominently in the theory. Just as the market is viewed as optimizing social utilities by economists, organizational ecologists view competitive processes as optimizing fitness. If this is true, one might be tempted to view organizational ecology as a subfield of microeconomics. This is incorrect.

Fundamentally the two approaches differ because economists do not usually focus on population phenomena. Their unit is most often the individual firm (Blau and Scott, 1962, p. 215). The subject of interest is the behavior of that firm as it varies the level of its production in response to variations in price. It is the production of goods and services that is the central interest, not the firm itself. Economists usually attribute *rational* behavior to firms in addition to profit motives. Organizational ecologists make no such attributions. Organizations may compete successfully without maximizing any observable utility, unless the term "utility" is tautologically defined to mean any consequence of organizational action. It is not even the case that the probability of survival is maximized. Ecological concern is most heavily concentrated on the probability of survival of the organizational form, not the individual organization.

Perhaps the differences can more clearly be seen if we examine the model of pure or perfect competition. This model is usually presented in terms of the following four characteristics:

1. Products of various sellers must be substitutable for each other.
2. Each buyer and each seller must be so small compared with the market that no single buyer or seller can affect the price by its own actions.
3. Resources such as labor must be perfectly liquid in the sense that they can instantly and costlessly be reallocated from one use to another.
4. All buyers and sellers must have complete knowledge of both current and future prices and alternative uses for resources that they allocate.

Ecological theory as discussed here makes no such assumptions. In fact, it tends to dispute all of the above.

Economists seem primarily interested in the production of standardized commodities. Pork bellies and pig iron are the sort of items that concern them. When products are not substitutable for each other so that each producer is a near monopolist, economic theory has little to say. Similarly, unique contributions of individuals in the labor market and idiosyncratic work are not easily analyzed using standard economic theories. This suggests that economists tend not to be interested in dynamic issues in general or in forces that produce differentiation in particular. Such issues are precisely the central interest of ecologists. Ecologists want to explain diversity—speciation. They do not assume the existence of anything like a single price for a given commodity at any one point in time.

Biologists have built population theories by relying in part on the strong knowledge base provided by researchers focusing on the ways in which individual organisms reproduce, feed, and change over their lifetimes. In other words, they know much about the life cycles of the organisms they study. In the next section we take up the internal political economies of organizations. Our purpose is to show that it represents a complementary view, not an alternative to be applied to a different class of organization or organizational phenomena.

THE DYNAMICS OF POLITICAL ECONOMY

In sociology, the study of formal or complex organizations had its origins in political sociology more than in any other field. Its emergence as a distinct specialty is a rather recent event. In the index to the *American Journal of Sociology* that covered the period of its publication from its founding in 1895 to 1947, there were no subject references to "organizations" or "formal organization" or "complex organization." The subject heading referring to "bureaucracy" in fact had no entries and simply referred the reader to "government" or "institutions" (1950). The index to the *American Sociological Review,* published 6 years later, had six articles under the heading of "bureaucracy" and the admonishment to the reader to look under "political sociology." Again, there was no reference to any of the modern headings under which organizations research is currently reported. It was not until 1966, that the next index to the *American Journal of Sociology* listed "organization" as a subject category. Under the editorship of Peter Blau (1966), it had emerged as one of the larger literatures of the time, or so it was reported. It is not surprising, given these strong early links to political sociology, that pioneers in the field saw organizational phenomena as highly politicized. Such works as Selznick's *TVA and the Grass Roots* (1949), Dalton's "Conflicts Between Line and Staff Managerial Officers" (1950) and *Men Who Manage* (1959), Gouldner's *Patterns of Industrial Bureaucracy* (1954), and Lipset, Trow, and Coleman's *Union Democracy* (1956) placed heavy emphasis on conflict as an endemic feature of organizational life. They stressed power phenomena in studies of structural formation and change within the organization as well as in establishing ties with the environment. Published earlier in German, but available in translation in 1949, Michels' *Political Parties* should also probably be included in this group.

Most of these books and papers were based on extended case studies that used an historical perspective. In consequence, these analysts took a dynamic approach to studying organizations. More recent efforts by researchers taking a political economy perspective are decidedly less concerned with organizational dynamics. Perrow (1967), March and Olsen (1976), and Pfeffer and Salancik (1978) all essentially concern themselves with the stable constraints on choice and on the resultant distribution of reward and punishment. Each of these researchers is primarily interested in the organization as an arena for decision making. Zald's work (1970b) tends to be more historical in approach, and more concerned with the evolution of the organization or kind of organization under study.

All of these researchers step back from the usual functionalist argument that organizations are structured so as to maximize the attainment of explicit goals. Most, however, substitute some sort of covert goal for the publicly stated goals. That is, they all realize that what the organization tells the world it is trying to do may differ from what it is really trying to do. This may be because the organization has a hidden agenda of goals that it cannot legitimate in the broader society or because its "dominant management coalition" (March and Simon, 1958) creates covert goals in the process of its own machinations. While this position is clearly the one adopted by Pfeffer and Salancik (1978) and Pfeffer (1981), other work published by them on "needs" theories of job motivation such as those advanced by Maslow (1954) and Herzberg (1966), attacks those writers for functionalist theory that is untestable due to its teleology (Salancik and Pfeffer, 1977). If organizations have goals, even covert ones, and their structure is developed in response to the requirements of goal attainment, needs of organizations or coalitions of individuals are being substituted for needs of individuals.

Aside from these objections, political economy approaches to studying organizations are complementary to studies using a natural selection logic. In fact, political economy may well provide a theory of functioning of individual organizations that life cycle accounts require to provide linkage with studies of organizational populations. That is, political economy may do for the study of organizational populations what physiology does for bioecology. Much of what political economists take as problematic, population ecologists take as given.

There are several commonalities. First, conflict is endemic to all organizations. It is as common as cooperation; it is not an abnormal or deviant state of affairs. Organizations can be seen as facing an environment in which others continually demand that they justify their existence. When seen as concentrations of resources, the more successful any organization is, the more others are drawn to attack it. This is one of the many ways in which nothing fails like success. In this sense, an entropic process characterizes a society made up of organizations.

Second, within organizations, resources are variably scarce. In one, space will be at a premium. In others, it will be finances. In still others, personnel "slots" serve as the major subject of dispute.

Third, both the political economy and ecological approaches deny that choice within organizations is necessarily rational in the sense of utility maximization. In addition to the usual observations about decision in organizations as a process in which information limitations and computational complexity create conditions of "bounded rationality" (Simon, 1957), population ecologists stress that organization observed today is a residue of prior selection processes. Even if it were true that organizing is done to maximize utilities, the inertial processes that limit subsequent adaptation make it quite likely that an organization observed today will be suboptimal with regard to its current circumstances.

If we examine the flow of resources into organizations, we see that over time the flow is uneven, but more so for some organizations than for others. Although this observation is probably valid for any imaginable resource, it is perhaps most obvious with regard to the product markets in which profit-making firms are typically involved. The business cycle is one way in which demand varies over time. A second mode of variation involves the concentration of demand transactions. Some organizations sell their product in a small number of large orders. "Large" in this sense is defined relative to the productive capacity or average yearly sales of the firm. Aerospace companies frequently commit very large shares of their total capacity with each sale or order. Demand is cyclical, depending on government arms expenditures and airline purchasing. Automobile companies, on the other hand, process orders that are, by and large, for single vehicles. Automobile sales are also notoriously subject to business cycles effects. They go through sales cycles that correspond to model year. In contrast, cigarette manufacturers experience smooth demand for their product. Cigarettes are sold in small amounts and sales are not cyclical.

When demand for product is experienced in peaks and valleys, two political phenomena are generated within the organization. The first involves performance assessment in crises. When demand is at maximum, failure to perform in ways that satisfy more powerful decision makers result in the strongest negative sanctions because it is precisely under these circumstances that the powerful other decision maker is likely to be watched most intensely by third parties. This provides an incentive for units to maintain sufficient excess capacity (slack) to meet peak demands (Cyert and March, 1963). Managers and other administrative officials husband reserves in ways that other claimants, arguing from a short-run perspective, view as highly wasteful. Excess capacity often does not vary sensitively with demand. This creates lags between claims and allocations of resources (Wildavsky, 1964; Downs, 1967). To maintain political stability, organizations attempt to manage cycles in the supply of resources. Thompson argues that this is the central reason for the organization's staff structure. Pfeffer and Salancik (1978) argue that such structures are used by dominant management coalitions to reduce dependencies on resource suppliers.

Second, variable demand patterns generated by large and erratic orders create short-run commitments to organizations and individuals. Long-run commitment and loyalty are unlikely when orders create heavy demand for finite, and known, periods. As indicated earlier, this gives

competitive advantages to firms that can lay off employees. It generates
entrepreneurs, however, and it increases the potential for internal opportunities for elites. Indeed, this is the singular feature of the draft-
based army, with its volatile participant base. Loyalty to the organization
is lower and therefore is less reliable as a tool for internal repression.

It is frequently unclear, however, whether observed trends are cyclical
or secular. It is to the advantage of agents defending resource domains
to argue that downturns are cyclical. The result is that cutbacks are put
off according to subunits' political strengths. Important among these are
the difficulty of reconstruction during subsequent periods of expansion
(Freeman and Hannan, 1975; Downs, 1967). The result of this is that
parts of the organization whose activities are most in line with what is
claimed to be organizational goals or missions are cut back before parts
performing peripheral or support functions.

Such cyclical patterns may themselves be generated by population
dynamics. Organizations are started in periods of resource munificence.
How rapidly this happens and the number of organizations founded depends on the technology and capital requirements, among other things.
The rapidity with which niches open and the information efficiency that
limits lag structures create more or less distinct waves of organizing.
They result in cyclical growth and decline processes within organizations.

An example of such a repeated phenomenon is in California egg production. Egg ranching is certainly one of the most notable examples of
technical innovation in agriculture. Since the Second World War, egg
production has evolved from labor-intensive farming to mechanized industry. Chickens are fed by machines. Their guano is carried away by
machines. Eggs are removed by machines. Chickens have been selec-
tively bred so that ranchers now know rather precisely how many eggs
they will produce, what grade, and when all of this will happen. This
means that egg ranchers who wish to start production can buy chicks
that will produce after a known time interval. Ranchers also know when
the hens will become too old to produce. This creates a lag between
profitable prices and the entrance of small firms. Small egg ranches are
typically family operations. They jump into the market when prices are
high and go out of business when prices are low. In fact, this mode of
adaptation is what generates the price fluctuation. At the other end of
the size spectrum are the very large corporately run egg ranches—often
with several million birds. These ranches cannot simply close down when
prices are low. They can, however, smooth out such fluctuations by
writing long-term contracts with supermarket chains and by investing in
freezing plants to store eggs for use in baking. They gain efficiency by
maintaining the age mix of their flocks to take advantage of high prices.
They continuously produce extra-large eggs whereas the small producers

must wait until their flocks reach the proper age for producing eggs of this kind.

The medium-sized ranches can take advantage of neither strategy. This suggests that the middle position on the size continuum is not viable. The growth path is blocked.

The point of this discussion is to show how cyclical patterns are created by organizational populations and how those patterns then represent niches to which the various forms are adapted. All of this depends on the ease with which births and deaths can be brought about. It would not work if there were no lag in those processes. Then the productive capacity of the industry would be kept in equilibrium with demand. Similarly, without lags generated by the productivity (and value) of the flock in its age distribution, ranches would close down as soon as the price approached the break-even point. Flocks could be reduced rather than organizational populations. So the population patterns depend on the life cycle characteristics of the individual organizations.

CONCLUSION

We have been exploring the relationship between life cycle phenomena in individual organizations and natural selection processes which are manifested by organizational populations. Natural selection involves fertility and mortality variations across organizational forms in varying environments. In a given environment, some forms out-compete others and thereby become more numerous. Variables that describe the environment have their effect, then, in combination with the variables that describe the differences among the various forms that have survival implications. So variations in net mortality result from nonadditive effects of these two classes of variables—interaction effects. But it is not survival itself, or failure, which is of central interest. Rather, it is the distribution of the organizations on the variables that define the forms resulting from the process that is the salient issue. Our purpose remains to understand why organizations are the way they are. The merit of this approach lies in its consideration of organizations that did not survive as sources of information about the morphology of those that did survive.

If we look about for new kinds of organizations, we can see them easily. In the restaurant business we see corporately run chains competing in the expensive dinner market (e.g., the Victoria Station chain). Twenty years ago, a person wishing to purchase a dinner in such a restaurant would have to look hard to find one. Similarly, a person wanting to work in a restaurant would not have found many dinner houses with corporate management styles (including the fringe benefits usually associated with corporate management structures).

A more specialized example that is currently flourishing in northern California is cookie bakeries, usually making only variations of chocolate chip cookies. They seem to be appearing everywhere. One may ask what has changed to bring about such organizational innovations. Have people suddenly decided that they desire chocolate chip cookies? Has there been a wave of entrepreneurial zeal among cookie bakers? Perhaps there has been an in-migration of people with high need for achievement in the cookie baking profession. What seems striking is that whatever the cause, it is happening in different cities and towns in a rather compact period in time. This commonality begs explanation, and that is what we are about.

This does not mean, however, that conventional organizational theory is irrelevant or that we are proposing a way of looking at organizations with a competing theory. We do propose a way of looking at the entire universe of formal organizations, not just the big ones and not just the profit-making ones. Our approach must make assumptions about how individual organizations function, just as bioecologists must make assumptions about how organisms function when proposing models to explain such phenomena as explosions in the population of some parasite. This article represents an attempt to show some of the ways in which what happens to individual organizations bears on what happens to populations of those organizations. *Sturm und drang* can hardly occur at one level and not at the other.

ACKNOWLEDGMENTS

The work reported here is supported by National Science Foundation grant SES79-12315. Michael T. Hannan, Jack W. Brittain, Douglas Wholey, Barbara Dohrn, and this series' editors all made comments on drafts of this paper. Their help is gratefully acknowledged.

NOTES

1. Not all population models are dynamic. In fact, arguments about equilibrium distributions of organisms across species are common. Natural selection processes underlie virtually all ecological analyses, but their role is frequently that of assumption.

2. Classic citations in this line of work are Perrow (1967), Cyert and March (1963), Thompson (1967), Hage and Aiken (1970), Lawrence and Lorsch (1967), Weick (1969), and, more recently, March and Olsen (1976).

REFERENCES

Aldrich, H. E. *Organizations and Environments.* Englewood Cliffs, N.J.: Prentice-Hall, 1979.
Aldrich, H. E. & Pfeffer, J. Environments of organizations. *Annual Review of Sociology,* 1976, 2, 79–105.

American Journal of Sociology: Index to Volumes I-LII, 1895–1947. Chicago, University of Chicago Press, 1950.

Blau, P. M. (ed.), *Cumulative Index to the American Journal of Sociology: Volumes 1–70, 1895–1965.* Chicago: University of Chicago Press, 1966.

Blau, P. M., & Scott, W. R. *Formal Organizations.* San Francisco: Chandler, 1962.

Brittain, J. and Freeman, J. H. Organizational proliferation and density dependent selection: organizational evolution in the semiconductor industry. In J. R. Kimberly and R. H. Miles (Eds.), *The Organizational Life Cycle,* San Francisco: Jossey-Bass, 1980.

Burns, T. and Stalker, G. M. *The Management of Innovation.* London: Tavistock, 1961.

Caplow, T. Organizational size. *American Sociological Review,* 1957, *1,* 484–505.

Carroll, G., & Delacroix, J. Organizational mortality in the newspaper industries of Argentina and Ireland: an ecological approach. Organization Studies Section, Institute for Mathematical Studies in the Social Sciences, Technical Report No. 3, Stanford University, 1981.

Churchill, B. Business population by legal form of organization. *Survey of Current Business,* U.S. Department of Commerce, 1955, *35,* 14–20.

Collins, R. Crises and declines in educational systems. Unpublished paper, Department of Sociology, University of Virginia, 1980.

Cyert, R. M., & March, J. G. *A Behavioral Theory of the Firm.* Englewood Cliffs, N.J.: Prentice-Hall, 1963.

Dalton, M. Conflicts between staff and line managerial officers. *American Sociological Review,* 1950, *15,* 342–51.

Dalton, M. *Men Who Manage.* New York: Wiley, 1959.

Downs, A. *Inside Bureaucracy.* Boston: Little Brown, 1967.

Freeman, J. H. The unit of analysis in organizational research. In M. W. Meyer (Ed.), *Environments and Organizations.* San Francisco: Jossey-Bass, 1978.

Freeman, J. Going to the well: School district administrative intensity and environmental constraint. *Administrative Science Quarterly,* 1979, *24,* 119–33.

Freeman, J. The Unit Problem in Organizational Research. In William M. Evan (Ed.), *Frontiers in Organization and Management,* New York: Praeger, 1980.

Freeman, J., & Hannan, M. Growth and decline processes in organizations. *American Sociological Review,* 1975, *40,* 215–28.

Gouldner, A. W. *Patterns of Industrial Bureaucracy.* Glencoe, Illinois: Free Press, 1954.

Hage, J., & Aiken, M. *Social Change in Complex Organizations.* New York: Random House, 1970.

Haire, M. Biological models and empirical histories of the growth of organizations. In M. Haire (Ed.), *Modern Organization Theory.* New York: Wiley, 1959.

Hannan, M. T., & Freeman, J. Environment and the structure of organizations. Paper presented at the annual meetings of the American Sociological Association, Montreal, Canada: 1974.

Hannan, M. T., & Freeman, J. The population ecology of organizations. *American Journal of Sociology,* 1977, *82,* 929–64.

Herzberg, F. *Work and the Nature of Man.* Cleveland: World, 1966.

Hirschman, A. O. *Exit, Voice and Loyalty.* Cambridge, Mass.: Harvard, 1970.

Ijiri, Y., & Simon, H. A. Effects of merger and acquisition on business firm concentration. *Journal of Political Economy,* 1971, *79,* 314–22.

Index to the American Sociological Review: Volumes 1–20, 1936–1955. New York: New York University Press, 1956.

Lawrence, P. R., & Lorsch, J. W. *Organization and environment: Managing differentiation and integration.* Boston: Graduate School of Business Administration, Harvard University, 1967.

Lipset, S. M., Trow, M. A., & Coleman, J. S. *Union Democracy.* Glencoe, Illinois: Free Press, 1956.

Mansfield, E. *The Economics of Technological Change*. New York: W. W. Norton, 1968.

March, J. G., & Olsen, J. P. *Ambiguity and Choice in Organizations*. Bergen, Norway: Universitetsforlaget, 1976.

March, J. G., & Simon, H. A. *Organizations*. New York: Wiley, 1958.

Maslow, A. *Motivation and Personality*. New York: Harper, 1954.

McKelvey, B. *Organizational Systematics: Taxonomy, Evolution, Classification*. Los Angeles, University of California Press, in press.

Meyer, M. W. Bureaucracy reconsidered. Unpublished manuscript, Department of Sociology, University of California at Riverside. 1980.

Michels, R. *Political Parties*. Trans. by E. and C. Paul. Glencoe, Illinois: Free Press, 1949.

Penrose, E. T. *The Theory of the Growth of the Firm*. Oxford, England: Basil Blackwell, 1959.

Perrow, C. A framework for the comparative analysis of organizations. *American Sociological Review*, 1967, *32*, 194–208.

Pfeffer, J. Some consequences of organizational demography: potential impacts of an aging workforce on formal organizations. Presented before the Committee on Aging, National Research Council, National Academy of Sciences, 1979.

Pfeffer, J. *Power in Organizations*. Marshfield, Mass., 1981.

Pfeffer, J., & Salancik, G. R. *The External Control of Organizations*. New York: Harper and Row, 1978.

Pianka, E. R. *Evolutionary Ecology*. 2nd ed., New York: Harper and Row, 1978.

Ricklefs, R. E. *Ecology*. Newton, Mass.: Chiron, 1973.

Salancik, G. R., & Pfeffer, J. An examination of need-satisfaction models of job attitudes. *Administrative Science Quarterly*, 1977, *22*, 427–56.

Scott, W. R. *Organizations: Rational, Natural and Open Systems*. Englewood Cliffs, N.J.: Prentice-Hall, 1981.

Selznick, P. *TVA and the Grass Roots*. Berkeley: University of California Press, 1949.

Simon, H. *Administrative Behavior*. New York: Macmillan, 1957.

Simon, H., & Bonini, C. The size distribution of business firms. *American Economic Review*, 1958, *48*, 607–17.

Stanley, S. M. *Macroevolution: Pattern and Process*. San Francisco: Freeman, 1979.

Starbuck, W. H. Organizational growth and development. In J. G. March (Ed.), *Handbook of Organizations*. Chicago: Rand McNally, 1965.

Stinchcombe, A. L. Social Structure and organizations. In J. G. March (Ed.), *Handbook of Organizations*. Chicago: Rand McNally, 1965.

Thompson, J. D. *Organizations in Action*. New York: McGraw-Hill, 1967.

Wedervang, F. *Development of a Population of Industrial Firms*. Oslo, Norway: Universitetsforlaget, 1965.

Weick, K. E. *The Social Psychology of Organizing*. Reading, Mass.: Addison-Wesley, 1969.

Wildavsky, A. B. *The Politics of the Budgetary Process*. Boston: Little, Brown, 1964.

Williamson, O. E. *Markets and Hierarchies*. New York: Free Press, 1975.

Zald, M. N. Political economy: a framework for comparative analysis, in N. Zald (ed.), *Power in Organizations*. Nashville, Tenn.: Vanderbilt University Press, 1970.

Zald, M. N. *Organizational Change: The Political Economy of the YMCA*. Chicago: University of Chicago Press, 1970.

THE EVOLUTION OF
ORGANIZATIONAL FORMS:
TECHNOLOGY, COORDINATION,
AND CONTROL

Howard Aldrich and Susan Mueller

ABSTRACT

The population perspective explains organizational change by focusing on
the distribution of resources in environments and the terms on which they
are available. Variation within and between organizations provides the
occasion for selection criteria to make their presence felt, and retention
mechanisms preserve the selected variations. In this paper, we examine
changes in environmental selection criteria from the early nineteenth century until the present, relating changes in these criteria to changes in
organizational forms. Forms are defined along three dimensions: technology, coordination, and control. We show that systematic change in organizational forms has been associated with a number of long term evolutionary changes in the social, political, and economic environment of the
United States.

Research in Organizational Behavior, Vol. 4, pages 33–87
Copyright © 1982 by JAI Press Inc.
All rights of reproduction in any form reserved.
ISBN: 0-89232-147-4

In the last century and a half, organizational forms have undergone substantial transformations. Beginning with a population of basically small enterprises that serve local markets and are under the direct control of the founding entrepreneur, organizational types have become increasingly heterogeneous. The population now consists of millions of small scale enterprises, similar in many respects to their predecessors of more than a century ago, plus hundreds of thousands of enterprises organized along substantially different lines. In this article, forces leading to such transformations in organizational forms will be explored, using a population perspective. This analysis builds on earlier applications of the population perspective; these focused on the distribution of resources in environments and the terms on which they are available, by dealing more explicitly with the political economy of change. The interrelation between social, political, and economic changes in the United States and the growth of new organizational forms will be examined.[1]

USING THE CONCEPT OF FORM TO STUDY ORGANIZATIONAL CHANGE

For the purposes of this study, the concept of organization developed by Aldrich (1979) will be used; therefore, we define an organization as a "goal-directed, boundary-maintaining, activity system." The three elements in the definition of an organization imply three dimensions of organizational form: (1) "goal-directedness" implies the *coordination* of activities toward a unity of purpose, and at least the appearance of pursuing a collective objective (this implies nothing about member consensus on objectives); (2) "boundary maintenance" requires authoritative *control* over entry into and exit from an organization, and control over the labor of those persons within the boundaries; and (3) an "activity system" is fundamentally a set of processes for accomplishing tasks, with production-related processes constituting the *technology* of the organization. The interest of this research lies chiefly with those organizations whose goals are directed toward the production of goods or services for purposes of exchange in a market. The existence of a capitalist economy is taken as a given, that is, a market context in which exchanges are undertaken with the aim of realizing and accumulating surplus (Wallerstein, 1974). Within the category of profit-oriented organizations, industrial or producing organizations will be the main focus, devoting only passing attention to organizations whose major activity is distributing and selling goods and services.

Research on organizational forms is part of the more general line of inquiry labeled "organizational systematics" by McKelvey (forthcoming). This field encompasses three related areas of investigation. *Tax-*

onomy refers to the development of a theory of differences among organizational forms, which, together with a theory of *Classification,* enables the researcher to determine when one form should be formally recognized as different from another. *Evolution* refers to the tracing out of the historical origins of different lineages of organizational forms, with the objective of explaining how forms have evolved and why certain groupings have emerged. The field of organizational systematics is in its infancy, and this article is not intended as a contribution to that field. Rather, some of the already developed ideas have been borrowed for assistance in organizing this work.

TAXONOMY

The concept of form is an extremely useful tool for studying the process of organizational change, as McKelvey (forthcoming) has so persuasively argued. A comprehensive taxonomy provides a conceptual framework for describing and understanding the diversity of organizational populations, guiding us in our search for the answer to the question, "Why are there so many different kinds of organizations?" (Hannan and Freeman, 1977). The identification of forms allows the categorization of information in a much more parsimonious way and allows us to make sense of the massive amounts of information presented to us by the historical record.

Unfortunately, the numerous dimensions on which organizations may vary makes the identification of a simple taxonomic scheme extremely difficult. Instead, we have chosen to identify three major dimensions of organizational variation and to discuss the organizations prevalent during any given historical period in terms of their positions on these three dimensions. For purposes of this analysis, an organization's form is defined by the conjunction of the technology, coordination, and control mechanisms involved in its on-going activities.

Technology. An organization's technology is the set of processes involved in the way tasks are carried out.[2] Some theorists have defined technology in terms of the operations required to perform tasks, focusing on the degree of continuity in the production process or on the degree of automaticity in the operations (e.g., Woodward, 1965; Hickson, Pugh, and Pheysey, 1969). Others have defined technology in terms of the type of knowledge involved in the production process or in terms of the degree to which tasks are well understood (e.g., Perrow, 1967; Lynch, 1974).

Another way of conceptualizing technology uses the proportions in which various types of resources are combined—labor versus capital intensive production, or primary (unprocessed) versus secondary (man-made, processed) inputs—and the flexibility permitted before the limits of efficient production are exhausted. Our interest lies in fairly broad-scale, long-run changes in technology, rather than in fine distinctions among technologies at any given time.

Coordination. Coordination structures and processes, within and between organizations, are the social arrangements for allocating resources across various uses. Resource allocation may be a matter of negotiation and bargaining between autonomous or semi-autonomous units, in which case we speak of coordination through *markets*. Coordination among the units emerges from compromises between units, and resource allocation within units is more or less directly shaped by the nature of the external compromises. Microeconomic theory of the firm has assumed that external pressures in a competitive market are so coercive and thus determinative of a firms' conduct and performance that it has paid little attention to internal organizational structure. Developments in industrial organization theory and business history have remedied this oversight [see Caves (1980) for a review of some of this literature].

When resources are allocated by directives or plans issued by central authorities, either from an organization's management or from state officials, coordination is achieved through *hierarchy*. Coordination is hierarchically rather than market directed because all units are constrained to abide by principles laid down by those superordinate to them, instead of being allowed to act autonomously. Organization design theorists often refer to market-like arrangements within work groups as coordination via feedback and authoritatively directed integration as coordination via planning. Weberian ideal–typical "bureaucracy" is the archetypical example of achieving coordination through the hierarchical structuring of authority relations (Perrow, 1979, Chapter 1).

Distinctions between "market" and "hierarchical" forms of coordination have appeared fairly frequently in the organization's literature, albeit often with different labels. As argued by Chandler (1977) and others, the long-run trend has been the replacement of market-directed coordination by hierarchical arrangements, with organizations internalizing transactions whenever feasible.[3] Hierarchical coordination *between* organizations has become an increasingly important factor of economic life in the modern American economy, although explicit direction by semi-independent planning authorities has so far occurred only during times of significant national stress.

Control. Control structures shape the way persons who are carrying out tasks are directed, evaluated, and rewarded (Edwards, 1979). *Simple* control has characterized work relations and the labor process in most eras, as supervisors and subordinates have been in face-to-face relations with only custom as a guide to proper behavior. When intermediaries are placed between the ultimate authority and the worker, we speak of *hierarchical* control, most notably in the form of foremen and supervisors. Simple and hierarchical control sufficed as modes of labor control until the late nineteenth century, but then a crisis of control led to the development of *technical* and *bureaucratic* modes of labor control.

Technical control involves designing machinery and planning the flow of work to reduce the need for direct supervision of labor, as well as maximizing the purely physically based possibilities for achieving efficiency. When properly done, technical control embeds the direction and evaluation of labor directly in the organization of production. *Bureaucratic control* goes beyond technical control in that control is embedded not only in the technology but also in the rules and regulations, procedures, job titles, pay grades, and other structural features of an organization. Such control establishes the impersonal force of "company rules" or "company policy" as the basis for control and institutionalizes the exercise of hierarchical power in organizations.

A fourth form of control structure is based on a deeply held *consensus* on the fundamental principles under which the organization operates (Ouchi, 1980). The important role played by ideological or cultural uniformity in this form of control structure is signified by labels such as "clan" or "commune" (Ouchi and Williamson, 1980; Butler, 1980). Such control is most applicable to the producers' cooperative form and to collectivistic–democratic organizations when a participatory–democratic culture has been established.

In addition to their descriptive utility, the three elements of organizational form may be interpreted as defining a matrix of constraints within which an organization must operate. Once in place, organizational forms constrain responses to new problems that arise. Whether such responses will be effective or whether new structures will be forthcoming are empirical questions (Heydebrand, 1977).

The three elements of form do not exist independently of one another within a given organization. Coordination needs may be achieved by arrangements that alter the technological aspects of an organization, or its control structure, or both. Thus, organizational forms may be viewed as arising from a dynamic interplay of developments and feedback effects across the three dimensions. This view obviates the question of whether technological change is a purely autonomous phenomenon or whether its direction is structured by such sociopolitical considerations as control and coordination.

The three main dimensions of organizational form and the terms associated with each are summarized in Table 1. Conceivably, organizations may incorporate any combination of characteristics from these three dimensions. Indeed, contemporary research on industrial organi-

Table 1.   Dimensions of Organizational Form

Technology	Coordination	Labor Control
Low capital/ labor ratio	Market-induced	Simple; consensual
	Hierarchical	Hierarchical—use of intermediaries
High capital/ labor ratio	State planning	
		Technical
		Bureaucratic

zations, using a large number of descriptive dimensions, has uncovered extensive heterogeneity between organizations in the same industry (Baron and Bielby, 1980). Our objective of pointing out fairly general long-term trends necessarily prevents us from giving detailed treatment to each specific organizational form. In our discussion of organizational development in the American context, our main themes will be the transition from handicraft to machine technology, from simple to bureaucratic control structures, and from market to hierarchical forms of coordination.

EVOLUTION: THE ANALYTIC FRAMEWORK

In the population–ecology model, *niches* constitute the intersection of resource constraints sufficient to support an organization and reflect the interaction of choices made by organizational members and the constraints imposed by the terms on which resources are available. An examination of changes in organizational forms necessarily requires the investigation of changes in niches. We follow McKelvey in distinguishing between niches and environments: An environment is composed of non-manipulable attributes or forces, whereas a niche is a dynamic set of manipulable environmental attributes that change as an organization adapts to environmental constraints by "carving out a niche." Organizations can only work with the resources made available to them by environments, but the concept of a niche as a *result* is an attempt to sensitize investigators to the local (and sometimes widespread) changes wrought in environments by organizations.

An entrepreneur interested in locating a grocery store in a newly developed suburban area must deal with many constraints set by the local environment: (1) demographic features of the population, such as the proportion of families at different stages of the life cycle, population density, and racial composition; (2) geographic features, such as the highway system and provisions for public transportation; (3) political–legal features, such as the permissible uses of the site under local zoning ordinances and the quality of police and fire protection; and (4) economic features, such as the presence of potential competitors and the possible benefits derived from the nearby location of businesses offering other goods and services. Carving out a niche will involve a choice between specializing in a limited line of goods or acting as a generalist, a choice between operating as a discount-price, low-overhead store or a full-service store, and a choice of normal or "24-hour" business hours. Whether the choices made are correct, that is, create a viable niche for the business, can only be known after the fact. However, some choices are clearly suicidal, such as opening a general, full-service grocery store, open normal hours, immediately adjacent to an "A & P" or Kroger operation in a suburban shopping mall. Accordingly an observer will have some basis for deciding whether many choices have been "strategic" or not.

Our approach to organizational forms and their development is an evolutionary one, as we explain the origins of forms and differences between them using principles of natural selection (Aldrich, 1979). In a dynamic analysis of the adaptation of organizations to their environments, we try to trace current organizational forms back to their common ancestors. In the language of evolutionary theory, we examine descent with modification (McKelvey, forthcoming). The population ecology model has been developed as a convenient means for conceptualizing these processes in the three stages of variation, selection, and retention. As these are discussed more fully in Aldrich (1979), we give only a brief outline of them here.

Variation refers to the results of mechanisms generating variation and diversity in organizational populations. Sources of variation include conflict over the control of resources within an organization, ambiguity in the definition of organizational reality, accidents, errors, tactical or strategic moves, creativity, and just plain luck. Whatever variation's source, differences across behaviors, roles, or subunits of organizations provide the raw material for potential changes in form.

Selection refers to the external pressures exerting influence on organizations and posing contingencies resulting in population differentiation. Those organizations surviving are those that are *relatively* more effective at achieving their goals, within the constraints set by the environment, than their competitors. Because the organizations relevant to this discussion are primarily privately owned, profit-seeking entities operating within the context of a modified free-enterprise market structure, the driving force of the selection process involves economic viability within a competitive context.

Williamson (1980a,b) has argued that many of the organizational changes identified by Chandler (1977) and others can be explained using a transactions cost approach. In this view, the selection pressures exerted on businesses to efficiently use their resources lead to "governance structures" in which transactions costs are minimized. Three dimensions are posited as determining how an organization deals with contractual relations: uncertainty, the frequency of transactions, and the level of transaction-specific investments required by a transaction. Using this scheme, Williamson has examined some of the same organizational changes discussed in this article. His application of the argument is restricted because of the paucity of information available in the historical record, but he nonetheless demonstrates the usefulness of viewing changes as a response to selection pressures rewarding efficient transactions, both with labor and suppliers/customers.

Edwards (1979) has pointed to a distinction between economic efficiency (as it is commonly understood) and "profitability" as the key factor in determining which forms will be abandoned or retained in any given historical context. Whether a distinction can legitimately be made between these two concepts depends upon the strength one attaches to the political rather than the competitive market forces at any given time. Although recognizing the possible importance of such a distinction, we will avoid an explicit choice on this issue by retaining a broad view of economic viability as the ability to satisfy certain minimal standards of economic return, without going into further detail on how or by whom such standards are established.

Given this loosely defined economic framework, the key environmental factors are the availability of the financial capital, the raw materials, and the labor required to generate the desired goods or services and the means necessary to transport both material inputs and finished products to the sites where they will be processed or consumed. Environments may be characterized by both the level and accessibility of economically relevant resources in terms of the dimensions in Table 2. As James Baron (personal communication) has noted, other organizations are a very salient feature of modern organizations' environments, and environments could be conceptualized as giant matrices of interorganizational relations (see, for example, Aldrich and Whetten, 1981). Using interorganizational matrices, *capacity* refers to an organization's relative position within networks of transactional dependence; *stability* refers to the continuity of matrix patterns over time; and *concentration* refers to the connectedness and density of local portions of the matrix.

The nature of the resource environment will have certain systematic effects on the activities of economic organizations attempting to adapt themselves to such environments. For example, stable concentrated en-

Table 2.   Dimensions of Environments

Environmental capacity (scarce, abundant): The relative level of resources available to an organization within its environment, varying from lean or low capacity to rich or high capacity environments.

Environmental stability–instability: The degree of temporal fluctuation in environmental elements and resources. Note that high turnover may still be patterned and thus predictable, or it may be unpatterned and therefore highly unstable.

Environmental concentration–dispersion: The degree to which resources, including the domain population, are evenly distributed over the range of the environment. Varies from random dispersion to high concentration in specific locations.

---

vironments are more likely to provide support for large, complex organizations, whereas unstable or highly dispersed environments (relative to the ease of transport) are likely to be more highly populated by smaller and simpler forms (Aldrich, 1979). Furthermore, organizations that are highly adapted to a particular resource environment may be adversely affected by any significant changes in that environment. As will become evident in the succeeding pages, the American economy has undergone substantial changes in the relative availability of human and material resources, and these changes have played an important role in the nature and timing of key changes in the form of organized economic activity that predominated in any given historical period.

Selection is obviously not an entirely unilateral process: organizations may interact with their environments to discover niches reducing detrimental environmental shocks. In this manner, through feedback or exchange processes, organizations or action sets may act on their environments and create niches more conducive to their own needs. Opportunities to modify environmental constraints are more readily available to large, powerful organizations, although even they often bow to external forces. A few years ago, United States auto manufacturers would have been cited as examples or organizations able to exercise strategic choice and dominate their environments—today we recognize the shortsightedness of such a vision.[4]

In historical terms, the nature of the selection process can be posed as the relative balance between choice and constraint. Pfeffer and Salancik (1978, p. 18), following March and Simon (1958), argued that prior decisions or compromises among competing interest groups structure subsequent organizational changes. Pursuing their analysis, Dawson (1980, p. 52) noted that this model "allows for iteration between choice and constraint over time and acknowledges that what is an unalterable constraint for one person, group or organization is in fact the result of the 'choices' of others exercised on the basis of power and influence in accordance with perceptions of interest." In one sense, this assertion is true by definition, for all human action can be described in terms of "choices" and it is unlikely that people make decisions *not* perceived to be in their interest, just as it probably is true that the powerful have their way more often than the weak. *Why* people perceive particular decisions as "in their interest," however, is often problematic (Bacharach and Lawler, 1980). An even more serious problem with posing the issue in Pfeffer and Salanciks' terms, however, is that they are concerned with change in *particular* organizations, whereas we are interested in *populations* of organizations. Our concern is with the forces that change the relative distribution of organizational forms in populations rather than with explaining a specific instance of change in a given organization.

Retention refers to the mechanisms and processes that facilitate the persistence of selected forms, unchanged, over time. Forms may persist because the niches they occupy have not changed, because they are protected against environmental changes by legislation or powerful sponsors, or because of internal structures that constrain departures from previously selected forms. The latter possibility is, of course, the focus of most research on bureaucratization and the extent to which bureaucratic forms inhibit organizational variation. One of the most significant developments in twentieth century managerial ideology was the growth of the "systematic management" movement and its concern for preserving successful managerial routines discovered through hard-won everyday experience.

The three stage model of variation, selection, and retention helps us understand how the historical process works in such a way that the myriad of possible organizational forms is reduced to a smaller range of those fulfilling the "relative effectiveness" criterion at any given point. Variation between organizations provides the occasion for selection pressures to make their weight felt; and if retention mechanisms are effective, the selected form will persist. New forms may replace earlier ones because existing organizations adopt new modes of technology, coordination, and control, because new organizations arise that embody new forms, or because of a combination of these reasons. The distribution of organizational forms at any given time affects the environmental constraints within which forms operate in subsequent periods, and thus outcomes from previous periods must be considered an additional constraint on organizational forms in succeeding periods (Heydebrand, 1977).

We turn now to an examination of organizational forms and their evolution during three historical epochs: (1) the transition from the pre-factory to the factory system, occurring in the early to mid–nineteenth century; (2) the transition from competitive to monopoly capitalism, also known as monopolistic competition, occurring in the late nineteenth and early twentieth centuries; and (3) the transition from early to "mature" monopoly capitalism. Each of these periods shows distinct variations in resource environments and in dominant organizational forms, and our task will be to identify those elements of the selection process that were important in determining which variant forms were retained under changing environmental conditions. In this way we hope to demonstrate something of the manner in which organizations interact with their environments by means of variations in form, as well as demonstrating the contribution that the population perspective makes to our understanding of the historical pattern of organizational change.

THE MERCANTILE-COMMERCIAL PERIOD: HANDICRAFT TO FACTORY PRODUCTION

From colonial times until after the Civil War, most production organizations in the United States were oriented toward local markets and operated on a very small scale with a heavy reliance on handicraft techniques. Such organizations controlled the activities of their employees (if they had any) through direct face-to-face relations and through a reliance on the internalized role requirements acquired during long periods of apprenticeship in the acquisition of a particular craft. Organizations were created within an environment characterized by an already high and still increasing degree of inequality in the distribution of wealth and by very low levels of worker organization or collective resistance.

The Resource Environment

Four characteristics of the environment were of particular importance for organizational forms in this early period: (1) the development of communication and transportation networks; (2) the distribution of natural resources; (3) a chronic shortage of unskilled wage labor; and (4) the uneven distribution of wealth in the United States.

Initial pressures for changes in organizational forms came not from technological improvements in production processes but rather from changes in the organization of production made possible by expanding markets. Market expansion, as Chandler (1977) has documented, was facilitated by gradual but far-reaching changes in transportation and communication networks. Canals and turnpikes were significant for a time on the East Coast and the North Central Region, but by the midnineteenth century they were eclipsed by the railroads. Producers in the early stages of industrialization who wanted to reach regional or national markets made use of the distribution networks originally created to market imported goods. Later, improvements in transportation and communication mechanisms permitted some producers to create their own distribution networks and others to use the services of middlemen distributors. The opening up of local markets to outside forces increased environmental instability for local business organizations.

The organizational carrying capacity of the environment was quite high as a result of the extraordinary abundance of natural resources in North America. Unskilled wage labor, however, was chronically in short supply. These two factors were closely related because the government's liberal land policies kept land prices under $2.00 an acre in the decades before the Civil War. It has been estimated that between 1820 and 1850 it would take a person with average wage and employment experience fewer than 5 years to accumulate sufficient savings to purchase 160 acres of Federal land (Brownlee, 1974, p. 121).

Scarcity of wage labor affected not only the growth of factory production but also the organization of agricultural production. Agriculture was the dominant industry in the American economy, accounting for more than 55 percent of the nation's output and 53 percent of the labor force at the time of the Civil War. Attempts to establish farming on a large-scale manorial style as had been commonplace in Europe were largely failures prior to the introduction of slavery, primarily because the high wages that would have been needed to retain laborers would have made production of the dominant cash crops of that time (e.g., cotton and tobacco) economically unfeasible. Similarly, the opportunities available at the frontier maintained a steady pressure on aspiring industrialists to enhance labor productivity and kept wages in the industrial sector well above those paid by competing manufacturers in England and on the Continent. Factory employment during this period was drawn largely from the "secondary" work force, including unmarried women, children, and new arrived immigrants without sufficient capital to purchase land.

This situation can be contrasted with the more familiar model of industrial development in an economy in which agricultural production contains a high degree of labor surplus or "hidden unemployment." Kindleberger (1967) built on earlier work by Lewis concerning the possibilities of growth in such a "dual economy." He suggested that an economy benefiting from a highly elastic source of labor supply during a period of rapid economic growth will face substantial cost increases once the underemployed labor surplus has been exhausted. These cost increases, if not accompanied by sufficient productivity increases through the application of physical or human capital investments, will result in a reduced rate of profit and a slowdown in the rate of economic growth. The lack of such an elastic labor supply in the American setting may help explain the relatively slow growth of the American industrial sector during the antebellum period.

The shift to factory-based production that began toward midcentury did not represent a major shift in the nature of American consumption patterns. American incomes were already high by the standards of that time, and a wide range of non–necessity items were already being provided locally by craftsmen or small-scale factory production. The shift to large-scale factory production was conditioned primarily by the geographic growth of markets and the rapid declines in transportation and communication costs that occurred (Chandler, 1977). Enlarged markets made it possible to reduce unit production costs by introducing new techniques of production. However, these techniques also required a greater use of unskilled relative to skilled labor, a factor that was already in short supply in the American setting. Thus the shift to factory production was encouraged by changes in the resource environment leading to reduced transportation costs, but the nature of American industrialization continued to be conditioned by the relatively high costs of unskilled labor in the American context.

The fourth environmental factor affecting organizational creation during this period was the high level of concentration in wealth holdings. The distribution of wealth is significant for the creation of organizational forms because any large-scale new venture (e.g., the railroads or oil production) can draw capital from two sources: government and private investors. Government investment in the nineteenth century was limited to a fairly narrow range of economic activities (e.g., the railroads), and so the bulk of investment necessarily came from private investors, both foreign and domestic.

How concentrated was wealth prior to the Civil War? Inequality in family wealth-holdings has evidently always been high in the United States, beginning in the agricultural–commercial era and continuing into the industrial era. Based on estimates by Alice Hanson Jones, Lindert and Williamson (1976, p. 99) concluded that the wealthiest 10 percent of potential wealth-holders in the United States in the early 1770s held a little over 60 percent of all personal wealth. (This figure appears not to have changed much from the previous century.) By 1860, samplings from the manuscript census by Lee Soltow and Robert Gallman indicate that the upper 10 percent controlled over 70 percent of all wealth. Lindert and Williamson posit that wealth inequality reached its all-time high in the 1880s.

The extent of wealth inequality is conveyed more sharply by figures from urban samples. Soltow and Gallman, studying Baltimore, New Orleans, and St. Louis with the 1860 census, found that the top 20 percent of the population held over 90 percent of the wealth, whereas the bottom 60 percent held essentially no wealth at all (Turner and Starnes, 1976). As long as most organizations were quite small and few barriers to entry existed, wealth inequality's affect on organizational creation was slight. However, as the scale of enterprise began to increase with industrialization, entrepreneurial opportunities were undoubtedly limited to persons having access to wealth.

Technological Change

In the American context, the abundance of resources such as wood, coal, and iron expanded the scope of technological choices available to organizations, while labor scarcity meant that production technologies would be oriented toward capital or resource-intensive methods (Rosenberg, 1977). American entrepreneurs and inventors were much less constrained than Europeans in their use of resources, as witnessed by power sources such as high pressure steam engines or the overbuilding of railroads, representing an extremely resource-intensive mode of transportation.

However, the shift to mechanized production also required a great use of unskilled labor, in contrast to the earlier reliance on skilled labor in the handicraft mode of production. This kept factory wages high relative to European competitors because of the wide range of alternative opportunities open to unskilled labor in the American context. It also meant that American ingenuity would be turned toward developing labor-saving innovations in production techniques imported from England during this period. As Gunderson (1976, p. 173) noted, "those processes where American technology was considered to be superior in the antebellum period were universally characterized by a saving on labor, often at the cost of using somewhat more capital or natural resources."

Industrialization, above all, meant the breakdown of tasks and the mechanization of production. Hirsch (1978), in her study of the process of industrialization in Newark, New Jersey, during the first half of the nineteenth century, identified three stages in the transition from the traditional craft organization of production to the factory system (see also Braverman, 1974). First, tasks were differentiated and work fragmented, as production processes were made more complex. Expanding markets meant that output could increase enough to justify a much finer division of labor than previously. Piece rates were replaced by a wage system, although the attempted abolition of piece rates provoked such conflict that the system persisted in some industries until the end of the century (e.g., boot and shoe manufacturing) and in others well into the next century (e.g., machine tools). Second, simple machines were introduced to perform tasks that were easily routinized. With the increased use of machinery, jobs could be filled by unskilled, lower-paid labor.

Third, after tasks were fragmented and machines developed to perform the simpler jobs, nonhuman power sources became more important. Firms dependent on water power concentrated in regions with easily harnessed streams and rivers, but the more important constraint was the inefficient transmission of power from source to machine. Even firms using steam power were forced to contend with linking all their machines to a central power source. Improvements in reducing the size of steam power sources (coal and oil fired) and, eventually, the introduction of electric motors, made possible the development of free-standing machinery. These developments, in turn, dramatically hastened the mechanization of production in mass production industries. Some industries made the transition from craft to factory production by midcentury (such as in the manufacture of hats, trunks, and leather goods), whereas others were almost untouched by mechanization (such as blacksmithing or carpentry). Clearly, not all tasks lent themselves to industrialization, and in some instances worker resistance inhibited the introduction of new technology, as in boot and shoe manufacturing (Yellowitz, 1977).

Coordination

In this early period, very little coordination between organizations existed above the enterprise level. Until the 1860s, agriculture dominated in the national economy, and production in this sector was primarily on a small-scale, highly competitive level. Throughout most of the early period of industrialization, the manufacturing sector produced only a small proportion of the total national income, and most manufacturing firms were relatively small. Production was carried out in these small units—with dozens as opposed to hundreds of workers that followed later—using traditional power sources: water, wind, animal, and human. Decisions on investment and production were made by these thousands of small producers in response to market forces, with most producers quite specialized and therefore dependent upon other producers and suppliers for essential goods and services (Chandler, 1977).

As transportation costs began to fall, business organizations that previously enjoyed a somewhat protected existence in semi-isolation found themselves exposed to the bracing effect of competition from nonlocal organizations. Selection pressures changed and business failures increased. Economic development in particular communities became intimately related to regional and national—business cycle—developments. Depressions and panics in 1837 to 1843, 1854–1855, and 1857 made their mark throughout the economy. Integration into a network of expanded markets by no means homogenized the environment or the organizational population, as differences remained in the extent of nonlocal orientation, technological flexibility, access to markets, and so forth.

Labor Control

Some theorists have described labor's fate in the process of industrialization as the "deskilling of labor," but this phrase conceals more than it conveys. Industrialization created new forms of organization *and* new forms of work, including thousands of jobs that had no precedent in the preindustrial economy. Over three-quarters of the labor force of 1.9 million persons in 1800 were in agriculture, with probably less than 50,000 in "manufacturing." By 1840, there were one-half million jobs in manufacturing and by 1850, over one million. As these jobs were being created, the process of task fragmentation, job specialization, and deskilling was already underway. While many workers experienced industrialization as a transformation of their traditional livelihood, the bulk of the industrial labor force came to their jobs from the agricultural sector or from abroad.

Control of labor throughout this early period of transition was primarily via simple control, involving face-to-face relations between owners and employees. Most employed persons worked on farms or plantations, where personal contacts presumably were frequent and remuneration only partially in the form of wages. In the rest of the economy, relations between owners and employees rested on a more explicit wage-labor foundation, with landless workers having no alternative but the selling of their labor power. "Simple control" therefore should not be taken to mean the *absence* of control mechanisms, and certainly for workers in cities, the periodic economic crises reminded them of their dependent status.

A comparison of traditional craft production with factory organization (Hirsch, 1978) highlights the *new*—not necessarily transformed—status of labor in the United States economy by 1860. (We emphasize the novelty of this status to reinforce our point that widespread wage-labor employment in nonprimary sector enterprises represented a new development in national economic organization.) Craftsmen knew their products completely and served long apprenticeships to acquire such knowledge. The factory system (and employment in the distributive trades as well) made apprenticeships irrelevant, as production (or distribution) was broken down into many separate tasks. Craftsmen worked with their own hand tools, whereas industrialization meant the use of machines owned by employers. Self-employed craftsmen set their own remuneration schedules, and farm laborers often shared in the fruits of their labor, whereas factory employers controlled remuneration and resisted bargaining over wages.

Although there were various workingmen's political movements during the early period of industrialization, most were short-lived and none coalesced into a unified working class movement. Most working class movements were highly localized, rarely spreading beyond a city or cluster of cities. Strikes by shoemakers in Geneva, New York, during the 1830s, for example, were confined to that locality. Most labor organizations were founded by skilled craftsmen, not common laborers, as for example the National Trades' Union. Founded by a loose federation of city labor councils in 1834, it did not survive the economic panic of 1837. The "friendly and benevolent societies" founded by workers' associations throughout this period limited themselves mostly to providing sickness and death benefits (Miller, 1980). Lack of a significant organized challenge from labor allowed entrepreneurs wide latitude in their use of resources, perhaps setting the stage for the violent confrontations that occurred late in the nineteenth century.

Summary

By the conclusion of the first era of transition, organizational forms had been transformed along three dimensions. First, some production organizations were becoming larger and more capital intensive, with a sharp discontinuity developing between manufacturing organizations using machines and nonhuman power sources, and other organizations, especially in the distributive trades, finance, services, and agriculture, relying on traditional small-scale, labor-intensive technologies. Second, the scale of organizational niches was increasing, with most entrepreneurs still relying on rather unsystematic management practices to achieve coordination of their organizations' activities. Few organizations, except in the transportation and communications industries, were large enough or well-organized enough to avoid going into the market for most of their essential resources. Third, simple control sufficed to handle most of the labor relations of the typical organization. Continuing immigration and the absence of a strong labor movement made labor compliance nonproblematic.

EMERGENCE OF THE INDUSTRIAL GIANTS, 1870–1920

During the second era of transition, major sectors of the United States economy were gradually dominated by large, technologically sophisticated firms with fairly complex structures for administratively coordinating resource allocation. Most organizations in most industries retained many of the attributes of organizational forms from the earlier period, however, as coordination was via markets and labor control was fairly simple.

The Resource Environment

Three developments in the post-Civil War period were particularly significant for organizational forms: (1) the heightened availability of capital; (2) a rapid increase in the flow of labor from abroad; and (3) the enlarged scope of markets resulting from the consolidation of earlier advances in transportation and communication technology. Following the Civil War, the industrial sector began to overtake agriculture as the major focus of American economic activity. The economy experienced an accelerated rate of economic growth, an increasing degree of instability, and a major shift in its relationship with world markets.

The Civil War marked a watershed with respect to capital resources, signaled initially by a dramatic increase in domestic saving. Savings rates rose from 15 percent prior to the war to a high of over 28 percent during the 1880s.[5] During the 1870s the substitution of capital for labor became a central feature of economic growth in the United States as the increase in the nation's capital stock exceeded growth in output levels from the 1870s till the 1920s.[6] Of special significance was the growing importance of financial intermediaries, such as banks and insurance companies, as mobilizers of capital. Prior to the 1870s investment bankers, particularly international bankers, had concentrated on railroad stocks, whereas following the panic of 1873 they moved increasingly into industrial securities and began to exert significant influence not only on the direction of investment but on the nature of corporate structure as well (Brownlee, 1974, p. 190–198).

With regard to natural resources, the gradual depletion of empty lands in the frontier areas reduced the attractiveness of small-scale farming relative to wage labor and led to a reversal in the flows of internal migration toward urban rather than rural areas. In the last few decades of the nineteenth century, almost two-fifths of United States counties lost population. A report by the Director of the Census in 1890 announced the disappearance of the American frontier and sparked an increased awareness of natural resource limitations and the need for conservation.

Reduced transportation costs, as well as the continuing attraction of relatively higher wages in American industry, contributed to a strong increase in the rate of net immigration during this period. During the last decades of the 1800s and the first decade of the twentieth century, immigrants accounted for about 40 percent of population growth and a disproportionally larger share (over 70 percent) of the increase in the industrial labor force. Thus immigration began to supply a much higher degree of labor elasticity during this period and may account for the steady increases in economic growth that distinguish this period from the more gradual industrialization process observed during the prewar years.[7] The high level of geographic mobility of labor lessened the possibility for working-class solidarity and indirectly decreased worker resistance to industrialization (Thernstrom, 1968).

The working population was not totally unaware of the competitive threat arising from free immigration, and during the early years of the twentieth century several attempts to limit immigration were passed by the Congress, only to be defeated by Presidential opposition. Following the First World War, however, national sentiment coalesced behind antiimmigration sentiments, and the series of Quota Acts passed between 1921 and 1919 virtually eliminated immigration as a reserve source of flexible labor suppy (Higham, 1955).

Thus, the balance of resources available for economic activity in the years following the Civil War differed from those of the antebellum period primarily in terms of the greater amounts of capital and unskilled labor available for industrial activity. Combined with the enlarged scope of consumer markets achieved by the earlier investments in the transportation and communication services, these factors provided a congenial environment for the acceleration of industrial growth that occurred during this period.

Technological Change

Changes in technology (defined to include the technology of information processing as well as materials processing) were a source of *variations* between organizations and industries, with selection criteria favoring innovations that increased the speed and scale of output. Our review of technological change in this era is colored by a debate over the forces generating continual technological innovation and also the factors leading to the implementation of new technologies. At the extreme, the argument separates theorists who see innovation and rationalization of organizational processes as the result of a highly autonomous, even immanent, force, and those who view these processes as closely linked to the distribution of power and wealth in societies. We cannot resolve this debate here, nor would it be fruitful to structure our review in such stark terms. Instead, we will try to give the flavor of both positions.

Technological change, as a semiautonomous force, was carried along by the capital goods industry and by the growth of institutions and associations promoting "scientific" research and its application. The capital goods industry was extremely important for the emergence of new organizational forms because new product innovations and improvements depend upon the ability of the capital goods producers to make a machine that can turn out the new product (Rosenberg, 1963). In the earlier period of industrialization, machines were made by the firms that used them to turn out their final product, whereas by 1880 a separate machine tool industry had evolved. This industry was the source of the continual diffusion of innovations to other industries and was partially responsible for the highly cumulative nature of technological change in the late nineteenth century.

Firms in industries producing dissimilar products nonetheless used highly similar production processes, and this similarity was an important contributor to the continual growth of the machine tool industry. Even though firms were producing for highly differentiated markets, and industries began to vertically disintegrate as markets expanded (firms made components of products rather than entire products), there was still a convergence toward the use of similar technology. For example, many industries had to make use of metal-cutting and metal-shaping machinery. So, the development of new techniques was assisted by the size of the market for machine tools and the core function served by the machine tools industry. The skills and technical knowledge used in this industry were relevant throughout all machine-using sectors, and thus it played an accidental but vital role in the transmission of technological innovations from one industry to another.

An emphasis on standardization and interchangeability vastly simplified the tool and machine-makers' jobs, and United States machine tool design (in contrast to European) stressed specialized, high-speed machinery (Rosenberg, 1977). A mass production orientation toward sales and marketing rather than one of market segmentation meant that firms like American Tobacco, Singer, and McCormick were continually searching for techniques to boost production. Associated with this orientation, of course, were heavy demands on managers' abilities to coordinate high-volume flows of raw materials to finished products.

In addition to the continuous generation of technological innovation from the cumulative feedback between tool-using and tool-making firms, "science" itself was harnessed to the yoke of organizational needs. Braverman (1974), Noble (1977), and others have argued that under nineteenth century industrialization, science was rationalized and made subservient to the requirements of industry. Previously, "science" was mostly the trial-and-error learning of persons working on immediate production problems. First in Germany and then in the United States, government and industry established research units that made natural science a cornerstone of industrial development. National differences persisted, however, and the United States was slow in breaking away from an empiricist, pragmatic approach to science: the Germans had Hegel, whereas the United States had Dewey!

Land-grant colleges, technical instututes, colleges of engineering, and the growth of professional associations of applied scientists (e.g., mechanical engineers and chemical engineers) all contributed to a stock of technical knowledge from which entrepreneurs and managers could draw. In Braverman's felicitous phrase, *science* was "transformed into a commodity," bought and sold like the other factors of production. The difficulty with Braverman's phrase, however, is that it implies much more organizational control of the process than the historical record can support, *if* we take it literally. The last few decades of the nineteenth century were tumultuous times for business firms, as bankruptcies, mergers, and general turnover in the organizational population were extremely high. A more reasonable reading of Braverman indicates that he is referring to the industrial environment, in which science and engineering were becoming integrated into the production system just as much as traditional resources, such as labor and capital. Indeed, Braverman argued that science itself was transformed into capital.

United States manufacturers surged far ahead of their European competitors in interchangeability and precision of the production process, but the archetypical example of industrialization—the assembly line— was perfected relatively late. Ford began experimenting with the assembly line production of parts and then in 1913 began building complete automobiles on a line. Production skyrocketed: 170,000 in 1912, 300,000 in 1914, 0.5 million in 1915, and 2 million in 1923. Throughout this time, the price was dropping and in 1924 a Ford cost only $290. Technological innovation in this key United States industry had a ripple effect that spread through other industries, forcing change in their technologies as well. Mass production (on the assembly line and elsewhere) speeded everything else up, and suppliers and distributors had to adopt new techniques to keep up, as in the glass and steel industries.

The technology of office work changed as well, although not nearly as dramatically as production technology. The development of the telegraph, typewriter, practical carbon paper, and other office machinery allowed offices to bureaucratize their information-processing procedures and thus expand their operations. Such operations remained very labor intensive, as was true of the techniques used by the vast majority of organizations throughout this period, as most retail and service units retained traditional methods of purchasing, stock control, and selling. Even this generalization must be qualified by recognition of those manufacturers who integrated forward into their own retail sales outlets. Nonetheless, widely divergent rates of variation and of change in selection criteria between industries, especially between capital versus labor intensive ones, contributed to the increasing heterogeneity of forms in the organizational population.

Coordination: The Significance of Hierarchy

Changes in the economic environment and in the technology and scale of internal organization confronted owners from the 1860s onward with problems of coordination on two fronts: managing complex interdependencies with other organizations and maintaining an effective degree of integration of increasingly dissimilar internal activities. As Chandler (1977), Litterer (1961, 1963), Pollard (1960), and others have noted, the consequence of organizational responses to these problems was the rise of a professional managerial class and the development of systematic management techniques. Interdependencies with other organizations were dealt with by internalization of some transactions, mergers, joint ventures, and the development of action sets linking organizations in a common response, such as trusts and cartels. At the national level, coordination was facilitated by the growth of a national banking system and a national industrial securities investment system, both increasingly government regulated, for example, by the Federal Reserve System and the Securities and Exchange Commission. Problems of internal coordination eventually led to the development of complex managerial hierarchies and the bureaucratization of organizational processes.

Why didn't a science of management develop during the initial period of United States industrialization? In the earlier age of basic structural changes in technology, it was difficult to isolate the "managerial" function from that of technical supervision or commercial control (Pollard, 1960). All the functions we think of today as comprising the "managerial function" were combined in the entrepreneurial role, and the scale of enterprise was typically too small to permit the employment of managers. Manufacturers tended to borrow practices from the past, such as adopting the accounting practices of merchants and underestimating or leaving out charges for depreciation of their capital.

Needs for orderliness and a system of practices didn't go unnoticed by owners, as exemplified in the use of printed forms by early manufacturers. Systematic planning of factory layouts took place before building, and plans had to be drawn for the flow of work in buildings such as iron works, breweries, and multistory cotton mills. A division of "managerial" labor, to the extent that it occurred, took place either through a division of labor among partners or through the creation of new roles: managing director and subordinate directors and managers. The latter development marked the beginning of a true hierarchy (Pollard, 1960).

Most coordination, however, was a result of an organization's dependence on other organizations, or, in short, the market. Efficient coordination was achieved to the extent that orderly procedures were followed in adjacent organizations and industries—among suppliers and customers. As Chandler (1977) noted, most large traditional enterprises, such as the cotton plantations of the South, were at the mercy of external forces, and exhibited little concern for rationalized labor or cost control.

As markets expanded and product technologies became more oriented to high volume output, selection criteria began to reward those enterprises that used *internal* mechanisms to keep track of resource allocation. By 1860, owners of integrated textile mills were using accounts to determine the unit costs of their production processes. Chandler (1977) cited the Springfield Armory, created after the War of 1812, as an example of an early prototype of the modern factory, as it had extensive controls over accountability for materials, quality, and piecework wages. However, this information was not really used to make decisions about the reorganization of production.

As long as most organizations relied on nonsystematic management and market-induced coordination of resource allocation, the organizational population remained a heterogeneous mixture of fairly small organizations run by owners and their close relatives or a few highly trusted employees. Economic conditions after the Civil War intensified competition between organizations and began to drive producers to seek new markets, expand production, and find ways to reduce costs. The aggregate effect of many individual firm's survival strategies were cycles of consolidation, expansion, overproduction, failure, merger, and so on. Evidence of competition's effect can be seen in falling prices for many goods.

In 1870 there were still only a handful of large factories, concentrated in textiles: in cotton goods, an average of 142 workers per plant; in worsted goods, 127; and in iron and steel, 103 (Nelson, 1975). Average plant size in most other manufacturing industries was well under 100. By 1900 more than 400 firms had 1000 or more workers, with the largest plants still in a relatively small group of industries: textiles, metals, machinery. Average size was over 300 in cotton and worsted goods, and in iron and steel, and over 50 in many other industries. Increased size and complexity created problems that were met by changes in organizational form.

Internally, administrative coordination via managerial directives permitted greater productivity, lower costs, and higher profits than coordination via transactions negotiated with external agents. Functions previously handled by an owner or a close associate were delegated to centralized functional departments for purchasing, production, marketing, transportation–distribution, and other specialized activities. The careers of the salaried managers who ran these departments became increasingly technical and professional, selection and promotion were on the basis of merit, career ladders developed, and professional associations formed. The greater effectiveness of organizations adopting professional managerial hierarchies versus those persisting in traditional methods was vividly illustrated in higher profitability for the former, for example, the Pennsylvania versus the New York Central railroad systems.

By twentieth century standards, the size of the professional managerial staff was fairly small. A rough indication of the size of the managerial class is given by the number of clerical workers—the office support staff. In 1870 there were 82,000 clerical workers in a labor force of about 12 million. By 1900 the number had climbed to about 900,000 (or 3 percent of the labor force), and by 1970 to 14 million (or 18 percent of the labor force). Although the managerial hierarchy was thin at first, it was the nucleus of power and continued growth of a new class that did not fit neatly into the traditional "owner" or "worker" classes.

In many cases increased internal complexity was created when manufacturing firms abandoned arms-length market transactions with retailers and integrated forward into final sales. As Williamson (1980b) pointed out, the added organizational costs of internalizing such transactions made economic sense only under certain conditions; for example, the failure of the existing distribution network, the marketing of a product that required extensive point-of-scale demonstration and service, or the marketing of a product whose quality was difficult to control. For example, Gustavus Swift found a great deal of resistance to his proposed long-distance shipment of dressed beef to the East Coast and so constructed his own distribution network, complete from refrigerated railway cars to delivery vans. When manufacturers whose environments did not warrant forward integration attempted it anyway, selection pressures forced the abandonment of the effort, often at great cost. American Sugar Refining, manufacturer of an undifferentiated durable consumer staple, attempted forward integration as a competitive strategy but had to give up after large losses (Porter and Livesay, 1972). Large brewers in the late nineteenth century attempted to create a system of tied houses, along the lines of the English system, with bars and taverns selling only one brewer's products. The maintenance of the system was too costly and brewers went back to selling to independents (Cochran, 1948).

Externally, coordination was achieved through new forms of interorganizational arrangements, resulting in the increasing concentration of capital. The corporate, limited liability form of organization broke the previous barriers to consolidation, and the liberalization of laws of incorporation in New Jersey, New York, and Delaware permitted a widespread merger movement in the last decade of the nineteenth century. Liberalized laws and the growth of another new form, investment banking, together with the public acceptance of industrial securities, made possible the growth of truly giant corporations.

The increase in merger activity was not much affected by the Sherman Antitrust Act of 1890, as it was strictly interpreted to cover only trusts.

Thus, corporations by-passed this weaker interorganizational form and moved directly to mergers. Moody (1904) estimated that more than 5000 independent manufacturing firms disappeared by merger between 1880 and 1904, and the resulting 300 companies controlled about 40 percent of all manufacturing capital by 1904 (cited in Boyle, 1972, p. 31).

Growth in economic concentration, in the form of giant firms in some industries with enough market power to control large portions of their environment, was opposed by a growing working class movement and a multiclass coalition of small capitalists, farmers, intellectuals, and middle class and professional groups (Edwards, 1979). The coalition was divided by its stand on unions, but it did succeed in pushing the Justice Department to file a series of anti-trust suits prior to World War I: Standard Oil was broken into ten parts, American Tobacco was broken into four parts, and suits filed against U.S. Steel, Armour, Dupont, ALCOA, and others may have discouraged some mergers. In the long run, however, the coalition was only partly successful, as during and immediately after World War I large firms used the power of the Federal Government to solidify their dominant positions, as on the War Industries Board and in eliciting government's support in defeating strikes.

Control: The Rise of Technical Control

In the late nineteenth and early twentieth century, "labor" was becoming a problem. A variety of responses by organizations, mostly large corporations, indicate the extent to which organized labor and market pressures were transforming mechanisms of labor control (Bendix, 1956). Welfare capitalism, technical control, and "scientific management" were the results of a wide variety of tactics adopted by managers to cope with such pressures.

As the trends toward larger workplaces and the replacement of the craft system by the factory system continued into the last decades of the nineteenth century, labor militancy grew stronger. From shop floor resistance to collective struggle, managers of firms in many industries found they had to concern themselves with the control of their work force. Additionally, traditional methods of labor control were inefficient relative to the rationalized methods advocated by proponents of "scientific management."

Many firms had made the transition from simple control to some form of hierarchical control in which foremen, managers, and supervisors exercised direct control over workers, rather than allowing craft-control or supervision by owners themselves. Hierarchical control operated on the principles of vertical lines of communication and discouraged lateral contacts. The system left a great deal of discretion in the hands of lower level supervisors, who were generally untrained in managing other persons and whose approach consisted of demanding that the work be carried out. This loosely coupled arrangement encouraged arbitrariness and thwarted top management's attempts at tighter control over labor costs.

Unlike employers in the earlier era of industrialization, late nineteenth century managers were confronted with a labor force that included many second or third generation industrial workers plus immigrant workers from societies with histories of working-class activism (Montgomery, 1976). These workers were familiar with the demands of factory work, including timeliness and discipline, and most accepted their status as employees rather than owners. However, they resisted the adoption of new technologies and modes of organization that reduced or eliminated workers' control over immediate decisions on how work was to be performed. Workers in particular firms fought new modes of control through output quotas, sabotage, and wildcat strikes, while actions were also taken by unions to unite workers across all firms within an industry.

Collective labor action included attacks on subcontracting (used by employers to get around union rules), stringent efforts to enforce union rules regarding the use of helpers, hours, piece rates, etc., and strikes. Strikes were obviously most effective when they were coordinated across all the firms in a locality and when a union could induce other unions to come out "in sympathy," in effect creating a labor cartel. During the 1880s, the percentage of strikes called by unions increased as the number of strikes increased, and issues involved not just wages but also union recognition, rules, and working conditions. Two crests of sympathetic strikes occurred between 1886 and 1892, but by the mid-1890s such strikes decreased (most were defeated). Montgomery (1976) noted that the AFL encouraged coordinated strikes, whereas other powerful craft unions were not sympathetic, such as the Iron Moulders, the brick layers, and the stone masons.

Employer actions against such challenges to their control took the form of lockouts, legal prosecution, and court injunctions. Escalating conflict led to many major strikes during this period: the Pullman strike of 1894, in which "abuse of power" was the major issue and which was put down by government intervention; the Colorado mine strikes of 1903 and 1904; the bloody confrontation between coal miners and Rockefeller interests in 1914; the U.S. Steel strikes in 1919, and in which the union's existence was at stake; and periodic strikes by the IWW between 1909 and WWI, where the issue was explicitly workers' control of the production process. Thus, although unions never succeeded in organizing more than about one in ten of the potentially eligible members during this time, periodic highly visible confrontations made labor control salient to most employers. We must emphasize that, except for a few radical unions such as the IWW, labor organizations by the late 1890s no longer questioned the right of capitalists to own the means of production or to make decisions about what to produce and how much to invest. The Industrial Commission hearings of 1901 vividly demonstrated organized labor's acceptance of negotiation and collective bargaining as the normal relationship between capital and labor.

One organizational form that failed to gain a foothold in the last half of the nineteenth century was the producers' cooperative form (Aldrich and Stern, 1978). Producers' cooperatives are industrial organizations practicing a type of economic democracy in which workers jointly hold title to the firm's assets and collectively make decisions about production and management. Although producers' cooperatives received quite a bit of attention from the mass media and certain unions (Knights of Labor, Iron Moulders) in the last three decades of the nineteenth century, only a few hundred were created. The economic and legal environment of the times rewarded *individuals* who were entrepreneurs rather than groups. Ambitious and energetic persons who were interested in advancing their personal fortunes had nothing to gain by devoting their efforts to an enterprise in which the benefits were shared equally by all. Only when material incentives were supplemented by ideological-purposive or so-ciable-solidary incentives did cooperatives have a chance, and such op-portunities were very limited.

Technical control was both a cause and a consequence of labor strug-gles against management. Beginning first in the textile industry during the early era of industrialization, when spindles and looms were attached to a water-driven power shaft, industrial workers found the rhythm of work paced by machines rather than by their own desires (Edwards, 1979). In the textile industry workers were tied to a fixed station, and sociable interaction with other workers limited. Few industries could adopt such an extreme form of long-linked technology, and so most remained organized on a "shop" basis, using simple or hierarchical control, for example, the iron and steel and brewing industries. Ma-chinery that made craft skills obsolete was introduced in many industries, but the social organization of production was unchanged: firms still relied on foremen, inside contractors, or skilled workmen to control the be-havior of lower-level workers.

Gradually, however, as the intensification of competitive pressures drove managers to search for ways to cut costs and as labor control became increasingly problematic, machine-based control spread. Any variation in organizational processes that increased profitability by low-ering unit costs (rather than raising prices) gave a firm a selective ad-vantage over competitors, although the diffusion of innovations made the advantage short-lived. Industries where technical control was compatible with existing production technology included meat packing, electrical products manufacturing and automobile manufacturing. Production technology in other industries made strict technical control difficult, for example, where production was in single units or batches.

Technical control is based on the principles of providing unambiguous direction to workers of those operations they are performing next, thus establishing the pace at which work is carried out. A technological presumption in favor of the line's work pace is thus established, eliminating "obtrusive foremanship." Struggle between capital and labor was mediated by the production technology itself rather than by the human agents of capital. At the Ford factories in 1914, a work force of 15,000 was directed by just 235 persons, not counting top management (Edwards, 1979). Foremen's roles were transformed because they became the enforcer of the technical structure's needs, monitoring rather than initiating worker compliance. Workers' roles were transformed by their loss of autonomy, as technical control essentially isolated them from other workers through restrictions on movement and social interaction.

Paradoxically, while technical control made the direction and evaluation of worker behavior easier, it actually increased problems of rewarding and disciplining labor (Edwards, 1979). At first, the interchangeability of workers under technical control allowed managers to hire labor on a purely quantitative rather than qualitative basis. Employers could count on large numbers of unemployed persons to keep workers docile, as immigrants, blacks, and other marginal subgroups were employed. But large masses of workers in a shared subordinate position, technologically linked in the production process, are a receptive audience for appeals to worker solidarity. Management's vulnerability to collective labor action became readily apparent, as automobile manufacturers in the 1930s learned.

Scientific management, as represented by F. W. Taylor and his followers, tapped the same rationalizing spirit as technical control but was a much more self-conscious ideology. (Every text on organization theory includes a discussion of "Taylorism," so our review will be mercifully brief.) Scientific management developed in the last several decades of the nineteenth century at the Midvale and Bethlehem Steel companies, promoting a new conception of management and workers that required the application of "scientific methods to task analysis." Because scientific management required firms to commit resources to the study and redesign of tasks, it was mainly adopted by large firms. The principles of Taylorism were applicable to all types of work, not just machine-paced tasks, and thus it could both substitute for and complement technical control.

Braverman (1974) identified three principles of scientific management. First, the labor process was disassociated from the skills of workers, as management observed how work was carried out and then systematized this knowledge. Second, the conception of work was separated from its execution, on the grounds that time and money were saved by such segmentation. Third, management used the knowledge gained to control each step of the labor process and its execution, using step-by-step instructions.

Scientific management had several consequences for organizational forms. The labor process was divided between separate sites and separate bodies of workers, reducing labor control problems but increasing needs for coordination. New occupations were created to monitor work, or as Braverman puts it, to "maintain the paper shadow form" of production. Merkle (1968, 1980) argued that the new middle class gained substantially from Taylorism because of the new class of professionals required to implement it. Rising numbers of educated children of the middle class were absorbed, and as the spirit of work rationalization spread, more and more people were required in administrative services positions.

We think scientific management is less important as a body of techniques than as a tangible sign of a more fundamental change in managerial orientations toward labor. Problems of technological innovation and coordinating resource allocation had preoccupied owners and managers in the beginning phases of industrialization, but now another frontier of cost control had opened up—rationalizing the allocation of human resources.

Welfare capitalism, or "welfare work," was a third form of labor control that emerged in the late nineteenth century. It grew out of the activities of a few paternalistic employers and humanitarian reformers and diffused rapidly at first, with 10 percent of all wage earners in 1908 covered in some way (Wood, 1960). John Patterson (of National Cash Register) emphasized its role in reducing production costs and increasing profits, and the National Civic Federation formed a department to promote welfare capitalism in 1904 (Nelson and Campbell, 1972). Welfare capitalism was a rather diffuse system, but generally included special consideration for workers' physical comfort, opportunities for recreation, savings and borrowing plans, insurance and pensions, and provision of company-built homes. Advocates stressed its benefits in stabilizing labor forces and promoting worker loyalty, but clearly combating unionism and strikes were also important objectives.

Welfare capitalism developed in different environments than scientific management. Scientific management was introduced in department stores, textile mills, mines, and steel mills, while welfare capitalism was usually

found in firms employing large numbers of women or in plants that were
geographically isolated (Nelson and Campbell, 1972). Just as Taylorism
demonstrated management's concern for the rationalization of work, so
welfare capitalism was a reflection of another current in American ideology—concern for the destructive effects of industrialization on workers. For example, a high rate of accidents in 1903–1907 aroused public
opinion and led to many states passing workman's compensation laws.
States also intervened to protect the traditional status of families, passing
laws regulating working conditions for women and youth.

Whether welfare capitalism succeeded is an open question. Edwards
(1979) argued that it reflected management's awareness of the need for
positive incentives in systems of hierarchical labor control, but that it
did not deal with the basic issue of power relations. For example, U.S.
Steel invested heavily in welfare work and yet was rocked by a major
strike in 1919. Welfare capitalism, in this view, failed to bribe workers
into accepting a form of control that was authoritarian and paternalistic.
Nelson and Campbell (1972), however, argued that welfare capitalism
eventually merged with elements of scientific management and evolved
into the modern field of personnel relations. Edwards actually supports
this view, as he argued that welfare capitalism demonstrated the importance of positive incentives for conformity.

Summary

By the beginning of the last third of the nineteenth century, substantial
differentiation within the organizational population was becoming apparent. Critical features of the economic infrastructure had been laid
down: a network of rapidly growing urban centers, linked by water and
rail transportation, constituted a vast market for mass-produced consumer goods. Manufacturing firms whose products and technologies en-
abled them to do so adopted the technology of mass production, while
the producers' goods industries (machine tools, iron moulding, oil refining, etc.) expanded apace. Major sectors of the United States economy
were dominated by large, technologically sophisticated firms with fairly
complex structures for administratively coordinating resource allocation.
Growth in the scale of organizations from dozens to hundreds, and then
thousands, of employees posed enormous problems of internal coordination and control for the newly emerging managerial class. Some of this
growth was simple expansion following existing structures, but much of
it involved vertical and horizontal integration as organizational elites
pushed for the internalization of problematic transactions.

Coordination of resource allocation proved less troublesome than control of labor as a "problem," with unions growing powerful enough in
some instances to challenge the power of management. Firms with mass

production or continuous process technologies had adopted technical control of the labor process, whereas others relied on welfare capitalism or scientific management. Certainly most organizations did *not* fit this description as they operated on a small scale and were at the mercy of market forces. Labor control in most organizations was still of a simple or hierarchical nature, as welfare capitalism and scientific management were too costly for them to implement.

Some sections of the capitalist class in the 1870s and 1880s had been fearful of a working class or socialist revolution, but by the turn of the century, labor, capital, and the state were operating in fundamental agreement on the structure of the economy. Periodic challenges continued into the 1930s, but large, imperatively coordinated organizations were an accepted feature of American life. Thus by the end of the nineteenth century, the United States economic structure of monopoly capital was fairly well in place, with monopoly firms dominating many industries, organized labor at a temporary peace with capital, and new forms of coordination and control firmly entrenched in the organizational populations.

POST-WORLD WAR I: THE RISE OF THE MANAGED MARKETPLACE

By 1920 the United States economy had undergone major changes in the type of goods and services produced and in the nature of the economic organizations involved in their production. Most gainfully employed persons now worked for employing organizations rather than for themselves, producers increasingly served national rather than local markets, and a growing number of businesses in the distributional industries were directly affiliated with major manufacturers. The federal government was still quite small by European standards, but the mobilization demands of WWI had brought innovations in both the form and substance of federal economic management, many of which were eventually incorporated in the more lasting reforms of the New Deal and the post-WWII period.

Thus, at the eve of the modern age, the population of economic organizations had become highly differentiated, primarily due to the increasing scope and magnitude of organizational activity. However, increasing scale was accompanied by an increasing degree of economic risk that could only be reduced through regularization of factor and product markets. As the opportunities for monopolistic control were exhausted, in part by legal restriction, innovation shifted in the direction of new techniques for stabilization of the business environment. Organizational efforts to gain mastery over the environment were vigorously pursued not only at the enterprise level but also through the activities of action sets and the nation-state as well. These efforts may be credited, in part, for the relatively uninterrupted prosperity of the post-war period and justify the characterization of this period as "the rise of the managed marketplace" (Brownlee, 1974). Although we cannot hope to analyze all the forces that have influenced organizational development since the 1920s, this section will highlight a few of the more significant environmental and organizational changes during these years.

The Resource Environment

The major characteristics of the economic environment during the post-WWI period have been (1) increasing organizational control over capital and labor markets, (2) the dominant role played by the United States in international finance, and (3) the changing economic role of women and blacks within the domestic labor force. During the 1970s, changes in each of the three main environmental factors may have signaled the start of a new period in American economic and organizational development, although it is as yet too early to assess the precise significance of these events.

With respect to capital resources, WWI marked a turning point for the United States, which became a net exporter rather than importer of investment capital for the first time in its history. Despite the heavy responsibilities imposed by its position as the major creditor within the world economy, the United States chose to pursue a strongly protectionist policy at this time, combining demands for rapid debt repayment with highly restrictive tariffs on imports. Some authors have suggested that such policies, combined with the erratic performance of the Federal Reserve system during these years, were responsible for the extent and duration of economic distress that characterized the 1930s. Whether financial conditions were in fact responsible for the Great Depression or not, this period marked a great increase in domestic control over capital resources. This control was further enhanced by modifications in the banking system introduced during the New Deal years.

Following WWII, American foreign and economic policy demonstrated a more balanced posture toward the economic concerns of America's major trading partners, even when continued restraint meant, at times, a somewhat slower rate of growth in the domestic economy. In the 1970s, the United States consciously abandoned its financial leadership position, and the rapid accumulation of capital resources in the oil-producing states has provided further confirmation of the altered nature of the economic environment during this decade.

With respect to natural resources, the economy continued to benefit from a rich endowment, although with the exception of Alaskan oil, no major new domestic discoveries of commerical value were made during this period. The consumption of raw materials grew less rapidly than total output, indicating a more intensive use of the available materials (Brownlee, 1974, p. 337). Over the course of the postwar period, the United States gradually became a net importer rather than exporter of raw materials, particularly in a few areas such as fish, certain metal ores, and crude petroleum. The decade of the 1970s brought an abrupt appearance of international shortages in several key import areas, particularly oil and food, with major consequences for the international business climate.

In the area of labor supply, major changes have occurred in the employment patterns of blacks and women, resulting from the labor shortages generated by the ending of free immigration in the 1920s. For women, who had supplied an important proportion of unskilled factory labor during the antebellum period (prior to the rapid increase of European immigration), the ending of immigration brought tightened labor markets during the war years of the 1940s and 1950s and a corresponding increase in female labor force participation, particularly among married women (Easterlin, 1968). Women's share of the labor force rose at a rate of between 1 and 2 percentage points per decade between 1890 and 1930, while during the 1940s it rose more than 5 percentage points, and has gained approximately 4 percentage points or more in each succeeding decade. In remarking on the economic consequences of these changes, Brownlee's comments (1974, p. 218) are reminiscent of Kindleberger's hypothesis of the relationship between labor supply and economic growth, as he noted that "without this expansive source of female labor, mainly white, the nation would have had to look abroad once again for its labor supply, make heavier investments in enchancing the quality of labor, introduce further labor-saving technology and organizational change, or accept a slower pace of economic growth."

The role of blacks in the United States economy has also been substantially altered in the years since WWI. Conditions for blacks in the North between 1900 and 1940 have been described in terms of a "split labor market" (Bonacich, 1976) because of the use of black workers for strike-breaking purposes, but these decades did mark the first significant penetration of blacks into the major goods-producing sectors of the economy. With the regularization of labor relations that occurred during the 1930s and 1940s, blacks were incorporated into the major industrial unions and the "split market" conditions of the early 1900s were substantially curtailed (Geschwender, 1978). However, as with women workers, blacks remain concentrated in certain less preferred job categories of "occupational ghettos" within the economy. Such job segregation, or "segmentation," has been held responsible for the continued differential between black and white earnings and employment experience, despite major equalization of educational attainments over this period (Harrison, 1972).

Workers in core firms of the United States economy have enjoyed increased employment security and enhanced earnings through the application of ever greater amounts of capital investment. One of the outstanding features of labor relations during this period was the increased length and stability of employment contracting which, although it provided a less risky environment for human capital investments, also reduced the organization's ability to respond flexibly to new and anticipated economic conditions.

Some labor force flexibility was provided by black migration and increased female labor force participation, but this was reduced as these groups began to apply organized political pressure to gain access to preferred jobs in sheltered labor markets. Viewed in this light, the renewal of large-scale immigration during the 1970s, this time from Southeast Asia and Latin America, may introduce a significantly greater degree of flexibility or response to changing economic environments, which the Kindleberger hypothesis would suggest might be an important precondition for renewed economic growth. As with other environmental changes that have occurred within the past decade, however, it is difficult to judge how prolonged or widespread the economic impact of such changes will be.

Technology

Chandler's (1977, p. 298–299) argument, which we are inclined to accept, is that new forms of coordination were much more important than further mechanization once capital-intensive technologies permeated manufacturing industries. Organizations gained selective advantages not through mechanization but through coordination (and control).

The technical core of manufacturing firms certainly continued to evolve, as managers used machines to replace human labor whenever they could. In contrast to European manufacturers, who used machines to rough out products that were then hand finished, United States manufacturers used hand labor only when absolutely required (Litterer, 1961). Manufacturers worked for interchangeability, requiring extremely close tolerances, and the continued vitality of the United States capital goods industry supplied the machines to make this possible. United States workers were not more "skilled" than Europeans; their skills were simply used for different ends, as United States manufacturers concentrated on the process while Europeans concentrated on the product. Rosenberg (1977) has also noted that the openness of United States manufacturers to external relations, especially with the capital goods sector, facilitated a mass production orientation.

In addition to the trend toward greater capital intensity of production, there was increasing differentiation between industrial sectors in the levels and rates of increases in capital intensity. Averitt (1968) characterized this period as one of increasing differentiation between "core" and "periphery" *firms,* whereas Galbraith (1967) wrote of the widening gap between the planned and competitive *sectors.* Core firms exhibited distinctive forms of technological development, as well as sophisticated control and coordination processes. Periphery firms tended to retain older forms of production technology and organization structure. Averitt stressed that "core" firms are found in any industry, but they are most often in the durable manufacturing, resource extraction, and regulated industries.[8]

Coordination

The two early waves of merger activity (occurring at the turn of the century and during the 1920s) emphasized first horizontal and then vertical coordination of firms with closely related or overlapping economic interests. The third great wave of mergers, beginning during the 1950s and continuing through the 1960s, emphasized product diversification and the growth of large conglomerate ventures. This increase in the scope and diversity of economic enterprise was accompanied by increasing Federal attention to and regulation of such activities, although the actual impact of such regulation and its expressed intent were not always in the closest correspondence. In 1890, the Sherman Antitrust Act prohibited individuals or firms from engaging in cooperative behavior "in restraint of trade," although its major initial effects were on unions and industrial trusts, not corporate mergers. In 1914, the Clayton Act and the creation of the Federal Trade Commission strengthened the legal basis of antitrust actions, but actual antitrust actions were quite limited because of the courts' conservative interpretation of the law, and so market functioning was only marginally affected. In the 1920s and 1930s the Webb-Pomerene Act, the Miller-Tydings Act, and the Robinson-Patman act weakened antitrust efforts by allowing combinations among firms in export markets, allowing agreements between manufacturers and retailers to fix retail prices, and by "prohibiting price discrimination in such a way that it often prevented price competition" (Weiss, 1971). In the 1940s and 1950s, however, prosecution of firms under the antitrust laws became more vigorous, the courts revised some of their earlier interpretations, and new attitudes toward corporate mergers came close to prohibiting any merger among substantial and viable competing firms, even in moderately concentrated markets. Yet these regulations have not been interpreted in ways that hinder merger activity resulting in corporate diversification, regardless of the overall size of the resulting conglomerate.

Why concentration has tended to increase, with giant firms dominating many industries, is an unsettled question, mainly because organization theorists seem to have taken for granted the significance of "strategic choice" within the successful firms. Alternative models positing a significant component of randomness in growth processes (such as Gibrat's law) do not seem to have been taken seriously, and yet some simulations have shown quite a good fit to actual trends (Prais, 1976). Until the population ecology model's emphasis on random variation within and between organizations is given more empirical attention (Aldrich, 1979), we must rely on the more orthodox accounts of organizational evolution. In any event, whether a particular organization prospered because of strategic choice or blind luck is not as significant as the fact that most successful organizations exhibited similar characteristics.

The large firms that emerged from the period of transition from competitive to monopoly capitalism were successful in integrating mass production with mass distribution, in coordinating resource flows within the enterprise, and in administering services internally that required large staffs of professionals. Integration was achieved by firms in a wide variety of industries, demonstrating that selection criteria had been modified across-the-board in the span of four to six decades, an incredibly short era in sociohistorical time. Chandler's studies (1962, 1977) emphasized the externally directed nature of the changes that occurred—whereas first mover advantages gave the first firms in a niche an enormous advantage, identifying promising niches was a formidable task.

Functions internalized by large firms included advertising, marketing and sales, financing from internal funds rather than capital markets (when profits and cash flow warranted internal financing), and selling on credit. Firms in industries producing semiperishable products where continuous process machinery permitted massive output from a few plants faced problems of buying raw materials in large quantities and expanding their sales organization to dispose of output: cigarettes, breakfast cereals and other grain products, canned soups, milk, pickles and other foods, soap, film, chewing gum, yeast, and soft drinks fall into this category. Firms producing perishable products needed transportation departments to ensure rapid shipment of scheduled deliveries, as in the meat packing industry. Firms that sold products requiring extensive point-of-sale set-ups and servicing had to create their own retail sales networks, as in the sewing machine and agricultural machinery industries. Firms selling producers goods, such as generators, motors, printing presses, and shoe machinery, had to compete both in servicing and engineering quality.

All these functions lay outside the core production process, and their coordination required increasing numbers of middle managers who created systematic procedures that could be formalized and thus used again and again. Because traditional management practices relied on custom and a "personal" type of supervision, the persistence of organization structure was very much dependent on consistent external pressures and low levels of turnover among managers and supervisors. As the scale of operations increased under monopoly capitalism, communication gaps opened between levels and departments, leading to problems of "control loss" (Williamson, 1975). The management literature of this period described problems of internal disorder, confusion, and waste (Litterer, 1963)—retention of selected processes had become problematic.

From management's perspective, the problem was how to transfer information from one level to the next and from one generation of managers to the next. Internalization of a host of transactions created scattered, loosely coupled organization structures, and management literature gradually focused on some prescriptions hard-won from experience: develop standardized ways to handle routine, create repetitive tasks, use specialists to free top executives for other tasks, define subordinates' scopes of responsibility, and follow universalistic policies in promoting managers (Litterer, 1961). In short, what emerged from a self-conscious examination of successful management practices were recommendations to *bureaucratize* organizational coordination processes (Perrow, 1979).

Production-control, cost-accounting, and wage systems were proposed to promote the vertical and horizontal flow of information and to give management a mechanism for predetermining the decisions of lower management and workers. Curiously enough, Braverman (1974), Marglin (1974), Stone (1974), and others have argued that specialization and fragmentation were often deliberate management policies, aimed at wresting control of production from workers, whereas the early management literature identified fragmentation and loose-coupling as serious barriers to gaining control over costs. As the issue here concerns both the *motives* and the *consequences* of management policies and as our interest in this article is in aggregate outcomes, we will not choose sides. Case studies of the labor process, such as those Pfeffer (1977) and Burawoy (1979), indicate how much we have to gain from further empirical work in this area.

From the population ecology model's perspective, the elaboration of hierarchical coordination mechanisms can be understood as the selective retention of an organizational form that met three criteria. First, systematic management techniques allowed managers to account for every last scrap of resources and every hour of labor time, thus meeting pressures for cost cutting that constituted the new mode of oligopolistic competition. Second, new methods of coordination permitted departmentalized and then divisionalized structures, in which coupling between units was loose enough to buffer the nonproduction units from the impact of continual technological innovation but tight enough to cope with the constantly changing nature of interdependencies and information needs (Thompson, 1967). Third, organizational forms under monopoly capitalism—in many industries, but not all—were highly complex, compared to their ancestors of the early nineteenth century. Their persistence in a form suited to their environments was made possible by internal retention mechanisms. Moreover, the new form was widely copied, and because selective elimination or retention depends on variation in the forms of a population, diffusion of the new practices created some homogeneity of form across rather divergent industries.

Many of the cost savings achieved by these techniques could only be maintained within the context of a fairly high and stable rate of capacity utilization. Therefore, extreme fluctuations in the level of production placed a constraint on the adoption of such organizational forms. Extreme fluctuations in demand can create such a high level of risk and uncertainty, even for large firms, that internalization of transactions is foregone in favor of subcontracting with independent producers. In a discussion of large firms in Italy and France, Berger and Piore (1980, p. 107) pointed out that economic uncertainty has given firms an interest in preserving the autonomy of traditional firms rather than integrating them: "despite technological backwardness, lower productivity, and even sometimes the inferior quality of their output, they still provide an essential flexibility. How valuable this flexibility is to the modern firm has been underscored by developments over the past few years in Italy, where, despite the economic crises, the quota of work subcontracted out of big plants has risen, not fallen." The efficacy of specific organizational forms can only be assessed with regard to specified environmental conditions.

Once made, managerial decisions to internalize previously independent activities may give firms a stake in protecting such costly investments (Williamson, 1975). For firms unable or unwilling to divest themselves of accumulated activities, the pursuit of economic stability can become an important end in its own right. For this reason (among others), as greater numbers of firms in the post-World War I era adopted highly complex, interdependent structures, they exhibited an increasing interest in coordination of economic activity *outside* the boundaries of the enterprise. Much of this interest was channeled into attempts at enlisting governmental support for economic stabilization.

As the first major American experiment in coordination of economic activity through federal administration, the mobilization for World War I could not be termed an unqualified success. Yet it did demonstrate that industry-wide coordination was possible under conditions of national emergency. A large proportion of the staff for the over 5000 administrative agencies created during this period were drawn from the managerial ranks of the private sector and returned to this sector when the mobilization effort was abruptly dismantled following the ending of the hostilities. Efforts in monitoring and forecasting production trends continued to be supported by the private sector through research foundations such as the National Industrial Conference Board and the National Bureau of Economic Research.

During the Depression, further attempts were made to provide a stable basis for business activity under the authority of the National Industrial Recovery Act. The concept of industry-wide coordination of forecasting and production planning received widespread initial support from such diverse interest groups as the Chamber of Commerce, the National Association of Manufacturers, and the leaders of the industrial union movement. However, political deadlock between these groups led to indecision, vacillation, and eventual failure to achieve effective coordination of production, well before the Supreme Court announced its decision on the question of constitutionality. In contrast, the institutions and programs created by the Agricultural Adjustment Act and the National Labor Relations Act were substantially more effective in reorganizing and regularizing market demand conditions of concern to commercial farmers and organized labor.

In the period since WWII, major advances in forecasting capability have been introduced through such innovations as input–output analysis and electronic data processing, as well as through major new undertakings in data collection by both federal and private agencies. Private support for coordination and planning of economic production has continued to be expressed by lobbying groups such as the Committee of Economic Development and the National Planning Association. Nevertheless, federal commitment to the discretionary use of fiscal and monetary policy for promoting conditions of stable economic growth has been far more tentative in the United States than among many other western economies. During the 1960s a consensus appeared to be developing over the uses of tax cuts and "full employment" budgeting, but the stagflation of the 1970s brought many of the accepted axioms of macroeconomic theory into question, and political opinion today on the appropriate role of government in the private sector remains diffuse.

As the above discussion demonstrates, organizations have increasingly reacted to problems to managing external environments by a collective

response, chiefly through forming *action sets*. An action set is a group
of legally distinct units that are oriented toward providing a mutually
supportive environment (Aldrich, 1979). Trade associations or business
interest associations have formed within industries, with peak associations as the Chamber of Commerce of the National Association of Manufacturers cutting across industries. These organizations exemplify the
collective response of business to competition, labor problems, and state
regulation in the United States, but a major difference between Western
Europe and the United States remains in the number of such associations,
their strength, and their functions (Offe and Wiesenthal, 1979; Schmitter,
1974; Staber, 1980).

New Forms of Labor Control

By the early decades of this century, technical control had substantially
replaced simple hierarchical structures in the mass production industries.
But as Edwards (1979) noted, technical control cannot by itself constitute
an adequate labor control system. Such control is not relevant to all
forms of production, and it tends to homogenize the work force, making
a firm vulnerable to unionization. A major distinction between labor
control systems of the nineteenth and twentieth centuries is the present
accommodation of labor organizations within a legally sanctioned collective bargaining framework. Federal recognition of the right to union-
ize, combined with the success of industry-wide organizing by the CIO,
produced a major change in the climate of labor control during this
century. In addition to wage demands, job security gained emphasis, and
organizational attention turned to reducing the costs of labor turnover
through better market forecasting and stabilizing production.

The major developments in internal coordination and market management introduced by bureaucratic organizations led to a shift in emphasis
from labor control per se to the enhancement of stable conditions of
production. Effective organizations were not simply those that had
adopted hierarchical coordination of their many subunits but were those
characterized by effective retention mechanisms. Selection of appropriate
processes was not enough; they had to be retained so that workers could
call on them again when required. From a population ecology perspective, improvements in retention mechanisms raised the standard of relative efficiency that organizations had to meet to remain viable. Large,
vertically integrated organizations with a complex division of labor were
most affected, whereas small organizations on the economy's periphery
were touched only indirectly through their dealings with larger firms or
through the invasion of their domains by large firms (as in food retailing).
Although the precise origins of these new forms of labor control may

be obscure, both the environmental climate (unionization) and the increased interdependency of labor tasks within a highly coordinated organizational superstructure raised the costs of replacing workers and provided an incentive for innovations aimed at reducing labor turnover within the enterprise.

Bureaucratic control evolved from the same rationalization of organizational processes that spawned Taylorism and scientific management, perhaps owing more to Taylorism than to technical control for its birth. It emerged most visibly in forms large and powerful enough to allow top management a free hand in introducing new methods, such as IBM and Polaroid. New procedures were introduced piecemeal (in response to problems rather than as a grand plan) and did not completely eliminate older forms. Where unions already existed, bureaucratic control's evolution was colored by the different interests of the two parties: management wanted to use it to limit union power and to draw them into the joint disciplining of workers, whereas unions saw bureaucratization as codifying and thereby protecting negotiated gains.

Edwards (1979) argued that bureaucratic control first emerged in the office, where it was applied to white collar work, and then was applied on the shop floor. However, Stone's (1974) case study of the steel industry makes it clear that one aspect of bureaucratic control—an internal labor market—was adopted at an early stage by firms, after the defeat of the Amalgamated Association of Iron, Steel and Tin Workers.

Just how does "bureaucratic control" operate, and in what ways is it distinguishable from simple or technical forms of labor control (Edwards, 1979)? Perhaps most characteristically, bureaucratic control establishes the impersonal force of "company rules" or "company policy" as the basis for labor control, and thus institutionalizes the exercise of hierarchical power in organizations. Perrow (1979), summarizing March and Simon's argument (1958), has called this "unobtrusive control," contrasting it with more visible forms of labor control.

It affects all three aspects of a firm's labor control practices: direction of tasks, evaluation of performance, and rewards and discipline. Work tasks are defined and workers directed within a highly stratified job structure. Job descriptions create a finely graded division of labor and break up the homogeneity of the work force. Many separate strata, lines of work, and foci for job identity result from a systematic analysis of all tasks in an organization. Job descriptions set out what constitutes a "fair day's work," and managers and supervisors can settle arguments by merely pointing out, "It's a rule."

Evaluation and supervision of workers' performance is on the basis of the job description. Comprehensive job descriptions constrain not only workers but also those persons responsible for evaluating them, that is, supervisors, foremen, lower-level managers. Thus, the entire evaluation process is brought under strict control from above, in contrast to the high level of evaluator arbitrariness under earlier forms of control.

Rewarding and disciplining workers is now a matter of eliciting co-operation and enforcing compliance with impersonal rules. Earlier forms of control relied heavily on negative sanctions, whereas the new system emphasizes positive (as well as negative) sanctions. Employees who are favored with high marks on standardized employee-evaluation forms can look forward to such benefits as higher pay, promotions, jobs with more responsibility, cleaner jobs, vacations, and so on.

Internal career ladders, or what Doeringer and Piore (1971) labeled "internal labor markets," are an essential aspect of bureaucratic control. Linking jobs in a hierarchy of job grades (each successive job with higher pay but not necessarily more rewarding content) rewards workers for remaining with a firm. Not only does this mechanism reduce labor turn-over and induce workers to acquire firm-specific skills, but it also reduces worker solidarity by increasing competition among workers for jobs of a higher grade.

One interesting organizational consequence of bureaucratic control has been the creation of new units within large organizations, i.e., personnel and industrial relations departments. Personnel management developed as a specialty around the time that "welfare capitalism" and "scientific management" were finding their way into organizational practice. Personnel selection, training, time and motion studies, job standardization, accident prevention, and other functions were taken up by the fledging specialty (Wood, 1960). Many personnel departments were eliminated in the years immediately after WWI, but by 1928 they had made a comeback, and more than one-third of the plants with more than 250 employees had such a department. Today, no sizable organization can be without such a department, given state and federal laws governing employment and compensation.

Bureaucratic control differs from previous forms of control in that it is an indirect path to the intensification of work (Edwards, 1979), creating a formalized structure and then rewarding conformity to it. Three principal types of behavior are sought and are rewarded accordingly: an awareness of the rules and willingness to follow them; habits of predictability and dependability; and, ideally, internalization of an organization's objectives. Internalization, if fully realized, would actually transform bureaucratic control into consensual control, creating a "clan" or "commune" structure.

Bureaucratic control enjoys a selective advantage over other forms because it depersonalizes the exercise of power, making power appear to emanate from organizations themselves, rather than from those persons issuing orders. Costly struggles over the legitimacy of orders are thus avoided, and the processes of coordination and control merge imperceptibly into one another. Underlying this form of control, of course, is the requirement that workers be predisposed to accept the legitimacy of such elaborate structures. Bowles and Gintis (1976), among others, have argued that United States institutions, especially the educational system, are structured so that people learn to take the existing system as given. Certainly United States labor unions after the early 1900s accepted the principle that ownership of capital carried with it privileges not open to workers. As Stone (1974) pointed out, unions have cooperated with the elaboration of internal labor markets, for they view it as a more universalistic way of allocating pay and fringe benefits. In the steel industry, unions cooperated in the rationalization of job classifications after WWII and backed policies that preserved job ladders and the principle of seniority in access to higher job grades.

Thus, the introduction of bureaucratic forms of labor control can be viewed in light of the general shift toward more managed and more predictable market conditions that has characterized the post-war period. It should not be inferred from this, however, that all jobs within the economy, or even within the bureaucratic firm itself, can profitably be set up along these highly inflexible lines. In fact, highly structured internal labor markets may generate a complementary need for loosely structured or unstructured markets to absorb unavoidable fluctuations in production levels that would be too costly to accommodate within the regular or primary job structure. Giddens (1973) noted that government and major corporations have a joint interest in promoting stable economic growth and regulating inflation. Unions' support for the necessary policies has been bought, he argued, by long-term contracts, generating a core labor force economically committed to the corporations. Left out of this contract, of course, are many workers in periphery firms, which tend not to be unionized.

Job security benefits, such as long-term contracts, are thus extended to a particular group of workers on the basis of their willingness to make a long-term commitment to the firm. This contrasts with the traditional practice, at least with craft workers, of dispensing job benefits on the basis of skill possession. Thurow (1975) suggested that firms may later make specific training investments in these workers, generating a degree of skill justifying their higher contract costs, but such skills are not the rationale for the contract. The offer of preferred working conditions to some nonskilled workers within the enterprise is made on the basis of their potential for employment stability and "trainability."

Evidence of job-related differentiation between workers who are otherwise equal in skill and educational preparedness remains fraught with controversy over methods and measurement. Attempts to "explain" earnings differentials in terms of an accumulation of returns from prior human capital investments fail to account for interindustry differentials between individuals who are homogeneous with respect to human capital characteristics. Although such differentials appear to be reduced when characteristics such as sex and race are taken into account (Weiss, 1966), it is unclear whether such findings should be interpreted as evidence of employment discrimination or unmeasured productivity differentials. Although interpretations vary, empirical estimation of earnings functions consistently show interindustry and interfirm differentials that are independent of the available measures of personal productivity.

Other studies provide corroboration for the hypothesis that firm-specific characteristics, such as firm size and organizational form, condition the quality of employment experience for otherwise homogeneous workers. Alexander's (1974) study of the "average firm mobility" of workers in 76 industries showed that internal labor markets were most prevalent in large firms: in industries in which interfirm moves were under 10 percent of total employment, over half the employees worked in establishments employing 1000 or more persons. By contrast, over half the workers employed in "unstructured" labor markets (interfirm moves exceed 20 percent of industrial employment) were employed in establishments with fewer than 50 employees. Masters' (1969) analysis indicates that plant size is an important determination of interindustry earnings differentials, independent of other possible influences, such as the degree of product market concentration, unionization, or capital-intensive production techniques. Furthermore, Masters suggested that the high-wage strategy pursued by larger firms may tend to dominate the wage structure of the industry, particularly where unions are strong, and collective bargaining is handled on an industry-wide basis. In this way the labor market behavior of the large firms may set the pattern for the smaller firms in the industry, even though the economic rationale (i.e., complex, bureaucratic organization) for such labor control practices is not as appropriate to the situation of the smaller firms.

Summary

Organizations using highly capital-intensive technologies, bureaucratized methods of labor control, and complex administrative allocation of resources now dominate the economy in terms of assets and receipts (Aldrich, 1979, p. 40–49). Government is a massive presence in the environments of all organizations, large and small, whereas organized labor affects mostly the core firms in the economy. Changes in the resource environment of the United States organizational population that generated new organizational forms by no means eliminated earlier forms of organization. Earlier forms, using labor-intensive technologies and simple labor control and relying on market-induced coordination, continue to exist, especially in the retail and services sectors.

CONCLUSIONS AND IMPLICATIONS

Interest in organizational change has always been high, but only a narrow range of the spectrum of change has been covered. Few investigators have risked taking the sweep of time covered by Chandler (1962, 1977) or Edwards (1979), concentrating instead on quite limited time spans (Aldrich and Reiss, 1976) or ignoring the issue of a proper time span altogether. Resource availability problems have apparently limited most investigators to case studies of one or a handful of organizations, and the full range of possible variation in organizational characteristics (size, mode of labor control, etc.) has rarely been captured.

The population ecology model's treatment of forms requires theoretically informed, historical investigations. We have been restricted to a selective review of secondary sources, using three characteristics of form suggested by Aldrich's (1979) definition of an organization: a goal-directed [coordination], boundary-maintaining [control], activity system [technology]. This scheme is also suggested by the attention devoted to technology, coordination, and control in the recent literature in labor, economic, and social history, industrial economics, and organizational sociology. Because research funds are likely to be scarce for the foreseeable future, we suspect that most persons interested in the evolution of organizational forms will focus on secondary analysis of existing literature, as we have.

Our discussion of the characteristic forms of economic organization over more than two centuries of American experience has demonstrated the high degree of variation and innovation present in this organizational population. From a relatively homogeneous population of small, simply organized, and highly specialized enterprises, the American economy has developed into a highly diversified organizational population with enterprises that run the gamut from small, self-owned and operated activities to large, diversified, and bureaucratically managed conglomerates. But while innovation and variation have been important factors in this developmental process, environmental factors unique to each historical period have conditioned and channeled the direction of this development.

Table 3 presents in schematic form the main elements of environmental influence for each of the historical periods we have discussed. Table 4 shows the characteristics of the dominant forms among industrial organizations in each era, using the three dimensions of form: technology,

Table 3. The Evolution of Organizational Forms, 1800–1970

Period	Production Factor	Environmental Characteristics			Organizational Developments
		Resource Capacity	*Temporal Stability*	*Resource Concentration*	
Pre-Civil War	Natural resources	Abundant	Stable	Highly dispersed	Slow growth in small firms, high risk
	Labor	Scarce	Fluctuating	Moderately dispersed	
	Capital	Scarce	Fluctuating	Moderately dispersed	
1870–1920	Natural resources	Abundant	Stable	Dispersed (accessible)	Rapid growth, increasing firm size, high risk
	Labor	Abundant	Fluctuating	Concentrated	
	Capital	Moderate	Fluctuating	Increasing concentration	
1920–1970	Natural resources	Moderate	Stable	Increasing concentration	Moderate, stable growth, led by large firms, low risk
	Labor	Moderate	Stable	Increasing concentration	
	Capital	Moderate	Stable	Concentrated	
1970–?	Natural resources	Scarce	Fluctuating	Concentrated	Slow growth led by small firms, high risk
	Labor	Moderate	Stable	Concentrated	
	Capital	Moderate	Stable	Concentrated	

Table 4. Dominant Forms Among Industrial Organizations, by Era

Era	*Organizational Forms*
Pre-Civil War	Many small, handicraft-based organizations, using the simple mode of labor control and little internal hierarchy. Coordination induced internally via external market relations.
Post-Civil War to WWI	Growing differentiation within the industrial organization population, with a minority of organizations growing quite large. The dominant group of organizations use more capital intensive technology. Labor is controlled through hierarchical authority structures and the technical relations of production. Some larger organizations adopt internal hierarchical coordination of resource flows to achieve transactions cost efficiencies.
Post-WWI	The population is further differentiated, within and between industries. Most organizations are still small (100 employees or less), but most assets and profits are controlled by the minority of large organizations. Most large organizations have adopted hierarchical coordination of internal resource flows, but modes of labor control differ by factors such as technology and degree of unionization.

coordination, and control. Overall, the population is characterized by increasing diversity over time. In this model, the pre-Civil War period is characterized by an abundance of natural resources with a high degree of geographic dispersal, a moderate degree of available investment capital, with the major environmental constraint on new activity introduced by the scarcity of wage labor. Small firms and simple forms of coordination and control were best suited to such an environment in which an appropriate match of natural resources, capital, and labor could only be accumulated in relatively small amounts at any particular time or location.

In the period between the Civil War and the first World War, the major environmental constraints of the earlier period were reduced by improvements in geographic accessibility and major injections of labor resources produced by the closing of the frontier and mass European immigration. This period was characterized by an increased number of larger firms, increasing reliance on hierarchical and technical forms of coordination and control, and rapid rates of growth in overall enonomic activity. However, instability remained an important feature of economic activity, not only because of fluctuations in product demand, but also because of unstable conditions in capital and labor markets as well.

The period immediately following the First World War brought major institutional changes, adding greater stability and predictability to the economic environment. Labor supply was regularized by the ending of free immigration and the institutionalization of collective bargaining, while the maturation of the Federal Reserve System and new responsibilities in the international financial community brought increased stability to the capital market. Larger, bureaucratically organized firms not only prospered in this newly stabilized environment but furthered this development by introducing greater stability in internal relations and in their control over product markets. Finally, the federal commitment to maintenance of economic stability through manipulation of fiscal and monetary policy introduced expectations of greater stability of overall consumer demand. Small, simply organized firms, although they retained an advantage in marginal, high risk areas of the economy, could not take full advantage of the unique opportunities for growth during this period.

Although attempts to characterize the historical period in which one is currently involved are always risky, many observers would agree that the early 1970s marked a watershed in modern economic activity and signaled the end of the so-called "post-war prosperity" enjoyed by Western free-enterprise economies. The most outstanding characteristic of the new economic climate is a severe reduction in the level and predictability of natural resource supplies. Increasing attention is being devoted to what is termed "supply-side economics," and institutions that were considered capable of guaranteeing a secure and stable environment for economic growth are coming under fire as the major causes of organizations' inability to respond to changing environmental conditions. The move toward deregulation, the decline of organized labor, the call for constitutionally mandated budgetary restraint all represent attempts to inject greater flexibility into the institutions that condition the economic environment. Concern over the declining levels of capital investment has led to modifications of the tax structure, new depreciation allowances, and other means of reducing investment risk. In this new climate of high investment risk, small firms seem to have had a developmental advantage, with the bulk of new job growth during this period confined to industrial sectors in which smaller firms predominate. Overall, this period would seem to be most similar to the antebellum period in which a chronic scarcity of factor inputs (in that case labor, in this case natural resources) produced a period of slow economic growth localized in smaller firms that were sufficiently flexible to take advantage of the dispersed and intermittant quality of growth opportunities.

It is far too early to tell whether the current economic environment is merely transitional in nature or represents the beginning of a prolonged period of slow and intermittant growth. Should this period be prolonged, we may speculate that such conditions will have a chilling effect on the spread of bureaucratic forms of economic organization, and that innovation will tend in the direction of increasing flexibility in both capital and labor markets to offset the instability in the natural resource area. Although conglomerates already provide a means of diversification of fixed capital resources, labor markets have tended to become increasingly sheltered and inflexible over the postwar period, with high levels of "human capital" investments introducing a degree of fixity in the allocation of labor that will make rapid redeployment of the labor force both economically and politically costly. Unfortunately, at the individual level, there is nothing analogous to conglomerate structure that would allow workers to diversify their human capital investments in order to become more responsive to rapid and unexpected shifts in economic conditions. New federal initiatives in the area of "human resource management" have brought much needed attention to the problems of career planning, training, and transitional services. Nevertheless, until new institutional mechanisms are developed that can provide greater flexibility and reduced risk in human capital markets, fears of massive unemployment effects are likely to inhibit needed organizational reforms and attempts to redirect the structure of economic activity.

Research Implications

We hesitated in drawing up our agenda of research implications, as such obligatory closing exhortations to one's colleagues are properly ignored unless the preceding text has laid out an argument coherently and critically. At the risk of thus needlessly expanding our paper by a page or so, we offer the following suggestions.

First, we certainly need more historically sensitive research on organizational change. Business historians have bequeathed a wealth of material to us, mostly ignored, and organizations' archives contain information almost completely ignored by organizational researchers. True longitudinal designs that follow a panel of organizations over time are rare indeed. Doubtless much of this neglect of historical research stems from the profession's reward structure, which motivates young investigators to emphasize easily executed cross-sectional research designs. Historical research, whether from archives or surveys, is extremely time consuming, with a long lead time to pay-offs (Kimberly, 1976). Established scholars will have to lead the way in conducting such research and in encouraging greater rewards for high-quality (but low-quantity) historical research.

Second, as McKelvey (forthcoming) and Aldrich (1979) have noted, much more attention should be paid to the conditions under which our research results are valid. Contingency theories have made inroads into the implicit assumption that "all organizations are alike," but we lack an historically informed taxonomy of organizational forms that would tell us *which* organizations are alike. In the absence of such a taxonomy, cumulation of research results is nearly impossible. An historically informed taxonomy would allow investigators to make rigorous decisions about sampling frames for their studies. Currently investigators appear to give little or no thought to the question, "Which population, or set of forms, is my research generalizable to?" "Samples" are taken haphazardly as they are available to the investigator, whether through consulting contacts, geographic proximity, or the physical endurance of the research assistants! Recognition that differences across organizational forms set boundary conditions on our generalizations would heighten investigators' concerns for a reliable and valid typology.

Third, much more attention must be paid to organizational failures, i.e., the organizations and organizational forms that are selected out of the population. Almost all of the current literature is based on studies of surviving and at least moderately successful organizations. This is particularly true of the business policy journals, but the problem pervades our field. By definition, the failures are not around for study, and many vanish without a trace. Some potential failures are caught in cross-sectional designs, but without a followup we cannot identify them. The population perspective emphasizes that we can learn as much about organizational change from failures as from successes, for the failures reveal the nature of the selection criteria and their effect on variations. Growing interest in the topic of organizational decline (Whetten, 1980) may spill over into an overt concern for failures, but a more direct approach is through the mounting of more historically sensitive research.

ACKNOWLEDGMENTS

James Baron, Joan Brumberg, Bill McKelvey, Bill Ouchi, Charles Perrow, Dave Ulrich, and the editors provided useful comments on earlier drafts of this paper. Sally Day, as usual, brought everything together in a finished final draft.

NOTES

1. Much of this article is written in a speculative vein, as we recognize the extent to which our arguments require further research and documentation. We hope that our analysis will be taken as suggestive of what a population–historical perspective on organizational evolution can accomplish. Readers troubled by loose ends in the arguments should rest assured that we are similarly concerned.

2. In the early nineteenth century, identifying an organization's primary technology was fairly straightforward, as few produced more than a limited range of products or services. In the twentieth century, however, matters are not so simple, as very large organizations are internally heterogeneous, owning establishments in a variety of industrial groups and running multiplant operations (Prais, 1976). For this reason, analyses of tech-

nology and its correlates in modern organizations typically focus on *establishments* or operations at a single site, treating a local unit as "an organization" regardless of its legal status vis-à-vis some larger entity. Because most organizations are small and operate from only a small number of sites, this problem mainly arises in analyses of large organizations (Aldrich, 1979).

3. Hierarchy, of course, was the dominant principle of economic coordination until markets began to predominate in the "long sixteenth century," from 1450 to 1650 (Wallerstein, 1974). Under feudalism and other precapitalist modes of production, producers were *not* free to enter into exchanges with the objective of realizing the maximum possible surplus. "Surplus," in the precapitalist era, was pumped out of primary producers through a variety of coercive political and social relationships (Anderson, 1974).

4. Early critical reaction to the population ecology perspective indicates that some organization theorists are reluctant to accept the argument that environments play a dominant role in organizational change (Van de Ven, 1979; Astley, 1980).

5. Interestingly enough, the increased rate of domestic saving may have contributed to the success of another new type of organization: religious voluntary associations. Joan Brumberg (personal communication) has noted that women volunteers' efforts at raising money were much more successful after 1870 than earlier.

6. Brownlee (1974, p. 191) suggested that the expansion of capital stock may have accounted for most of the growth of real product during this period.

7. The flexibility of immigration as a reserve labor supply may also help explain why labor unrest remained relatively insignificant throughout much of this period, since immigration flows tended to decline dramatically in response to economic slowdowns in the 1870s and 1890s.

8. Although Averitt (1968) argued that *firms* and not industries were the critical units of analysis, Galbraith (1967) ignored within-industry differences.

The population perspective's emphasis on the historical roots of diversity in organizational populations has obvious implications for contemporary debates on the relationship between segmentation of the business population and social stratification (James Baron, personal communication). Currently a great deal of effort is devoted to assigning specific Standard Industrial Classification code groupings of industries to "core," "periphery," or any number of other sectors. The population perspective emphasizes how fluid organizational segmentations have been historically, suggesting that understanding how "segments" (such as "core" and "periphery") have evolved is a prerequisite to assessing their effect on social stratification.

REFERENCES

Aldrich, H. E., *Organizations and Environments*. Englewood Cliffs, New Jersey: Prentice-Hall, Inc., 1979.

Aldrich, H. E., & Reiss, A. J. Jr., "Continuities in the study of ecological succession." *American Journal of Sociology*, 1976, *81*, 846–866.

Aldrich, H. E., & Stern, R. N. *Social Structure and the Creation of Producers' Cooperatives*. Paper presented at the IX World Congress of Sociology, Uppsala, Sweden, August 1978.

Aldrich, H., & Whetten, D. Organization sets, action sets, and networks: Making the most of simplicity. In P. Nystrom and W. Starbuck (Eds.), *Handbook of Organization Design*. New York: Oxford, 1981.

Alexander, A. Income, Experience, and the structure of internal markets. *Quarterly Journal of Economics*, 1974, *88*, 63–85.

Anderson, P. *Passages from Antiquity to Feudalism*. London: New Left Books, 1974.

Astley, G. Review of organization and environments. *Organization Studies,* 1980, *1,* 285–288.

Averitt, R. *The Dual Economy.* New York: W. W. Norton, Inc., 1968.

Bacharach, S. B., & Lawler, E., III. *Power and Politics in Organizations.* San Francisco: Jossey-Bass, 1980.

Baron, J. N., & Bielby, W. T. Bringing the firms back in: Stratification, segmentation, and the organization of work. *American Sociological Review,* 1980, *45,* 737–765.

Bendix, R. *Work and Authority in Industry.* New York: John Wiley & Sons, Inc., 1956.

Berger, S., & Piore, M. *Dualism and Discontinuity in Industrial Societies.* London: Cambridge, 1980.

Blau, P. M., & Scott, W. R. *Formal Organizations.* San Francisco: Chandler Publishing Co., 1962.

Bluestone, B., Murphy, W. M., & Stevenson, M. *Low Wages and the Working Poor.* Ann Arbor: University of Michigan, 1973.

Bonacich, E. Advanced capitalism and Black/White relations in the United States. *American Sociological Review,* 1976, *41,* 34–51.

Bowles, S., & Gintis, H. *Schooling in Capitalist America.* New York: Basic Books, 1976.

Boyle, S. *Industrial Organization: An Empirical Approach.* New York: Holt, Rinehart, and Winston, Inc., 1972.

Braverman, H. *Labor and Monopoly Capital.* New York: Monthly Review Press, 1974.

Brito, D. L., & Williamson, J. Skilled labor and nineteenth century Anglo-American managerial behavior. *Explorations in Entrepreneurial History,* 1973, *10,* 235–251.

Brownlee, W. E. *Dynamics of Ascent: A History of the American Economy.* New York: Alfred A. Knopf, 1974.

Burawoy, M. *Manufacturing consent: Changes in the labor process under monopoly capitalism.* Chicago: University of Chicago Press, 1979.

Butler, R. J. *Control Through Markets, Hierarchies, and Communes: A Transactional Approach to Organizational Analysis and Quasi Markets.* Paper presented to the Conference on Markets and Hierarchies, Imperial College, London, January 1980.

Caves, R. E. Industrial organization, corporate strategy, and structure. *Journal of Economic Literature,* 1980, *18,* 64–92.

Chandler, A. *Strategy and Structure.* Cambridge, Mass.: The M.I.T. Press, 1962.

Chandler, A. *The Visible Hand.* Cambridge, Mass.: Harvard University Press, 1977.

Cochran, T. C. *The Pabst Brewing Company.* New York: New York University Press, 1948.

Collins, R. *The Credential Society: An Historical Sociology of Education and Stratification.* New York: Academic Press, 1978.

Collins, N. R., & Preston, L. E. The size structure of the largest industrial firms, 1909–1958. *American Economic Review,* 1961, *51,* 986–1011.

Dawson, S. Natural selection or political process: The dynamics of organizational change. *Personnel Review,* 1980, *9,* 49–54.

Doeringer, P., & Piore, M. *Internal Labor Markets and Manpower Analysis.* Lexington, Mass.: D. C. Heath, 1971.

Easterlin, R. *Population, Labor Force, and Long Swings in Economic Growth.* New York: National Bureau of Economic Research, 1968.

Edwards, R. *Contested Terrain.* New York: Basic Books, 1979.

Etzioni, A. *A Comparative analysis of complex organizations.* New York: The Free Press, 1961.

Galbraith, J. K. *The New Industrial State.* Boston, Mass.: Houghton-Mifflin, 1967.

Geschwender, J. *Racial Stratification in America.* Dubuque: William Brown Company, 1978.

Giddens, A. *The class structure of the advanced societies.* New York: Harper and Row, 1973.

Gunderson, G. *A new economic history of America.* New York: McGraw-Hill Co., 1976.

Hall, R., Haas, J. E., & Johnson, N. J. Examination of the Blau-Scott and Etziono Typologies. *Administrative Science Quarterly*, 1967, *12*, 118–139.

Hannan, M., & Freeman, J. The population ecology of organizations. *American Journal of Sociology*, 1977, *82*, 929–964.

Harrison, B. *Education, training, and the urban ghetto.* Baltimore, Maryland: The Johns Hopkins Press, 1972.

Heydebrand, W. Organizational contradictions in public bureaucracies. *The Sociological Quarterly*, 1977, *18*, 85–109.

Hickson, D., Pugh, D., & Pheysey, D. Operations technology and organization structure: An empirical reappraisal. *Administrative Science Quarterly*, 1969, *14*, 378–397.

Higham, J. *Strangers in the land.* New Brunswick, New Jersey: Rutgers, 1955.

Hirsch, S. *Roots of the American working class.* Philadelphia: University of Pennsylvania Press, 1978.

Jones, A. H. *Wealth of the colonies on the eve of the American Revolution.* New York: Columbia University Press, 1976.

Kimberly, J. Issues in the design of longitudinal organizational research. *Sociological Methods and Research*, 1976, *4*, 321–348.

Kindleberger, C. *Europe's postwar growth: The role of labor supply.* Cambridge: Harvard University Press, 1967.

Litterer, J. Systematic management: The search for order and integration. *Business History Review*, 1961, *35*, 461–476.

Litterer, J. Systematic management: Design for organization recoupling in American Manufacturing firms. *Business History Review*, 1963, *37*, 369–391.

Lindert, P., & Williamson, J. Three centuries of American inequality. In P. Uselding (Ed.), *Research in Economic History* (Vol. I). Greenwich, Conn.: JAI Press, 1976.

Lynch, B. An empirical assessment of Perrow's Technology Construct. *Administrative Science Quarterly*, 1974, *19*, 338–356.

March, J. G., & Simon, H. A. *Organizations.* New York: John Wiley & Sons, Inc., 1958.

Marglin, S. What the bosses do: The origins and functions of hierarchy in capitalist production. *Review of Radical Political Economics*, 1974, *6*, 60–112.

Masters, S. An interindustry analysis of wages and plant-size. *Review of Economics and Statistics*, 1969, *51*, 341–345.

McKelvey, B. Guidelines for the empirical classification of organizations. *Administrative Science Quarterly*, 1975, *20*, 509–525.

McKelvey, B. *Organizational Systematics.* Berkeley, Calif.: University of California Press (forthcoming).

Merkle, J. The Taylor strategy: Organizational innovation and class structure. *Berkeley Journal of Sociology*, 1968, *13*, 59–81.

Merkle, J. *Management and ideology: The legacy of the international scientific management movement.* Berkeley, University of California Press, 1980.

Miller, M. *American trade union attitudes toward worker producer cooperatives.* Unpublished paper, NYSSILR, Cornell University, 1980.

Montgomery, D. Workers control of machine production in the nineteenth century. *Labor History*, 1976, 17, 485–509.

Moody, J. *The truth about trusts.* New York: Moody Publishing Co., 1904.

Mueller, S. *Industrial structure and low-level earnings.* Unpublished Ph.D. Dissertation, NYSSILR, Cornell University, 1978.

Nelson, D. *Managers and workers: Origins of the new factory system in the United States, 1880–1920.* Madison, WI.: University of Wisconsin Press, 1975.

Nelson, D., & Campbell, S. Taylorism versus welfare work in American industry. *Business History Review,* 1972, *46,* 1–16.

Noble, D. F. *America by design: Science, technology, and the rise of corporate capitalism.* New York: Oxford University Press, 1977.

Nutter, G., & Einhorn, H. *Enterprise monopoly in the U.S.: 1899–1958.* New York: Columbia University Press, 1969.

Offe, C., & Wiesenthal, H. Two logics of collective action. *Political Power and Social Theory,* 1979, *1,* 67–115.

Ouchi, W. Markets, bureaucracies, and clans. *Administrative Science Quarterly,* 1980, *25,* 129–141.

Ouchi, W., & Williamson, O. *Markets, hierarchies, and clans.* Paper presented to the Conference on Markets and Hierarchies, Imperial College, London, January 1980.

Parkin, F. *Marxism and Class Theory: A Bourgeois Critique.* New York: Columbia University Press, 1979.

Perrow, C. A framework for comparative organizational analysis. *American Sociological Review,* 1967, *32,* 194–208.

Perrow, C. *Complex organizations: A critical essay.* Glenview, Ill.: Scott, Foresman and Company, 1979.

Pfeffer, J. Power and resource allocation in organizations. In Barry Staw & Gerald Salancik (Eds.), *New Directions in Organizational Behavior.* Chicago, Ill.: Clair Press, 1977.

Pfeffer, J., & Salancik, G. *The external control of organizations.* New York: Harper and Row, 1978.

Pollard, S. *The genesis of modern management.* Cambridge, Mass.: Harvard University Press, 1960.

Porter, G., & H. C. Livesay. *Merchants and manufacturers.* Baltimore, Md.: Johns Hopkins, 1971.

Prais, J. J. *The evolution of giant firms in Britain.* Cambridge, Mass.: Cambridge University Press, 1976.

Pugh, D. (et. al.). Dimensions of organizational structure. *Administrative Science Quarterly,* 1968, *13,* 65–104.

Rosenberg, N. Technological change in the machine tool industry. *Journal of Economic History,* 1963, *23,* 414–443.

Rosenberg, N. American technology. *American Economic Review,* 1977, *67,* 21–26.

Rothschild-Whit, J. The collectivist organization: An alternative to rational bureaucratic models. *American Sociological Reveiw,* 1979. *44,* 509–527.

Scherer, F. *Industrial market structure and economic performance.* Chicago, Ill.: Rand McNally, 1970.

Schmitter, P. C. Still the century of corporatism? *Review of Politics,* 1974, *36,* 85–131.

Staber, U. H. *The organizational structure and functions of trade associations.* Ph. D. dissertation proposal, Cornell University, 1980.

Stone, K. The origins of job tructures in the steel industry. *Review of Radical Political Economics,* 1974, *6,* 113–173.

Thernstrom, S. Urbanization, migration, and social mobility in late nineteenth-century America. In Barton J. Bernstein (Ed.), *Towards a New Past: Dissenting Essays in American History.* New York: Pantheon, 1968.

Thompson, J. D. *Organizations in action.* New York: McGraw Hill, 1967.

Thompson, W. *A preface to urban economics.* Baltimore, Maryland: The Johns Hopkins Press, 1965.

Thurow, L. *Generating inequality.* New York: Basic Books, 1975.

Turner, J., & Starnes. *Inequality: privilege and poverty in America.* Pacific Palisades, Calif.: Goodyear, 1976.

Van de Ven, A. Review of organizations and environments. *Administrative Science Quarterly,* 1979, *24,* 320–326.

Wachtel, H., & Betsey, C. Employment at low wages. *Review of Economics and Statistics,* 1972, *54,* 121–129.

Wallerstein, I. *The modern world system: Capitalist agriculture and the origins of the European world-economy in the sixteenth century.* New York: Academic Press, Inc., 1974.

Weiss, L. Concentratrion and labor earnings. *American Economic Review,* 1966, *56,* 96–117.

Weiss, L. *Case Studies in American Industry* (2nd Ed.). New York: John Wiley and Sons, Inc., 1971.

Whetten, D. Sources, responses, and effects of organizational decline. in John Kimberly & Robert H. Miles (Eds.), *The Organizational Life Cycle.* San Francisco: Jossey-Bass, 1980.

Williamson, O. E. Organizational innovation: The transaction cost approach. Center for the Study of Organizational Innovation, University of Pennsylvania,Discussion Paper, Number 83, 1980b.

Williamson, O. E. The organization of work: A comparative institutional assessment. *Journal of Economic Behvior and Organiztion,* 1980a, *1,* 5–38.

Wood, N. Industrial relations policies of American management, 1900–1933. *Business History Review,* 1960, *34,* 403–420.

Woodward, J. *Industrial organization: Theory and practice.* London: Oxford University Press, 1965.

Wool, H. *The labor supply for lower level occupations.* Washington, D.C.: U.S. G.P.O., 1976.

Yelowitz, I. Skilled workers and mechanization: The lasters in the 1880's. *Labor History,* 1977, *18,* 197–213.

"BUREAUCRATIC" VERSUS
"PROFIT" ORGANIZATION

Marshall W. Meyer

ABSTRACT

Theorizing and research comparing 'bureaucratic' and 'profit' organizations
are reviewed. Generally, sociologists have minimized and economists exaggerated differences between the two types, which arise from differences
in purpose and in formal organizational structure. Suggestions for further
research are made.

Research in Organizational Behavior, Vol. 4, pages 89–125
Copyright © 1982 by JAI Press Inc.
All rights of reproduction in any form reserved.
ISBN: 0-89232-147-4

89

This essay compares "bureaucratic" and "profit" models of organization. The distinction between bureaucratic and profit organizations is of nebulous repute in the social sciences. At one pole bureaucracy is seen, principally by sociologists, as embodying values of rationality and efficiency hence typifying modern organizations whether in the private or public sector. At the opposite pole bureaucracy is viewed as antithetical to these values. The conservative economists and political scientists holding this position therefore make much of the distinction between bureaucratic and profit organizations, arguing that the scale and scope of the former ought to be severely limited because of their inherent inefficiencies and potentially antidemocratic tendencies. Not all sociologists have claimed bureaucracies to be efficient and rational—there is a wealth of sociological literature on bureaucratic dysfunctions and pathologies, some of which is reviewed later—and not all economists accept the claim of their conservative brethren that bureaucratic and profit organizations can be sharply distinguished. Nonetheless, ideology and disciplinary affiliation have in the past largely determined the tenacity with which the bureaucratic/profit distinction is maintained or denied. One purpose of this essay is to assess, based on a review of theories and pertinent empirical research, the relevance of differences between bureaucratic and profit organizations for organizational theory as well as for some more general concerns of the social sciences.

Another purpose of this essay is to contribute to the understanding of several issues that are at the conjunction of organizational theory and public policy. One such issue is the extent to which public regulation of private enterprise is desirable. Another is the degree to which unchecked or self-sustaining bureaucratic growth occurs in *both* the public and private sector organizations and whether such growth can be curtailed only through fiscal constraint or strangulation. These questions cannot be answered definitively in a relatively short article. But, at a minimum, it may be possible to develop a theoretical framework or context that might contribute to answers to such questions.

Both bureaucratic and profit considerations motivate this article and are reflected in its organization. I begin with the discussion of the doctrinal background of the bureaucratic/profit distinction. We should not deceive ourselves or our students concerning the role of beliefs in social science theories, at least in this instance: Max Weber, although a passionate advocate of value-free science, rather shared the Prussian enthusiasm for stable, well-ordered, rule-bound democratic systems. Ludwig von Mises, a representative of the Austrian school of economics, did not. The views of Weber and von Mises continue to influence debate on the appropriateness of bureaucratic versus profit organization and will therefore be laid out in some detail in the following section. The next section summarizes theorizing and research in the Weberian tradition. Some of Weber's intellectual heirs are less convinced of the virtues of bureaucratic organization than Weber was, but like Weber, they do not distinguish bureaucratic from profit types. In the following section, the work of economists and others sharing Mises' neoclassical orientation to bureaucracy will be reviewed; the bureaucratic/profit distinction is maintained in most of this work. An extended digression follows. Research comparing explicitly or implicitly bureaucratic and profit organizations will be summarized in the next section. The final section will discuss whether preferences for bureaucratic as opposed to profit organization depend more upon beliefs about how major institutions should be governed than upon considerations of efficiency, and will also discuss possible directions for new research.

The reader is cautioned that the term "bureaucratic" is used in two ways throughout this article, as it is in the literature. "Bureaucratic" in the Weberian sense connotes modern, rational, and efficient organization and is in contrast to traditional forms of administration. "Bureaucratic" in the argot of neoclassical economics connotes rule-bound inefficient organization and is in contrast to efficient "profit" organization. One thesis of this essay is that the two usages of bureaucratic have led to both lacunae and confusion in research: the former because explicit comparison of bureaucratic versus profit organizations (in the neoclassical sense) are rare, and the latter because research results have shown obviously bureaucratic organizations (in the neoclassical sense) to be less bureaucratized (in the Weberian sense) than others. The implication is that we should move somewhat away from the Weberian framework. Modern organizational forms may differ substantially, one key difference being whether they are organized bureaucratically (in the neoclassical sense) or for profit.

DOCTRINAL BACKGROUND

"Precision, speed, unambiguity, knowledge of the files, continuity, discretion, unity, strict subordination, reduction of friction and of material and personal costs—these are raised to the optimum point in the strictly bureaucratic administration . . ." (Weber, 1946, p. 214). In these terms, Weber extolled the virtues of the bureaucratic form of organization. Although only a fragment of his massive delineation of social and institutional structures of all types, Weber's essay "Bureaucracy" signaled the historical shift from administration based on tradition to administration based on rational procedures and law. The characteristics of bureaucratic administration distinguishing it from earlier forms are familiar: division of labor, hierarchy of authority, fixed rules and regulations, written files, and a "staff of scribes and subaltern officials of all sorts" to maintain them, selection and advancement according to qualifications, careers moving from lower to higher offices, and guaranteed pensions. As I have argued elsewhere (Meyer, 1979a, Chapter 1), one can draw hypotheses from this model of bureaucracy despite Weber's assertion that the ideal–typical construct consists only of analytic description. The first hypothesis posits that organizations have become increasingly bureaucratic over time. If the transformation from traditional to rational bureaucratic organization has occurred historically as Weber described, then one would expect to find elements of the bureaucratic model more frequently represented later in time and in newer organizations. This, in fact, turns out to be the case; pertinent findings are reported in Stinchcombe (1965) and Meyer and Brown (1977). A second hypothesis arising out of Weber's work is that bureaucratized organizations, whatever the constellation of elements constituting bureaucratization, are more efficient than others. Weber does not, however, state with respect to what outcomes they are efficient. Various subsidiary propositions might be drawn from the essay "Bureaucracy," for example, hypotheses concerning relationships among the elements of the bureaucratic model such that change in any one leads to change in some or all of the other elements. Although central to certain endeavors, such as comparative organizational research, these subsidiary hypotheses are relatively unimportant to the present discussion.

Weber denies rather emphatically fundamental differences between public and private enterprise, bureaucratic and profit organizations. The key characteristics of the bureaucratic model, Weber argues, are present in both. "In public and lawful government these . . . elements constitute 'bureaucratic authority.' In private economic domination they constitute bureaucratic 'management.' Bureaucracy, thus understood, is fully developed . . . only in the modern state, and, in the private economy, only in the most advanced institutions of capitalism" (1946, p. 196). Basic social and economic forces contributing to bureaucratization (the development of money economies, literacy, norms of impersonality and calculability, and the rationalization of law and of administrative codes) contribute equally to facilitation of administrative activities in public and private bodies. Weber recognizes that officials in public bureaus are granted tenure and a modicum of social esteem, which, at least in Europe, are not features of private enterprise. But overall, Weber finds more similarities than differences between bureaucratically organized administration in the public sector and bureaucratic management of private capitalist enterprises.

Two comments about Weber's work are also in order. First, Weber believed modern capitalistic enterprise and bureaucracy to be products of the rationalization of almost all social institutions that began in the sixteenth and seventeenth centuries. Just as capitalism introduced rationality into acquisitive and entrepreneurial activities, bureaucracy rationalizes administrative work and thereby contributes to capitalism to the extent that the latter requires orderly administration. Second, although Weber's concept of democracy was limited, he perceived a close link between bureaucratization and democratic governance of the nation-state. Equal treatment of citizens before the law, Weber argued, is ensured by bureaucracy but not by earlier administrative form. Weber did not think that democracy required direct participation in governance by the government. He called this mob rule or rule by the *"demos."* For this reason, he saw no inconsistency between the permanence and power of the bureaucratic apparatus of the state, on the one hand, and democracy, on the other. The conservative critics of bureaucracy disagree on this point, although this is by no means their only disagreement with Weber's analysis.

Mises, a staunch opponent of socialism and Nazism, found the roots of all forms of totalitarian governments in the extension of the administrative apparatus of the state. For this reason, his factual judgments also differed from Weber's: Bureaucracy's origins were ancient rather than modern. Rather than functioning as the instrumentality through which administration of the modern state becomes possible, bureaucracy had in the past "resulted in a complete disintegration of political unity and in anarchy" (1944, p. 23). Bureaucracy succeeds in the modern state, therefore, only to the extent to which the latter "is built upon the ruins of feudalism" (1944, p. 17). Mises does not take issue with Weber concerning the surface characteristics of bureaucracy (division of labor, hierarchy, administrative staff, etc.), but he does disagree profoundly as to their consequences. Whereas Weber viewed the existence of bureaucracy as necessary to the development of capitalism, Mises treats the two as inimical; and whereas Weber finds consistency between bureaucracy and democratic principles, Mises finds potential antipathy. I shall first review Mises' distinction between bureaucratic and profit organization—the title of this article was taken from his chapter on the topic—and later I shall turn to Mises' analysis of the consequences of bureaucracy for democracy.

The key characteristics of capitalistic or profit organization, according to Mises, differ substantially from those of bureaucracy. The capitalistic system is driven by the market or consumers' preferences. "Every penny gives a right to vote" (1944, p. 31). Planning and assessment of results under capitalism are done entirely in terms of profit. In the argot of modern economics, prices serve as sufficient statistics. Management relies principally upon modern bookkeeping and accounting as means of organizational control, and supervision consists, for the most part, of calculating the profitability or productivity of subordinates. Both consumers and producers are therefore sovereign: the former because they are free to make choices in the market, and the latter because they are also free to make choices, the consequences of which will be reflected in profit. Bureaucratic organizations, according to Mises, function quite differently. Bureaucratic management is "bound to comply with detailed rules and regulations fixed by the authority of a superior body. The task of a bureaucrat is to perform what these rules and regulations order him to do" (1944, p. 58). Rules rather than market prices drive bureaucrats because their work has no cash value on the market. Mises points out that this does not mean that the work of bureaucracies is without value, but it does mean that the market cannot determine its value. In the absence of market prices, the efficiency of bureaucratic organizations is impossible to determine, and attempts to improve efficiency usually prove futile. Two key characteristics of bureaucratic management, then, are dependence upon rules and incalculability of results.

Mises, like Weber, acknowledges that democratic governance requires bureaucratic administration because the latter is an effective check upon arbitrary actions of rulers. The extension of bureaucracy into other spheres is of substantial concern, however. Bureaucratization of enterprises that could conceivably be managed for profit impairs their efficiency; bureaucratization induces mindless conformity that makes men risk averse; ultimately, bureaucratization substitutes political for economic logic, thereby subordinating individual interests to the interest of the state. Mises claims also that modern totalitarian nations have consolidated their power exactly through bureaucratic regulation of individual enterprise, thus raising at least a potential contradiction in his arguments. While acknowledging that bureaucratization limits arbitrariness in government, Mises views extension of the bureaucratized state as threatening arbitrary and unwarranted control of individuals and subgroups. But a similar contradiction may also be seen in Weber's work. According to Weber, bureaucracy ensures democracy by maintaining formal equality among citizens, but citizens are rendered substantially powerless in the face of the resources of expertise of the bureaucratic apparatus of the state.

One could, if he wished, reconcile the descriptive accounts of bureaucracy given by Weber and Mises. One could not, however, reconcile their assessments of the role of bureaucracy in capitalist enterprise, nor could one reconcile their evaluations of the two forms of organization. Ultimately, according to Weber, bureaucratic organization maximizes rationality and efficiency. For Mises, bureaucracy, when extended beyond core administrative activities of the state, impedes rationality and efficiency in comparision with profit organization. Both Weber and Mises are aware of the power potentially wielded by bureaucracies, although they differ substantially in their degree of concern about the consequences of such power. Two questions seem to be raised by these conflicting analyses of bureaucracy. The first falls in the domain of organizational theory: Are bureaucratic organizations substantially different from profit organizations? The second question, which does not presume an affirmative answer to the first, is more in the realm of politics than of administration: Whose values, whose interests, and whose power are served by these competing forms of organizations? Ironically, economists objecting to bureaucracy on ideological grounds have treated differences between bureaucratic and profit organizations largely as matters of administrative organization, whereas sociologists have been much more sensitive to the question of power.

THE WEBERIAN TRADITION

Weber's work, including the essay "Bureaucracy" was not immediately translated into English and became known in the United States principally through the writings of Talcott Parsons and Robert K. Merton. Both Merton and Parsons accepted Weber's assertion of the efficiency and rationality of bureaucracy compared to earlier organizational forms, but they also raised some issues not addressed by Weber. Parsons, for example, questioned whether professionalization is not an alternative to bureaucratic authority in modern society (1958, p. 58) and pursued his subject in a number of essays (see especially Parsons, 1960, Chapters 1 and 2). Merton (1958) raised a wholly different question, namely whether bureaucracy, which is conducive to efficient administration in general, does not tend toward inefficiency in specific instances. Merton's work and the work of his students deals more directly with the central concern of this article than does Parsons'—indeed, it could be interpreted as sustaining the economists' negative evaluation of bureaucracy—and for this reason I shall address mainly the former.

The Bureaucratic Personality

The sociologist Robert K. Merton, in his essay "Bureaucratic Structure and Personality" (1958), observed a discrepancy between Weber's treatment of bureaucracy as the quintessence of rationality in administration and the popular view of bureaucracy as clumsy and inefficient. Merton posed the issue as follows: Could organizational practices intended to contribute toward efficient performance tend toward inefficiency in specific instances? In particular, is it possible that bureaucratic procedures, which are means, become ends in themselves as a result of overtraining and overconformity among officials? Such "displacement of goals," Merton reasoned, could occur as a result of a number of conditions. First, in order to ensure conformity with rules, officials in bureaucratic organizations are indoctrinated in them to a somewhat greater degree than is demanded by the technical requirements of their jobs. Second, career advancement depends somewhat upon compliance with bureaucratic rules, also promoting overconformity. Third, knowledge of bureaucratic regulations constitutes the special technical competence of officials, hence the informal social organization and occupational esprit de corps of bureaucrats is tied with compliance to rules. Peer pressure resists deviation strongly. Fourth, because public agencies rarely have competitors, clients are not lost by sticking to the rules.

Merton's essay makes no mention of the bureaucratic/profit distinction but its explanation of goal displacement would appear to apply to organizations, or to segments of organizations, where there is no profit motive. This is especially the case for the third and fourth conditions, rules constituting the expertise of bureaucrats, and the monopoly power of bureaucracies. Most likely, Merton was not concerned with the bureaucratic/profit distinction largely because his objective was explanation of the discrepancies between the formal rationality of public agencies and certain nonrational aspects of their behavior. The same analysis could be applied to private firms: Not only may there be overindoctrination in rules, but overindoctrination may occur in other respects (loyalty to the firm, conventions of appearance, interpersonal style, and sensitivity to the whims of the boss). Career advancement may depend heavily upon conformity; knowledge of formal procedures as well as of informal ones (the latter form of expertise constituting political acumen) may be an employee's unique competence; and the same arrogance that characterizes some public officials due to their monopoly situation may operate with equal or greater force in the monopoly segments of the private sector. Two issues then arise. One is the extent to which bureaucratic mechanisms, especially detailed regulations, are required for efficient operation of firms. The second is the extent to which allegedly profit organizations experience "displacement of goals," which detracts from efficiency.

Whereas simple observation confirms that all large firms are rule-bound to a considerable extent, indicating some link between extensive regulations and efficiency or effectiveness outcomes, there have been few studies of why such regulations were implemented initially. It may be that the needed evidence can be obtained only from historical analysis or intensive observation of individual cases. The historical Alfred Chandler (1978) argued, for example, that both market forces and technology have contributed to the bureaucratization of firms, whereby full-time salaried managers who are either entrepreneurs or workers took charge of internal administration. Myriad examples are given in his work. Railroads, for instance, could not traverse substantial distances without careful planning and scheduling; otherwise collisions would result. Large industrial firms operating in national markets also developed staffs in charge of planning and coordination so that orderly flows of raw materials and intermediate products could be maintained. The sociologist Alvin Gouldner (1954) viewed bureaucratic regulations as instruments used by managers to consolidate control when informal means failed. Specifically, Gouldner argued that rules were more effective than command authority in breaking an entrenched "indulgency pattern" in an industrial firm he observed. More generally, Gouldner claimed as did Blau (1955) that bureaucratization promoted efficiency by depersonalizing relationships that would otherwise be fraught with tension and conflict. Therefore, the historical work of Chandler, as well as the case studies of Gouldner and Blau, would appear to suggest the dependence of many if not all types of organizations upon bureaucratic regulations.

Behavioral studies have not addressed, however, the second issue posed earlier, namely, whether, under what conditions and to what extent, bureaucratic regulations that are implemented to promote efficiency become ends in themselves, thereby impairing efficiency. Behavioral studies are rife with illustrations of nonrationalities and subgoal pursuit in supposedly rational organizations, but there has been little explanation of how rules themselves may impair efficiency. (See, for example, Roethlisberger and Dickson, 1939; Dalton, 1959; Whyte, 1948; Whyte and Hamilton, 1964.) The concept of "informal organization," elaborated by Barnard (1938), carries a suggestion that workers' sentiments are often in opposition to formally stated objectives. Little is known, however, about the conditions promoting harmony or antagonism between the former rationality of larger organizations and what workers actually do. Perscriptive theorists, especially those in the human relations tradition, have claimed the virtues of participative management (Likert, 1961, 1967), but the empirical basis for these assertions has been questioned; for example, Perrow's (1970) comments on Likert, as well as critiques of Rothesburger and Dixon by Landsberger (1958) and Carey, (1968). In other words, despite the wealth of work on "informal organization" and related topics, Merton's hypothesis identifying the source of bureaucratic dysfunctions as the very mechanism intended to promote rationality in organizations has not been subject to much empirical testing.

The "Vicious Circle" of Bureaucratic Dysfunctions

The French sociologist Michel Crozier (1964) has extended both Merton's and Parsons' theoretical treatments of organizations, but in so doing he discarded the Weberian view of bureaucracy as the embodiment of rationality and administration. Crozier instead defined bureaucracy as dysfunctional or pathological organization that cannot correct its own errors. Numerous theoretical questions are addressed in Crozier's work. Of greatest importance for present purposes are his theoretical models of bureaucratization as a function of internal forces in organizations and of the manner in which external forces accelerate or impede this process. Crozier's book *The Bureaucratic Phenomenon* is based on "clinical" observation and analysis of a clerical agency and an industrial monopoly, both of which were state-run enterprises. Similar patterns of low morale and indifference toward authority were observed in both, but in the industrial monopoly there was also considerable antagonism between production workers and maintenance personnel responsible for upkeep and repair of machinery. Crozier took the latter as evidence of parallel, that is nonhierarchical, power and attempted to reconcile this observation with the bureaucratic ideal of impersonality and with the bureaucrat's aversion to influence. Crozier argued as follows: Bureaucratic rules have their intended effect of depersonalizing decisions, but only by removing authority from the line of command and reserving discretionary judgment to managers at the apex of organizations. The weakness of line authority renders hierarchical strata isolated from one another, and power then can be exercised only in areas not covered by rules, particularly by workers such as the maintenance personnel whose jobs cannot be wholly rationalized. The exercise of power, however, usually leads to demands for further rules to restrain the exercise of influence, leading to further centralization and the erosion of line authority and increasing the likelihood of "parallel" power in the few remaining areas that cannot be regulated. Positive feedback relationships leading to a casual spiral among these four elements (rules, centralization, strata isolation, and parallel power) constitute a vicious circle of bureaucratic dysfunctions.

Although vicious circles may exist in any organization, Crozier notes a number of conditions that may affect their intensity. One is the nature of beliefs concerning authority shared in the larger society. Frenchmen are notably wary of face-to-face authority relationships for numerous reasons that are mainly historical, hence their bureaucratic pathologies are likely to be somewhat exaggerated compared to other nations'. Another condition affecting the intensity of the vicious circle is the nature of an organization's more immediate environment. The continued existence of the public agencies studied by Crozier is assured. So are the jobs of their workers who are tenured civil servants. Such is not the case for private firms in France as elsewhere; for this reason top management decisions pose substantial uncertainties for workers in firms that they do not pose in bureaucracies. The ability of management to control uncertainty, or at least to define it for workers, gives private firms a modicum of power lacking in bureaucratic settings, and the vicious circle of bureaucratization is somewhat attenuated, allowing for orderly change. As a sociologist, Crozier is not principally interested in efficiency outcomes, but his model of the vicious circle does carry the implication that organizations wholly protected from uncertainties arising externally will inevitably prove less efficient than others. Croziers' model of the vicious circle, however, has not been subjected to rigorous empirical tests other than the observations provided by Crozier himself, nor have research studies addressed the question of whether intrusion of external uncertainties dampens or exacerbates the operation of the vicious circle.

Institutionalized Organizations

A third strand of organizational theory in the Weberian tradition begins from altogether different premises. Whereas both Merton and Crozier focused entirely upon the negative consequences of bureaucratic structures, the theory of institutionalized organizations anticipates inefficiencies and discrepancies between "formal" and "informal" organizations as entirely a function of conditions external to organizations. Unlike most theories treating coordination and control, hence efficiency, as the major achievement of modern organizations, institutional theory treats organizations as successful to the extent that they embody societal myths concerning rationality.

The theory of institutional organizations, elaborated by the sociologist John W. Meyer and his associates (Meyer and Rowan, 1977, 1978; Meyer, Scott, Cole, and Intili, 1978) is based on the following observations: There is often dissent as to both procedures and objectives in organizations. Activities in organizations are rarely well coordinated, even though the formal categories used to describe work roles and relationships are extremely orderly. (This is sometimes called "loose coupling"; see Weick, 1976.) Furthermore, assessment of performance is normally avoided or ignored altogether. Together these observations suggest that *legitimacy,* as opposed to efficiency, of highly rationalized formal organizations accounts for their pervasiveness in modern societies. The idea that rationalized organizations are the appropriate means for accomplishing collective activity is widely accepted. Indeed, other means are normally considered illegitimate. Because modernity is closely associated with legitimation of rationalized authority structures, the more modern the society, the greater the number of domains of action for which highly rationalized organizations are created; and the more elaborate are societal beliefs concerning what organizations ought rationally to do, the more complex the structure of individual organizations. The greater the extent to which the formal structure of organizations mirrors societal beliefs about what it ought rationally to do, the more easily the organization evades assessment of its outputs. Avoidance of evaluation, in turn, allows greater leeway for ambiguity and "loose coupling" while preserving legitimacy, thereby enhancing survival prospects.

The theory of institutionalized organizations does not specify which organizations are highly "institutionalized" and which are not, but it carries the implication that all organizations whose activities are directed toward social and political purposes rather than toward profit will exhibit certain attributes—proliferating categories of structure, disarray, inefficiency, yet persistence. It differs from other perspectives in treating the legitimation of rationalized authority structures rather than the emergence of large-scale bureaucracies themselves as the key organizational transformation of the twentieth century. It also differs from other theories in viewing organizational rationality as more symbolic than substantive and in anticipating substantial rates of apparent (if inconsequential) change in categories used by organizations to describe their activities rather than dogged resistance to such change. Like Weber's work, institutional theory is written as if it applied to all organizations generally, yet like Merton, Crozier, and other theorists, its implications suggest differences between bureaucratic and profit organizations. Bureaucratic organizations, one might imagine, seek institutionalization by cultivating beliefs concerning their legitimacy and rationality. They are able to do so precisely because their core activities tend not to be of an economic nature and are not easily assessed or evaluated. The same strategy is not so easily available to organizations seeking profit, for the test of their rationality is in the attainment of explicit goals of growth and return on investment. A paradox is suggested: Bureaucratic organizations, which may be inherently inefficient for several reasons, benefit little by attempting reduction of internal inconsistencies, improvement of coordination, and assessment of outputs, for to do so would impair public confidence by exposing their irreconcilably diverse goals. Institutionalization thus poses a potential trap for organizations. As in the fable of the emperor's clothes, organizations garbed in the cloak of legitimacy may find rational management and accountability increasingly costly to implement. Myth and ritual justifying existing practices are elaborated instead, resulting in further declines in actual effectiveness but ensuring organizational preservation. A circle of bureaucratic dysfunctions, similar to Croziers' "vicious circle" is thus suggested.

THE NEOCLASSICAL TRADITION

The economists' approach to bureaucracy differs substantially from sociologists' in that it assumes the primacy of acquisition in contrast to more complex social and political forces shaping organizations. Mises, to be sure, focused almost entirely upon bureaucracy's deleterious impact upon profit enterprises, but modern economic theory has attempted to identify conditions giving rise to bureaucracies in the first place, explain differences between rational (i.e., maximizing) patterns of actions of bureaucrats as opposed to profit seekers, and predict conditions causing bureaucracies to fail. The economists' stance is generally this: Remove imperfections in the market and bureaucracies would not arise in the first place. Remove peculiarities of the budgeting process whereby bureaus derive income, and rational bureaucrats would behave much like rational businessmen. And remove the inability to assess effectiveness in terms of profit, and organizational alternatives available to private firms could be implemented in bureaucracies, rendering gains in efficiency relatively easily achieved. Some of the arguments are derived from Mises, but some are not. Mises acknowledged that certain functions of bureaucracy are legitimate, hence one can regard economic theories accounting for the existence of bureaucracy as an elaboration of Mises' work. That bureaucratic organizations may be less efficient than profit firms was acknowledged by Mises, but Mises did not consider what bureaucrats in fact do maximize. Finally, Mises also did not consider the possibility that the hierarchical structure of bureaucracies themselves can become, past a point, an impediment to efficiency.

Elaboration of Mises

Some economists share Mises' definition of bureaucracy as organization that does not enter into market transactions, hence cannot gauge its performance. Usually profit and bureaucratic organizations are further distinguished by whether or not transactions are coerced. Business transactions are presumed voluntary whereas transactions in bureaucratic settings are not. The economist Anthony Downs (1967) thus defines bureaucracy as organization that does *not* enter into voluntary quid pro quo transactions in the marketplace.

Downs cites several reasons for the existence and proliferation of large government bureaucracies. To begin, substantial *externalities* (or external costs) are attached to many activities in society. An externality is a cost or benefit not reflected in market prices but experienced by persons not party to a transaction. For example, externalities are involved in the control of automobile emissions. A motorist may incur virtually no costs and possibly save money should his smog equipment fail, yet those who must breathe the air he has fouled may pay dearly for his carelessness. No simple market mechanism can correct this inequity. As a result, governmental agencies are created with power to coerce compliance with automobile emissions standards. Some economists claim that there are alternatives to government regulation in such instances. It is argued, for example, that polluters should be taxed or fined to provide compensation for those whom they injure; the errant motorist could choose between repairing his smog gear and paying for his negligence. Unfortunately, a government bureaucracy would be needed to levy taxes or fines. Other economists claim that citizens anticipate pollution costs in choosing homes or jobs, discounting land and inflating wage demands accordingly. (This assumes that citizens can change homes or jobs freely.) No bureaucratic intervention is needed under these assumptions, provided, of course, that one is not concerned about equity considerations, that is, whether it is acceptable to subject the poor and those who cannot relocate for other reasons to unpleasant and unsafe levels of pollution.

The extreme form of externality is the *public good*. Public or collective goods exist to the extent that one person's benefit benefits all, regardless of who pays. Many general government functions, such as police and public health protection, can be construed as public goods; some nongovernment organizations, such as trade unions, provide indivisible goods to members that can be construed as collective goods. As Mansur Olson (1965) has pointed out, public and collective goods normally raise the problem of "free riders." A person may be tempted not to pay for police service, knowing that patrol activities for which his neighbors have paid would also protect his property; a worker may be similarly tempted not to pay union dues, knowing that his wages will be the same as those of dues-paying members. Normally, there is no market solution to the free-rider problem, and compulsory payment, which must be administered bureaucratically, is imposed.

Other circumstances may also require bureaucratic administration. Market forces are rarely able to provide the framework of law that governs most peoples' day-to-day activities. Similarly, markets rarely are able to fix conventions such as currency regulations, allocation of broadcast frequencies, and the control of airways without which some confusion and danger would result. By definition, redistributive policies cannot be implemented through market means, nor can markets regulate monopoly firms such as utilities. Bureaucratic organizations, then, are unable to gauge their performance in market terms precisely because their activities are of the sort for which markets do not exist or function imperfectly. Because, following Downs and others, the nature of their work is different from firms, one would expect that substantial differences would obtain between bureaucratic and profit organizations.

Bureaucrats as Maximizers

A wholly different approach to the behavior of bureaucracies has been proposed by the economist William Niskanen (1971). Bureaucrats, Niskanen argues, are, like other economic actors, purposeful maximizers. They cannot maximize profit because their agencies do not operate for profit, but they can attempt maximization of salary, perquisites of office, prestige, power, and outputs of their agencies. Importantly, almost all of the things bureaucrats seek to maximize (except, perhaps, the ease of their jobs) increase with the level of budgetary support according to Niskanen. For this reason, budget maximization may be taken as the proximate goal of most bureaucrats. "The most distinguished public servants of recent years substantially increased the budgets for which they were responsible. . . . bureaucrats who do not maximize their budget will have an unusually short tenure" (Niskanen, 1971, p. 39–41).

Not only are bureaucrats maximizers like business people, but bureaucrats also engage in exchange relations like firms. But the conditions surrounding exchanges in which bureaus engage are quite different from those for firms. First, following Niskanen, most, although not all, bureaucracies are monopoly suppliers of services to their "sponsors" who are department heads, legislative bodies, and the like. Second, the sponsor is somewhat passive, that is, he understands less well than the bureaucrat the minimum feasible costs of resources and he has little incentive to find these costs. Indeed, the sponsor himself may be a budget maximizer. Third, the exchange between sponsors and bureaus is one of *budgets* for a promised *set of outputs or activities,* not an exchange of a marginal *price* for an incremental *unit* of output or activity. Following Niskanen, we can assume that there is a budget–output function of the following form:

$$B = aQ - bQ^2 \qquad 0 \leqslant Q \leqslant a/2b \tag{1}$$

where B = maximum budget granted by sponsor, and Q = expected level of output or activity. This equation states, simply, that up to a point ($a/2b$), the value of the total expected output increases, but at a decreasing rate. The marginal value of each *unit* of output V is thus

$$V = a - 2bQ \qquad 0 \leqslant Q \leqslant a/2b \tag{2}$$

A cost-output function of the following form also exists:

$$TC = cQ + dQ^2 \tag{3}$$

where TC, the minimum total payment to factors (suppliers) of a service increases at an increasing rate with expected levels of output. The marginal cost of each unit of output is

$$C = c + dQ \tag{4}$$

The budget sought by the rational bureaucrat will be the maximum budget that is sufficient to cover the costs of output expected by the sponsor at the budgeted level. Formally, since $B \geqslant TC$, a bureau's *maximum* budget will be at $Q = a/2b$, and its minimum budget (where $B = TC$) will be at $Q = (a - c)/(b + d)$. The minimum and maximum levels of Q are equal at $a/2b = (a - c)/(b + d)$, or $a = 2bc/(b - d)$.

Figure 1 illustrates the equilibrium levels of output for bureaus following Niskanen's model. At the lower output level $[Q = (a_1 - c)/(b + d)]$, the total budget just covers minimum costs, and no cost-benefit analysis would reveal any "fat" or slack in the budget. However, at $Q = (a_1 - c)/(b + d)$, the marginal value of a unit of output to the sponsor is substantially less than the marginal cost of producing it. Conventionally, in markets equilibrium output occurs for a monopolist at a point where marginal value (or price) equals marginal cost [as $Q = (a_1 - c)/2(b + d)$]. This appears not to be the case for bureaus where the exchange for budgets for promised output yields, at a minimum, levels of output that will exhaust the available budget even though the marginal cost of the last unit of output exceeds substantially its marginal value to the sponsor.

Should the value of each unit of output to the sponsor be high, that is, should the magnitude of the coefficient a be high, demand rather than budget will constrain total output. As Figure 1 shows, total output will

Figure 1.   Bureaucratic Outputs

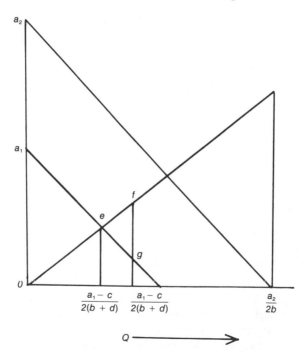

rise to $a_2/2b$, and the budget allocated to the bureau by its sponsor will exceed the minimum costs of producing the promised level of output, although the sponsor will not know this. Niskanen concludes that regardless of whether total output is constrained by budget [at$(a_1 - c)/(b + d)$] or by demand [at $a_2/2b$], all bureaus will be too large, that is, both budget and output will be larger than that which maximizes net value to the sponsor.

While not necessarily yielding inefficiency, the exchange of budgets for promised outputs, which is characteristic of bureaucratic organizations, leads to overproduction of public services compared to levels that would result from market transactions. A number of secondary consequences follow from this primary characteristic of bureaus, according to Niskanen. First, factors (suppliers) profit handsomely from the large output of bureaus, hence factors tend to be among the most vocal supporters of government programs. Second, improvements in efficiency, while decreasing per unit costs of output, will tend to increase total budgets and outputs because sponsors are willing, up to a point, to pay some additional increment for increased outputs. Third, bureaucrats will tend to overinvest in capital goods because they are budget maximizers. (Bureaucracy thus is in opposition to the labor-intensive spoils system whose main function is to employ friends of elected officials.)

The Managerial Discretion Hypothesis

Niskanen's model of bureaucratic behavior has been the subject of considerable discussion and criticism among economists and others who believe that managers in both bureaucratic and profit organizations may choose between maximizing a number of outcomes, including profit, which is not available in the public sector, and "rents" or perquisites of office and outputs, which are available in both public and private organizations. The concept of managerial discretion was originally developed by the economist Robin Marris (1964); among the antecedents to Marris' book is the classic work of Berle and Means (1932), which first argued that managers do not always maximize return to stockholders.

The concept of managerial discretion can be applied to the behavior of bureaucratic organizations in the following way: Assume, following Migué and Bélinger (1974), that bureaucrats are not constrained to maximize budgets. Assume instead that budgets are somewhat discretionary and can be apportioned between producing outputs and other utility-producing expenditures or "rents." Assume further, using Niskanen's terminology, that the marginal demand for the output of a bureau is $a - 2bQ$, and that marginal cost is $c + 2dQ$. Marginal demand equals marginal cost at $Q = (a_1 - c)/2(b + d)$, or at one half the lower level of output one would expect based on Niskanen's model. (See Figure 1.)

The manager's discretionary budget, which would be returned as profit were he a discriminating private sector monopolist, is also maximized at this point. Output beyond $Q = (a_1 - c)/2(b + d)$ decreases discretionary resources. Migué and Bélinger argue that since managers may value output beyond that which would maximize the discretionary budgets, a bureau may produce any level of output between that of a price-discriminating monopolist and that of an output-maximizing bureau. Where in this range actual output will fall depends greatly upon personal preferences. There is some likelihood, however, that the equilibrium level output of a bureau may not differ appreciably from that of monopoly firms in the private sector. This conclusion is at sharp variance with Niskanen's. Migué and Bélinger claim further that bureaus differ from firms in that they generate substantial benefits or rents from managers in addition to their intended outputs, and that bureaus for this reason are not cost-effective. Again, the conclusion differs from Niskanen. Migué and Bélinger also argue that increases in demand, that is, in budget, tend to increase the proportion of expenditures supporting managerial rents as opposed to outputs; costs rise faster than outputs. (The algebra used in deriving this conclusion is straightforward but will not be reproduced here.) This observation is somewhat consistent with Niskanen's, as the Niskanen model does demonstrate declining efficiency when output moves from the budget-constrained to the demand-constrained region. Migué and Bélinger conclude that "the citizen has good grounds for holding bureaucrats in suspicion" (1974, p. 34).

More recently, Niskanen (1975) has proposed a general model of bureaucrats as utility as opposed to budget or "rent" maximizers. Starting from the assumption that bureaucrats' utilities are functions of both outputs and discretionary income appropriated by their agencies, Niskanen derives equations reproducing his earlier result $[Q = (a - c)/(b + d)]$ where outputs but not discretionary income contribute to bureaucrats' utilities, but Migué and Bélinger's result $[Q = (a - c)/2(b = d)]$ where discretionary income but not output contributes to utilities. The algebra used to derive this result need not be reproduced; suffice it to say that the model indicates bureaucrats to be neither pure budget nor pure "rent" maximizers.

The debate over whether bureaucrats maximize budgets, in which case they overproduce, or maximize rents, in which case they overspend, cannot be resolved without substantial empirical evidence, and perhaps may never be. Budget maximization, following Niskanen, is characteristic of organizations operating from budgets; hence to the extent that the Niskanen model holds, bureaus suffer in comparison with profit organizations. Because discretion is not limited to firms, any conclusions regarding the relative advantages or disadvantages of bureaucratic versus profit organizations depends upon the extent to which managers' preferences for perquisites of office remain unchecked in the former. An approach to organizations that focuses principally upon the costs of conducting transactions both between and within firms carries the implication that, at least under some circumstances, profit organizations may limit managerial discretion somewhat more effectively than bureaucratic types. The theory of transaction costs has been developed most fully by the economist Oliver Williamson (1975). The basic theorem is this: Organizations arise when markets fail, and vice versa. Market failures occur when the costs of conducting transactions between firms (or individuals) exceed the costs of internalizing them in organizations; organizations fail when a market *or an organizational alternative* offers lower transaction costs. Transaction costs are functions of several conditions: the conjunction of uncertainty with bounded rationality and of small numbers conditions with opportunism (or lying). Williamson's theory outlines several organizational alternatives for firms, including simple hierarchy, vertical integration, and multiunit and conglomerate forms. The multiunit and conglomerate alternatives are of special interest because they are decentralized. Under multiunit or conglomerate organization, a firm is divided into quasi-autonomous units, each with responsibility to profit. Profit responsibility and associated monitoring by the central office minimize the possibility for managerial discretion and extraction of rents. Other organizational forms do not have these and other advantages, according to Williamson, and for this reason there is a tendency for multiunit and conglomerate firms to displace other types.

As already noted, Williamson's is a theory of organizations attempting if not achieving profitability. One key difference between bureaucratic and profit organizations is that the latter have a range of structural alternatives that the former do not (Meyer, 1979a, Chapter 7). In particular, decentralization and profit responsibility at lower levels, which are characteristic of multiunit and conglomerate firms, cannot occur in bureaucracies. Simple hierarchy is the only structural form available to bureaus. This is the case almost by definition. Profit is not central to public agencies and other types of organizations where maximizing financial results is not a principal objective, and other quantitative measures of performance may be flawed or contradictory. (Certain public hospitals may, for example, admit patients for routine physical examinations so as to minimize costs per patient-day.) Remove valid performance measures, and responsibility for results cannot be delegated downward and direct supervision abandoned; separation of strategic planning and evaluation from operational concerns is difficult. Because decentralized multiunit and conglomerate organizations are, according to Williamson, most likely to limit managerial discretion, the absence of these alternatives from bureaucratic organizations would suggest that their potential for least-cost, maximally efficient behavior is limited.

One further issue surrounding the Niskanen model should be reviewed, although it does not fall strictly within the rubric of the managerial discretion hypothesis. A number of economists (Tullock, 1965; Williamson, 1964) as well as behavioral scientists (Tannenbaum, 1968) have raised the issue of control loss in organizations whereby discrepancies between wishes of superiors and actions of subordinates increase with size and layers of hierarchy. Typically, antidistortion and control devices are introduced to thwart the natural tendency toward control loss. Breton and Wintrobe (1975) have argued that such antidistortion and control devices may have the additional effect of curbing budget maximization by revealing to sponsors bureaus' true costs of supplying outputs, and that sponsors will invest in control devices to the point where their marginal benefits equal the marginal costs of control. Toma and Toma (1980) use the term "shirking control devices" to describe practices that may limit bureaucrats' rents. Toma and Toma note that the response of bureaucracies to tax limitations may depend very much on the effectiveness of such controls—the more effective the controls, the greater the potential efficiencies—suggesting that no simple link between fiscal constraints and the performance of bureaucratic organizations may be anticipated.

COMMENT

Bureaucratic and profit organizations are distinguished by both sociologists and economists—grudgingly by the former, enthusiastically by the latter. This occurs because, from the sociologists' perspective, bureaucratization is a comparatively recent development marking the application of rational concepts to administration, whereas, for many economists, bureaucratic agencies of government serve mainly to interfere with efficiency, hence rationality, of market exchanges. Ideology may also play a role in these different assessments of bureaucracy. Economists normally evaluate collective benefits in terms of efficiency, whereas sociologists focus on other outcomes, sometimes unspecified.

With a few exceptions, sociologists attacked the problem of bureaucracy long before economists. Indeed, bureaucracy was considered to be the exclusive domain of sociology until almost a decade ago. Sociologists concerned with bureaucracy have focused principally upon the causes and consequences of formal structure and regulations, whereas economists treating bureaucratic organization as somewhat aberrant compared to profit organization have asked what anomolous market conditions give rise to bureaucracies in the first place and how acquisitive motives of officials sustain bureaucracies once established. Sociologists' insights into bureaucracy have been largely the result of observation, both qualitative and quantitative, whereas the recent work of economists has been largely formal, drawing inferences from abstract but simple mathematical models whose assumptions remain largely untested. Finally, sociologists' interest in bureaucracy, as opposed to organizations generally, appears to have waned in recent years, while economists have been increasingly active in this area; economists tend to cite the work of sociologists where the reverse tends not to hold (see Breton and Wintrobe, 1975; Williamson, 1975).

Despite the fact that sociologists' interest in bureaucracy has not flourished as has economists', some questions arising almost exclusively in the sociological literature persists as a result of either the inability of economists' tools to cope with them or inconsistencies in the economists' approach. Of particular concern are issues revolving about questions of power—the persistence of bureaucracies and citizens' subordination to them despite substantial decoupling of activities from formal rules and structures and the increased power and scope of bureaucratic systems. Economists have rarely been comfortable with concepts describing intangibles such as power, yet the logic of certain economic arguments leads inescapably to the conclusion that intangibles operate with much greater force in bureaucratic compared to profit organizations because of the conditions giving rise to the former in the first place. To the extent that activities and services of bureaucracies cannot be adequately gauged in markets and are thus dependent upon political support and legitimacy, the attention of bureaucratic officials may be diverted toward maximizing support and legitimacy regardless of individual avarice. Put somewhat differently, bureaucrats' utilities may be more tied to political and social outcomes and somewhat less to personal gains than businessmen's. The fate of an entrepreneur may be inextricably tied to growth and aggrandizement of his enterprise, but the same does not hold with equal force for the bureaucrat, Niskanen notwithstanding. Indeed, it may be that persistence and proliferation of bureaucracies whose actual activities may be decoupled from formal representation of what they do is the result of a political process that is attempting to be maximally responsive to noneconomic demands.

In sum, the appropriateness of economic models as descriptions of organizations whose functions are not principally economic is questioned. In the next section, it will be argued that while certain research results can be interpreted as confirming the economists' view of bureaucratic organizations as excessively large and wasteful as compared to profit types, the sources of large size and inefficiency can be traced to the nature of the social and political processes in which bureaus are embedded rather than the personal utilities of bureaucrats.

THE RESULTS OF RESEARCH

Given the theoretical and practical implications of the bureaucratic/profit distinction, one might imagine that considerable research on the subject has been undertaken. That this is not the case is explained in part by the history of research in organizations as such (as opposed to research on people in organizational settings). Until recently this work was dominated by sociologists who, while recognizing bureaucratic dysfunctions and pathologies, considered Weber's model to be prototypical of all modern organizations. Early research compared sets of organizations considered homogeneous using Weber's categories (division of labor, hierarchy, etc.) and was insensitive to bureaucratic/profit differences. Another explanation lies in the inherent limitations of the research enterprise. If wholly exogenous conditions determine which activities are organized bureaucratically and which are organized for profit—for example, the military is extremely bureaucratized because the market will not sustain it, but car washes are rarely run as public agencies—then comparison of observable organizational characteristics cannot identify causes of bureaucratization. Indeed, comparison of observable markets or environments may also explain little, given that past market successes or failures determined whether an activity is organized bureaucratically or for profit. Clearly, a good theory is needed, but even now such a theory barely exists. The work of economists suggests conditions leading to bureaucratization and attributes of bureaus such as large size and inefficiency, but it says little about how the conditions cause bureaus to differ *organizationally* from profit firms. This section, then, is titled somewhat whimsically. Research results, many of which do not deal directly with bureaucratic/profit differences, are used to construct a somewhat heterodox argument about these differences. While I am concerned principally with organizational concomitants of the bureaucratic/ profit distinction, effects of societal conditions upon the two types of organizations are also discussed below.

Organizational Concomitants of Bureaucracy

A number of organizational features may distinguish bureaucratic from profit types. To begin, I shall return to the argument made earlier that bureaucracy is tied to simple hierarchy, whereas other organizational forms are available to profit organizations. This has consequences for elaboration of structure, rates of organizational change, and, possibly, formalization. I then turn to differences in accounting procedures between bureaucratic and profit organizations—simple hierarchy is associated with complex accounting. From these organizational concomitants of bureaucracy, I derive large size and high costs as likely consequences. This is confirmed in empirical research. Some sociological work on correlates of bureaucratization is then reviewed.

Simple Hierarchy.   Bureaucracy is tied to simple hierarchy, whereas alternatives to hierarchy are available to profit firms. Simple hierarchy is the organizational form described by Weberian and classical organizational theory: each official or organizational unit is linked to one and only one person or unit at the next highest or more inclusive level of organization. Simple hierarchy is thus a structure of command that facilitates execution of directives and insures accountability because each official's actions are subject to appeal and review by higher authority. Weber and other classical organizational theorists claimed that simple hierarchy facilitates rational administration because it fixes duties and reporting relationships.

Several consequences appear to flow from the unavailability of alternatives of hierarchy in bureaucratic organizations. First, organizational structure proliferates with size, given the absence of alternatives to hierarchy. There is a voluminous literature on the subject (see Kimberly, 1976, for a succinct summary). Generally structural differentiation is treated as a function of size (Blau, 1970; Meyer, 1972), but the only evidence from time series suggests that the opposite relationship may hold, that is, organizational size is a result of proliferation of hierarchy and specialized subunits (Meyer, 1980b). Second, the reliance upon simple hierarchy deprives organizations of effective buffering mechanisms and thereby opens them to change; organizational change, in turn, accelerates with levels of hierarchy. It may be that the same conditions giving rise to bureaucracy in the first place (namely, the absence of markets hence of reliable means of assessing their own performance) render bureaus unusually vulnerable to shifts occurring in the environment (Meyer, 1977, 1979a). Alternatively, the principle of subordination whereby change at any level of hierarchy is a function of endogenous change plus change at all higher levels may account for increased rates of change as one moves from higher to lower levels (Meyer, 1980a). Third, hierarchy tends to substitute conformity for efficiency criteria. The extensiveness of written rules and regulations increases with levels of hierarchy (Blau, 1968; Meyer, 1968), although formalization may be more cause than effect of hierarchy (Meyer and Brown, 1977). Hierarchy may also produce a communication distortion, either positive (telling the boss what he wants to hear) or negative (concealing what he does not want to hear), which is exacerbated when conformity displaces efficiency as a value. Finally, because control loss (whereby policies and directives emanating from top management are distorted and eventually lost in transmission from level to level of organization) increases almost inexorably with hierarchy, managers of multitier bureaucracies must often short-circuit formal hierarchy in order to preserve their effectiveness (Downs, 1967).

Whether alternatives to simple hierarchy, which are available to some firms but not at all to bureaus, in fact enhance efficiency and effectiveness remains a subject of debate. Chandler's (1962) study *Strategy and Structure* argues that the survival of major United States industrial firms in the 1920s depended critically upon their capacity for organizational innovation. General Motors, Dupont, Sears Roebuck, and Standard Oil of New Jersey weathered the post-World War I financial crisis that preceded the Great Depression by moving from unitary organizational structures based on functional division of labor to multiunit structures composed of quasi-autonomous units charged with profit responsibility. Contemporary empirical evidence yields less certain results, however. Weston and Mansinghka (1971) adduce evidence showing conglomerates to be significantly more profitable than other firms in similar industries. Armour and Teece (1978), however, present evidence that I (although not they) find ambiguous. Their time series comparisons of oil firms show multiunits to have been the most effective performers until 1958 but no more effective than others since. Armour and Teece state that multiunits could not be expected to be significantly advantaged in the later years of their series after the preponderance of firms had changed to the multiunit structure. A number of alternative explanations might be imagined, however, for example, (1) changed external conditions (such as regulation), which compromise advantages of the multiunit firm, and (2) effective recentralization of control by management without corresponding shifts in formal structure. (That such has occurred at General Motors is argued by Wright, 1979). On balance, it may be that the availability of organizational alternatives to simple hierarchy may advantage profit in comparison to bureaucratic organizations, but these advantages may diminish over time due to both internal and external changes.

Complexity in Accounting.   Neither organizational theory nor research have been particularly attentive to the details of organizational systems for financial accounting, preferring instead to describe entire organizations by their degree of formalization or standardization (see, for example, Hickson, Pugh, and Pheysey, 1969). This is unfortunate because whereas the degree of formalization of accounting procedures varies little across organizations of different types, the substantive content and categories used in accounting vary greatly. Almost universally, profit organizations report operating results in consolidated balance sheets. A single column of figures, beginning at the top with revenue and ending with net income at the "bottom line" normally suffice to describe operating results of a firm. Nonbusiness organizations, especially governments, do not normally provide a single consolidated statement, and if they do, the reader is warned that the statement is not in conformity with generally accepted accounting principles. Instead, fund accounting is the accepted method of financial reporting for other than profit organizations. Under fund accounting, revenues, expenditures, and balances are reported by funds, which reflect both the diverse purposes of government and nonprofit organizations as well as legal restrictions prohibiting co-mingling of funds intended for different purposes. Typically, a municipality will have a general fund covering common services such as police, fire protection, and public works. Each separate district (for example, a street lighting or mosquito abatement district) maintains separate funds, as does each city-run enterprise (for example, transit systems and parking facilities), and separate "sinking" funds are also maintained for short- and long-term indebtedness as well as for obligations secured by future revenues of municipal enterprises.

Complexity is introduced into fund accounting not only by the large number of funds ordinarily maintained by bureaucratic organizations, but also by transfers between funds. General fund revenues, for example, are used to amortize long-term debt and may also be used to subsidize money-losing enterprises, or, conversely, net enterprise revenues may be transferred to the general fund. With interfund transfers, which are nowadays common, revenues and expenditures of separate funds do not sum to total revenues and expenditures. Interfund transfers must be removed before separate fund accounts can be consolidated into a single financial statement. But the absence of such transfers renders a consolidated statement out of conformity with accounting principles because bureaucratic organizations must demonstrate both financial condition and the propriety of expenditures (whether funds were spent as specified in appropriation and budget ordinances), whereas profit organizations are not subject to the latter constraint.

The accounting profession continues to debate the usefulness of distinguishing fund from consolidated accounting. Several critics suggest that fund accounting poses needless complexity. Coopers and Lybrand (1976) and Green, Hellerstein, Mandansky, and Weil (1977) argue that fund accounts elude comprehension to all but experts. (I concur.) Anthony (1980) claims further that the financial condition of nonbusiness organizations can be ascertained only with consolidated accounts and, furthermore, that such accounts would be as comprehensible as those of business. Dreben (1979, 1980) notes, however, that many businesses adopt what is in effect fund accounting by issuing separate statements for a parent corporation and its subsidiaries, and sometimes doing so inconsistently. Additionally, segment reporting requirements, imposed recently as a result of concern that consolidated statements of large conglomerate firms potentially conceal monopolistic practices, have made separate statements, including entires for transfers between units, mandatory in some instances. Critics of fund accounting may also underestimate its importance in insuring financial compliance (Herzlinger and Sherman, 1980). How ever this debate is resolved—if it ever is—it is clear that the further from the profit model and the closer toward bureaucratic organization one moves, the greater the intricacy of financial accounting. In all likelihood, other forms of accounting such as personnel and other organizational records are also much more elaborate in bureaucratic compared to profit organizations.

There is no need to dwell on the consequences of fund accounting for bureaucratic organizations, substantial paperwork among them. What is important is that simple hierarchy and complex accounting persist in bureaucracies for similar reasons. Bureaus cannot be decomposed into quasi-autonomous, self-contained units with "bottom line" responsibility for profit or anything else because their purposes are highly differentiated and profit is not among them. An authority structure must therefore be maintained. Again, because profit is not among their purposes, bureaus find little indication of the adequacy of their performance in consolidated accounting. Much more intricate methods are needed to test whether funds have been maintained and expended in compliance with statutory requirements. The bureaucratic/profit distinction should not be overdrawn as many organizations contain elements of both models, and increasingly so. Nonetheless, it appears to be the case that the closer an organization moves toward the bureaucratic model, the fewer alternatives to simple hierarchy it has and the more detailed the accounting of its activities it must provide. Formal organizational structure—the availability of alternatives to simple hierarchical structure—thus may be closely related to the detail with which activities are reported. Where performance is ascertainable, organizational structure is constructed so as to maximize performance, and organizational accounts of activities are relatively simple and straightforward. Where compliance must be ascertained because performance cannot be, there is no alternative to simple hierarchy, and accounts of activities assume substantial complexity. The nature of demands placed on organizations, then, determine not only how they are organized internally but also the complexity with which they report their activities.

Growth and Inefficiency.   Growth is characteristic of bureaucratic organizations. Government expenditures in the United States have increased
more than 5 percent annually in real (i.e., deflated) dollars from the
beginning of this century to 1970 (Borcherding, 1977b). Federal employment in the same period has moved from less than 2 to more than 8
percent of the labor force, although it did not increase substantially after
the late 1950s. Since that time, however, the rate of growth of local
government employment, much of which has been supported by federal
subventions, has accelerated (Borcherding, 1977a; Meyer, 1979b). In
industry, the ratio of administrative to production workers, which is the
conventional index of bureaucratization, has also increased rapidly. Bendix (1956) provides basic data on ratios of administrative to production
workers in several Western nations for the first half of the twentieth
century. These ratios were generally below 10 percent in 1900 and above
20 percent in 1950. Using census data, Meyer (1979b) shows that the
administrative/production ratio has increased further since 1950, ex-
ceeding 30 percent in multiunit firms in 1972, the last year for which
Census of Manufactures series are presently available.

Although comparisons of public- and private-sector organizations are
hazardous because of differences in their activities, almost all such comparisons that have been attempted show public organizations to be less
efficient than their private-sector counterparts. The classic comparison
of a public and private organization, which corresponds closely but not
exactly to the bureaucratic/profit distinction is Davies' (1971) study of
Australia's two trunk airlines: Trans Australian Airways (TAA), a government firm, and Ansett Australian National Airways (Ansett ANA),
a private firm. The two airlines have similar routes and equipment and
they charge equal fares. Per employee, Ansett ANA carried more than
twice as much freight and mail, 21 percent more passengers, and had
13 percent greater revenues than TAA over an 11-year period beginning
in 1958. Had the two airlines not been constrained by law to be similar
in every respect, Davies notes, the efficiency advantage of the private
carrier might have been greater. Municipal utilites tend to have costlier
plants and higher operating costs than privately owned utilities, although
much of this difference is a result of the small scale of many municipal
power plants (Spann, 1977). Private provision of fire protection in Scotts-
dale, Arizona, is substantially less expensive than in other Arizona cities
when relevant community characteristics are controlled (Ahlbrandt,
1973). Private scavengers operate at substantially lower costs than public
refuse collection (Savas, 1977), although these differences diminish in
suburban communities compared to central cities (Hirsch, 1965).

Economic analysis may not adequately explain the growth and low
efficiency of bureaucratic compared to profit organizations. The high

growth rate of public agencies, which cannot be wholly explained as a function of population increase and wealth (Borcherding, 1977b), is consistent with Niskanen's (1971) model of bureaucrats as simple budgets maximizers, but the impaired efficiency of bureaucratic compared to profit organizations is inconsistent with the model. (It will be remembered that budget maximization renders bureaus too large but not inefficient in terms of cost per unit output.) Inefficiency of bureaus is consistent with Migué and Bélanger's "rent" model of bureaucratic behavior, but the "rent" model does not necessarily imply constant growth. These models, it will be noted, assume bureaucrats to be principally economic actors, whose utilities are associated with either budgets or "rents." Meyer's (1980a) research renders this assumption questionable. Historical time series describing municipal agencies in three large United States cities showed survival of organizational units to be a function of extensiveness and rates of change in administrative structure. (Quantitative change in organization is not precluded by invariant organizational form; indeed, the absence of alternatives to simple hierarchy for bureaus may stimulate high rates of organizational change.) Units with extended hierarchies and substantial variability of organizational structure had significantly higher probabilities of surviving than others. Moreover, organizational size had only a slight or nonsignificant effect upon survival. To the extent that organizational persistence is a utility for bureaucrats, managers at all levels will foster development of subordinate layers of organization. A proliferation of offices results in growth (Meyer, 1980b) rather than the reverse, suggesting that budget maximization is only a secondary utility. Meyer's results may also help explain the apparent inefficiency of bureaucratic compared to profit organizations. To the extent that proliferation of offices serves bureaucrats' utilities, slack resources or "rents" will be used for building and maintaining organization. A simple evolutionary principle, as opposed to economic maximization, may account for this pattern of empirical results. In an environment characterized by extreme uncertainty as to both objective conditions as well as to objectives, variety, and variability (or what Hannan and Freeman, 1977, call generalism) may better suit organizations for survival than specialization and stability. Alternatively, social or political maximization may account for these results. If the most visible action of a public or not-for-profit agency in response to external demand is creation of an organizational unit in order to represent that a problem is being attended to, as suggested by institutional (Meyer and Rowan, 1977) and signaling (Meyer, 1979c) theories, then managers maximize their constituencies by proliferating and varying organizational categories. To the extent that the environment consists of constituencies and that organizational–environment exchanges are mediated by political processes, the predictions made by evolutionary and institutional/signaling theories converge. Noneconomic theories, in short, offer potentially much richer explanations of bureaucratic growth and inefficiency than economic explanations, although they do not so readily admit of formalization. That these theories have not been tested rigorously in research may reflect the difficulty of obtaining intricate data on organizational patterns over extended intervals—economic models do not require such detailed data—but it may also reflect sociologists' reluctance to test the proposition that the same social and political processes that gave rise to rationalized bureaucracy almost a century ago nowadays propel both its growth and its downward spiral of efficiency.

A Note on Sociological Research on Bureaucracy.   Much early sociological research on organizations was concerned with delineation and measurement of elements of organizational structure, especially those elements identified by Weber (1946) in his classic essay "Bureaucracy." Not surprisingly, this research classifies organizations as bureaucratic to the extent that their characteristics fit Weber's ideal–typical model: division of labor, hierarchy of authority, administrative staff, and so forth. Some scholars, such as Udy (1959) and Stinchcombe (1959), found bureaucratic to be a subset of all rational organizations, the difference between the two types determined by the existence of formal hierarchy and written records. Others, such as Hall (1963; see also Hall and Tittle, 1966) and the Aston group (Pugh, Hickson, Hinings, and Turner, 1968; Pugh, Hickson, and Hinings, 1969b, 1969c) attempted to construct scales measuring bureaucratization in terms of structural attributes. Hall and Tittle (1966), for example, measures bureaucratization in terms of impersonality, hierarchy, division of labor, task specificity, and complexity of rules. Two of their empirical results should be noted. First, when bureaucracy is treated as a set of structural characteristics, a large number of profit organizations appear to be highly bureaucratic. Although 10 of the 25 organizations studied by Hall and his colleague were public or not-for-profit agencies, 5 of them were among the 7 least bureaucratized organizations and only 2 were among the 9 most highly bureaucratized (see Table 1 of Hall and Tittle, 1966). Second, and not surprisingly given the first result, of five predictors of bureaucratization used by Hall and Tittle, the best was orientation to objects as opposed to ideas. (The second best predictor was size, and the third was *low* degree of "people orientation.") The Aston researchers also generated counterintuitive results by defining bureaucracy in terms of structural attributes. Pugh, Hickson, and Hinings (1969a) attempted a typology of organizations using three key dimensions: structuring of activities, concentration of authority, and line control, as opposed to impersonal control of work flow. Their research was based on 52 organizations in the British Midlands, few of which were government agencies. "Full bureaucracy" was defined as a high structuring of activities and concentration of authority, and low-line control (i.e., impersonal control) of work flow. The two categories furthest removed from "full bureaucracy" were characterized by personal control of work flow regardless of other characteristics. Most government organizations fell into these two categories because work flow in them was controlled by supervisors. One should not conclude from these studies that organizations regarded as bureaucratic by economists least conform to Weber's model of bureaucracy. Their implication seems instead to be as indicated above: complex organizational forms used by profit organizations are not available to bureaucratic organizations, which are constrained to simple hierarchy.

The only sociologist to combine measurement of structural properties of organizations with explicit consideration of the bureaucratic/profit distinction is William Rushing. Rushing studied short-stay profit and nonprofit hospitals, reporting the results in two articles (1974, 1976). While his data analysis was complex, there was one persistent result: associations among measures of structure and performance were uniformly higher for profit than nonprofit hospitals. For example, the impact of occupancy rates upon proportions of production (as opposed to administrative and "hotel") personnel was higher in profit hospitals as was the correlation of community wealth with average daily patient costs (Rushing, 1974). Associations of occupational differentiation with measures of coordination were also significantly higher in profit compared to nonprofit hospitals. Rushing observed that profit/nonprofit differences in hospitals may be important theoretically because the results anticipated by rational models of organization are confirmed in the former but not the latter. After questioning the applicability of much of organizational theory to organizations whose goals are not economic, Rushing concluded that there ought to be more research on the profit/nonprofit or bureaucratic/profit differences in organizations. (I concur.)

Summary.   I have shown that bureaucratic organization is tied to simple hierarchy but at the same time must provide extremely detailed accounts of its activities in comparison with profit firms. These constraints impose substantial liabilities upon bureaus, and it is therefore not surprising to find bureaucratic organizations to be disproportionately large and inefficient compared to profit types. The same constraints also yield the paradoxical result that when bureaucracy is treated as a unitary concept and measured in terms of structural characteristics of organizations, many public agencies that are by any common sense definition bureaucratic score low on measures of bureaucratization. The problem here is not one of measurement but rather one of language, namely sociologists' penchant for using the term bureaucracy as synonymous with modern organization and their inattention to bureaucratic/profit differences. At the same time, I have indicated that economic models do not adequately account for long-term patterns of bureaucratic growth and change, and that recent sociological theories of organizations, which are attentive to details of structure, are potentially richer and more insightful than economic models in exploring and explaining modern bureaucracy. Organizational theory generally and an understanding of bureaucratic/profit differences in particular require a melding of the two disciplines.

Societal Concomitants of Bureaucracy

Even now relatively little is known about the impact of political and social forces at the societal level upon bureaucratization and the balance of bureaucratic versus profit organizations. The social conditions contributing to high rates of organizational formation are identified by Weber (1946) and elaborated by Stinchcombe (1965). These include literacy, urbanization, a money economy, political revolution that upsets vested interests, and a high density of social life, especially of organizing experience. The density of bureaucratic organization increases, of course, with the extensiveness of the nation-state. The greater the degree to which government is centralized and the more areas of economic activities subject to state control, the larger the bureaucracy (La Polombara, 1963). Large-scale profit organization does not exist in most communist nations.

Social and political forces affect the degree to which bureaucratic elements are incorporated into all organizations. Meyer and Brown's (1977) study of local government finance agencies linked their personnel regulations to federal actions, all of which were in the direction of increased formalization of procedures. Newer local agencies were found more likely to have extensive personnel procedures than older ones, and over the 6-year study interval all agencies moved toward greater formalization, suggesting extreme openness to the environment at the time of formation. No research is needed to document that federal regulations governing occupational health and safety, workers' pensions, and equality in employment practices have required extensive reporting to determine compliance and hence have incurred bureaucratization in all organizations. Service delivery in hospitals is now largely governed by Medicare regulations, and the Department of Energy presently mandates types of fuels that may be used by industrial firms. In each of these instances, extension of the nation-state into areas previously unregulated or left to the individual states is accompanied by creation of a federal

bureaucracy, complex reporting requirements, and the threat of substantial fines or loss of federal contracts for noncompliance. Compliance
reporting is a form of nonfinancial accounting but is unrelated to performance for profit firms. Massive penalties associated with noncompliance may compel firms to recentralize and retreat into simple hierarchy,
because managers held accountable solely for profit under decentralization may be tempted to behave opportunistically with respect to regulations and allow the larger corporation to suffer the consequences if
caught. To date, there has been no systematic research on the impact
of regulation on the internal organization of industrial firms.

As Weber noted, bureaucracy remains the principal guarantor of formal
equality before the law in modern societies. Demands for equality and
fairness may result in the creation of new agencies (e.g., the Office of
Civil Rights), and in this sense bureaucratization is often viewed as a
positive outcome of a political process. Once established, bureaucratic
agencies have the capacity to mobilize constituencies in support of their
budgets, rendering continued and augmented appropriations highly likely.
Thus, whereas there may be some agreement among citizens that taxes
are too high and the government too intrusive, proposals to reduce government programs and regulation almost always meet stiff resistance.
The taxpayer revolt is in opposition not only to bureaucrats but also to
single-issue politics that creates a mutuality of interests among constituencies, Congressional committees, and federal agencies. The vulnerability of elected representatives to interest groups renders a strengthening
of the political parties in the United States necessary before demands
for creation of new agencies and expanded authority for existing ones
can be resisted. Again, little systematic research concerning the relationship of political processes to the creation and growth of bureaucracy
has been conducted to date.

STUDYING "BUREAUCRATIC" AND "PROFIT" ORGANIZATIONS

Lord Keynes observed that most people are slaves of some defunct
philosopher. His dictum holds for social scientists as well as others, at
least with respect to the study of bureaucratic versus profit models of
organization. Basically, sociologists have been trapped by Weber. Because Weber asserted his model of bureaucracy to be descriptive of
modern organizations generally, sociologists have employed their full
array of measurement and estimation techniques to ascertaining the fit
between extant organizations and Weber's model, not pusing to consider
whether or not alternative and often opposed models of organization are
equally products of modernity. Economists have been trapped in their

metatheory, which asserts that conditions surrounding an exchange, whether of goods or services for a price or of promised outputs for a budget, determines its efficiency. This metatheory is at once insufficiently macroscopic in ignoring social and political values that are central to bureaucratic behavior and insufficiently microscopic in not attending to details of internal structure and procedure that distinguish bureaucratic from profit organizations. (The latter criticism merely echoes Williamson's (1975) comments on the industrial organization literature.)

Ultimately, bureaucratic organization operates in an arena where noneconomic values of compliance, propriety, and equity are paramount because they enhance legitimacy, hence sustain the enterprise. Profit organization maximizes long-run tangible results, which sustain the enterprise by augmenting its assets. At the highest level of generality, then, bureaucratic and profit organizations operate similarly, garnering resources in order to ensure continued existence. But in their details the two types differ substantially. There are differences in organizational structure and accounting procedures. The values of compliance, propriety, and equity constrain bureaucratic organization to simple structures and complex accounting, yielding large size and, possibly, inefficiency. The emphasis on results encourages structural innovation in profit firms and allows simple accounting. To ignore these differences is folly, but to treat bureaucrats as principally economic actors is equally so.

Research, then, should proceed in several directions simultaneously. To begin, there needs to be careful study of the link between organizational purposes and values on the one hand and internal structure and accounting on the other. I recognize that purposes and values may prove elusive in the extreme, given peoples' tendency to attribute purpose and value to their actions after the fact. Nonetheless, the tie between what organizations are expected to do and their internal structures and processes bears close examination. Of particular importance is the conflict between tangible economic and other goals: Are they inconsistent such that organizational mechanisms implemented in pursuit of one detract from the other? Cross-sectional comparisons of organizations are unlikely to prove useful in this regard. Indeed, microscopic examination of several organizations over time may be necessary. The observer cannot prescribe what purposes and values organizations ought to hold, but he can identify conflicts and tensions among them, thereby contributing to intelligent decisions. The issue, again, is whether organizational mechanisms implemented in pursuit of one purpose or value are inconsistent with other purposes or values. A second issue, linked to the first, is that of growth of bureaucratic organizations. For profit firms, excessive growth of staff is checked by its adverse effect upon performance and, in the long run, assets. For bureaucratic organizations the same does not hold, and the opposite may in fact be the case if, as noted earlier, the creation of an organizational unit is the most tangible outcome of the political process and is evaluated positively. Bureaucratic growth, then, may be ceaseless to the extent that efficiency considerations are subordinated to other values. The task of research is to identify the forces promoting growth with greater specificity than I have done. Again, long-term microscopic studies are needed to supplant the cross-sectional research relying upon gross indicators that economists have undertaken to date. One conceivable result of such studies is that no one, save for taxpayers, is benefited by restraining the size and elaborateness of public bureaucracies. Certain implications for policy and for political action would be inevitable. A third strand of research should focus upon the impact of long-term social and political change upon the balance between bureaucratic and profit forms of organization and vice versa. An acquisitive, individualistic society will not be a highly bureaucratized society. The question is whether a highly bureaucratized society, as is ours, so subordinates acquisitiveness and individual gain to other considerations that productive capacity is severely sapped and competitive advantage in a world economy compromised. Again, long-term relatively microscopic analysis is needed to supplement the macroscopic work conducted to date.

The bottom line is this: The distinction between bureaucratic and profit organization is one of values, but it is also consequential and thus is properly the subject of scientific study. Neither a denial of bureaucratic/ profit differences nor the application of inappropriate models (and, possibly, inappropriate formalization) to the behavior of bureaucrats will contribute to understanding the problem. Instead, economists' insight that there is a difference between the two types must be combined with sociologists' insight that political and social rather than economic processes propel most bureaucracies. Research comparing either explicitly or implicitly the two types must be long-term and more microscopic than heretofore so as to focus upon the *organizational* mechanisms distinguishing them and their effects. Not only will such research contribute to the theory of organizations, but it may also suggest as-yet-untried organizational alternatives.

REFERENCES

Ahlbrandt, R. An empirical analysis of public and private ownership and the supply of municipal fire services. *Public Choice,* 1973, *16.*

Anthony, R. Making sense of nonbusiness accounting. *Harvard Business Review,* 1980, *58,* 93–93.

Armour, H., & Teece, D. Organizational structure and economic performance: A test of the multidivisional hypothesis. *Bell Journal of Economics,* 1978, *9,* 106–122.

Barnard, C. The functions of the executive. Cambridge: Harvard University Press, 1938.

Bendix, R. Work and authority in industry. Berkeley: University of California Press, 1956.

Berle, A., & Means, G. The modern corporation and private property. New York: McMillan, 1932.

Blau, P. The dynamics of bureaucracy. Chicago: University of Chicago Press, 1955.

Blau, P. The hierarchy of authority in organizations. *American Journal of Sociology*, 1968, *73*, 453–467.

Blau, P. A formal theory of differentiation in organizations. *American Sociological Review*, 1970, *35*, 201–218.

Borcherding, T. One hundred years of public spending, 1870–1970. In T. Borcherding (Ed.), Budgets and Bureaucrats: The Sources of Government Growth. Durham: Duke University Press, 1977a.

Borcherding, T. The sources of growth of public expenditures in the United States, 1902–1970. In T. Borcherding (Ed.), Budgets and Bureaucrats: The Sources of Government Growth. Durham: Duke University Press, 1977b.

Breton, A., & Wintrobe, R. The equilibrium size of a budget maximizing bureau. *Journal of Political Economy*, 1975, *83*, 195–207.

Carey, A. The Hawthorne studies: A radical criticism. *American Sociological Review*, 1968, *32*, 403–416.

Chandler, A. *Strategy and Structure*. Cambridge: MIT Press, 1962.

Chandler, A. *The visible hand*. Cambridge: Harvard University Press, 1978.

Coopers, & Lybrand, and the University of Michigan. Financial Disclosure Practices of American Cities: A Public Report. New York, Coopers and Lybrand, 1976.

Crozier, M. The bureaucratic phenomenon. Chicago: University of Chicago Press, 1964.

Dalton, M. Men who manage. New York: Wiley, 1959.

Davies, D. The efficiency of public versus private firms, the case of Australia's two airlines. *Journal of Law and Economics*, 1971, *14*, 149–165.

Davidson, S., Green, D., Hellerstein, W., Mandansky, A., & Weil, R. Financial Reporting by State and Local Governmental Units. Chicago: University of Chicago Center for Management of Public and Nonprofit Enterprise, 1977.

Downs, A. Inside bureaucracy. Boston: Little-Brown, 1967.

Dreben, A. Governmental versus commercial accounting: The issues. *Governmental Finance*, 1979, *8* (3), 3–8.

Dreben, A. Letter to editor. *Harvard Business Review*, 1980, *58* (6), 216–221.

Gouldner, A. Patterns of industrial bureaucracy. Glencoe: The Free Press, 1954.

Hall, R. The concept of bureaucracy: An empirical assessment. *American Journal of Sociology*, 1963, *69*, 32–40.

Hall, R., & Tittle, C. A note on bureaucracy and its 'correlates'. *American Journal of Sociology*, 1966, *72*, 267–272.

Hannan, M., & Freeman, J. "The Population Ecology of Organizations." *American Journal of Sociology*, 1977, *82*, 929–964.

Herzlinger, R., & Sherman, H. Advantages of fund accounting in 'nonprofits'. *Harvard Business Review*, 1980, *58* (3), 94–105.

Hickson, D., Pugh, D., & Pheyrey, D. Operations technology and organizational structure: An empirical reappraisal. *Administrative Science Quarterly*, 1969, *14*, 378–395.

Hirsch, W. Cost functions of government service: Refuse collection. *Review of Economics and Statistics*, 1965.

Kimberly, J. Organizational Size and The Structuralist Perspective: A Review, Critique, and Proposal. *Administrative Science Quarterly*, 1976, *21*, 571–597.

Landsberger, H. Hawthorne revisited. Ithaca: New York State School of Industrial and Labor Relations, 1958.

La Polombara, R. Bureaucracy and political development. Princeton: Princeton University Press, 1963.

Likert, R. New patterns of management. New York: McGraw-Hill, 1961.

Likert, R. The human organization. New York: McGraw-Hill, 1967.

Marris, R. The economics of "managerial" capitalism. New York: Free Press, 1964.

Merton, R. Bureaucratic structure and personality. In Social Theory and Social Structure, 2nd edition. New York: Free Press, 1958, 195–206.

Meyer, J., & Rowan, B. Institutionalized organizations: Formal structure as myth and ceremony. *American Journal of Sociology,* 1977, *83,* 340–363.

Meyer, J., & Rowan, B. The structure of educational organizations. In M. Meyer, (Ed.), Environments and Organizations. San Francisco: Jossey-Bass, 1978.

Meyer, J., Scott, W. R., Cole, S., & Intili, J. Instructional Dissensus and Institutional Consensus in Schools. In M. Meyer (Ed.), Environments and Organizations. San Francisco: Jossey-Bass, 1978.

Meyer, M. Two authority structures of bureaucratic organizations. *Administrative Science Quarterly,* 1968, *13,* 211–228.

Meyer, M. Size and the structure of organizations: A causal analysis. *American Sociological Review,* 1972, *37,* 434–440.

Meyer, M. Theory of Organizational Structure. Indianapolis: Bobbs-Merrill, 1977.

Meyer, M. Change in public bureaucracies. New York: Cambridge University Press, 1979a.

Meyer, M. Debureaucratization? *Social Science Quarterly,* 1979b, *60,* 25–34.

Meyer, M. Organizational structure as signaling. *Pacific Sociological Review,* 1979c, *22,* 481–500.

Meyer, M. The bureaucratic structure hypothesis. Unpublished manuscript, 1980a.

Meyer, M. Persistence in change in bureaucratic structure. Unpublished manuscript, 1980b.

Meyer, M., & Brown, M. C. The process of bureaucratization. *American Journal of Sociology,* 1977, *83,* 364–385.

Migué, J., & Bélanger, G. Toward a general theory of managerial discretion. *Public Choice,* 1974, *17,* 27–47.

Mises, L. Bureaucracy. New Haven: Yale University Press, 1944.

Niskanen, W., Jr. Bureaucracy and Representative Government. Chicago: Ardine-Atherton, 1971.

Niskanen, W., Jr. Bureaucrats and politicians. *Journal of Law and Economics,* 1975, *18,* 617–643.

Olson, M., Jr. The Logic of Collective Action. Cambridge: Harvard University Press, 1965.

Parsons, T. "Introduction" to M. Weber, Theory of Social and Economic Organization. New York: Free Press, 1958.

Perrow, C. Organizational Analysis. Belmont, California: Wadsworth, 1970.

Pugh, D., Hickson, D., Hinings, R., & Turner, C. Dimensions of organizational structure. *Administrative Science Quarterly,* 1968, *13,* 65–104.

Pugh, D., Hickson, D., & Hinings, R. The content of organizational structures. *Administrative Science Quarterly,* 1969a, *14,* 91–114.

Pugh, D., Hickson, D., & Hinings, R. An empirical taxonomy of work organizations. *Administrative Science Quarterly,* 1969b, *14,* 115–126.

Roethlisberger, F., & Dickson, W. J. Management and the Worker. Cambridge: Harvard University Press, 1939.

Rushing, W. Differences in profit and nonprofit organizations: A study of effectiveness and efficiency in general short-stay hospitals. *Administrative Science Quarterly,* 1974, *19,* 474–484.

Rushing, W. Profit and nonprofit orientations and the differentiation-coordination hypothesis for organizations: A study of small general hospitals. *American Sociological Review,* 1976, *41,* 676–691.

Savas, E. An empirical study of competition in municipal service delivery. *Public Administration Review,* 1977, *37,* 717–724.

Spann, R. Rates of productivity change and the growth of local government expenditure. In T. Borcherding, (Ed.), Budgets and Bureaucrats: The Sources of Government Growth. Durham: Duke University Press, 1977.

Stinchcombe, A. Social structure and organizations. In J. March (Ed.), *Handbook of Organizations*. Chicago: Rand McNally, 1965.

Stinchcombe, A. Bureaucratic and craft administration of production. *Administrative Science Quarterly*, 1959, *4*, 168–187.

Tannenbaum, A. Control in Organizations. New York: McGraw-Hill, 1968.

Toma, M., & Toma, E. Bureaucratic responses to tax limitation amendments. *Public Choice*, 1980, *35*, 333–348.

Tullock, G. The Politics of Bureaucracy. Washington: Public Affairs Press, 1965.

Udy, S., Jr. 'Bureaucracy' and 'rationality' in Weber's organization theory. *American Sociological Review*, 1959, *24*, 791–795.

Weber, M. Bureaucracy. In H. Gerth & C. W. Mills (Eds.), From Max Weber: Essays in Sociology. New York: Oxford University Press, 1946, 196–244.

Weick, K. Educational Organizations as Loosely Coupled Systems. *Administrative Science Quarterly*, 1976, *21*, 1–19.

Weston, J., & Mansinghka, S. Tests of the efficiency performance of conglomerate firms. *Journal of Finance*, 1971, *26*, 919–936.

Whyte, W. Human Relations in the Restaurant Industry. Chicago: University of Chicago Press, 1948.

Whyte, W., & Hamilton, E. Action Research for Management Homewood, Illinois: Irwin-Dorsey, 1964.

Williamson, O. The Economics of Discretionary Behavior. Englewood Cliffs: Prentice Hall, 1964.

Williamson, O. Markets and Hierarchies. New York: Free Press, 1975.

Wright, J. On a Clear Day You Can See General Motors. Grosse Pointe, Michigan: Wright Enterprises, 1979.

THE MEANINGS OF ABSENCE:
NEW STRATEGIES FOR THEORY AND RESEARCH[1]

Gary Johns and Nigel Nicholson

ABSTRACT

The central thesis of this chapter is that the gap between experiential accounts of absence from work and the inferred accounts derived from conventional research should be reduced. First, six "propositions in use" that have tacitly guided conventional absence research are presented. These include the assumptions that empirically similar absence events have equivalent meanings; most absence is volitional; absence is best conceived as a function of individual differences; absence is a static phenomenon; absence is strictly an "organizational" behavior; absence occurs only among blue-collar and clerical workers. Second, six "counterpropositions" are introduced, which, if adopted, should lead to the use of new research methods and the development of fresh theory to study absence. Finally, seven research issues, which derive from the joint application of the counterpropositions, are presented to illustrate their value. These include a reevaluation of proneness; attribution processes and absence; the relationship between absence and other behaviors; absence and time allocation; absence as coin of exchange; normative control of absence; absence climates and cultures.

Research in Organizational Behavior, Vol. 4, pages 127–172
Copyright © 1982 by JAI Press Inc.
All rights of reproduction in any form reserved.
ISBN: 0-89232-147-4

I am sometimes prevented from attending work through no fault of my own.
You lack motivation to attend work regularly.
They are lazy malingerers, willfully milking the system.

Thus might a cynical grammarian conjugate the verb "to be absent from work." Cynicism aside, there is a grain of truth here: Accounts of absence often refer to a "generalized other," and one need not be a committed attribution theorist to see that the terms in which we explain our own behavior and that of people we know well differ from those we offer for strangers. It is the main theme of this chapter that the gap between behavioral scientists' accounts of absence as a "social problem" and its experiential reality to the worker should be closed by the adoption of new frames of reference for research and theory building.

Evidence of the need to close this gap is abundant if indirect. Concern about the social and organizational costs of absence has generated a vast amount of research and some theorizing. However, reviews of this work (Chadwick-Jones, Brown, & Nicholson, 1973a; Muchinsky, 1977; Porter & Steers, 1973; Steers & Rhodes, 1978) reveal a rather depressing state of affairs. Relationships of other variables with absence are often inconsistent. Even when well established and of practical magnitude, such relationships may be poorly understood (e.g., the tendency for women to exhibit more absence than men; Steers and Rhodes, 1978). In short, a heavy investment of research effort has failed to generate significant dividends, whether one's criterion is the prediction, explanation, or control of absence.

It is our contention that the implicit boundaries within which absence research has been conducted, drawn by metatheoretical assumptions and unstated premises, are overly restrictive and inappropriate. In turn, these boundaries have led to theoretical and empirical vacuity. In this chapter we shall first delineate these boundaries by presenting the hidden axioms of absence research in the form of six propositions in use (PIUs). We borrow here from Argyris and Schon's (1974) notion of "theories in use" to distinguish the premises that underpin action from those that may be "espoused" by actors. Following this, we shall outline six counterpropositions (CPs), which, if adopted, would radically reorient absence research toward theoretical innovation, fresh methodologies, and neglected content areas. Finally, we shall illustrate this consequence by discussing seven potentially fruitful approaches to the study of absence, each of which derives from our CPs rather than from the paradigms of the PIUs, which have long dominated the field.

The PIUs and CPs are developed first in outline form. This is done in anticipation of our intention to draw out their implications in the extended discussion of the seven research issues.

PROPOSITIONS IN USE IN ABSENCE RESEARCH

The PIUs that are discussed in the following paragraphs stem from our review of the methods behavioral scientists have used to study absence. In several cases these PIUs also correspond to managerial treatments of the "absence problem." This correspondence between research strategies and management interests is, of course, not uncommon (Nord, 1977).

PIU 1: *Empirically similar absence events have functionally and psychologically equivalent meaning for all workers.*

It is nearly universal for organizations to classify and label absences in accordance with this assumption. For example, the worker who misses a day and fails to offer an acceptable explanation or produce a medical certificate is likely to have his or her absence labeled "voluntary," "illegitimate," "unexcused," or "casual." Such labels impute motives, and it is apparent that supervisors and personnel managers often exercise extreme discretion in assigning absence to these or other categories. Moreover, there are indications that such judgments and assignments are frequently unreliable (Ilgen, 1977; Latham & Pursell, 1975) and culture-bound (Smulders, 1980). Despite this, it is common for absence researchers to adopt organizational measures of absence without comment or criticism (see Rhodes and Steers[2] for documentation of the prevalence of this practice).

Even when researchers adopt more objective criteria for absence classification, such as frequency and time lost, the naming of the resultant absence classes sometimes "smuggles in" causal attributions (e.g., Huse and Taylor, 1962, "Attitudinal Index" denoting short-spell frequency; see also Chadwick-Jones, Brown, Nicholson, and Sheppard, 1971). In other cases, researchers have made use of less value-laden distinctions, such as "medically certificated" versus "uncertificated," or "paid" versus "unpaid." However, often these are then adopted as operationalizations of *causal* categories, notably the "voluntary" versus "involuntary" distinction. The operationalizations upon which these distinctions are made are likely to tell us more about organizational and external controls than about the causal dynamics of the behavior.

PIU 1 is also evident in the great favor with which the notion of "withdrawal" is embraced to encompass not only different types of absence but also to link it with other behaviors such as turnover and lateness (Beehr & Gupta, 1978; Bernardin, 1977; Waters & Roach, 1971; Gupta & Jenkins, 1980[3]). This label imputes similar motivational states to superficially similar behaviors.

PIU 2: *Individual volitional processes underlie most psychologically interesting and potentially controllable forms of absence.*

While it is a profound misreading of motivational theory to assume that *motivated* behavior is *willed* behavior, it is commonly assumed by otherwise sophisticated scientists that most absence is provoked by desires to avoid work and to "consume" alternative satisfaction (Argyle, 1972). Indeed, this assumption is enshrined in the use of the term "voluntary" to describe unsanctioned absence (Behrend, 1959) and in managerial treatments of control strategies (CBI, 1970). Despite this, the hedonistic, rationalistic, and normative character of "push–pull" or "pain avoidance" treatments of motivated behavior has not gone unchallenged (Nicholson, 1977). It is now widely recognized that feelings of satisfaction and dissatisfaction may be peripheral to the core motivational process, as in expectancy theory, where they are cast in the role of potentially transient outputs (cf. Campbell & Pritchard, 1976). Similarly, rational calculations of subjective utilities and the probabilities of outcomes may be less important than behavioral and attitudinal commitments to habitual acts or constructions of the situation. Such relatively unconsidered factors are important and relevant motivational dynamics, yet ones that may only be obliquely glimpsed when the focus is fixed on conscious volitional states.

There is a curious exception to this emphasis on the volitional aspects of absence: the problem of bypassing significant motivational processes for those absences that have the appearance of being "involuntary." Even where the locus of control for absence can be attributed to factors external to the person, they are nonetheless mediated by the person's construction of reality, and their impact may be significantly moderated by the person's motivational state (as in the case of much nonchronic illness).

PIU 3: *Absence is essentially an individual-level phenomenon, best predicted and explained via individual differences.*

The reviews of the literature show that two strategies have dominated absence research. On one hand, absence has been correlated with personal characteristics such as age, sex, and family size. On the other, it has been associated with individually generated measures of work attitudes and perceptions, such as job satisfaction and job characteristics. The individualistic paradigm has proved so pervasive as to even lead researchers to apply explanations appropriate to individual variations to data in which groups are the operational units of analysis (e.g., Dittrich & Carrell, 1979; Kerr, Koppelmeier, & Sullivan, 1951).[4] As Hulin and Rousseau[5] point out, individual responses and rates of behavior do not tap the same pool of variance, and certainly in the absence literature there has been a relative neglect of factors potentially underlying sources of variation in group-level absence, such as norms, cohesiveness, and climate.

In their review of studies of absence and job satisfaction, Nicholson, Brown, and Chadwick-Jones (1976) found that 13 of 29 studies based their conclusions about the potency (or otherwise) of dissatisfaction as a cause of absence upon analytical techniques that took no account of individual variance on either variable. That is, all were group level investigations that resorted to individualistic explanatory frameworks. A related logic may be observed in many research treatments of job characteristics. Instead of viewing absence in light of workplace structural influences that distinguish *work roles,* job characteristics are abstracted as psychological dimensions that attach to *jobholders* (e.g., Turner & Lawrence, 1965). Although some positive findings have been reported by such studies, their efficacy is directly limited to those features that are suitable for psychometric analysis (i.e., displaying reliably quantifiable individual variation). They typically tell us little about other dimensions of jobs that may be of crucial relevance to understanding absence (e.g., payment systems and supervisory regimes), and that may underlie relationships between perceived job characteristics and absence behavior. These considerations suggest that subjective perceptions of job dimensions and work attitudes should be restored to their logical research roles as individual-level *intervening* variables, lying between the structure of work environments and worker behavior, rather than treated as intrapsychic *independent* variables without reference to their situational antecedents.

PIU 4: *Absence is a static phenomenon.*

Although fairly wide variations may be observed in rates, absence is almost always sufficiently infrequent among employee populations to be considered a low base rate phenomenon. A recent Canadian report judged the average industrial time lost rate to be around 4 percent of scheduled working days, with a range of approximately 1 to 10 percent ("Absenteeism," 1980), and one writer has recently assessed the United States average time lost to be 3.5 percent (Hedges, 1977). As Rousseau[6] and Hulin and Rousseau[5] have pointed out, a consequence of this has been the common practice of aggregating absence data over time (usually 6 to 12 months) to yield sufficient reliable variance for conventional analyses. The conceptual corollary of this, to which many researchers are prey, is to discuss absence as if it were timeless and absolute (i.e., an attribute or property of an individual or an organization): this person "has" high absence; that organization "has" low absence. Changes in absence levels are usually treated as problems of reliability (Chadwick-Jones et al., 1971; Huse & Taylor, 1962; Latham & Pursell, 1975). However, as Hulin and Rosseau[5] argue, the unreliability of behaviors such as absence may be a function of "lawful changes," meaning that the occurrence or nonoccurrence of the behavior may increase or decrease its probability in the future.

PIU 5: *Absence is best viewed as strictly an "organizational" behavior.*

In urging managers and researchers to measure work *attendance* rather than absence, Latham and Pursell (1975) state that "absenteeism is a *nonevent* in that no behavior can be observed or recorded *on the job*" (p. 369, italics added). This statement is a truism, and it indicates the profound lack of interest exhibited by researchers in the extraorganizational factors that may influence absence. For example, in their review of the absence literature, Porter and Steers (1973) partition the investigated correlates into four categories, three of which are solely concerned with the organization (organization-wide, immediate work environment, and job-related). Similarly, a later summary compiled by Rhodes and Steers[2] divides the factors associated with absence into seven categories, five of which are exclusively organizational.[7] When one examines individual studies more closely, this extreme "organization-centric" perspective is confirmed. Let us consider briefly how this arises.

In most regular employment, workers enter into a quasi-contractual exchange of a fixed quota of time to fulfill organizational goals for a schedule of rewards. Within this framework, unscheduled absence becomes deviant behavior in relation to organizational expectations, because it imposes direct costs upon organizational efficiency and profitability. This often leads to absence being viewed as an index of organizational effectiveness and individual performance, and as a criterion for the success of change programs (many basic organizational behavior texts stress this point of view). The assumption underlying this kind of treatment is that absence is "management's problem" (see Fox and Scott, 1943, for an early influential stimulus for this view), and that it falls within the organization's sphere of legitimate and intended control (Gaudet, 1963). In other words, there is a logical drift from awareness of the significance of absence for organizational functioning to a belief that causes and corrections lie within the workplace. A stimulus for this logical drift is the very ease with which absence is quantifiable as a performance measure, and the legalistic, contractual terms in which it is interpreted. Unfortunately for would-be agents of organizational control, however, absence events that are responses to aspects of work experience are identical in appearance to those that are prompted by extraorganizational factors.

PIU 6: *Absence occurs only among blue-collar and clerical workers.*

In treating absence as "management's problem," commentators usually mean that it is a problem for the regulation of managers' *subordinates*. The mechanisms organizations institute to record and discipline absence are applied primarily to those areas of the enterprise where it is visibly related to output and requires adjustment to the programming of work systems (e.g., rescheduling tasks, reallocating manpower). For these reasons, reliable records of employee absence are usually only maintained at the lower levels of organizations. This is reflected in the great volume of research data pertaining to blue-collar and some lower level white-collar populations, and the dearth of information about higher level employees (consult the reviews cited earlier). The relative "invisibility" of absence among managers, professionals, and entrepreneurs has meant that these groups are generally exempted from generalizations about the causes of absence, and it seems to be assumed that no comparable "problem" exists among them. Among blue-collar workers the problem is often cast as one of "malingering" (Dennett, 1978), whereas among executives "stress" is the fashionable explanation for aberrant behavior, even though close scrutiny of the evidence shows that stress symptoms are in fact most prevalent among lower level occupations (Fletcher, Gowler, & Payne, 1979). As we shall be arguing in due course, one may certainly expect absence to have different meanings for people in contrasting occupational circumstances, but this in no way buttresses the fiction that absence is a problem or a behavior peculiarly characteristic of lower organizational levels.

It should be recognized that the six PIUs presented do not constitute a coherent "theory in use." Strictly interpreted, there are logical inconsistencies among them. For example, the normative view of absence causation seen in PIUs 1 and 6 is contradicted by methodologies that individualize its causation in accordance with PIU 3. Similarly, seeing absence as a means of fulfilling various conscious purposes (PIU 2) is potentially at odds with the assumptions underlying its aggregation in measurement (PIU 4) and its treatment as a species of organizational performance (PIU 5). Why should this be so? First, all these PIUs are supportive of the traditional positivist ethos of investigative methods. Each derives from the assumption that absence is a "problem" that can be "solved" by the application of normal science treatments, characterized by a value-free orientation, an acultural and ahistorical perspective, an emphasis on quantitative rather than qualitative explorations of data, and the application of the logic of hypotheticodeductive verification. For positivist methods to succeed, it is necessary that they be applied within carefully bounded limits that are specified by subtopic areas and internally consistent partial models of the phenomena in question. The result is a fragmentation of different approaches to absence, each invoking a different set of supportive PIUs. Some aspects of absence may be illuminated by such approaches, though it is our contention that alternatives are necessary to advance understanding in areas where research has reached an impasse or where there has been neglect by researchers.

Absence research, like much other research in organizational behavior, is method-driven. The ease with which absence data may be collected at different levels of analysis suggests facile possibilities for data analysis at these various levels. Consequently, the multiplexity of absence causes is simplified, and questions about its social and personal meanings are shelved in the interests of easy data manipulation and hypothesis confirmation. In a manner similar to job satisfaction researchers (as charged by Locke, 1969), absence investigators have "measured and correlated" absence with whatever other variables are available and avoided the more fundamental questions about what it is they are measuring.

Our counterpropositions are thus intended as antidotes to this tradition. We are not trying to level one set of deities to erect another, but seeking to enlarge the possibility for useful future research by bringing to the fore some little considered alternative perspectives on absence.

SOME VIABLE COUNTERPROPOSITIONS

In this section we present six counterpropositions regarding the nature of absence that are intended to demonstrate that new approaches to research are possible. These CPs avoid, but do not preclude, a managerial orientation toward the control of absence.

CP 1: *Absence events are phenomenologically unique.*

The personal significance of each absence event has distinctive properties according to the shifting interaction of personal factors and environmental constraints. Put another way, absence means different things to different people at different times in different situations. We do not deny that valid generalizations may be made about absence behavior, as there are numerous regularities in personal and organizational life. However, there is no law of permanence for such regularities, and we should expect generalized predictions to be unreliable—as indeed they are. This is reflected in small amounts of variance in absence behavior that studies have usually been able to predict, and the instability of these relationships (as is the case of job satisfaction and absence). In order to better explain absence, this more closely contingent approach is needed, in which we attempt to uncover the specific contextual conditions that apply to individual absence episodes. This demands more painstaking investigation, in which idiographic techniques are used to correctly specify the boundaries that are appropriate to explaining episodes and which will enable us to judge when similar explanations are valid for individual actors and episodes. Phenomenological strategies that explore the significance of absence events within the life-space of individuals are an essential prerequisite for the development of grounded theory about individual absence causation.

CP 2: *Much absence is not the result of conscious choice but is the result of nonvolitional forces.*

It is evident that absence is often purposive and environmentally adaptive. Morgan and Herman (1976) have shown how absence can be seen as constructive goal-seeking behavior, directed at fulfilling aspirations and obligations outside the sphere of the organization rather than simply fulfilling a need to escape the discomforts of work. However, this does not constitute confirming evidence for the assertion that most absence is a conscious and calculated act. Even when workers take advantage of a sick pay scheme or take a day off to attend to pressing business affairs, the decision may take place within a "bounded rationality" (Simon, 1957) of rules, constraints, and introjected norms whose potency as guiding forces is largely unseen by the person. More common is the attribution of absence to involuntary factors—usually illness. The pervasiveness of medical criteria for absence legitimation and the extensive penetration of medical etiology into everyday thought and language has meant that the purposive nature of absence is often disguised from the consciousness of the absentee and those close to him or her. Psychological medicine has established that a great deal of common illness has strong psychogenic elements, an insight that has consistently eluded the consciousness of industrial and organizational psychologists! By the same token, most *attendance* is not the result of a daily "decision" of any conscious kind but is behavior executed in accordance with established norms, routines, customs, and habits. The attendance behavior of most employees is effectively on "automatic pilot," and indeed their conscious decisional processes will probably have played only a small part in the original setting of the normative controls that thereafter guide their behavior. A corollary of this view is the suggestion that some individual differences in absence will be due to variations in personal "habit strength." Such strength is probably a function of both the degree of compulsive "attachment" to work (Nicholson & Payne)[8] and external constraints on perceived decisional freedom.

CP 3: *Valid generalizations about absence often require a sociocultural perspective.*

There is increasing recognition in the field of organizational behavior that different work environments may provoke different psychological reactions, often researched under the heading of "organizational climate" (Payne & Pugh, 1976). The psychological environment that is created by structural conditions, by the framework of rules, norms, and customs, and by the values of influential organizational members may be pervasive in its impact on employee thought and action. Comparative research has shown that the absence profiles of individual organizations are indeed highly distinctive, and that the correlates of absence vary widely from plant to plant (Chadwick-Jones, Brown, & Nicholson, in press). We may learn significantly more about absence behavior by moving our focus to encompass absence "cultures," that is, the set of shared understandings about absence legitimacy in a given organization and the established "custom and practice" of employee absence behavior and its control (e.g., predominant supervisory styles and worker beliefs about co-workers' attendance behavior). If one accepts that behavior is mediated by the sociopsychological environment, then it is necessary to establish as a baseline for causal analysis the unique normative constraints that distinguish absence patterns across organizations and their subunits.

CP 4: *Absence is temporal behavior and continually subject to dynamic change.*

By definition, absence reallocates the distribution of time from work to nonwork. Thus, the meaning of absence events to both absentees and others in their social framework may be distinguished by duration as well as perceived causes. Given that absence *a priori* restructures the work week, it follows that this may be the primary outcome for which absence is instrumental; i.e., to autonomously change the schedule of working hours. In expectancy theory terms, the valence of this outcome will derive from the valences of the uses of reallocated time. This compels us to view absence causation as a recursive learning process, and in the words of Hulin and Rousseau[5], to expect "lawful changes" in absence behavior over time and from episode to episode. The longitudinal "dialectic" of attendance behavior has been neglected by research, apart from those studies that have looked for changes in employee attendance following organizational changes. The implication of this CP is that research should attempt more continuous monitoring of feedback and change in employee absence behavior and not merely view such change as a source of unwanted error variance.

CP 5: *Absence represents nonwork behavior and is subject to major causal influences from variables that transcend the workplace.*

By defining the behavior in terms of its obvious organizational impact, the word "absence" involves the same conceptual snare as the term "withdrawal." This perspective neglects the fact that when a person is absent from work he or she is *present* somewhere else, and far too little attention has been paid to the impact of forces outside the workspace. When studies have incorporated work-transcending variables, such as domestic circumstances, they have contributed significantly to absence prediction (e.g., Morgan & Herman, 1976). Staw and Oldham (1978) make a similar point when they charge that too little attention is paid to the complex meaning of our dependent variables in organizational research, and, in the case of absence, how its maintenance functions for individual adjustment should be considered in addition to its more common construal as dysfunctional performance. In short, we need to know more about the barriers to attendance and the incentives to absence that exist beyond organizational boundaries and outside the purview of management controls.

CP 6: *Absence occurs throughout the world of work, and research should reflect this fact.*

Wherever people are subject to the quasi-contractual exchange of time and effort for rewards, there will be occasions when they seek to unilaterally effect a temporary change in their side of the bargain. In short, managers and other higher level organizational members are not immune from the need or desire to take time off work in addition to that scheduled in the work contract. Whether this is viewed as unproblematic or defensible is irrelevant to the fact that such behavior is generically identical to what is considered problematic at lower organizational levels. It only shows that different assumptions, attributions, and controls are thought to be applicable. Researchers' neglect of managerial absence (and that of the self-employed) may be attributable to the paucity of data available in readily analyzable form, though this must be considered a poor excuse for scientific omissions and should only serve as a spur to fresh initiatives. Unfortunately, it has not. In particular, we do not know to what extent absence has common costs, causes, and controls at different organizational levels or in different occupational settings. There is good reason to expect that people who occupy different roles and hold different statuses will differ systematically in motive structures, habits, normative imperatives, and external constraints. A comparative approach that captures the variance in these factors may be an especially effective strategy for exploring the various meanings of absence.

These six CPs do not constitute a more coherent "theory" of absence than the PIUs that they are intended to supplant. However, in our view, they do suggest more complex, realistic explanations of absence and invoke more challenging methodologies than their well-worn predecessors. These methods include phenomenological approaches to dispositions toward absence (e.g., illness behaviors); ethnogenic strategies at various levels of analysis (e.g., work group interpretations of member behavior); longitudinal analyses of cause-effect relationships; the investigation of new variables that surface as a result of the previous techniques. There is growing recognition (among social psychologists in particular) that strategies of this nature are necessary to cope with the historical complexity of social behavior and to encompass the subjective meanings that link it with its context (cf. Gergen, 1973; Harré & Secord, 1972; Pepitone, 1976).

In the sections that follow we consider seven research areas that are suggested by the selective joint application of the CPs. Juxtaposed as they are, it will be apparent that there is some overlap among them, with the consequent potential for eventual theoretical synthesis. First, some basic issues regarding absence are considered. Second, absence as a form of personal control is explored. In conclusion, the social aspects of absence are examined.

SOME BASIC ISSUES

This section considers three fairly basic research issues that stem from the adoption of the CPs. In a sense, work in these areas should "clear the decks" and generate needed information for investigating other substantive topics regarding absence. In two cases (absence proneness and absence and alternative behaviors), we take a new look at old issues. In the other case (the attribution process and absence), we examine a basic issue that has been neglected by previous research.

A Fresh Look at Absence Proneness

Although absence is a universal organizational phenomenon and is exhibited wherever people are employed, it is also a low base rate phenomenon (i.e., a relatively small number of instances are distributed among work forces). At very low levels, the distribution of absence takes the form of the *J*-curve or Poisson distribution (Walker, 1947), with "the many" having few or no spells of absence and "the few" accounting for the remainder. From an observer's point of view, this may have two consequences. First, the visibility of the few is accentuated by figure–ground contrast. Second, a dispositional explanation of absence is invited. These consequences circumscribe what might be called the classical view of absence proneness. Were absence more or less common than it is, it could be accepted as normal or dismissed as aberrant. But absence, being a phenomenon that is readily observable and measurable in all industries but not among all workers, is optimally visible, thus arousing attention and concern.

It is often argued that a small core of workers accounts for a disproportionate share of absenteeism, with 10 to 20 percent of the work force accounting for 80 to 90 percent of time lost (Robinson, 1980; Yolles, Carone, & Krinsky, 1974). Indeed, careful empirical studies provide support for the disproportionate occurrence of absence, although the magnitude of the effect appears to vary with the time frame over which data are aggregated and the specific absence measure used. In a Cardiff, Wales, study of 16 organizations (Chadwick-Jones et al., in press) it was found that 10 percent of the workers were responsible for 25 to 40 percent of 1 year's total absence frequency. This finding was remarkable for its consistency across quite disparate employee populations and quite independent of wide variations in absolute levels of absence. On the other hand, Garrison and Muchinsky (1977), using a 3-month time frame, found that 17 percent of the work force accounted for 90 percent of paid time lost whereas 31 percent accounted for 90 percent of unpaid time lost.

Such findings tend to fuel the common supposition that absence is due to some malaise in disposition or malignancy of constitution on the part of the offenders. Once set apart from their fellow workers in this manner, it is logical to try to "normalize" the distribution by means of various sanctions. In this common managerial strategy we see several of the PIUs exhibited: equivalent meaning among the absences of the core; the assumption that absence reflects a static, volitional personal property; and the notion that absence is widely susceptible to organizational control.

Our CPs suggest that the PIUs are loaded in favor of discovering proneness but ill-suited to explore its nature once identified. Where this reasoning prevails, there is a need to examine empirically the premises upon which it rests and then look at the whole question of proneness afresh. First, there is a need to establish whether absence occurs among the few *more often* than might be expected. The Poisson distribution is, after all, the normal distribution writ small, and the laws of chance alone predict a core at the upper asymptote. Second, it must be established that the core remains *constant,* for there are two alternatives to the attribution of proneness to people. One is that there is a different core each time behavior is sampled. This would be expected if a small number of absences were allocated totally randomly each year across a work force. The other is that apparent proneness is a function of some fairly constant factor such as personal attributes or role requirements.

There have been studies that shed light on these issues. Arbous and Sichel (1954) and Froggatt (1970) have found that statistical proneness clearly exceeds chance expectations. However, even when one accepts this point, it may be reasoned that only a proportion of those who are statistically prone are prone by disposition or constitution. Many of those at the high extreme can still be viewed as merely unlucky rather than culpable, because although curve-fitting reveals significant deviations from chance, these are not sufficiently dramatic to support a dispositional explanation for *all* absence-prone persons. A secondary source of evidence regarding proneness is the incidence of "repeaters." Few studies have quantified this, although it does seem that one of the best predictors of a person's absence spell frequency for one time period is his or her spell frequency for an adjacent period: interyear correlations between .5 and .7 are typical (Froggatt, 1970; Morgan & Herman, 1976; Nicholson & Goodge, 1976; Waters & Roach, 1979). A more differentiated approach has been taken by Garrison and Muchinsky (1977), who showed that proneness was a relatively short-range phenomenon because interperiod correlations declined over time until returning to chance levels. Thus, the core may change, but slowly. However, this does not tell us *what* determines absence proneness, for the factors that lead to a shifting core of prone persons in one setting may not be found in others, e.g., changes in job content, payment systems, supervisory regimes, and the like. In a stable environment, the only predictable changes are in personal characteristics: the effects of aging, increasing job tenure, and variations in domestic circumstances. Relative stability in such factors is the norm, and hence changes in them causing increases or decreases in susceptibility to high levels of absence will be uncommon or very gradual. It would seem then that in most industrial settings proneness will be demonstrable for a given time period, but its immutability cannot be assumed.

Let us now turn to a brief examination of the possible causes of proneness, for ultimately it is upon knowledge of these that inferences about its generality must rest.

Walker's (1947) explanation of the *J*-curve was social. Its clearest manifestation at the subunit level was interpreted as symptomizing emergent patterns of conformity and deviance. There are at least three explanations for deviance: constitutional or character traits, environmental circumstances, or interactions reflecting person–environment mismatches. Conventional correlational studies have implicated all three; though not surprisingly (in view of the highly skewed distribution of absence frequency), they have failed to account for much variance. Neither is this approach able to tell us specifically about the "hard core" absentees. It is plausible that their absence is generated by causes that are different from the majority of absentees who have only one, two, or three spells a year. Cross-sectional correlational studies may confound these different causes, with the very small number of high level absentees submerged in the general mass and with predictions statistically geared to distinguishing the "lows" from the "zeros."

Clearly there is considerable scope for a fresh approach to the question of proneness, for example, by deliberately setting out to analytically isolate the chronic repeaters or employees who deviate radically from subunit norms and *then* commencing the search for causes. However, it is unlikely that research strategies that treat the prone as homogeneous will succeed. As a group they may be few relative to the employee population, but there is good reason to assume that individual differences will distinguish them from each other in as many ways as from their less prone colleagues. For example, if prone workers are deviant relative to low absence norms because of personality characteristics, they are in all probability an aggregate of highly differentiated "characters." In addition, given the multiplicity of potential causes of absence, prone individuals are likely subject to the interactive influence of several factors, and for each person this subset of causes will be unique (e.g., work dissatisfaction × susceptibility to minor illness; domestic anxieties × transportation problems; poor co-worker relations × strong external leisure interests). In short, in most of the directions one may speculatively search for causes of proneness, it would seem advisable to commence by treating the prone as unique cases, searching for the singular meaning of their proneness, and relating affect and behavior to singular contextual characteristics. Much of this work could be accomplished by using timely interviews and diary techniques.

As we have noted, there is no reason to believe that the causes of absence are unvarying over time (CP 4). The Garrison and Muchinsky (1977) findings suggest that investigators should pay particular attention to characteristics that change gradually or continually, such as domestic circumstances, which may give rise to a shifting core of prone workers. Thus, a joint phenomenological and historical approach is needed to decompose the absence patterns of the prone. Only when this has been achieved can individual histories be collated into more general accounts of proneness. Such collation should avoid regenerating a static vision of proneness, one which effectively ignores "time and space." Specifically, the broader concern of proneness research should be the extent of its spatiotemporal stability, its propensity to endure as people move from setting to setting. Are those who are prone in school also prone in subsequent employment settings? Are those who are absent from work also absent from other social obligations? Principally and initially, however, it remains to be discovered whether transituational proneness is normal or whether it is more useful to conceive of proneness within the context of specific absence climates or cultures (to be discussed later).

In summary, we know little about absence proneness, and its examination from the perspective of our CPs may enable us to better understand the behavior of those who contribute disproportionately to the total volume of absence.

Attributional Processes and Absence

In line with CP 2, Nicholson (1977) has argued that there is far less rational calculus preceding most absence events than a process of succumbing to potential risks or barriers deflecting the person from the norm of habitual attendance. In that paper Nicholson described how researchers might develop risk profiles based on objective characteristics such as age, work setting, and family circumstances. Each profile would quantify how employees differ in their susceptibility to proximal causes of absence, such as injury, illness, fatigue, family demands, and personal business. In this section, we take this argument a step further by exploring individual differences in the *interpretation* of these proximal causes. For example, how is it that one worker with a mild head cold manages to come to work whereas another finds this an adequate reason to remain at home?

The preceding suggests that conventional attitudinal and motivational constructs may serve less as direct predictors of absence than as mediators of potential proximal causes. Support for this can be found in an ingenious study by Smith (1977), who showed that job satisfaction predicted absence among managers on the day of a heavy snowfall in Chicago but did not do so on the same day in snow-free New York. The point here is that psychological processes may create individual differences in the threshold of susceptibility to causes lying more or less outside the employee's control. In order to explore this, we advocate the investigation of the attributional process behind absence from the perspective of both absentees and observers.

Attribution is the process of imputing motives or explanations for observed behavior. Attribution theory has been applied to the analysis of various forms of organizational behavior, including leadership (Calder, 1977), performance (Mitchell, Green, & Wood, 1981), and turnover (Steers & Mowday, 1981).[8] However, we are not merely jumping on the bandwagon. Because absence is a particularly public behavior and because it is frequently viewed as significant behavior by both actors and observers, it seems especially likely to provoke attributed explanations. In many cases, absence is a behavior that *demands* explanation or justification. Additional interest in an attributional analysis of absence stems from CP 1, which suggests that absence may have a variety of meanings for individuals. Insight into these meanings seems accessible through the explanations given for absence. Although such explanations may not be directly predictive of absence, and may indeed be manifestly inaccurate, they should provide a picture of the phenomenal field within which absence occurs.

There are several key questions to be answered regarding the attribution of causes of absence behavior: What are the processes that individuals use to explain discrete episodes of their own absence behavior? What are the processes that observers (superiors, co-workers, family) use to explain discrete episodes of absence on the part of others? To what extent do people harbor *generalized* attributions about the "typical" causes of absence, and when might such attributions be employed? Under what conditions might attributions regarding absence be more or less accurate? How do attributions change over time? Although no single theory of attribution provides the answers to these questions, we hope to demonstrate that the eclectic utilization of several extant theories (Bem, 1972; Jones & Davis, 1965; Kelly, 1972) can provide a good starting point.

There are at least three sources or formats for the exploration of explanations for one's own absence behavior. The first of these involves having organizational officials accurately and completely record the stated explanations provided by absentees. It is reasonable to expect that such reports will be distorted by ego-defensiveness, social desirability, and general self-interest. In fact, exit interview evidence suggests that such motives affect explanations for turnover (Hinrichs, 1975; Lefkowitz & Katz, 1969), and there is every reason to believe that similar forces would be at work in the case of absence. However, such reports should reveal workers' beliefs about what the organization considers to be legitimate reasons for absence. These reasons provide input for the attributions made by organizational observers of absence, including those found officially categorized in personnel records.

It would also be useful to have workers explain in general terms, under research conditions, why they are usually absent from work. As will be discussed later, Nicholson and Payne[9] have done this. Retrospective accounts of "typical" reasons for one's usual absence seem especially likely to reveal what Nisbett and Wilson (1977) have termed *a priori causal theories*. That is, such explanations, removed in time and context from actual proximal stimuli, may invoke accepted cultural or subcultural notions about why absence is likely to occur. Although such theories may be probabilistically accurate, they should inadequately analyze the causes of distinct absence episodes. Yet, as will be pointed out shortly, there may be conditions under which individuals adopt such theories to explain a series of ostensibly poorly justified absences to themselves.

The third and most interesting manner of gathering data to study self-attribution would be to have workers keep diaries of the proximal causes of discrete absence episodes. Alternatively, timely interviews might be arranged with persons who fail to report for work. While there is currently a debate raging in the literature concerning the accuracy of introspective verbal reports (Nisbett & Wilson, 1977; Smith & Miller, 1978; White, 1980; Ericsson & Simon),[10,11] there is apparent consensus that data collection methods that are closer to "real time" should reduce distortions due to the passage of time. If this is so, timely accounts of reasons for absence should have more variance than generalized retrospective reports and relevant context effects should be more readily accessible.

Aspects of extant attribution theories could be incorporated into timely studies of absenteeism. The theories proposed by Kelly (1972) and Jones and Davis (1965) are complementary, because the former involves the temporal and contextual cues that precede a given absence episode, whereas the latter involves cues derived from the consequences of the episode. Thus, perceptions of the consistency, consensus, and distinctiveness of absenteeism could be measured (Kelly, 1972), and the perceived work and nonwork (CP 4) consequences of absence episodes could be obtained (Jones & Davis, 1965).

Just what could the preceding three types of analyses be expected to demonstrate? First, it is reasonable to expect the reversal of the well-established "fundamental attribution error" (Ross, 1977). That is, self-attributions should reveal a disproportionate tendency to invoke circumstantial, rather than dispositional, causes for absenteeism. Such attributions should be supported by the relevant consensus, consistency, and distinctiveness cues. Of course, the circumstances invoked to explain an absence episode to company representatives would often differ from those marshaled to explain the episode to oneself.[12] Obviously, none of this is very surprising. However, there are conditions under which the timely longitudinal study of self-attributions may reveal the tendency to adopt dispositional explanations for one's absence. We now turn to this issue.

There is one type of introspective tendency that may be especially prevalent in probing absence: the unlikely attribution of "large" effects to "small" causes (Nisbett & Wilson, 1977). If this is so, relatively trivial proximal stimuli (the alarm clock failing to go off, an interesting program on television, a slight hangover, a mild cold) may be reinterpreted even under conditions favoring accurate reportage. This situation corresponds to the well-known "insufficient justification" paradigm, especially if the perceived consequences of absence are strongly negative. In this case, Bem's (1972) self-perception theory suggests that actors are likely to adopt the attribution process of external observers and infer that some intrinsic, dispositional motive prompted their behavior. Such an attribution is especially likely if unjustified absence is repeated over time (Jones and McGillis, 1976; Kelly, 1972). For example, the individual who is frequently absent in response to a series of disconnected minor ailments, especially at the expense of negative consequences, may come to perceive himself or herself as constitutionally unfit, effectively adopting a "sick role" (cf. Levine & Kozloff, 1978). Thus, the criteria by which one judges one's fitness to attend work may be altered over time. This attribution may be "borrowed" from an *a priori* causal theory that is approved by the culture or subculture. In fact, this scenario synchronizes nicely with Nicholson and Payne's[8] study of retrospective reports of reasons for typical absence events; this study showed a strong tendency for individuals to invoke medical explanations. Different individuals encountering different proximal stimuli should develop different attributions. For example, a more culturally independent person who experiences a series of hangovers and alarm clock failures may adopt a "deviant" role to account for his or her absence. In fact, these kinds of attributional processes may be characteristic of certain classes of proneness, as discussed earlier.[13]

Before leaving the topic of self-attribution, it is worthwhile to consider another example of the value of this approach. There has been a surprising neglect of a decision with which every absentee is faced: when to *return* to work. We are in agreement with Smulders (1980) that conventional research has been more oriented toward predicting the *inception* of absence rather than its *duration* (consistent with the "withdrawal *from*" argument: PIU 2). Thus, it may be no accident that predictions of frequency of absence (literally, number of inceptions) are consistently stronger than those for time lost (loading on duration) (Johns, 1978; Metzner & Mann, 1953; Nicholson, Brown, & Chadwick-Jones, 1977). While the argument that time lost is "contaminated" by serious sickness may have some validity, such a position ignores the determinant nature of the chosen predictors and ignores the fact that the seriousness of sickness is itself a relative, interpreted, and attributed matter (Smulders, 1980). In his current doctoral research at the University of Sheffield, Chris Brewin is examining the duration of absence following industrial accidents. Preliminary results indicate that individuals who are high on internal locus of control (Rotter, 1966) are more likely to accept a measure of self-blame for their difficulties and return to work earlier than externals, who are less ready to accept such blame. These fascinating results are exactly in line with the earlier arguments concerning the mediation of proximal causes via psychological states through the attribution process. That is, two individuals with objectively similar injuries (proximal cause) who differ in locus of control (psychological state) attribute the reasons for their absence to different causal factors.

In addition to self-attributions, the attribution processes used by observers of absence episodes should be examined. Such observers may include friends and family members, as well as organizational members. The attributions of observers are important because they determine in part the consequences that absence will have for the actor. Again, the theories proposed by Kelly (1972) and Jones and Davis (1965) provide helpful guidelines for such research. Presumably, because observers will usually be in possession of fewer relevant cues than actors, their explanations should reveal more stereotyping. The form of this stereotyping may depend, however, on the location of the observer. Specifically, observers inside and outside of the organization should possess substantially different cues regarding the circumstances of a specific absence episode. These cues should often lead them to provide substantially different explanations for absence. In particular, organizational observers may be especially likely to commit the "fundamental attribution error" (Ross, 1977) of overemphasizing dispositional motives for absence. This may occur because such observers will be unaware of mitigating off-the-job circumstances that preceded an absence event. Furthermore, if these observers are superiors of the absentee, a dispositional attribution enables the superior to discount his or her own role in provoking or preventing absence. Such dispositional explanations should be especially likely when strong sanctions against absence exist, when absence is exhibited steadily (high consistency), when co-workers are seldom absent (low consensus), and when the person is known to have exhibited high absence on previous jobs (low distinctiveness). In fact, this may be just the case in which proneness is most likely to be invoked to "explain" absence.

Some important questions regarding attribution of the absence behavior of others include: What other cues do observers use to explain or classify absence events? Which combinations of cues are associated with "acceptable" and "unacceptable" absence? Is one's explanation of the absence of others related to one's own absence behavior? In addition, CP 6 suggests that it would be illuminating to examine such attributions under systems that differ in expectations regarding attendance or that differ in the extent of formal sanctions against absence (e.g., university professors, the self-employed, and factory workers).

In concluding this section, it seems worthwhile to reverse the coin, as it were, and mention observers' attributions regarding *attendance*. Specifically, it might be hypothesized that a certain proportion of good attendance represents an attempt on the part of subordinates to *ingratiate* themselves to their superiors. Ingratiation tactics are employed to enhance one's attractiveness to others, and as Wortman and Linsenmeii (1977, p. 135) point out, "the ingratiator's task is primarily one of manipulating the attributions made by the target person he is trying to impress." If the likelihood of such strategies is dependent upon their probable success, there is ample reason to believe that good attendance is a frequent ingratiation tactic in work settings. Wortman and Linsenmeir (1977) argue that because of the power differential subordinates must avoid obvious ingratiation tactics such as direct praise and slavish opinion conformity. While good attendance fulfills these criteria, it has some other characteristics that are generally associated with successful ingratiation. First, it is nonverbal. Second, it may represent a subtle, indirect form of opinion conformity with the boss. Third, by making the superior look effective as a leader, it may act as a form of favor rendering for which it is difficult to find an ulterior motive. Good attendance would seem to be an especially effective technique for manipulating the superior's attributions when performance criteria are otherwise vague, when there are few formal sanctions against absence, and when peers exhibit a high level of absence.

Absence and Behavioral Alternatives

If we are to accept CP 1 (that absence benefits from being viewed as phenomenally unique), logic compels us to extend the same courtesy to other employee behaviors. A corollary of this is that an individual absence incident may have more in common with an instance of lateness, slacking off on the job, or similar behavior than it does with many other absence incidents. The reasons for absence are likely to change over time as a function of variations in environmental pressures and personal goals. The same is true for other employee behaviors, and the failure of absence to correlate with these other behaviors in aggregated data sets (across time and across persons), as in the case of absence and lateness (Nicholson & Goodge, 1976), does not mean they are unrelated. Rather it suggests that any such relationships will be subtle and individually differentiated. The likelihood of different behaviors may be under the partial control of similar individual dispositions at a given point in time but subject to quite distinct environmental contingencies. For example, lateness or absence may be equally sufficient responses to a nasty hangover. However, differential organizational sanctions may prompt one reaction rather than the other. The point here is that, whatever behavior we choose to examine, it is for the person an adaptive or proactive response to the unique configuration of the life space at that time. It is thus axiomatic that various work and nonwork behaviors are systematically linked via the "personal system" but that the causal history of each will be different. The real nature of relationships among such behaviors can thus only be revealed by a closer focus on individuals and instances. The same arguments apply to both the relationships between different so-called "types" of absence and between different instances of absence that are classified as similar.

It is not surprising that researchers have shunned this methodologically and theoretically thorny path and found it more attractive to assume that absences themselves share a causal unity (PIU 1), albeit a loose one, and that other employee behaviors exhibit parallel or similar causal coherence. This is usually argued under the rubric of PIU 2, that absence is a motivated "withdrawal" from (negative aspects of) the workplace, as are other behaviors such as turnover, lateness, and some accidents. It has been argued elsewhere (Nicholson, 1977) that this reasoning is the product of the logical fallacy of identifying *physical* withdrawal with *motivated* withdrawal and that the attractiveness of this idea is partly ideological, seeking to keep absence within the zone of managerial control (PIU 5). An opposite fallacy can be seen in the contrasting orientation of some social scientists whose ideological stance leads them to view work behavior in conflict terms, with absence portrayed as "unorganized conflict" sharing common causes with the organized conflict of strikes and other protests (cf. Barbash, 1980; Hyman, 1972). For these writers, absence and industrial action are functionally equivalent responses to similar employment circumstances. Both are manifestations of alienation or of divergent employee–employer goals.

There seems to be little empirical support for either proposition. No research has demonstrated the viability of the "withdrawal" hypothesis. Even between such allegedly similar behaviors as absence and turnover, the evidence does not indicate stable interrelationships or consistently common causes (Lyons, 1972). Data purporting to support the "conflict" hypothesis are even more insubstantial, usually deriving from industry-level data aggregations, where all variance is conveniently eliminated, and where a host of mediating influences could be adduced to account for what tenuous relationships are obvious. At a trivial level, absence may be a form of industrial action, as in cases of "blue flu" where clauses in the labor contract prohibit strike action. Where such constraints do not apply, there is no evidence for any kind of reliable relationship between absence and different forms of industrial action at the plant level (Kelly & Nicholson, 1980).

Let us be clear that in making these points we are not arguing that absence and other behaviors are unrelated. However, we are arguing that to advocate such relationships in general terms is meaningless, for there are as many possible relationships as there are shared causes and conditions. To illustrate this, it is useful to consider the case of absence and turnover. First, these variables may be positively correlated because similar conditions of employment induce both, in which case a quasi-cultural analysis of employment "cultures" is prescribed (CP 4). Second, they may be correlated at the individual level because a spate of absences precedes (as it would in job-seeking behavior) the decision to quit (Burke & Wilcox, 1972). Third, in the long term, they may be disjunctively related as absence substitutes for unfavorable opportunities to quit (Hill & Trist, 1955). Which of these possible relationships receives empirical support can be expected to depend upon the salient causes of behavior in the particular circumstances under consideration (personal, occupational, and cultural factors) and the chosen mode of analysis (group or individual level, cross-sectional, or longitudinal). For example, the capacity for absence to substitute for turnover may depend upon perceived opportunities for alternative employment, as reflected in local levels of unemployment. The likelihood of absence preceding the act of quitting will depend partly on job search opportunities in one's present job (e.g., access to a telephone). The correlation of absence and turnover at the plant level will be a product of intraorganizational homogeneity and interorganizational differentiation (e.g., the existence of clear-cut differences in job characteristics between firms). Obviously, the discovery of such relationships requires specifically tailored research strategies, and any given strategy may necessarily preclude the detection of other possible associations.

This does not mean that research should retreat from the linkage issue. Rather, absence and other behaviors should be treated as lenses through which more fundamental processes of employee motivation and work relations can be observed. There are signs in recent work that this is taking place. Gupta and Jenkins[3] have attempted to use the concepts of "binding" and "distancing" forces between the person and the organization to predict a continuum of withdrawal ranging from estrangement and frequent work breaks, to tardiness and alcohol consumption, to chronic absence and turnover. However, their intent to retain a conceptual unity under the rubric of "withdrawal" from "aversive" conditions owes more to our PIUs than our CPs. Thus, we are unoptimistic about the possibility of meaningful research strategies being evolved to test a general withdrawal model or of its finding consistent empirical support. Nonetheless, it may prove useful to draw attention to a wider range of potential behaviors than are commonly studied in organizations, and use them as vehicles for fresh approaches to social and psychological processes in organizations (e.g., deviance, effort–reward relations, and role stress).

In summary, the connection between absence and other behaviors should be studied as a contingency developing from the operation of universal psychological and social processes under *unique* circumstances. It is worth noting that this approach corresponds to recent arguments for more fine-grained analyses of the typical dependent variables used in organizational behavior research (Moore, Johns, & Pinder, 1980; Staw, 1980; Staw & Oldham, 1978). Cognitive consistency needs aside, we have not been well served by the implicit stereotype of the good worker as one who is highly productive and satisfied, never late or absent, and consistently striving for long tenure. Such a stereotype neglects the fact that the expected probabilities of various attitudes and behaviors are differentially responsive to circumstantial constraints.

ABSENCE AS A MECHANISM OF CONTROL

We do not reject the notion that a certain proportion of absence is volitional or calculated. However, past attempts to explain absence from a personal motivational perspective have been extremely general in focus, relying on some version of need theory and investigating the relationship between absence and job satisfaction. Unfortunately, the generality of the notion that workers are motivated to absent themselves from jobs that fail to meet their needs is equivocal at best (Nicholson et al., 1976). Thus, in the following two sections we partially forsake CP 2 in order to examine two specific intentional functions that absence might serve: the manipulation of work versus nonwork time and the fulfillment of implicit contracts of exchange. In each case, the use of absence can be hypothesized as centering on the notion of *control* over the temporal or socioeconomic environment. Also in each case, CP 5 figures heavily as employees strive to balance work and nonwork demands.

Absence and Time Allocation

Absence researchers have made remarkably little use of one of the few incontrovertible associations in organizational behavior: the negative relationship between work and nonwork time. PIUs 1, 4, and 5 have conspired to treat absence as a static property of individuals that is relevant only to what happens behind organizational walls. The approach we adopt here asserts that absence temporarily redraws the boundaries between work and nonwork time. As such, it is a dynamic response (CP 4) that depends on the interplay between work and nonwork experiences (CP 5). In addition, its personal significance (CP 1) for certain workers may be the purposive restructuring of time that is more or less necessary or possible across various populations (CP 6).

At the outset, it should be recognized that many studies confound factors that may be relevant to the association between absence and time allocation strategies. This is especially true of large-scale projects such as national absence surveys and research concerning the relationship between organizational size and absence. Despite this confusion, there are four classes of studies that may bear upon this issue. These include studies of (1) the association between absence and nonwork variables, (2) the occurrence of absence under various formal work schedules, (3) the temporal location of absence in the work cycle, and (4) the nature of absence under systems that vary in discretion between work and nonwork time. As will be seen, the use of absence as an intentional time control mechanism must be *inferred* from this work rather than be accepted as *demonstrated*.

As discussed earlier, researchers have frequently examined the association between absenteeism and personal variables. Reviews indicate that frequency of absence decreases with age (Nicholson et al., 1977), that women exhibit more absence than men (Steers & Rhodes, 1978), and that workers with larger families tend toward more absence (Muchinsky, 1977). Such findings have often been interpreted from a time allocation perspective. It has been argued that older workers have fewer extracurricular demands for their time than younger workers or that women and those with large families must often allocate more time to family needs. Clearly, these interpretations can be challenged by plausible hypotheses that have little to do with purposive time allocation. However, two studies have specifically explored the relationship between absence and off-the-job experiences. Using an expectancy theory framework, Morgan and Herman (1976) found that absence was strongly associated with the anticipated achievement of off-the-job social outcomes and leisure time. On the other hand, absence was unassociated with anticipated organizational deterrents. It should be emphasized that the *quality* of off-the-job experiences may influence the allocation of time between work and nonwork. Rousseau (1978) found that frequency of absence among employees of a radio station and an electronics firm was negatively related to reports of challenge experienced in nonwork activities.[14] Thus, attendance patterns may reflect an attempt to balance the quantity *and* quality of time spent in various endeavors.

If absence is influenced by off-the-job experiences and demands for time, it should also be affected by the manner in which working time is scheduled by the organization. The majority of research in this area involves the incidence of absence within or across various shift systems. Some relationships between absence and shift systems appear to be attributable to differences in the personal characteristics of workers who are attracted to a particular system or to objective differences in job context or content (cf. Taylor, 1967). However, the consensus of research in this area suggests that the temporal boundaries of shift systems themselves exert an independent influence on attendance (Nicholson, Jackson, & Howes, 1978; Pocock, 1973). Nicholson et al. determined that both work and nonwork factors stimulate shift effects. Specifically, the length of the shift cycle was associated with the frequency of absence at different locations within the cycle. This finding implicates the influence of nonwork demands through the scheduling of leisure activities at different times of the day or on different days of the week. Also relevant here are studies of the impact of the shortened work week. One claimed advantage of this schedule is that it enables employees to meet personal obligations and arrange leisure activities in a manner that is less likely to impinge upon working time. The evidence on this is mixed. Nord and Costigan (1973) found reduced absence following the introduction of a shortened week, whereas Ivancevich and Lyon (1977) found no change in absence. Both of these studies were conducted in manufacturing environments, and it is possible that the longer days required by the shorter work week induce fatigue. If so, absence for recuperative purposes may sometimes offset expected attendance gains.

A third group of studies indicates that absences are distributed nonrandomly over time. While less common than work schedule research, these studies provide better evidence for the strategic, calculated use of absence to restructure work and nonwork time. Chadwick-Jones, Brown, and Nicholson (1973b) found that women's absence peaked at calendar points when competing domestic demands were greatest. Similarly, Nicholson and Goodge (1976) found that ostensibly casual absence was clustered around holiday periods, and Nicholson (1976) observed that it fell into numerical multiples of the working week. The strategic scheduling argument received additional support in the latter study, which recorded systematic changes in the *form* rather than *level* of absence following an escalation of management sanctioning procedures. This suggests that the volitional component of absence may relate less to the nature of the work experience than to variations in the personal value of nonwork time. Indeed, Rousseau (1978) found that the scope of off-the-job activities was a better predictor of absence than job scope.

There are no studies that directly explore the relationship between absence and discretionary temporal aspects of the work itself. However, the nature of the work cycle and the autonomy or discretion of the worker have been shown to discriminate strongly among jobs of varying status (Fox, 1974; Jacques, 1957). In occupations where effort–reward relationships are obscure and the boundaries between work and nonwork are highly discretionary or blurred by the nature of the task, absence may have an entirely different meaning from that exhibited by those engaged in typical industrial employment (CP 6). Professors, artists, basic scientists, and self-employed business persons often experience autonomy in goal setting and relative freedom from the employment contract, which should in turn influence their conception of absence. In fact, for many such individuals, failure to show up at the designated workplace may be equated with actually accomplishing a greater amount of work. It might be argued that the autonomy inherent in such jobs finds parallel expression in some of the casual absence exhibited by workers with less freedom. Indirect evidence for this can be found in absence reductions that are claimed to follow increases in opportunities for the autonomous scheduling of work tasks and leisure, as in flex-time systems (Golembiewski & Proehl, 1978). Under flex-time, employees can fulfill personal business and leisure pursuits during traditional working hours and still meet attendance obligations.

Research has barely scratched the surface of the function of absence as a mechanism of time allocation. Macroscopically, there is a need for comparative studies that treat the "shape" of work and nonwork boundaries as an independent variable and as a factor mediating the relationship between absence and work and nonwork time. Particular attention must be paid to the probability that the very *construct* of absence differs across occupational groups. Research in this area will have to come to grips with the admittedly knotty problem of distinguishing attendance from "motivation" or "performance" on jobs that are characterized by fewer organizational constraints to absence. Microscopically, there is a need for longitudinal studies of the specific time usage of individuals and the extent to which the inception and duration of absence represents an attempt to control or redefine the work/nonwork boundary. Such research should incorporate personal and work schedule variables as a means of exploring the conjectures presented earlier.

As society faces the prospect of declining hours of work and the increasing salience of leisure time and its uses, there would appear to be great social value in pursuing these themes. Action-research strategies might be contemplated to determine how working hours can best be structured to meet the goals of production and the needs of the work force.

Absence as Coin of Exchange

Absence might usefully be viewed as an attempt to fulfill or modify a series of implicit social contracts between the worker and the employing organization and the worker and relevant parties external to the organization. This point of view does not exclude the possibility that many instances of absence are responses to job dissatisfaction. Rather, it is congruent with CP 1 that absence has a variety of "meanings" or functions for individuals in various circumstances. Thus, absence as a response to job dissatisfaction may represent an attempt to adjust one's job inputs in response to a perceived inequitable exchange with the organization. On the other hand, a worker who is well satisfied with job circumstances may still exhibit considerable absence in order to fulfill perceived familial obligations. Although the meaning of absence differs radically for these individuals, both are using absence to redress or fulfill certain social contracts.

An exchange perspective suggests a number of alternative research strategies with which absence might be investigated. For one thing, it would be useful to explore employees' perceptions of the nature of the implicit social contracts that exist between themselves and the employing organization and the family, with special emphasis on the role of absence. Such a strategy would be the first step in isolating those situations in which absence is viewed as a *relevant* input to social exchange equations. For example, perceptions of the organization's expectations regarding attendance might be explored. Similarly, perceptions of the legitimacy of family demands on "working time" should be investigated, since there is evidence that the relevance of such demands for absence may be substantial (Morgan & Herman, 1976). In all cases, it would be useful to determine the extent to which absence is viewed from a moral perspective as being deviant behavior, rule-breaking behavior, or behavior that unfairly damages the interests of other persons.

The study of absence could also benefit from the application of equity theory (Adams, 1965). However, as might be imagined, we are not in particular sympathy with the notion that absence simply represents "leaving the field" in response to inequity. Rather, a key hypothesis here is that attendance may be used to modify an individual's input/outcome ratio, bringing it into line with expectations of "fair exchange." In fact, in some routine, structured jobs, variations in attendance may be one of the few readily available means of manipulating input to modify this ratio. One obvious implication of an equity perspective is the probability that the absence process differs considerably under different payment systems. When payment is not a direct function of attendance, absence might serve to redress felt inequity stemming from perceived underpayment or some other factor. In this case, outcomes remain constant while input is reduced. When payment is closely associated with attendance, behavior other than absence may be necessary to achieve "fair exchange." Evidence linking perceived inequitable pay with absence has been reported by Patchen (1960) for oil refinery workers and by Dittrich and Carrell (1979) for clerical personnel. In line with the input reduction argument, Patchen reported that 75 to 80 percent of absences in the refinery were paid absences. Dittrich and Carrell did not report the relationship between pay and attendance.

There is, of course, a caveat to be observed here. Equity theory does not do a particularly good job of specifying the boundaries that define a particular social exchange. Furthermore, most experimental tests of equity theory have severely and artificially restricted these boundaries. However, as indicated earlier, absence behavior may have a simultaneous impact on several exchange systems. Thus, the *net* effect of absenteeism on these systems must be considered in order to obtain optimal predictive power. For example, even when absence does not appear to be the appropriate response to maintain fair exchange in the *job* system, off-the-job outcomes derived from absenting oneself to nurse a sick child or spouse may mandate this response. What research needs to do, then, is determine the complete phenomenal payoff matrix surrounding absence and attendance.

Moving beyond strict equity considerations, there is considerable scope to examine absence from a more abstract notion of socioeconomic exchange. That is, under what conditions do attendance patterns reflect the desire to establish, maintain, or regain a particular economic position? For example, it would be useful to examine attendance patterns before, during, and after the imposition of mandatory shortened work weeks or threatened layoffs and plant closures. In these cases, we might expect attendance to reveal anticipatory economic maximization; that is, employees should respond to economic threats with improved attendance. Steers and Rhodes (1978) review several studies that suggest that regional unemployment is associated with decreased absenteeism but point out that the attendance of individuals threatened with *personal* unemployment may vary with their expectations of finding another job. Thus, those whose skills are in demand may continue their usual attendance behavior, whereas those whose skills are not may absent themselves to engage in job searches. This qualifier corresponds with Hulin and Rousseau's[5] recent caution about inferring individual effects from rates of behavior.

Under more steady economic conditions, there is the distinct possibility that absence may be associated with those conditions that favor economic "satisficing" rather than "maximizing." For example, we have heard anecdotes about workers restricting their income through absence in order to maintain a favorable tax bracket status. Also, the well-established fact that younger workers tend to exhibit more casual absence than older workers (Nicholson et al., 1977) might be partly attributed to a satisficing strategy. Certainly, the response, "I work 4 days a week because I can't earn enough in 3," would seem to reflect this goal.

Other economic factors that may influence absence involve the degree of autonomy in the rate at which income can be earned or the manner in which it can be earned. Evidence from the Cardiff study (Chadwick-Jones et al., in press) suggested that workers under piecerate payment systems exhibited more absence than those under hourly payment. Under piecerate, the autonomy in the rate at which income can be earned may enable workers to maintain a desired level of income while taking off "deserved" time from work. Similarly, there is some evidence to suggest that workers may substitute lucrative overtime work for regular working hours, exhibiting more absence from scheduled work under conditions of readily available overtime (Gowler, 1969; Martin, 1971). Finally, individuals with outside sources of income may be able to justify absence from their primary jobs. Notice that each of these examples may also reflect the operation of a satisficing motive, and in some cases may reflect equity motives. Also, notice here the delicate interplay between economic autonomy and the structuring of work and nonwork time discussed earlier.

In passing, it is worth mentioning that we have chosen to present the relevance of exchange theory to absence research from a personal motivational perspective rather than an explicitly normative perspective. Whereas the same arguments could have been presented in terms of equity norms, fairness norms, and norms of social comparison, the interpretation of exchange theory from a personal motivational perspective corresponds more closely to the way exchange notions have usually been applied to organizational phenomena. However, as will be demonstrated in the next section, an explicit normative perspective can be utilized to sharpen our understanding of the absence process.

ABSENCE AS A SOCIAL PHENOMENON

Thus far we can hardly be accused of ignoring social influences upon absence. However, in the following two sections, the issue is confronted directly by discussing the normative control of absence and the notion of absence "climates" or "cultures." We confess some ignorance about just when norms begin to constitute climates or cultures. Somewhat arbitrarily, this problem is circumvented by examining absence norms in discrete portions of the employee's role set (co-workers, management, off-the-job parties). Then it is argued that, in part, the net interactive effect of these norms may define an absence climate or culture for a particular subset of employees, an organizational subunit, or the organization as a whole.

Normative Control of Absence

This section is concerned with social norms that have as their explicit content the regulation of work attendance. The exploration of absence from such a perspective follows most directly from CPs 3 and 5. Respectively, these CPs suggest that absence is susceptible to collective influence and that nonwork forces may influence attendance.

While we are unaware of any research that conclusively demonstrates the operation of normative constraints on absence behavior, evidence can be marshaled to suggest that this may be a fruitful approach. First, on an intuitive level, absence is among the most public of work-relevant behaviors in typical job settings. Thus, co-workers, official representatives of the organization, and relevant off-the-job parties can easily observe instances of absence. As such, it should be especially susceptible to potential normative sanctions. In contrast, behavior such as low performance may go unnoticed by persons external to the organization and be obscured from organizational members by "make work" or "cooperative" activities. Second, there is research to suggest that absence may be associated with small group experience and organization (Mann, Indik, & Vroom, 1963; Mayo & Lombard, 1944; Walker, 1947). Taken together, this circumstantial evidence points to the explicit normative control of absence.

In order to truly understand normative constraints on absence, it will be necessary to examine the attendance norms that exist in various portions of an individual's role set. As indicated earlier, the most reasonable partitioning of this role set would probably involve co-workers in the primary work group, supervisors and other official organizational representatives, and relevant family members and friends. Consideration of this fairly complete role set should enable researchers to obtain some notion of the ultimate extent to which normative constraints influence attendance. Perhaps more important, such a strategy should enhance our understanding of apparently anomalous absence patterns. For example, good attendance might prevail in spite of a primary work group norm that is supportive of casual absence. This contradiction might be explained by formal organizational norms and norms in the external community that encourage regular attendance. Because such contradictory norms may be the rule rather than the exception, it will be necessary to determine the attendance norms that may exist in each relevant portion of the role set. In each case answers to the following questions should be sought:

1. Under what circumstances are norms regarding attendance likely to develop?
2. Will developed norms encourage attendance or encourage absence?
3. What is the probability that violations of attendance norms will be detected?
4. What punishments are available for norm violation and what rewards are available for conformity?

Clearly, the answers to these questions may be interdependent. Notice, however, that the questions recognize that attendance norms will only develop if attendance behavior is of at least marginal importance to some portion of a role set. In addition, "attendance norms" may *en*courage or *dis*courage attendance. Furthermore, although absence is an especially public behavior, its ease of detection may vary across portions of the role set. Finally, even clear-cut norms whose violation is easily detectable may exert little influence on attendance if they are not backed by adequate punishment and reinforcement.

For that portion of the role set composed of co-workers or the main work group, the development of attendance norms is probably fairly complex. Important variables to be examined here would include the manner in which work is organized and the nature of the payment system. For example, a norm that favors regular attendance would seem likely when a high degree of interdependence is required for task accomplishment, especially under some form of group payment system. In some cases, even without task or economic interdependence, professional or collegial codes of conduct may encourage a similar norm. For example, whatever their other shortcomings, university professors are generally expected by their colleagues to show up to teach their classes.

Under what conditions might co-workers develop a norm that encourages absence? First, even under conditions of interdependence or professionalism, a depressed work ethic or an unfavorable labor climate might lead to the development of norms that condone, yet systematize, absence. Some explicit or implicit consensus may be reached regarding who can be absent and when absence is permissible. In this manner, workers can "cover" for each other without seriously threatening goal accomplishment or professional standards. In work settings where task interdependence, economic interdependence, or professionalism do not exist, a norm that actually encourages unregulated absence might develop if there is consensus concerning mitigating circumstances (poor labor climate, perceived inequity, job dissatisfaction) *and* if there is consensus that absence is an *appropriate* reaction to these circumstances. In this case, regular attenders might be labeled "suckers," whereas those who are frequently absent are esteemed. Of course, absence can be esteemed even when it is not an approved reaction to a negative environment. In some universities, absence incurred to present conference papers or to do consulting is seen as a sign of professional stature.

In the case of co-workers, the mechanics of detecting deviation from attendance norms and enforcing such norms are fairly obvious. Of all the portions of the relevant role set, this portion should be most aware of attendance patterns, with obvious occupational exceptions. In addition, the extraordinary range of norm enforcement mechanisms available to small groups in work settings has been well documented (e.g., Homans, 1950). Thus, it can be concluded that *if* the work group has developed attendance norms its members should be in an especially good position to enforce these norms.

A final point should be raised regarding the probable relationship between work group *cohesiveness* and attendance norms. Two of the best known "facts" regarding cohesive groups are that they are especially effective in developing and enforcing norms and in inducing active participation in group affairs. When other conditions favor the development of a "good attendance" norm, these characteristics are perfectly consonant and should be facilitative of the norm (cf. Mayo & Lombard, 1944). However, when other conditions favor the development of an "absence" norm, the required behavior would seem to be inconsistent with the participative characteristics associated with cohesiveness. In this case, of course, the requirement for participation might be fulfilled by group activities off the job. For example, a cohesive group might absent itself *en masse* to go hunting or fishing.

Let us now turn to attendance norms that might be developed and sent to organizational members by that portion of the role set consisting of supervisors and other organizational officials. It is important to distinguish between these (latent) norms and official rules and policies regarding absence. Although these concepts are by no means independent, there are organizations that "say" one thing about absence (via rules and regulations) and "do" something else (via informal normative mechanisms). This point will be developed shortly.

Official organizational representatives should be especially likely to develop norms that favor attendance in the presence of certain financial, technological, strategic, or moral imperatives. For example, increased concern with attendance is a frequent outcome of cost-cutting programs or escalating labor costs. In addition, technologies that require the presence of key persons or that require workers on one shift to relieve those on the next should prompt a similar outcome. The strict attendance rules seen in military settings probably result from a combination of strategic and moral imperatives. In contrast to these situations, university professors and administrators seldom develop norms regarding the classroom attendance of students because such imperatives are largely irrelevant in the classroom setting.

In theory, official organizational representatives should be in a good position to monitor deviations from developed attendance norms, especially those prompted by technological or strategic concerns, where absence actually affects operations. In fact, however, there is good reason to believe that the monitoring of absence by this portion of the role set is often unreliable. In some cases, workers may be able to "cover" for each other without detection. In any situation, employees may be motivated to disguise the true reason for their absence. This motivation, coupled with the need for organizational representatives to engage in some attributional process to designate a particular absence event as "voluntary," may further threaten the reliability of the monitoring process. Finally, there is considerable variation in the extent to which organizations actually record and study absence data, however collected, especially for salaried jobs (PIU 6). Each of these factors may in practice limit the ability of organizational officials to accurately detect deviations from attendance norms. Of course, when such norms are strongly established, some (often arbitrary) mechanism may be invoked to bolster the monitoring process.

Organizations may systematize a range of control mechanisms such as disciplinary crackdowns and attendance bonuses. The effectiveness of these mechanisms is reviewed by Muchinsky (1977) and Steers and Rhodes (1978). It is at this enforcement stage, however, that the distinction between official rules and regulations and effective norms becomes apparent. The organization that has a "strong policy" against absence but offers its employees liberal "sick days" may be inadvertently encouraging absence. Similarly, the organization that implements strong sanctions against certain forms of absence may be signaling employees to adopt other forms of absence (Nicholson, 1976). Thus, although it is difficult to conceive of a norm held by official organizational representatives that *favors* absence, this may be the latent message sent to employees when the sanctioning system operates in an unintended manner.

Attendance norms that develop in that portion of the role set external to the organization are probably a function of the prevailing work ethic in the family or community and social and economic imperatives that increase the salience of attendance patterns. Put simply, a highly positive work ethic, coupled with strong economic needs and weak off-the-job demands on "working time" should lead this portion of the role set to develop a norm favoring attendance. The reverse of these conditions may lead to a norm supportive of absence. These perfect combinations are probably the product of unusual circumstances. In most cases, the conditions that increase external demands upon working time (e.g., a large family or dependents with chronic sickness) also increase economic needs that can be fulfilled by regular attendance at work. These conflicting demands suggest that the development of clear-cut attendance norms by off-the-job parties may be atypical.

The ability of external parties to monitor attendance varies with the nature of employment and what the absentee does when time is taken off work. If a worker remains home with the family, an absence episode is immediately detectable. However, absence may go undetected if the worker leaves home and "calls off" work. Such an incident may be detected after-the-fact if it affects a subsequent paycheck of if the organization contacts the home to verify the cause. Under normal circumstances, friends would find it more difficult than family members to monitor attendance behavior. In many cases, then, workers can probably disguise their attendance activities from off-the-job parties with greater ease than they can from organizational members.

Members of the external role set have available a full range of social mechanisms for enforcing developed attendance norms. However, the previous discussion suggests that the application of these mechanisms may often be delayed or confounded by the imperfect monitoring of attendance behavior. In addition, in contrast to the enforcement mechanisms of organizational members, there may be little *direct* connection between the reinforcers and punishment available and the specific acts of attendance or absence. In many cases, the worker who conforms to or violates an attendance norm held by a portion of the external role set may fail to understand that the ensuing consequences were specifically due to attendance behavior.

In summary, if the preceding notions are correct, the primary work group should be especially able to monitor attendance and enforce attendance norms if such norms are developed. Except under the imperatives mentioned, official organizational representatives may adopt a strategy of benign neglect in response to moderate levels of absence. If attendance norms are developed, their direct effectiveness is dependent upon the energy and care invested in monitoring and enforcement procedures. Finally, the development of attendance norms by parties external to the organization may often be precluded by competing social and economic motives. If such norms do develop, several weaknesses in monitoring and enforcement capability may reduce their effectiveness.

Absence Climates and Cultures

If the experiences of workers are constrained by common work environments, task interdependence, similar external socioeconomic circumstances, and a relatively uniform absence control system, it may prove unhelpful to restrict the search for explanations of absence to individual differences. More enlightening may be the identification of distinctions between identifiable aggregates (CP 3). As such, an "absence climate" or "absence culture" might be conceived as the net interactive effect of the normative forces that exist in the various relevant portions of employees' role sets and common nonnormative influences. Such an analysis could be applied to particular classes of employees (e.g., women), organizational subunits (e.g., departments or wards), or an entire organization.

This approach is in sharp contrast to the cumulative tradition that has dominated absence research and many other areas of organizational behavior. It has been assumed that one can understand the behavior of social units by aggregating information derived from individuals (PIU 3).[15] While this may be trivially true, it is likely to restrict the choice of predictors to intrapsychic constructs, job characteristics, and personal circumstances on which individuals may be contrasted, and to overlook those that distinguish between collectivities, including rules of conduct, organizational socialization practices, company ethos, and management style. Among such group level variables, one may also include the signal function served by absence levels themselves.

One reason why the individual level approach often accounts for relatively little variation in absence may be the fact that there are many work settings in which there *is* little variation in absence among employees. This restricted variation, of course, is just what one would expect if social norms from various portions of the role set operate to define an absence climate or culture, and absence at the individual level is thus poorly predicted. Where such cultures or climates exist, analyses between groups, subunits, or organizations, using predictors relevant to collectivities, might account for substantial variance between social units.

A complementary perspective suggests that the restricted variance of a low base rate behavior such as absence gives it by chance alone a spuriously normative appearance (the Poisson distribution). This appearance itself becomes part of the absence culture by providing normative grist. According to this view, the absence culture is the self-attribution by groups about the characteristics of their attendance that they infer from its configuration. Such a phenomenon is open to at least two interpretations, neither of which is exclusive of the other. From a sociological perspective, characteristic absence rates may be indicative of collective behavior that functions to clarify a situation in which there are few objective cues available concerning what is proper. Strike activities have often been interpreted from this collective perspective, and absence may be equally susceptible to collective social forces and definitions of behavior. From a more social psychological angle, we may find group-induced polarization (Lamm & Myers, 1978), in which employees act collectively to exaggerate and regularize their individual attendance patterns. Such a reaction may be reinforced by managers who claim that "most employees are responsible, but we have a core of malingerers" on the basis of absence distributions that do not actually deviate from chance. (In fact this *attitude* toward employee absence may itself be a product of group-induced polarization among managers). Here, we see the convergence of co-worker and management norms that would characterize an absence climate or culture.

Sex differences in absence may illustrate these points. Gender, a surrogate for a veritable stew of individual and social differences, reliably differentiates absence at the group level (Steers & Rhodes, 1978). It does not advance our understanding to attribute this to inherent differences in the susceptibility of the sexes, when our attention can more profitably turn to the convergence of community, work group, and supervisory norms and their effect on attributed legitimacy. For example, family, friends, and female co-workers might support a norm that encourages womens' absence based on a common belief that such work is "only temporary" or that the organization treats women inequitably. Convinced that female absence is a "special case," supervisors may then apply existing sanctions less rigorously, implicitly sending a similar normative message. As a culmination of this process, women employees acquire empirical evidence of the attendance behavior that is expected of them via the resultant absence level and proceed to polarize their behavior against this baseline.

The subcultural dimensions of absence at the organizational level have been revealed in several research investigations. One intriguing illustration is found in the study of epidemics. Colligan and Murphy (1979) have shown how environmental "triggers," such as the appearance of symptoms among workers involved in processes they don't fully understand (such as chemical processes), can lead to contagious mass psychogenic illness. This is characterized by the diffusion of symptoms and pseudo-symptoms across employee populations. Clearly, the capacity for such contagion is dependent upon the existence of intraorganizational networks of communication, as well as shared beliefs and values.

One of the principal general findings of Chadwick-Jones et al. (in press) was that the predictability of absence from work attitudes varied considerably across 16 investigated plants. In most they were unrelated, but in a few, attitudes were viable predictors. This seems to suggest that the plants differed in their "causal climates." Further analysis at the inter-plant level revealed that differences *between* organizations were often more interesting than differences *within* them and were predictable from a quite different range of variables, such as the role of unions, management sanctioning strategies, and spans of control.

Within most complex organizations, differences in subunit climate are likely to prove an important source of absence variation. In the Cardiff study cited above (Chadwick-Jones et al., in press), it was found in one plant that different shifts of workers on a Continental rotation system had significantly different absence levels. There were no objective differences in job content or personal characteristics, but workers did differ in attitudes toward supervision, with the high absence shift expressing *more* satisfaction. This ostensibly anomalous result is clearly open to a climatic explanation (Nicholson, 1975). The relative social isolation of shifts and their supervisors on continuous rotation systems constitutes an ideal condition for the development of a group climate. Similar conditions obtain in hospitals, where a system of relatively autonomous wards is operated. Under these circumstances it has been shown that objectively similar wards can generate markedly different climates, which are reflected in pronounced differences in absence patterns and levels (Clark, 1975).

It should prove especially valuable to examine the process by which new entrants are socialized into the ambient absence culture. That is, how does the new member learn just what constitutes "legitimate" expected attendance behavior? The sociological literature provides some useful perspectives here. For example, it was the study of interward differences in psychiatric care that led Strauss (1978) to develop the idea of "negotiated order" to describe the dynamic interplay of norm-inducing forces. This notion may be helpfully applied to understanding how norms that legitimate absence are communicated to new members and effectively enforced. Bensman and Gerver's (1963) participant observation study of the social rituals involved in inculcating deviant work behavior in an aircraft plant is also instructive. In the face of pressure for high productivity, experienced workers, supervisors, and government inspectors conspired to encourage the regulated use of shortcut techniques and teach them to novices. Absence, conceived as a deviant behavior, may be influenced through similar processes. Such a perspective suggests that qualitative observational techniques may be especially valuable in probing the nature of absence climates or cultures. This approach may permit an understanding of the complexity of normative forces operating in a situation that may be threatening or sensitive to those involved.

Socialization into an absence culture could also be explored quantitatively. CP 4 indicates that absence should be recognized as temporally structured behavior responsive to feedback over time. As such, the presence of differential absence cultures should be revealed by changes in the absence patterns of new recruits and in the regularization of absence over time. Furthermore, the new worker's first experiences with absence are seldom personal, but instead are observational: the contexts and consequences of co-workers' absences are observed. Relatively straightforward studies in the attributional tradition would be useful to explore this early learning process.

Over 25 years ago, Hill and Trist (1955) argued that at different stages of organizational careers there may be systematic variations in subcultural expectations and limitations surrounding the legitimacy of different forms of absence and alternative behaviors. Now seems like an appropriate time to explore these arguments empirically.

CONCLUSION

In this chapter we have argued for a number of new approaches to conceiving of and studying the meanings of absence. We have chosen the plural term "meanings" carefully in order to emphasize two points about past absence research.

In our opinion, most absence research has been essentially descriptive in nature rather than explanatory. Correlating absence with job satisfaction, job content, and personal characteristics simply has not told us much about what absence *means* nor has it accounted for much variance. For example, although dozens of studies have reported significant associations between absence and age and absence and sex, the *reasons* for these associations remain uncharted. We have emphasized the plurality of the meanings of absence in order to counteract some biases that appear to be held by both researchers and managers. For researchers, absence appears to be seen simply as "one more criterion variable" usually signifying individual withdrawal from aversive work conditions. For managers, absence is often seen merely as a threat to organizational effectiveness, motivated by something that is circularly labeled "proneness." These restricted meanings ascribed to absence by researchers and managers have unduly limited our understanding of the phenomenon.

Just what is new about what we have proposed? First, on the basis of various circumstantial evidence and the limitations of previous research, we advocate the adoption of a fresh series of propositions about the nature of absence behavior. In combination, these premises suggest a series of new research areas. In some cases, these new research areas require the adoption of methods not commonly used in investigations of absence. Let us review two examples of this process.

If absence events can be viewed as phenomenologically unique (CP 1), some way is needed to penetrate this phenomenology. One way to effect this penetration is to use attribution theory to explore the reasons individuals give for their own absence behavior. Such an approach may help us understand why objectively equivalent proximal stimuli (such as sickness, family demands, or bad weather) are differentially interpreted as just causes for absence. If absence is responsive to feedback over time (CP 4), such attributions should depend in part on the successive reactions of relevant observers of absence episodes. In turn, these reactions depend upon *their* attributions of the reasons for a particular episode. There is reason to believe that the details of these attributional processes will differ across occupational groups because of objective differences in the constraints and opportunities regarding absence (CP 6). In this example, we see several CPs marshaled to suggest a particular research area, namely, the study of attributions that underlie absence episodes. In turn, several particular research methods are indicated, including (1) the use of absence diaries, (2) the longitudinal application of conventional attribution theory methods, (3) the incorporation of multiple observers, and (4) comparisons of processes across populations.

Turning to another example, we have argued that absence may often be influenced by social mechanisms and that the study of absence may profit from an explicitly collective perspective (CP 3). In addition, there is reason to believe that some of the social forces that affect attendance behavior stem from parties external to the organization (CP 5). In order to pursue these themes, we have advocated the examination of attendance norms in various relevant portions of employees' role sets. In addition, it is necessary to understand the conditions that favor the development of such norms and the factors that contribute to their enforcement. In many cases, the net effect of a set of attendance norms may be the development of an absence climate or culture that varies across work populations, organizational subunits, or entire organizations (following in part from CP 6). Here, again, we see several CPs marshaled to suggest two new areas of study. In turn, several novel research strategies are indicated, including (1) the collection of data from a variety of source persons, (2) participant observation of absence cultures in action, and (3) longitudinal studies of the absence patterns exhibited by new members of a particular absence culture.

To be realistic in our aspirations, we are aware that it is easier to prescribe change than to bring it about. The paradigms of the PIUs continue to be reinforced by the terms under which researchers gain access to organizations, the methodologies with which we feel most competent, and the criteria by which scientific communication is evaluated. But change is necessary if we are to have any hope of gathering empirical data that will help to systematize the scattered insights about absence that are currently available. More importantly, we will stop doing violence to the experiential reality of the behavior and will achieve a clearer and yet more differentiated view of its personal and social meanings.

ACKNOWLEDGMENTS

The support of a Social Sciences and Humanities Research Council of Canada leave fellowship and research grant is gratefully acknowledged. We wish to thank Richard Mowday for valuable comments on an earlier version.

NOTES

1.   This chapter was drafted while the first author was Visiting Research Fellow at the Medical Research Council Social and Applied Psychology Unit, University of Sheffield, and completed while he was Visiting Associate Professor of Management at the University of Oregon.

2.   Rhodes, S. R., & Steers, R. M. *Summary tables of studies of employee absenteeism.* Technical Report No. 13, University of Oregon, 1977.

3. Gupta, N., & Jenkins, G. D., Jr. *Employee withdrawal: An expanded definition and conceptual framework.* Unpublished manuscript, The University of Texas at Austin, 1980.

4. For other examples of the interpretation of group-level data at the individual level of analysis, see Rhodes and Steers (Note 2). Also see Muchinsky's (1977) discussion of the association between absence and turnover at the individual and group level.

5. Hulin, C. L., & Rousseau, D. M. *Analyzing infrequent events: Once you find them your troubles begin.* Technical report 80-3, Department of Psychology, University of Illinois at Urbana-Champaign, 1980.

6. Rousseau, D. M. *Measuring exceptional behavior in organizations: Problems in aggregating low base rate phenomena.* Paper presented at the annual meeting of the American Psychological Association, Toronto, 1978.

7. These breakdowns actually represent conservative estimates of the attention that has been paid to the organizational correlates of absence. Both Porter and Steers (1973) and Rhodes and Steers (Note 2) include organizational tenure in categories that otherwise concern extraorganizational "personal factors."

8. Because absence and turnover are so often linked under the rubric of "withdrawal," it is instructive to compare our application of attribution theory to absence with Steers and Mowday's (1981) application to turnover. First, Steers and Mowday correctly point out that the resignation of a particular employee from a particular organization is a one-shot event. The singular nature of such an occurrence, of course, does not preclude an attributional analysis. It does, however, obviate the literal use of consistency cues (Kelly, 1972) by observers. On the other hand, the absence behavior of a particular person in a particular organizational setting may be recurrent, and consistency cues are thus available for use by observers. Steers and Mowday also point out that other perspectives on the attribution of turnover allow for the observation of recurrent behaviors. First, every turnover incident is preceded by a series of job behaviors on the part of the incumbent that may serve as attributional cues regarding the cause of resignation. Second, the observation of several incidents of turnover over some period of time may provide a basis for the explanation of a subsequent specific incident. In the case of attributions by observers, these perspectives are equally applicable to explanations of absence. However, we would point out that because turnover usually occurs less frequently than absence, and because relevant behavioral cues for turnover probably occur over a longer time period, a greater degree of retrospection may be necessary to isolate relevant turnover cues. This may cause turnover attributions to reflect more stereotyping, more ego-defensive bias, and more aspects of cultural approval than absence attributions. Steers and Mowday restrict their discussion of turnover to attributions made by observers, whereas we additionally emphasize the important role of self-attributions of absence. Their perspective would seem to reflect the one-shot nature of turnover. Our perspective stems from the notion that the personal meanings of absence can be partially understood by self-attributions and that these attributions are shaped over recurrent absence events by the consequences provided by observers. These consequences depend upon the attributions that are made by these observers.

9. Nicholson, N., & Payne, R. *Attachment to work and absence behaviour.* Medical Research Council Social and Applied Psychology Unit Memorandum No. 223, University of Sheffield, 1978.

10. Ericsson, K. A., & Simon, H. A. *Retrospective verbal reports as data.* C.I.P. Working Paper No. 388, Carnegie-Mellon University, 1978.

11. Ericsson, K. A., & Simon, H. A. *Thinking-aloud protocols as data: Effects of verbalization.* C.I.P. Working Paper No. 397, Carnegie-Mellon University, 1979.

12. Specifically, explanations given to organizational officials seem likely to involve "motivated" biases of an ego-defensive nature whereas those provided for oneself may

reveal "informational" biases (cf. Ross, 1977). Both phenomena are covered by Green-wald's (1980) neatly coined term "beneffectance"—the tendency to accept personal responsibility for positive outcomes and to reject such responsibility for negative outcomes.

13.   It may be useful to describe how the adoption of such dispositional roles could be detected. Suppose workers A and B exhibit typical absence behavior for their organizations at the beginning of our research. When they are absent, both tend to provide unelaborate medical reasons for organizational officials. Similarly, both tell us retrospectively that they are usually absent due to minor disconnected medical reasons. During this period, their timely introspective reports indicate a mixture of head colds, mild depression, family demands, hobby pursuits, alarm clock failures, and hangovers. In addition, their reports of consistency, consensus, and distinctiveness cues point to circumstantial attributions. Gradually, the timely reports of worker A begin to reveal more and more medical reasons for absence, whereas those for worker B reveal more and more alarm clock failures and hobby pursuits. Simultaneously, their cue utilization shifts from circumstantial to dispositional, and the absence of each begins to increase. In explaining his absence to organizational officials, worker A, adopting a "sick role," begins to provide elaborate medical reasons backed up by vague but supportive physicians' certificates. Worker B, adopting a "deviant" role, provides flippant reasons or simply reports that her absences can be considered unexcused.

14.   Rousseau's (1978) discovery of a negative correlation between off-the-job challenge and absence is open to several causal interpretations. One assumes that high quality nonwork experiences substitute for the quantity of such experiences and thus lead to better attendance. Another assumes that attendance behavior influences the descriptions of non-work experiences, perhaps via dissonance mechanisms.

15.   This is an example of what Roberts, Hulin, and Rousseau (1978) refer to as *conceptual* aggregation in that the theory used to explain the observations is "relatively distant from the observations" (p. 87).

REFERENCES

Absenteeism: The dimensions of the problem. *IR Research Reports*, 1980, *4*, 1–2.

Adams, J. S. Inequity in social exchange. In L. Berkowitz (Ed.), *Advances in experimental social psychology* (Vol. 2). New York: Academic Press, 1965.

Arbous, A. G., & Sichel, H. S. New techniques for the analysis of absenteeism data. *Biometrika*, 1954, *41*, 77–90.

Argyle, M. *The social psychology of work*. London: Penguin, 1972.

Argyris, C., & Schon, D. *Theory in practice*. San Francisco: Jossey-Bass, 1974.

Barbash, J. Collective bargaining and the theory of conflict. *British Journal of Industrial Relations*, 1980, *18*, 82–90.

Beehr, T. A., & Gupta, N. A note on the structure of employee withdrawal. *Organizational Behavior and Human Performance*, 1978, *21*, 73–79.

Behrend, H. Voluntary absence from work. *International Labour Review*, 1959, *79*, 109–140.

Bem, D. J. Self-perception theory. In L. Berkowitz (Ed.), *Advances in experimental social psychology* (Vol. 6). New York: Academic Press, 1972.

Bensman, J., & Gerver, I. Crime and punishment in the factory: The function of deviancy in maintaining the social system. *American Sociological Review*, 1963, *28*, 580–598.

Bernardin, J. H. The relationship of personality variables to organizational withdrawal. *Personnel Psychology*, 1977, *30*, 17–27.

Burke, R. J., & Wilcox, D. S. Absenteeism and turnover among female telephone operators. *Personnel Psychology*, 1972, *25*, 639–648.

Calder, B. J. An attribution theory of leadership. In B. M. Staw & G. R. Salancik (Eds.), *New directions in organizational behavior.* Chicago: St. Clair, 1977.

Campbell, J. P., & Pritchard, R. D. Motivation theory in industrial and organizational psychology. In M. D. Dunnette (Ed.), *Handbook of industrial and organizational psychology.* Chicago: Rand McNally, 1976.

Chadwick-Jones, J. K., Brown, C. A., Nicholson, N., & Sheppard, C. Absence measures: Their reliability and stability in an industrial setting. *Personnel Psychology,* 1971, *24,* 463–470.

Chadwick-Jones, J. K., Brown, C. A., & Nicholson, N. Absence from work: Its meaning, measurement, and control. *International Review of Applied Psychology,* 1973a, *22,* 137–156.

Chadwick-Jones, J. K., Brown, C. A., & Nicholson, N. A-type and B-type absence: Empirical trends for women employees. *Occupational Psychology,* 1973b, *47,* 75–80.

Chadwick-Jones, J. K., Brown, C. A., & Nicholson, N. *The social psychology of attendance motivation.* New York: Praeger, in press.

Clark, J. *Time out?* London: Royal College of Nursing, 1975.

Colligan, M. J., & Murphy, L. R. Mass psychogenic illness in organizations: An overview. *Journal of Occupational Psychology,* 1979, *52,* 77–90.

Confederation of British Industry. *Absenteeism.* London: Author, 1970.

Dennett, B. How to minimize malingering. *Personnel Management,* 1978, *10,* 5, 30–32.

Dittrich, J. E., & Carrell, M. R. Organization equity perceptions, employee job satisfaction, and departmental absence and turnover rates. *Organizational Behavior and Human Performance,* 1979, *24,* 29–40.

Fletcher, B., Gowler, D., & Payne, R. Exploding the myth of executive stress. *Personnel Management,* 1979, *11,* 5, 30–34.

Fox, A. *Beyond contract: Work, power and trust relations.* London: Faber and Faber, 1974.

Fox, J. B., & Scott, J. F. *Absenteeism: Management's problem.* Cambridge, MA: Harvard Business School, 1943.

Froggatt, P. Short-term absence from industry. III. The inference of "proneness" and a search for causes. *British Journal of Industrial Medicine,* 1970, *27,* 297–312.

Garrison, K. R., & Muchinsky, P. M. Evaluating the concept of absentee-proneness with two measures of absence. *Personnel Psychology,* 1977, *30,* 389–393.

Gaudet, F. J. *Solving the problems of employee absence.* New York: American Management Association, 1963.

Gergen, K. J. Social psychology as history. *Journal of Personality and Social Psychology,* 1973, *26,* 309–320.

Golembiewski, R. T., & Proehl, C. W. A survey of the empirical literature on flexible workhours: Character and consequences of a major innovation. *Academy of Management Review,* 1978, *3,* 837–853.

Gowler, D. Determinants of the supply of labour to the firm. *Journal of Management Studies,* 1969, *6,* 73–95.

Greenwald, A. G. The totalitarian ego: Fabrication and revision of personal history. *American Psychologist,* 1980, *35,* 603–618.

Harré, R., & Secord, P. F. *The explanation of social behaviour.* Oxford: Blackwell, 1972.

Hedges, J. N. Absence from work—measuring the hours lost. *Monthly Labor Review,* 1977, *100,* 10, 16–23.

Hill, J. M. M., & Trist, E. L. Changes in accidents and other absences with length of service. *Human Relations,* 1955, *8,* 121–152.

Hinrichs, J. R. Measurement of reasons for resignation of professionals: Questionnaires versus company and consultant exit interviews. *Journal of Applied Psychology,* 1975, *60,* 530–532.

Homans, G. C. *The human group*. New York: Harcourt, Brace and World, 1950.

Huse, E. F., & Taylor, E. K. Reliability of absence measures. *Journal of Applied Psychology*, 1962, *42*, 159–160.

Hyman, R. *Strikes*. London: Fontana, 1972.

Ilgen, D. Attendance behavior: A reevaluation of Latham and Pursell's conclusions. *Journal of Applied Psychology*, 1977, *62*, 230–233.

Ivancevich, J. M., & Lyon, H. L. The shortened workweek: A field experiment. *Journal of Applied Psychology*, 1977, *62*, 34–37.

Jacques, E. *Measurement of responsibility*. London: Heinemann, 1957.

Johns, G. Attitudinal and nonattitudinal predictors of two forms of absence from work. *Organizational Behavior and Human Performance*, 1978, *22*, 431–444.

Jones, E. E., & Davis, K. E. From acts to dispositions: The attribution process in person perception. In L. Berkowitz (Ed.), *Advances in experimental social psychology* (Vol. 2). New York: Academic Press, 1965.

Jones, E. E., & McGillis, D. Correspondent inferences and the attribution cube: A comparative reappraisal. In J. H. Harvey, W. J. Ickes, & R. F. Kidd (Eds.), *New directions in attribution research* (Vol. 1). Hillsdale, NJ: Lawrence Erlbaum Associates, 1976.

Kelly, H. H. Attribution in social interaction. In E. E. Jones, D. E. Kanouse, H. H. Kelly, R. E. Nisbett, S. Valines, & B. Weiner (Eds.), *Attribution: Perceiving the causes of behavior*. Morristown, NJ: General Learning Press, 1972.

Kelly, J., & Nicholson, N. Strikes and other forms of industrial action. *Industrial Relations Journal*, 1980, *11*, 5, 20–31.

Kerr, W. A., Koppelmeier, G. J., & Sullivan, J. Absenteeism, turnover and morale in a metals fabrication factory. *Occupational Psychology*, 1951, *25*, 50–55.

Lamm, H., & Myers, D. G. Group-induced polarization of attitudes and behavior. In L. Berkowitz (Ed.), *Advances in experimental social psychology* (Vol. 11). New York: Academic Press, 1978.

Latham, G. P., & Pursell, E. D. Measuring absenteeism from the opposite side of the coin. *Journal of Applied Psychology*, 1975, *60*, 369–371.

Lefkowitz, J., & Katz, M. Validity of exit interviews. *Personnel Psychology*, 1969, *22*, 445–455.

Levine, S., & Kozloff, M. A. The sick role: Assessment and overview. In R. H. Turner, J. Coleman, & R. C. Fox (Eds.), *Annual review of sociology* (Vol. 4). Palo Alto, CA: Annual Reviews, 1978.

Locke, E. A. What is job satisfaction? *Organizational Behavior and Human Performance*, 1969, *4*, 309–336.

Lyons, T. F. Turnover and absenteeism: A review of relationships and shared correlates. *Personnel Psychology*, 1972, *25*, 271–281.

Mann, F. C., Indik, B. P., & Vroom, V. H. *The productivity of work groups*. Ann Arbor: Survey Research Center, Institute for Social Research, University of Michigan, 1963.

Martin, J. Some aspects of absence in a light engineering factory. *Occupational Psychology*, 1971, *45*, 77–89.

Mayo, E., & Lombard, G. *Teamwork and labor turnover in the aircraft industry in Southern California*. Cambridge, MA: Harvard University Press, 1944.

Metzner, H., & Mann, F. C. Employee attitudes and absences. *Personnel Psychology*, 1953, *6*, 467–485.

Mitchell, T. R., Green, S., & Wood, R. An attributional model of leadership and the poor performing subordinate. In L. L. Cummings & B. M. Staw (Eds.), *Research in organizational behavior* (Vol. 3). Greenwich, CT: JAI Press, 1981.

Moore, L. F., Johns, G., & Pinder, C. C. Toward middle range theory: An overview and perspective. In C. C. Pinder & L. F. Moore (Eds.), *Middle range theory and the study of organizations*. Boston: Martinus Nijhoff, 1980.

Morgan, L. G., & Herman, J. B. Perceived consequences of absenteeism. *Journal of Applied Psychology,* 1976, *61,* 738–742.

Muchinsky, P. M. Employee absenteeism: A review of the literature. *Journal of Vocational Behavior,* 1977, *10,* 316–340.

Nicholson, N. *Industrial absence as an incident of employee motivation and job satisfaction.* Unpublished doctoral dissertation, University of Wales, Cardiff, 1975.

Nicholson, N. Management sanctions and absence control. *Human Relations,* 1976, *29,* 139–152.

Nicholson, N. Absence behaviour and attendance motivation: A conceptual synthesis. *Journal of Management Studies,* 1977, *14,* 231–252.

Nicholson, N., Brown, C. A., & Chadwick-Jones, J. K. Absence from work and job satisfaction. *Journal of Applied Psychology,* 1976, *61,* 728–737.

Nicholson, N., Brown, C. A., & Chadwick-Jones, J. K. Absence from work and personal characteristics. *Journal of Applied Psychology,* 1977, *62,* 319–327.

Nicholson, N., & Goodge, P. M. The influence of social, organizational, and biographical factors on female absence. *Journal of Management Studies,* 1976, *13,* 234–254.

Nicholson, N., Jackson, P. J., & Howes, G. Shiftwork and absence: An analysis of temporal trends. *Journal of Occupational Psychology,* 1978, *51,* 127–137.

Nisbett, R. E., & Wilson, T. D. Telling more than we can know: Verbal reports on mental processes. *Psychological Review,* 1977, *84,* 231–259.

Nord, W. R. Job satisfaction reconsidered. *American Psychologist,* 1977, *32,* 1026–1035.

Nord, W. R., & Costigan, R. Worker adjustment to the four-day week: A longitudinal study. *Journal of Applied Psychology,* 1973, *58,* 60–66.

Patchen, M. Absence and employee feelings about fair treatment. *Personnel Psychology,* 1960, *13,* 349–360.

Payne, R., & Pugh, D. S. Organizational structure and climate. In M. D. Dunnette (Ed.), *Handbook of industrial and organizational psychology.* Chicago: Rand McNally, 1976.

Pepitone, A. Toward a normative and comparative social psychology. *Journal of Personality and Social Psychology,* 1976, *34,* 641–653.

Pocock, S. J. Daily variations in sickness absence. *Applied Statistics,* 1973, *22,* 375–392.

Porter, L. W., & Steers, R. M. Organizational, work, and personal factors in employee turnover and absenteeism. *Psychological Bulletin,* 1973, *80,* 151–176.

Roberts, K. H., Hulin, C. L., & Rousseau, D. M. *Developing an interdisciplinary science of organizations.* San Francisco: Jossey-Bass, 1978.

Robinson, J. Goof-off champs! *Montreal Gazette,* July 5, 1980, p. 17.

Ross, L. The intuitive psychologist and his shortcomings: Distortions in the attribution process. In L. Berkowitz (Ed.), *Advances in experimental social psychology* (Vol. 10). New York: Academic Press, 1977.

Rotter, J. B. Generalized expectancies for internal versus external controls of reinforcement. *Psychological Monographs,* 1966, *80,* (Whole No. 609).

Rousseau, D. M. Relationship of work to nonwork. *Journal of Applied Psychology,* 1978, *63,* 513–517.

Simon, H. A. *Administrative behavior.* New York: The Free Press, 1957.

Smith, E. R., & Miller, F. D. Limits on perception of cognitive processes: A reply to Nisbett and Wilson. *Psychological Review,* 1978, *85,* 355–362.

Smith, F. J. Work attitudes as predictors of attendance on a specific day. *Journal of Applied Psychology,* 1977, *62,* 16–19.

Smulders, P. G. W. Comments on employee absence/attendance as a dependent variable in organizational research. *Journal of Applied Psychology,* 1980, *65,* 368–371.

Staw, B. M. The consequences of turnover. *Journal of Occupational Behaviour,* 1980, *1,* 253–273.

Staw, B. M., & Oldham, G. R. Reconsidering our dependent variables: A critique and empirical study. *Academy of Management Journal*, 1978, *21*, 539–559.

Steers, R. M., & Mowday, R. T. Employee turnover and post-decision accommodation processes. In L. L. Cummings & B. M. Staw (Eds.), *Research in organizational behavior* (Vol. 3). Greenwich, CT: JAI Press, 1981.

Steers, R. M., & Rhodes, S. R. Major influences on employee attendance: A process model. *Journal of Applied Psychology*, 1978, *63*, 391–407.

Strauss, A. *Negotiations: Varieties, contexts, processes, and social order*. San Francisco: Jossey-Bass, 1978.

Taylor, P. J. Shift and day work: A comparison of sickness absence, lateness, and other absence behaviour at an oil refinery from 1962 to 1965. *British Journal of Industrial Medicine*, 1967, *24*, 93–102.

Turner, A. M., & Lawrence, P. R. *Industrial jobs and the worker*. Boston: Harvard University Graduate School of Business Administration, 1965.

Walker, K. The application of the J-curve hypothesis of conforming behavior to industrial absenteeism. *Journal of Social Psychology*, 1947, *25*, 207–216.

Waters, L. K., & Roach, D. Relationship between job attitudes and two forms of withdrawal from the work situation. *Journal of Applied Psychology*, 1971, *55*, 92–94.

Waters, L. K., & Roach, D. Job satisfaction, behavioral intention, and absenteeism as predictors of turnover. *Personnel Psychology*, 1979, *32*, 393–397.

White, P. Limitations on verbal reports of internal events: A refutation of Nisbett and Wilson and of Bem. *Psychological Review*, 1980, *87*, 105–112.

Wortman, C. B., & Linsenmeier, J. A. W. Interpersonal attraction and techniques of ingratiation in organizational settings. In B. M. Staw & G. R. Salancik (Eds.), *New directions in organizational behavior*. Chicago: St. Clair, 1977.

Yolles, S. F., Carone, P. A., & Krinsky, L. W. (Eds.), *Absenteeism in industry*. Springfield, IL: Charles C. Thomas, 1974.

WORKERS PARTICIPATION IN MANAGEMENT:
AN INTERNATIONAL PERSPECTIVE

George Strauss

ABSTRACT

Formal schemes for workers participation in management (WPM) through elected representatives have been the focus of considerable interest and controversy throughout the world. This article reviews the research evidence with regard to how these schemes work in practice. It begins by discussing the difficulties of doing research in this area, particularly given the multitude of reasons for which WPM is introduced. It then examines the experience with WPM in Israel and Yugoslavia, in producers cooperatives, and in cases where employees have bought their plants to save them from being shut down. The discussion then reviews more generally the new role of the participative board member and the changed roles of labor and management. Next evidence is presented as to the impact of technology, values, and rewards on WPM success. Finally the article pulls the various themes together and concludes with an agenda for future research.

Research in Organizational Behavior, Vol. 4, pages 173–265
Copyright © 1982 by JAI Press Inc.
All rights of reproduction in any form reserved.
ISBN: 0-89232-147-4

Workers participation in management (WPM)—sometimes called industrial democracy—has become a major political, social, and economic issue throughout the world, particularly in Europe. A wide variety of forms of WPM exist, for example, workers' self-management (Yugoslavia), codetermination (Germany), works councils (in much of Europe), Scanlon Plan (United States), and producers cooperatives or PCs (in many countries). These various social experiments have in turn stimulated a growing stream of research utilizing many methodologies.

WPM's centrality as a social issue has made it a major OB research concern outside the United States. For United States scholars it provides a series of test cases for the participative theories so widely accepted in the OB community. After all, WPM has been prescribed as the solution of a wide variety of organizational problems: alienation, low productivity, autocratic management, poor teamwork, power imbalance, opposition to technological change, union–management conflict, and the like. Further, it represents a massive, presumably planned organizational change, which, if successful, introduces alterations not just in structure and attitudes but also in the variable of much current OB interest: power. Finally, for the industrial relations specialist, WPM provides an alternative to the primarily adversary system existing in the United States.

As an introduction to WPM, this article has two purposes. First, an attempt will be made to interpret the experience with WPM to date, with special emphasis on its significance for OB. The article will concern chiefly the problems encountered in making it "work," the extent of its "success" (by a variety of disputed standards), and the conditions favorable for "success." Second, the main research questions in this area and the kinds of research being done will be described.

Except occasionally for purposes of comparison, this article is concerned chiefly with formal schemes for participation at the plant and company levels, and so it largely ignores three other forms of participation that are already familiar to United States students: (1) job enrichment and autonomous work groups, (2) what might be called Likert-type informal participation in which workers preferences are relayed via linking pins from foremen to company president (rather than through elected representatives), and (3) collective bargaining—though this may be the most effective participation form of all.

The thesis of this article is that WPM should be evaluated in terms of its impact on society generally, not just on productivity and worker satisfaction. Thus, this article will view WPM from a variety of perspectives. It will start with two introductory sections. One will list the main forms of WPM and the conflicting reasons for which they are introduced; the other will deal with the difficult question of how WPM is to be researched. Next several forms of WPM in practice will be reviewed. The purpose here is to provide background for the heart of the article, which consists of two sections. The first one will examine how WPM affects the main interested parties; the second will look at various contextual issues affecting how WPM operates. Finally, some implications from the research as a whole will be offered.

FORMS OF WPM AND WHY THEY ARE INTRODUCED

This section will begin with an around-the-world tour, illustrating the range and forms WPM takes in various countries. Then this diversity will be related to the conflicting theoretical and practical justifications for introducing them in the first place. Finally, seeking to provide some illusory order out of this confusion, it erects a taxonomy of WPM forms that should further demonstrate that WPM is not a unitary concept.

International Diversity

Yugoslavia. Workers in each plant elect Workers Councils, which in turn (subject to some restrictions) hire and fire management. Both national law and the prevailing ideology stress active participation by workers in a variety of councils and committees. Important decisions require the consultation of rank-and-file workers in departmental shop floor meetings.

Germany. Codetermination has been a major political issue. Company boards of directors in the steel and coal industries include equal numbers of management and worker representatives. In other large companies, the current compromise calls for almost equal representation, with a management-selected chairman entitled to a tie-breaking vote. At the plant level, the approval of elected works councils is required for some personnel actions, whereas the councils must be consulted with regard to others.

Britain. Here too "industrial democracy" has been controversial. The Bullock Committee, appointed by the Labour Government in 1975, came out squarely for codetermination (Elliott, 1978). Meeting vehement management opposition and only mild union support, the issue was sidetracked and rests dormant under the Thatcher administration. On the other hand, there is a long tradition of at least partly worker-owned and worker-controlled businesses, some founded by paternalistic owners and others organized to forestall plants from being shut down altogether. Furthermore, worker directors sit on the boards of some nationalized companies. For most of industry, however, collective bargaining represents the main form of participation. Plant-wide bargaining through shop stewards has become increasingly important in recent years.

France. There is wide agreement on participation as a symbol, though not on its substance (Bornstein and Fine, 1977). As early as 1946, De Gaulle supported participation as a "third road" between communism and capitalism, although in practice this meant little more than profit sharing. The socialist unions are committed to "autogestion," worker-run enterprises, whereas the communists support indirect participation through a state-owned, centrally planned economy. Works councils, concerned with personnel issues, exist in most enterprises of any size, although they have less power than in Germany.

Sweden. Until recently Swedish unions sought to influence unemployment rates and the distribution of income through governmental policies, although Paragraph 32 of the national labor–management agreement guaranteed employers' rights to hire and fire workers and to direct and allocate work. The famous quality of worklife experiments at Volvo and elsewhere were largely management sponsored, with only union acquiescence. Then, a 1972 law put two union representatives on most company boards of directors; in 1977, the Employee Participation Act repealed Paragraph 32 and required employers to negotiate with unions before "any important . . . change of activity," with the union being given the power to block change before final resolution by strike, arbitration, or Labor Court decision. The union-backed Meidner plan would require 20 percent of company profits to be converted into stock to be given to union-run "wage earner funds" with the expectation that eventually workers would win majority ownership of most companies (Martin, 1977; Logue, 1978).

Norway. The history here parallels that of Sweden, except that, influenced by Thorsrud and Emery (1970), unions began early to concern themselves with ship-level quality of worklife questions, especially autonomous work groups.

Israel. The kibbutzim or agricultural cooperatives are worker owned and managed, with incomes being shared roughly equally. Many kibbutzim also operate small factories. The national union, the Histradrut, owns a substantial percentage of the country's economy. Various attempts have been made to increase worker participation in the management of this sector, but with little success, as we see later.

Spain. At least for its supporters, Mondragon, a system of Basque producers cooperatives, may provide one of the most successful examples of worker-owned and -managed enterprises today (Johnson and Whyte, 1977; Eaton, 1979).

The United States. Aside from UAW President Fraser's election as a Chrysler director, there has been little United States interest in Germany-style codetermination. United States labor leaders are virtually unanimous in their belief that collective bargaining is the best way to protect workers rights. At the shop level considerable interest has been given to "Quality of Worklife" change, although little of this involves participation in management, except at very low levels. More to the point have been several carefully monitored joint union–management experiments in which workers participated in what may be viewed as middle management decisions as to the type of worklife changes to be made (e.g., Goodman, 1979). The Scanlon Plan combines worker participation in production decisions with a group incentive bonus (Driscoll, 1979). Finally, there is a new-found interest in worker-owned producer cooperatives (PCs). As in Britain, some PCs have a long history whereas others were founded recently to stave off plant shutdowns and still others were organized by members of the counterculture. Related to worker ownership, much attention has been given to Employee Stock Ownership Plans (ESOPs).

Australia. There are few examples of WPM in practice; still it stimulates much controversy (Derber, 1978). The union movement has made it a major objective; the two largest political parties support it in principle (though with differing degrees of enthusiasm); and it is the leading subject for articles in the nation's academic industrial relations journal. Further, Australia—land of strange beasts—houses what is perhaps the most radical WPM experiment on earth, Dynavac, a high-technology business totally without formal leaders.

Latin America. The military regime in Peru passed a law requiring self-management in certain firms which it had expropriated, but with indifferent results (Berenbach, 1979; Stephens, 1980). A similar process occurred in Chile under Allende, but reportedly with greater success because there was a political movement at the rank-and-file level to support it (Espinosa and Zimbalist, 1978).

China. The late Maoist period (1968–1976) was marked by "two participations": (1) professional managers were partly replaced by Revolutionary Committees which included shop-floor representatives and (2) the remaining professional managers were expected to "participate" regularly in physical production work. In fact, Revolutionary Committees had little autonomy; however, work groups were allowed some freedom in *implementing* centrally imposed plans. Further, something akin to Japanese style quality circles were utilized to introduce technological change. Since Mao's death the emphasis has shifted toward representative plant-wide Workers Congress and individual election of supervisors and managers. It is still unclear whether the new approach will make any difference (Walden, 1981; Lockett, in progress).

Soviet Union. As in China, "participation" is widely used to mobilize mass support. Soviet workers attend considerably more meetings than do their Western counterparts. But participation consists chiefly of ratifying policies already decided upon, and of making suggestions as to how these policies may be implemented. Russian workers have little power to reject or modify policy itself (Lane and O'Dell, 1978; Little, 1980).

This is but a quick summary of the state of WPM in various countries. Studies have been completed in a number of other countries: Algeria (Clegg, 1971); New Zealand (Young, 1979); Malta (compare Kester, 1980 and Koziara, 1979); Denmark (Westenholz, 1979); Canada (Nightingale, 1979); Belgium (Jain, Vanachter, and Gevers, 1980); and the Netherlands (Mulder, 1971).

Reasons for Participation

Even more varied than the forms of WPM are the reasons for which it is undertaken. Dachler and Wilpert (1978) analyze the main theoretical justifications. The classification in this article is in terms of the interested parties.

WPM has been popular in older states with highly developed technologies, such as Britain, Sweden, and West Germany, as well as in newer nations, such as Israel and Algeria—and in pluralist democratic countries as well as in one-party states where individual freedom is limited. One reason for its popularity is that it represents a happy melding of the ideologies of socialism and human relations (Strauss and Rosenstein, 1970). Also in many cases it meets the political needs of union leaders and national governmental figures. Parenthetically, the situation today is very different from that of the early 1900s, when the idea of PCs "was opposed by capitalists, academicians, government and labor unions, although each held a separate rationale" (Aldrich and Stern, 1978, p. 7).

OB Experts. More of the impetus for WPM has come from intellectuals (both OB experts and socialists) and politicians than has come from the rank-and-file workers who are supposed to do the participating. So the attitudes of intellectuals, as change agents, are worth considering.

Participation is a central tenet in the managerial ideology taught in many capitalistic business schools. Beginning with Hawthorne the human relations (now OB) tradition placed high value on cooperation between subordinates and superiors. This emphasis has been reinforced by the findings of the Michigan school, by almost the entire OD movement, and most recently by advocates of job enrichment, autonomous work groups, and quality of worklife reforms. To be sure, the managerial version of participation assumes that participation will occur on a face-to-face basis, between individual bosses and subordinates; further it largely ignores unions and all issues of power. Nevertheless, in part as a result of the missionary efforts of such pioneers as McGregor and Likert, the ideology of participation is now at least superficially accepted by managers in most parts of the world (Haire, Ghiselli, and Porter, 1966).

The purported advantages of WPM in terms of OB theory have been described often (Lowin, 1968; Strauss, 1977; Locke and Schweiger, 1979). Very briefly they include

- To the extent that WPM improves *communications,* it raises productivity because (1) better decisions are made because (a) WPM allows subordinates to contribute important information and suggestions and (b) it permits a variety of sometimes conflicting views to be aired; (2) decisions are better implemented because (a) workers know better what they are required to do, (b) teamwork is facilitated, and (c) resistance to change is reduced.
- To the extent WPM involves *goal setting,* productivity is also raised because (1) individuals work harder for goals they have committed themselves to reach; (2) once attaining these goals they gain a sense of achievement; and (3) individual efforts are reinforced by group pressures.

Much of the above contributes to satisfaction. Beyond this WPM provides individuals a chance to express themselves and exercise power. Additionally it promotes individual growth, reduces alienation, and provides training for democracy (Pateman, 1970). Industrial relations scholars see it as reducing labor strife and substituting integrative for distributive bargaining. Finally, for some OB theorists, WPM is important because it leads to power sharing (Tannenbaum, Kovcic, Rosner, Vianello, and Wieser, 1974). Democracy, in other words, is a value in itself.

In short, for OB people the main values of WPM are productivity, satisfaction, human growth, and for some, power sharing or democracy. To various degrees of intensity, managers voluntarily instituting WPM share these views. In addition, some view it as a means of keeping unions out.

Socialists. Socialists have theories of their own. Presumably WPM helps eliminate the four causes of alienation that Marx saw as resulting from capitalism; meaninglessness, powerlessness, social alienation, and self-estrangement. "Workers control" has become a common goal of socialists of almost every persuasion, even though there is much difference as to what the term means. Disillusioned by socialism Soviet-style, many younger socialists are looking for a socialism with a "human face." They place a high value on "self-management," that is, freedom for workers to direct their own work on a democratic basis. By contrast Communists reject *shop-level* workers control, as did many older socialists, most notably Sidney and Beatrice Webb (1920). Workers control for these socialists means *public* control of the economy on a fairly centralized basis. Workers self-management, they fear, will be inefficient; further, workers in each shop are likely to favor their own narrow interests rather than those of the working class as a whole. All factions agree that workers control involves a rejection of capitalism and a substantial redistribution of power. As a distinguished Yugoslav scholar puts it, "The goal of self-management is above all the political emancipation of the working class" (Rus, 1979, p. 322; see also Mako, 1978, p. 8). Ironically, once socialists become managers themselves they begin to accept some of the human-relations OB values as their own.

Unionists. Unionists also disagree as to WPM. As mentioned earlier, United States and many right-wing British unions (Elliott, 1978) have generally opposed WPM, largely because they fear being co-opted and believe that collective bargaining better protects their members. United States unions are reluctant to become involved in "Quality of Worklife" programs, such as job enrichment or autonomous work groups, fearing that these will mute the demands for economic gains, lead to speedups, and weaken hard-fought-for work rules (for a more extensive discussion, see Strauss, 1977, p. 80). Interestingly, some left-wing and Communist-dominated unions also reject WPM, viewing it as a form of class collaboration.

In between are unions in Scandinavia, Germany, and some in the Netherlands (Albeda, 1977) and Britain who have come to support WPM with various degrees of enthusiasm. Their motivation for doing so is complex and varied, though, for the most part, it boils down to a desire to extend union power. Swedish unions, reacting to extensive wildcat strikes during the late 1960s, saw WPM as a means of reinvigorating plant-level unions in an era of centralized bargaining. Earlier many Swedish unions opposed WPM on the grounds that stronger plant-level unions would impede the drive toward nationwide wage equalization (Martin, 1977).

In Britain, under the Labour Party, the introduction of worker-directors at the firm level was seen as a means to plug the last gap in the network of industrial democracy, which already included shop steward representation at the shop and plant levels, industry-wide bargaining, and a nationwide social contract (Elliott, 1978).

On the continent, especially in Germany, collective bargaining traditionally has been conducted at the industry, rather than company or plant, level (and many unions have stressed national-level political roles). Further it has been concerned chiefly with overall wage levels. Thus WPM provides the opportunity to extend the scope of bargaining to subjects other than wages and to strengthen the union at the plant level. The German law, which requires management to consult with the works council or get its approval before engaging in discipline, layoffs, or significant technological change, brings to German industry the rough equivalent of United States-style, plant-level collective bargaining. However, codetermination goes beyond this. It allows some worker input into the investment policies that determine the level of employment. As a Swedish unionist put it, "our interest is seeing that capital is used to provide secure jobs, and that's what we need influence for. We can't trust management to do that" (Logue, 1978, p. 12).

Politicians. In many countries WPM has been introduced by law. Therefore, the motives of the politicians and public leaders involved should be examined. Often these combine various mixtures of the practical and the ideological.

In Germany, according to Hartmann (1970), codetermination was introduced after the war because of the fortunate juxtaposition of numerous interests: the British occupying power supported it as a means of curbing industrialists' power, managers hoped it would protect their plants from Allied dismantling, unions viewed it as a means of preventing the reestablishment of a management controlled nationalist party, whereas Catholic liberals found it consistent with papal encyclicals. (Cynically, one might add that Socialist leaders may have perceived support for WPM as a means of preserving their credentials as socialists while at the same time abandoning the class struggle and nationalization of industry as political objectives.)

Attempts by De Gaulle to introduce participation in the waning days of his administration may be interpreted as an effort to devise a new look for his regime and also to win support among increasingly militant students by proposing a seemingly leftist measure. The Giscard government also proposed some mild participatory measures, leading Bornstein and Fine (1977, p. 161) to conclude that "participation schemes function, for conservative governments, as a means of pacifying workers, separating them from their unions, and integrating them into a rationalized neocapitalist institutional framework."

In communist bloc countries, WPM programs existed for a while during the 1960s in Poland and Czechoslovakia; quite recently they have been revived in China and Poland. In all these cases, WPM reflected the intentions of the political leadership to decentralize and liberalize economic life. In Yugoslavia, workers self-management legitimated the return to a semimarket economy at the time of the split with Russia; in this way Tito's reforms could be treated as a new advance into socialism rather than a retreat to capitalism. In Britian (Jones, 1977), the Labour Government offered unions "industrial democracy" in part as a quid pro quo for acquiescence (through the social contract) in incomes policy; roughly the same deal was made in Sweden (Martin, 1977).

In Israel (as we shall see, the Histadrut leaders looked upon WPM as a means of closing the gap between their own ideological convictions and the reality that their union had become a business conglomerate. In Algeria and other developing countries, the problem was to endow economic activity with a patina of socialism and at the same time introduce industrial discipline. In India, government-introduced programs represented, among other things, a carry-over into mass industry of the gentle notions of Mahatma Ghandi.

Conflict Among Objectives. Clearly participation means all things to all people. For some it means increased motivation and productivity or, by contrast, protection of jobs and work rules. For various others it means personal growth, a defeat for capitalism, or the preservation of social peace.

In some cases (e.g., Germany) this very diversity of meaning helped make the formal institutionalization of WPM politically possible. WPM can be a convenient slogan around which many different interests may gather. Politicians especially may view it as a seemingly costless concession that can be made to have considerable symbolic value.

Yet many of the parties' objectives are mutually inconsistent. There is conflict, for example, between those who view WPM as a means of winning greater acceptance of organizational objectives and those who see it as a means of counterbalancing or weakening management. The first group tends to ignore power; for the second, power is the central issue. In a sense the difference is between those who view WPM as an integrative process and those who see it as distributive (Walton and McKersie, 1965).

Thus management may view WPM as a means of eliciting worker suggestions for improving productivity and generally for facilitating change, whereas, for many unionists its purpose is to protect job rights and work restrictions against unilateral management actions (Bull and Barton, 1978). These differences in expectations contribute to differences in their "vocabulary of participation" (Brannen, 1976), that is, the parties differ in the meanings they give to the same words and institutions, thus greatly frustrating communication. There is a tendency to assume that WPM will automatically solve real conflicts of interest, when, in fact, by creating an unrealistic assumption of mutuality, it may only sweep problems under the table. Thus the diversity of expectations that helps facilitate *formal* acceptance of WPM may actually hinder its successful *implementation*.

Objectives and Research Strategy. This diversity of objectives also creates problems for researchers. On what aspects of WPM should they concentrate: attitudes, strike rates, level of employee benefits, distribution of profits, or what? New left academic idealists—seeking a freer society—may stress different points than do hard-headed (hearted?) business school OB types. And by what criteria should WPM be evaluated? Obviously value judgments are involved here. OB reviews that examine participative decision making merely in terms of productivity and satisfaction (e.g., Locke and Schweiger, 1979) may be too narrowly focused. Perhaps the impact of WPM upon society generally should also be considered.

Forms of Participation: A Taxonomy

As the foregoing discussion illustrates, much of the confusion regarding WPM arises from the fact that the generic term covers a multitude of activities. Disagreement extends even to the appropriate name to use. Americans prefer "workers participation in management" (the term used here), whereas for some Europeans "participation" sounds too manipulative. They prefer "industrial democracy," "self-management," or "workers control," all terms that imply that workers have substantial power.

Given that WPM means so many different things to different people, it is understandable that much recent writing has been devoted to constructing taxonomies. This is no idle exercise because the various forms of participation have greatly varying impacts on organizational performance. Although there is as yet little agreement as to terms, most attempts at classification (Globerson, 1970; Walker, 1974; Bernstein, 1980; Espinosa and Zimbalist, 1978) involve one or more of four dimensions, which I shall call: organizational level, degree of control, issues, and ownership. Table 1 outlines the major dimensions.

Table 1.   A Taxonomy of Various Forms of Participation

Classification	Examples
Organizational Level	
Individual	Job enrichment
Small group	Autonomous work group
Departmental	Scanlon Plan production committees
Plant	German works councils
Company	Worker directors
Industry	Much European collective bargaining
National	Labor input into national economic planning
Degree of Control	
Joint consultation	French works councils
Joint decision making	Collective bargaining; codetermination in the German iron and steel industry
Self-management	Yugoslavia; producers cooperatives
Issues	
Wages	Collective bargaining in most countries
Personnel issues (e.g., layoffs, overtime)	Collective bargaining in the United States; works councils in Germany
Welfare benefits	French works councils' control over plant medical services
Production methods, job content	Scanlon Plan, autonomous work groups
Vacation schedules	Yugoslav zbors (shop meetings)
Selecting managers	Yugoslav workers council selecting a manager
Major investment decisions	Supervisory board under German codetermination
Ownership	
No worker ownership	Typical company
Some worker ownership	United States Employee Stock Ownership Plan (ESOP)
Completely worker owned	Producers cooperative

Organizational Level. This dimension requires little explanation. American academic interest in WPM has been at the departmental level and lower. European writing stresses the plant or company levels, with an increasing emphasis occurring at the national level.

Organizational level is related to the often-debated question of *direct* (face-to-face) versus *representative* (indirect) participation. The human relations arguments for WPM apply best to direct participation. Representative participation may be effective in protecting workers' economic interests and perhaps in giving them a sense of power. However, the sense of involvement and participation provided by direct participation is reduced when participation is handled indirectly. In theory, to obtain a fully participative organization, both forms of participation should be integrated. However, aside from the Scanlon Plan, few WPM schemes have successfully integrated the participative efforts of various organizational levels.

Degree of Control. This dimension is concerned with the subordinate's influence over decision making. With joint consultation (the most common form of WPM), management makes the final decisions, but workers have the right to be informed, to offer advice and objections, and even to make proposals. Joint decision making implies that the parties have equal power and that each side's consent is needed before action is taken. Self-management gives workers or their representatives final authority.

Only in joint decision making and self-management do workers have formal power to make or block decisions. Joint consultation depends on management's good will to make it work; management can (and frequently does) merely go through the motions and totally ignores the workers' input.

Each of the main categories can be further subdivided (e.g., IDE, 1981). Walker (1974), for example, notes three forms of what I call joint consultation: "Management decides unilaterally but workers are informed before decision is put into effect"; "Management decides after hearing workers' views"; and "Negotiations take place but management goes ahead if no agreement is reached."

Another distinction can be made between formal decision making and actual decision making. There appear to be numerous instances where one party (either workers or management) has the formal power but usually allows the other party to do what it wants. Thus the decisions of autonomous work groups may be subject to a rarely exercised management veto; by contrast Yugoslav workers councils typically give rubber stamp approval to most of management's recommendations.

As Locke and Schweiger (1979, p. 276) suggest, participative decision making "may be more effective at some stages than others." Motivated by decision-making theory, recently researchers have examined the various stages of the participative decision-making process. The Decisions in Organizations (DIO, 1979) group distinguishes among four stages: initiation, development, finalization, and implementation.

Issues. Compared with other dimensions, there is somewhat less agreement as to how to classify the subject matter covered by WPM. By contrast with the categories indicated for level and degree, which are meant to be fairly inclusive, those for issues are merely illustrative. Distinctions relevant to one country may be irrelevant in another. The main point is that some WPM schemes may be limited to purely personnel or shop-level production problems whereas others may cover the entire gamut of issues. If WPM deals only with personnel issues, it hardly extends beyond United States-style collective bargaining. Some British participative committees deal with such trivial issues that critics call them "tea and toilet" committees.

WPM advocates differ in the issues they stress. Human relationists have focused chiefly on production issues and some are disappointed when workers talk about wages. German and British union proponents of WPM, by contrast, have been interested mainly in long-run employment-related issues.

Obviously levels and issues are related. Different issues are likely to be handled at different levels. Major investments are more likely to be considered at the company level; shop-level WPM is more likely to be concerned with such issues as vacation schedules or production methods.

Ownership. The issue of participation is often connected with that of ownership. Employee Stock Ownership Plans have spread rapidly in the United States in recent years because of favorable tax treatment. Many producers cooperatives are purely worker owned; however, as we shall see, most of the employee-owned firms recently established in the United States to prevent plant shutdowns, in fact, have a high degree of management or outside ownership as well as little employee control. In Europe, employee ownership schemes, such as Sweden's Meidner Plan, have been widely proposed as a complement or even substitute for WPM, particularly to ensure the socially acceptable use of capital (Chamberlain, 1980).

LITERATURE AND RESEARCH

The growth of workers' participation in the real world has been matched by the development of a substantial literature (of uneven quality), only a small portion of which will be cited here. (For bibliographies, see Marclay, 1971; Williams, 1976; Maley, Dunphy, and Ford, 1979). Much of the early writing was speculative and normative, based on hopes and fears, because there was little evidence. Later authors described the background and details of participation schemes in individual countries as these were adopted (e.g., there have been a host of books and articles on Yugoslav self-management, German codetermination, and the British Bullock report). Some of these studies related the introduction of participation to the social, political, and economic conditions in the countries in which participation has been introduced (see especially Garson, 1977). In addition, as research data have accumulated, there have been several important studies that compare the experience of various forms of WPM in a conceptual manner. Pateman (1970), Walker (1974), Dachler and Wilpert (1978), and Bernstein (1980) deserve special note. Finally, there have been some valuable collections of articles (Vanek, 1975a; Hunnius, Garson, and Case, 1973; Windmuller, 1977; Garson, 1977; Lansbury, 1980).

Two streams of specialized normative literature deserve mention. The first, produced largely by trade unionists and academic union sympathizers, debates the question of what the union's attitude toward WPM should be (e.g., Webb and Webb, 1920; Clegg, 1960; Coates and Topham, 1968). The second, chiefly by radical political economists, seeks to determine optimum incentive, price, and investment policies for self-managing organizations (e.g., Wachtel, 1973; Vanek, 1977). Some of the articles involve mathematical economic theory, others analyze empirical data. (For a summary, see Steinherr, 1978.) Much of it appears in an English-language Yugoslav journal, *Economic Analysis and Worker Management*.

Aside from conceptual and normative studies, there is a growing stream of empirical studies. These fall into two main categories, behavioral and attitudinal–cognitive, each of which involves research problems.

Measures of Participation. Before going further, some conceptual questions, which are discussed at greater length elsewhere (Strauss, 1977, 1979a), should be considered briefly. Implicitly or explicitly, most studies (e.g., IDE, 1981) in this area examine aspects of two general questions:

1. To what extent is *proscribed* (intended or de jure) participation associated with *actual* (or de facto) participation?
2. To what extent is proscribed and/or actual participation associated with such *outcomes* as higher productivity, increased worker satisfaction, fewer grievances, or increased power for the working class?

Proscribed participation has been defined as referring to "all formal, written operative norms and rules governing the participation of various groups which result from the implementation of national laws, bargaining contracts, or managerial policies" (IDE, 1979, p. 274). It includes the various participative forms discussed in the taxonomy section.

Regarding actual participation, there are two main schools of thought. The first looks at participation as a resultant, the extent to which subordinates are able to *influence* decisions (or, more frequently, the extent to which they perceive themselves as influencing decisions). Many of the influence studies make use of Tannenbaum control graphs (e.g., Rus, 1970), which are based on respondents' responses to questions asking them how much "say" people at various organizational levels have with regard either to what happens in the organization *generally* or with regard to such *specific subjects* as task assignment. Influence studies typically make use of questionnaires.

The second approach views participation as a *decision-process* and is interested in how decisions are made, for example, by the boss, by subordinates, or jointly. Process, of course, is a behavior. Though some process studies involve questionnaires, they also include what I call "behavioral research."

Behavioral Research

Behavioral research consists chiefly of intensive studies, each of which looks at how WPM works in a small number of cases (usually just one). A few studies have included observation over years; when combined with interviews and historical records, the evolution of WPM in any one situation can be traced from its inception to the present. Some case studies are based largely on interviews and short plant tours (e.g., Eaton, 1979) whereas others make use also of available "hard" data such as production records or minutes of participative bodies (e.g., Rosenberg and Rosenstein, 1980).

More intensive case studies involve observation of participative bodies in action (for Dutch research, see Mulder, 1971; for a United States example, see Witte, 1980). Thus, Kolaja (1960) spent eight weeks in a Polish factory interviewing workers and managers and attending meetings of the workers council and then (1966) repeated his observation in two Yugoslavian factories, spending 4 weeks in each. Adizes (1971) also studied two factories, but for longer periods. Not only did he attend a broader range of meetings than Kolaja, but in each factory he was given a desk in a key department (legal in one and planning in the other), permitting him to observe decision making on a continuing basis, thus giving perhaps our most intensive view of WPM in action.

Obradovic (1975; see also Bertsch and Obradovic, 1979) and his colleagues observed workers council meetings in 20 companies over a 3-year period, accumulating data on over 900 hours of discussion. Coding their observations in great detail, eventually they were able to analyze 16,941 interactions.

Observational studies of this sort present difficulties. The observer's time is limited, so at best he can sample only a small portion of the activities of the organization being studied. Additionally, entree is always difficult. The most interesting organizations may be the ones that do not let you in; the ones that you can study may well not be representative.

Further, there is the problem of what to observe and record. Obradovic (1975) coded verbal interactions in workers council meetings, but according to Adizes (1971) some of the most important communications at these meetings took the form of low-level murmurs, body language, and facial responses. Finally, many decisions are made informally, in advance, making the discussion at the formal meeting merely a formality. Presumably none of this was recorded in Obradovic's statistics.

In an almost unique study, reminiscent of the Aston research, Espinosa and Zimbalist (1978) examined a stratified sample of 35 presumably worker-run firms that had been either expropriated or worker-seized during the Allende period in Chile. Key union and management informants were asked questions as to relatively objective factors, such as organization structure, attendance at meetings of participative bodies, productivity, accident rates, and the like. Unfortunately this remarkable study may be faulted for (1) relying excessively on somewhat biased observers, (2) mixing dependent and independent variables, and (3) basing its findings on a limited time frame and an unrepresentative sample.

Attitudinal Surveys

By contrast with case studies, which are based chiefly on observation and nonstandardized interviews, attitudinal surveys are based on standardized questions asked (either orally or in writing) of a variety of respondents, often at different organizations. The number of respondents is great enough and the alternate responses are sufficiently structured to permit quantification of the data. Among other issues, the questions relate to how much participation respondents have now, how much they want, their satisfaction with the participation, and their receptions of the behavior of others.

Unfortunately, "the predominant use of questionnaire and interview techniques in the study of mainly attitudinal–cognitive factors precludes deeper insights into the intensity of behavioral" change (Wilpert, 1975; p. 60) or the contingent factors (such as technology) affecting WPM success. Further, only a few studies permit comparisons, either among organizations that enjoy various degrees of participation or within given organizations before and after participation is introduced. Goodman (1979) provides one of the rare examples of a before and after study, here of the introduction of autonomous work groups by a joint union–management committee. In this study questionnaire data collected at five time periods is supplemented by "hard" (production, cost, accidents) data and actual observation.

There have been a variety of studies of desired and perceived actual participation (e.g., Tabb and Galin, 1970; Quinn and Staines, 1978; Wall and Lisheron, 1977; Witte, 1980; Rus, 1979), some of them based on nationwide samples. Nightingale (1979) compares 10 participative with 10 nonparticipative Canadian firms, collecting data from 50 respondents at 3 hierarchical levels in each firm.

More recently there have been several international studies comparing forms and extent of participation in various countries, each making use of an international team. Just organizing these international studies represented a participative triumph itself. Not only did the academicians concerned come from a variety of intellectual traditions, but measures had to be developed that would be appropriate in a wide variety of legal and industrial relations systems and that could be translated so as to be meaningful and equivalent in as many as ten languages.

Perhaps the first of these international teams, Tannenbaum, Kavcic, Rosner, Vianello, and Wieser (1974), made use of a number of measures, particularly the Tannenbaum control graph; thus making it possible to compare participation in three countries utilizing conventional management (the United States, Italy, and Austria) with two forms of WPM (the Israeli kibbutz and Yugoslavian self-management). Ten carefully matched factories were studied in each country. Members of this same team have joined with others in a new project, MPIO (Member Participation in Organizations), to compare matched participative and nonparticipative firms in six countries ($N = 70$ firms and approximately 3,500 respondents).

The Industrial Democracy in Europe (IDE) International Research Group consists of 25 scholars from 12 countries. Their study (IDE, 1981) involves 134 firms (matched as to technology) and nearly 9,000 individual respondents. This is not purely an attitudinal study because certain data were provided by "expert" respondents in each firm. However, respondents at all levels were asked a number of questions probing attitudes regarding issues such as actual and desired participation, satisfaction, and participation by others. A distinctive characteristic of the IDE study (as well as of Tannenbaum et al., 1974) is that WPM is viewed not in isolation but in terms of its impact on the distribution of power among organizational levels.

The work of the Decisions in Organizations group (DIO, 1979) is closely related to the IDE study. It involves overlapping questions and personnel. Its sample is smaller (three countries, seven firms, 988 respondents), but it is looking at some questions in greater depth. It employs longitudinal as well as cross-sectional measures and it observes decision making as well as asking questions about it.

Still another study, conducted by what has become known as the Vienna Center, was confined to automobile manufacturing, but covered 3,200 workers in 135 work places in 15 countries, including six behind the Iron Curtain (P. Jacob, Vez, Koval, Margulies, Rautalaiho, Rehak, and Weiser, in press). Again, though focused more on the impact of automation than on WPM as such, the survey asked numerous questions relating to participation.

Methodological Problems. Attitudinal studies are beset by methodological and conceptual problems. Many ask workers to indicate the extent and form of participation they *desire*. But answers to such questions are heavily subject to priming, salience, and attribution. Workers responses will be influenced by the rhetoric of their leaders, the values of their peers, and even by the way the question is worded (Salancik and Pfeffer, 1977).

Participation often takes on symbolic meanings and so the term evokes a broad range of connotations. As we have seen, in some European circles WPM means victory for the working class; in contrast, many United States labor leaders have learned to suspect it as a form of union busting. A French union, the CFDT, makes self-management a fundamental goal; not surprisingly, 82 percent of its leaders state that their preferred form of management would be one elected by the workers (Smith, 1977). But how deep a feeling is this? For decades the 30-hour week has been a widespread official United States union objective, yet rarely is it given high priority and many members of the few unions to win a 30-hour week have clamoured for guaranteed (but voluntary) overtime or second jobs. Until workers have a *real* need to make a choice, questions about priorities are not very meaningful. For workers who never have had any experience with substantial participation, questions as to desire for participation are essentially hypothetical. By contrast, the attitudes of workers in countries such as Germany or Yugoslavia, which already enjoy forms of participation, may be shaped by their particular experience and not indicate desire for participation in the abstract.

Responses may differ, depending on the context in which they are asked. More favorable responses may be given to formal survey questionnaires than in informal conversations with participant observers (Mulder, 1971). Daniel (1973) shows how workers may resist job enrichment in a collective bargaining context yet react highly favorably when asked about it in a different context 9 months later.

Small differences in the wording of questions may lead to substantial differences in response. Thus, Ramsay (1976) asked four different versions of essentially the same question regarding the desirability of participation at the company-wide level and got seemingly very different responses. Some day research should focus on these small differences, which have so great an effect. Or perhaps projective tests might be useful to uncover underlying perceptions and values.

Cross-national studies pose additional problem. According to Tannenbaum et al. (1974), United States workers report considerably less desire for participation (influence) than do those in Yugoslavia, even though in reported actual influence the two countries are roughly alike (with the United States making up in shop-floor informal participation what it loses in terms of plant-level formal participation). What does this apparent lesser United States desire for participation reflect? Are Yugoslav workers really so different? Does this difference reflect the fact that WPM plays a key role in Yugoslav national political ideology whereas it is less salient in the United States? Or, despite its apparent sophistication, does the authors' methodology try to compare the incomparable? How can the researcher determine whether a score of 4 on a seven-point scale means the same in one country as it does in another?

Questions as to actual (as opposed to desired) WPM face equal problems. If participation is won after a long fight (as codetermination was won in Germany), it may be more favorably evaluated than if it is merely a gift from a benevolent management (or a theory Y-oriented OD consultant) or imposed by the government. A good advertising program (or years of indoctrination, as in Iron Curtain countries) may persuade workers that they have more influence than they really have. Similarly, attention from visiting social scientists or newspaper publicity may make participation more salient to workers. On the other hand, unrealistic expectations as to what WPM may bring may lead to frustration and expressed dissatisfaction (Wilpert, 1975). It is possible, for example, that ideology has inflated Yugoslav workers' desire for participation, but the frustration they experience may reduce reported actual participation.

Given these problems, how does the researcher evaluate findings that Soviet workers report that they have "a lot of opportunity" to influence wage and production decisions (P. Jacob and Ahn, 1979); that Soviet unions score 90+ percent on perceived "adequacy," whereas capitalist unions rank much, much lower (B. Jacob, 1978); or that 80 percent of Russian auto workers are willing to take part in "decisions affecting the plant," as compared to 63 percent of Yugoslav workers, 34 percent of United States workers, and 24 percent of Swedish workers (Jacob and Jacob, 1979)? This latter study also finds perceived opportunities for participation to be greater in Czechoslovakia and the United States than in Yugoslavia and puts Sweden, home of the job-enriched assembly line, lowest of all. These findings, contrary to normal expectations, are not easy to explain.

A Caveat. The discussion that follows is based on the available evidence, but this is often sketchy and always incomplete. Many seemingly "hard" findings (based on large-scale attitude studies) are actually rather soft; only part of them are directed toward the critical issues. On the other hand, the behavioral research is often based on small, possibly nonrepresentative samples. Another problem: many of the original studies, especially of Germany and Israel, are not published in English. Consequently the discussion is based on English-language summaries.

WORKERS' PARTICIPATION AND OWNERSHIP: FOUR CASES

This section illustrates the chief problems faced by WPM as well as some of the major research approaches in this area. Space permits but four cases: (1) Israel exemplifies the range of WPM possibilities, from the relatively successful kibbutz cooperative farms to the relatively unsuccessful attempts to introduce WPM into firms owned by the country's dominant union. (2) By contrast with Israel's diversity, Yugoslavia has introduced workers self-management on a uniform basis as a matter of national policy. (3) Worker-owned, worker-managed producers cooperatives (PCs) exist in a variety of countries; some have been studied intensively. (4) Finally, we look at some examples of largely worker-owned firms, none of which enjoy substantial WPM; they are included here to illustrate the relative importance of worker ownership as contrasted to worker control.

Israel

Participation has a high value in Israel. Many early settlers were socialists; even nonsocialists were committed to common nation-building sacrifices. The discussion below deals with participation as it exists in three sectors of Israeli society: (1) kibbutzim or agricultural communes; (2) kibbutz industries, manufacturing operations run by the kibbutzim; and (3) manufacturing firms directly owned by Histadrut, the country's labor movement. The other forms of participation that exist in various cooperatives and the state and private sector industries will be ignored.

Kibbutzim. The 4 percent of the labor force who belong to kibbutzim represent the elite of Israeli society, contribute far more than their proportional share of the national leadership, and provide an ideological and behavioral model for the rest of society. In addition, there is a strong commitment to the value of hard physical labor as an end in itself.

Kibbutzim are highly equalitarian. Property is owned in common. Except for a small pocket money allowance, goods and services are allocated according to need. Communal dining rooms and nurseries are the norm. Nasty jobs and leadership positions are rotated, the first to prevent alienation, the second to avoid oligarchy.

Kibbutzim are small (averaging 200–300 members each), thus permitting a considerable amount of direct democracy. Daily work decisions are made either by elected committees (annually 50 percent of the membership serves on one committee or another) or by elected department heads, in consultation with other department members. More basic decisions are referred to weekly or monthly community-wide general assemblies.

Such is the ideal. In practice, there appears to be some erosion of these standards (Fine, 1973; Agassi, 1974). In some kibbutzim a revival of the nuclear family is occurring. Young people often reject their parents' strict ideals, try their wings in the outside world, and many never return. As kibbutz members get better educated, they become less enamored of physical labor. Technical skills are more and more required, and for technical jobs the norm of rotation is often ignored. In fact, most males become specialists, while women are often relegated to lower status domestic jobs. Volunteer and hired temporary laborers are excluded from the participative system.

Nevertheless, the basic ideals are still highly valued, and they are violated only at the cost of guilt, tension, and endless discussion.

Kibbutz Industries. Many kibbutzim engage in manufacturing, in part to earn extra income. Industrial plants are governed much like agricultural branches. Weekly or monthly assemblies of all members working in the plant make the major decisions not requiring approval of the entire community. Managers are elected, averaging 2–3 years in office before being rotated (Leviaton, 1978). Many managers do part-time physical work. Fifty percent of the membership belongs to one committee or another.

In practice, these ideals are violated more frequently than in farming (Agassi, 1974). Somehow factory work is seen as less ennobling than working with the soil. Further, the industrial kibbutz tends to have less of a sense of community than does its agricultural counterpart and it deals with a narrower, more technical range of problems (Rosner, forthcoming). Jobs are more specialized making rotation more difficult. Over 50 percent of the workers in many plants are hired nonkibbutz members who are excluded from self-government (though in some cases they have a separate union-like committee to represent their interests). Consequently "everyday life in some kibbutz plants . . . [is] nearly as undemocratic as the average plant anywhere" (Agassi, 1974, p. 70). Further, there are economic pressures for these plants to grow, despite the recognition that growth will further threaten the democratic ideal.

Despite these problems, kibbutz industries get high grades from Tannenbaum et al. (1974), who, however, confined their studies to plants in which all workers were kibbutz members. Compared to the other four countries studied, the kibbutz industries ranked highest on the Likert System 1–System 4 participativeness scale; its workers were least alienated and psychologically most healthy, and its managers were seen as most participative and supportive. On the other hand, workers felt that they themselves had less influence than did Yugoslav workers and only very slightly more than did American workers.

The kibbutz plants are the only group studied in which the workers "ideal" distribution of influence gives them more power than it gives management. All this means that kibbutz managers suffer: they are seen as having less power than those in the United States, Italy, or Yugoslavia (but more than in Austria).

Two other studies are relevant. On the basis of a comparison between six kibbutz plants and six matched conventionally managed Israeli plants, Melman (1971) concludes kibbutz plants "can be as efficient or more efficient, than managerial controlled units" (p. 212). In analyzing the impact of managerial rotation on kibbutz enterprises, Leviaton (1978) found that firms in which a high percentage of the work force consisted of present and former managers also tended to score high on various measures of economic efficiency, participativeness, and initiative-taking behavior.

Hevrat Ovdim. About 15 percent of the Israeli labor force work for plants owned by the national union, Histadrut. Theoretically this is very democratic. As union members, workers elect Histadrut's national council, which doubles in brass as the council for Hevrat Ovdim, the industrial division. In turn this council selects management. Thus, workers indirectly select their own bosses.

In practice, it doesn't make much difference. Not that elections are pro forma; quite the contrary, they are hotly contested. But the electorate consists of *all* Histadrut members, not just those working in union-owned plants; the issues are national party politics and members must choose from among slates representing the national parties; further, each slate runs at large so that no one person represents Hevrat Ovdim as such (Ben-Porat, 1979). All this reduces top leadership's sensitivity to shop-level concerns. Finally, not only is the union also management, but until the 1977 Begin government, the party controlling the union also controlled the government. The government was interested in reducing inflationary pressures, which in practice meant raising productivity and keeping a tight control over wages—neither typical union objectives. Contrasted with this was the ship-level "feeling that a worker employed in an enterprise that 'belongs to him' should be earning more than workers in other enterprises and not have to work so hard" (Tabb and Galin, 1970).

This might not make much difference were the Israeli industrial culture naturally participative; however, IDE (1981) ranked Israel and Italy as the lowest of the 12 countries studied on practically all of their many measures of worker and supervisory participativeness. Further, according to another study, Hevrat Ovdim managers exhibited a less democratic ideology than did managers of state and privately owned Israeli plants, perhaps because their experience with participation (discussed later) made them "disillusioned about the desirability of participative management" (Vardi, Shirom, and Jacobson, 1980).

In addition to voting for Histadrut's national leadership, workers elect a plant "workers committee" to handle grievances. Collective bargaining contracts themselves are negotiated on a nationwide basis through a process by which one section of the union in effect negotiates by itself, often without input from the workers involved. Workers committees behave like unions elsewhere, negotiating with local management over wages and working conditions and frequently using unauthorized strikes and slowdowns to bolster their position. [During 1960–1969, 76 percent of the strikes in the Histadrut sector were unauthorized, contrasted to only 39 percent in the private sector (Michael and Bar-El, 1977)]. Thus union ownership was irrelevant to shop-level behavior.

The Histadrut leadership was acutely aware of ironies involved: particularly for the older leaders this situation violated the socialist, equalitarian values they continued to espouse. The answer was to experiment with a series of forms of WPM. This would restore commitment to common objectives, raise productivity, and perhaps reconcile workers to the realities of a tough wage restriction policy.

Faced with the new state's need for dramatically increased productivity, in 1952 the order went out to establish shop-level Joint Productivity Councils in each enterprise. These were to seek means of "assuring cooperation between workers and management . . . increasing production and . . . determin[ing] appropriate methods of work." Though duly established, they were soon concerned primarily with negotiating piecework rates. Galin (1980) believes they make an "economic contribution by increasing efficiency and output" (1980, p. 185), but they hardly constitute kibbutz-style participation.

Having failed once, the Histadrut leadership tried again. This time the objective was to "turn the factories into social cells based on communal work, self-management and communal ownership" (Tabb and Galin, 1970, p. 103), the objective being primarily to reduce alienation (Galin, 1980). As a first step, half-labor, half-management Plant Councils were established with the authority "to discuss and decide all matters pertaining to the enterprise, except wages and social conditions" (Tabb and Galin, 1970, p. 104). Management engaged in "passive resistance" while works council discussions "often deteriorated into mutual accusations" (Galin, 1980, p. 186). By 1961 these Councils had petered out. Post mortems ensued, with the final decision being that another effort should be made, this time with more careful preparation.

The new attempt was called Joint Management. Again there were to be plant-level joint boards, this time accompanied by worker representatives on company-wide boards and some profit sharing. The first experiment with Joint Management largely failed (Tabb and Galin, 1970). Undaunted, Histadrut's top political leadership plowed on. By 1975, 32 Joint Managements has been set up. Galin and Tabb (1978, p. 20) summarize the results of two case studies: "The employees of both plants did not believe that there were any improvements due to the participating management, and even the most ardent supporters . . . could not point to a contribution of the joint managements to labour–management relations, worker morale or economic achievements."

So the experiment continues. Rosenstein (1977), once a sharp critic of Israeli participation, now concludes more moderately that "the program . . . reveals considerable variation in implementation. . . . Some boards are active and deal with important issues, while others merely have formal meetings and deal with marginal questions" (p. 119). But Agassi (1974, p. 78) calls it "an empty formality—if not . . . a bad joke."

What have been the main problems all along? Almost everything (Rosenstein, 1977; Tabb and Galin, 1970; Galin and Tabb, 1978). The various plans were initiated entirely by the top political leadership. Neither operational managers nor workers showed much enthusiasm. By the third time around, lack of enthusiasm turned to skepticism. Even at the beginning the expectations of the various parties differed; nevertheless, managers, engineers, technicians, and workers council members all suspected that participation would dilute their authority. Initial difficulties were compounded by political and ethnic rivalries. Rank-and-file workers were uninvolved. Unresolved differences arose with regard to distribution of profits.

"Yet participation plans are turned to repeatedly. One reason is undoubtedly the extent to which the residues of traditional ideology are yet part of Israel's political mythology" (Fine, 1973). Participation has become almost an exercise in nostalgia, an attempt to return to the days when Israel was smaller, its technology less complex, and its society more homogeneous. Alas, "the pioneering and intensely idealistic workforce of the early days has been replaced by newcomers for whom a Histadrut-owned plant is just another work place" (Rosenstein, 1977).

Some Lessons. Why was WPM more successful in the kibbutzim than in the Histadrut? Provisionally let me suggest that (1) kibbutzim were more autonomous and perhaps smaller; (2) WPM was introduced by the workers themselves, rather than from top-down; (3) plant-level WPM was extended to the shop; (4) there was no union to act as a rival power center; (5) workers rotated as managers; and (6) kibbutz members were much better educated and more ideologically motivated than the largely oriental workers in the Histadrut firms.

Yugoslavia

Yugoslavia is of interest not only because it involves an attempt to run an entire economy on a self-management basis but because of the exceptionally broad freedom given researchers during the 1960s and early 1970s. Yugoslav WPM research is probably richer than that of any other country.

Yugoslav self-management originated at the time of Tito's break with Russia in 1948. In an effort to win popular support for the break, Tito sought to reduce the typically tight centralized Stalinist controls that had been placed on the country immediately after the war.

Self-management initially meant that firms were allowed a certain amount of freedom in implementing plans set nationally. Over the years this freedom was enlarged. Individual enterprises were given increased discretion to choose what they would produce, to set prices, to allocate profits, and to select their own management. The share of profit claimed by the government declined, and each enterprise was set free to compete in a fairly unrestricted market—and increasingly against foreign competition. The main restriction was that since business property was "socially owned" by the *entire* society, individual enterprises were not permitted to sell their assets. To obtain money for expansion, they had to turn to the banks, thus making banks a major instrument of national planning.

Structure of Self-Management. Most of the published research was conducted during 1968–1973 (even if some is dated later), and the discussion that follows is based largely on this period.

During 1968–1973, the typical enterprise was organized as follows: The governing body is the Workers Council, of 30 to 120 members, elected on a rotating basis for 2-year terms, with (as in Israel) some restrictions to reelection that prevent oligarchy. The Council meets at least monthly. It elects a smaller Management Board and also appoints the plant Director, after an advertised search and some consultation with local authorities. In theory, the Council makes basic decisions, the Management Board the more routine ones, and the Director implements both. By contrast with the kibbutz, Directors are professionals, and many move from job to job.

Yugoslav firms tend to be larger than kibbutzim. Large enterprises are divided in Economic Units; each Unit elects its own Council, which makes Unit decisions (e.g., setting vacation schedules) and in some cases selects Unit management. Really important decisions, such as the annual production and investment plans, require successive approval of the Workers Council, the Unit Councils, and finally mass meetings of individual workers, often assembling on a department-by-department basis. In addition, the various councils spawn a number of committees, with perhaps 30 percent of the work force serving on some committee in any given year. Perhaps the most important of these is the Personnel Committee, which has the power to hire and discipline workers.

Finally, there are two other moderately important bodies: the League of Communists (the local unit of the governing party) and the union. Though most of the top enterprise leaders in fact belong to the League, the League as such played a rather low-keyed role in the plant during the early 1970s. Theoretically representing the interests of the larger society, it occasionally acts as a trouble-shooter, but mostly its role is to espouse values. Workers typically reported that it had much less influence than either the Workers Council or management (Rus, 1970). Unions, as we shall see, have less influence yet (Rus, in press).

Thus, except for fairly weak party and union organizations, the Yugoslav self-management structure closely approximates that of the kibbutz. The major differences relates to pay. The kibbutz is equalitarian. Yugoslav enterprises have pay differentials of 5 to 1 or more. Yugoslav pay consists of a number of complex elements: (a) base pay, set by job evaluation or by Council vote; (b) *individual* bonuses, based on performance; and (c) *Unit* and *enterprise* bonuses, depending on their respective profits. Each Unit serves as an accounting profit center; as production moves from one Unit to another, the sending Unit charges the receiving Unit a transfer price. Base pay, the allocation of profits among various uses, and inter-Unit transfer prices are all democratically determined, the latter technically requiring the concurrence of both sending and receiving departments (with elaborate provision for resolving deadlocks). All these details generate much paperwork and give participative bodies much to discuss.

How Workers Councils Operate. There is a voluminous evidence here. The ideal is that the Council's membership would reflect that of the work force generally. But, as Yugoslavian scholars keep rediscovering, skilled workers, managers, staff experts, League members, and well-educated people are more than proportionally represented—further, this disproportion increases over time (e.g., Jovanov, 1978; Baumgartner, Burns, and Sekulic, 1979). Actual participation tends to be even more elitist than membership in the Council itself. Though but 6 percent of the work force in the plants studied had college training, this group held the Council floor 65 percent of the Council time (Obradovic, 1975); similarly League members constituted but 13 percent of the workforce, but did 70 percent of the talking.

Actually different groups participate regarding different subjects, depending on their knowledge and interests. In a typical meeting, according to Kolaja (1966; see also Riddell, 1968), rank-and-file workers listened passively through management's presentation of the next year's production plan, then displayed a "lively reaction" to some new rules regarding incentive rate payments, but developed real enthusiasm only when debating the allocation of newly available apartment houses. More quantitative data confirms these observations (Obradovic, 1978). Marketing experts and top management dominate deliberations regarding marketing; participation regarding compensation issues is more evenly distributed with almost no correlation (.029; N = 1,825 individuals, 16,941 interactions) between the length of time any one individual spends discussing marketing and the time he spends discussing compensation (see also Wachtel, 1973: 91). Especially with regard to marketing and economic issues, the worker councillor's role is chiefly to ratify management's proposals (Ramondt, 1979).

Council sessions are often overloaded with trivia. The issues are often too complex for the average member to understand and rapid turnover of membership makes expertise difficult to develop. Sessions may last for up to 6 hours, well past dinner time. Council members become bored and side conversations are frequent. Attendance is often spotty, particularly because a high percentage of workers have second jobs. Except for a few activists who develop expertise, there are few rewards for Council membership. Further, fellow workers are likely to feel resentful when the Council votes against them. Given these frustrations, it is understandable that Obradovic (1970) found that Council members were more alienated than rank-and-file workers. Similarly, Yugoslav Council members have less "interest" in WPM and evaluate it less favorably than do their German counterparts; just the reverse is true at the rank-and-file level (IDE, 1981, Figures 8.6 and 8.7).

Contrasting Decision-Making Patterns. It would be misleading, however, to concentrate just on the Council's formal deliberations. As with legislative bodies everywhere, many of the important decisions are made behind the scenes. Further, there are sharp differences in decision-making patterns among organizations. Adizes (1971) provides a fascinating contrast between two textile firms that were similar in size and technology but very different in decision-making practices.

The Director of one firm, XYZ, was somewhat self-effacing. Major proposals were initiated in the Collegium, a group of top management officers, who might debate an issue for months in regular sessions before a rough consensus was reached. It would then be sent consecutively to (1) the Extended Collegium, a somewhat larger group including lower-level managers; (2) the Politikal Aktiv, which included key leaders from management, the Workers Council, the League, and the union; (3) meetings in the affected units; and finally to (4) the Workers Council for ratification. Substantial opposition at any level would hold the proposal up until appropriate modifications were made. But once a decision was made at one stage, those participating felt committed to defend it at later stages. Progress was slow, meetings were lengthy, and ideas were often dropped because consensus was not obtained. Agreement was particularly difficult regarding such issues as production work rates, transfer prices, and the transfer of work or workers from one department to another, all of which related to relative status and income.

To make the system work required political skills, manipulation of agendas, and much patience. Decisions were often delayed until crises made their logic overwhelmingly compelling. At worst, it sounds much like faculty self-governance; at best, like Japanese management.

The advantages of this system included high commitment and excellent communications (workers were observed debating plant investment issues on the bus and in social gatherings). Among the disadvantages were slow reactions to external pressures, perhaps heightened tension between groups, and decisional saturation (Alutto and Belasco, 1972) for some people. (Supervisors had to exert considerable pressure to round up workers for unpaid, after-work Zbor meetings.)

At a second firm, ABC, a young, charismatic director had important political connections in the community and with the local bankers. He initiated key decisions. His contacts with subordinates were on a one-to-one basis (rather than as a group), and he hired a much larger college-trained staff than in XYZ. Although decisions went through the same stages as in XYZ, meetings were formally conducted, with status differences much more obvious (top management had special, gold-plated coffee cups). The Director made his presentation, questions were answered, formal consent was obtained, and the meeting was fairly quickly adjourned. Though the Director was easily available to all levels of the work force, his rapid decision making short circuited the formal participatory process.

The results were as one might expect: quick decisions, but less development of middle management, poorer communications, technological change occurring faster than workers could be trained to handle, a high disciplinary rate, and a strike (by night-shift workers who failed to understand that their paycheck was low because the company had incurred a loss).

Which plant was more typical? To read Yugoslav sociologists, it was ABC. In several well-publicized cases (Adizes, 1971, p. 209–213), the Workers Council entered into a "contract" with its Director according to which the Council relinquished its power to interfere in operational management, in return for which the Director agreed to have this performance (and even compensation) judged strictly on results.

Staff and Middle Management. Self-management downgrades the legitimacy of the formal management hierarchy and makes managers uncertain of their roles. Even though workers councils can be manipulated, this takes time. Being weak in reward, coercive, and legitimate power, managers must rely heavily on their expert power. However, staff people resent being forced to make the often vain attempt to explain technical questions in language that the average worker can understand (Broekmeyer, 1977).

The Yugoslav system is highly legalistic. Each firm has a legal department. A "self-management lawyer" is normally present at every meeting to ensure that the rules are observed. Of the 12 countries studied by IDE (1981), Yugoslavia scored *by far* the highest on formalization, functional differentiation (Pugh, Hickson, Hinings, and Turner, 1968), and in the number of rules regulating participation.

Rather than undergo the frustration to make the rules work, managers are tempted either to pass the buck to the Council or to give only lip service to the rules (as Director ABC did). Either approach generates cynicism. Functional differentiation (i.e., the division of responsibility among middle managers) plus the need to use "illegitimate" means has the result that "effective influence and formal responsibility have been separated . . . top management remains the dominant group; it exerts influence without being subject to satisfactory control" (Rus, 1970, p. 160). (Although IDE, 1981, reports that Workers Councils exercise more influence than do directors, at least five others studies, including Tannenbaum et al., 1974, put directors first.)

Labor Relations. In theory, as a workers' state, Yugoslavia should be free of strikes. In fact, they are fairly common and have been extensively studied (Jovanov, 1978; Arzensek, 1978; Zupanov, 1973; Rus, in press). Strikes are often caused by the failure to consult a work group sufficiently before instituting a change (e.g., the night-shift strike at ABC). But on several occasions an entire plant (even management) has struck to protest high material costs or low prices for the product it makes.

From the Yugoslav point of view, strikes are illegitimate. Why should workers strike against themselves? On the other hand, given management's own shaky legitimacy and the ideological priority given workers' interests over management's, it becomes illegitimate for management to crush these strikes. Strikes are viewed as being caused by "bureaucratic deformations'' (Rus, in press) and are an embarrassment all around. (There is some similarity between Yugoslav and OD theory: both treat strikes as pathological occurrences to be cured by better communications.)

As a consequence neither side seeks an all-out battle. Most strikes are settled quickly. Few last more than a day; some consist merely of mass attendance at Workers Council meetings. Usually management concedes most of the workers' demands; sometimes all that is required is that management listens.

How about the union? As in other communist countries, Yugoslav unions are concerned chiefly with welfare and ceremonies, and at times the union and the personnel department are almost indistinguishable. Thus, the union plays little part in settling strikes; neither does the Workers Council. Third-party mediation, if any, comes from the political leadership in the outside community.

Attitudinal Impacts. Despite the problems mentioned earlier, self-management gave Yugoslav workers a sense of power and influence. Both Tannenbaum et al. (1974) and the IDE (1981) group placed Yugoslav workers first in terms of influence among the countries these groups studied. (Tannenbaum et al., 1974, put them even above kibbutz workers.) Apparently shop-floor ratification of major policy pays off, because of the 12 work groups studied by IDE, only Yugoslav workers were perceived to exert substantial influence on long-run issues. (Norwegian workers ranked higher on short-term, shop-level issues.) Yugoslav plants have the flattest control curves (Tannenbaum et al., 1974), and Workers Councils were the most influential of IDE's 12 national forms of participative bodies.

Though Yugoslav workers rank high on perceived influence, participation with regard to big issues does not translate into a participative immediate boss–subordinate relationship. Yugoslav managers are reported as being less participative than Danish (IDE, 1981), kibbutz, or United States managers (Tannenbaum et al., 1974). Neither has the opportunity to participate eliminated alienation or dissatisfaction. Yugoslav workers were the most alienated of those studied by Tannenbaum et al. (1974) and their job satisfaction is quite low compared to other countries (Jacob and Jacob, 1979, p. 35; Tannenbaum et al., 1974). Despite their relative sense of power and influence, few knew or cared much about what workers councils did (Riddell, 1968, p. 65–66; Kolaja, 1966, p. 60; Sachs, 1975). When asked how frequently they participated, the average response lay between ''very seldom'' and ''seldom'' (Rus, 1979, p. 226).

Although, as do workers in most other countries, Yugoslav workers expressed an abstract desire for more participation than they actually

had, their aspirations for equality declined during the experiences of the
1960s (Burt, 1972, p. 166). When asked *how* they would like to participate, over two-thirds wished "to be informed only" or "to discuss";
the percentage who wanted " to decide" or "to control implementation"
ranged from 12.5 to 31.1, depending on the issue (Rus, 1979, p. 232–233).
Although Yugoslav workers rate the consequences of participation higher
than do workers in other countries and a higher percentage of them are
willing to serve on participative bodies generally (IDE, 1981), the possibility of serving on such bodies was ranked as either fifth or sixth of
six possible sources of satisfaction (wages and physical conditions being
highest) (Obradovic, 1970). Further, the most frequently mentioned advantage of WPM was more equitable distribution of income (Burt, 1972).

Epilogue. During the early 1970s, self-management and Yugoslav society generally went through a crisis. As the economy became more
competitive and turbulent, it became increasingly obvious that the self-
management system had become too cumbersome. There was mounting
criticism that "technocrats" were usurping the power properly belonging
to workers. Competitive pricing and enterprise autonomy was widening
income differentials, not just within individual firms, but among firms
and above all among regions. (Income in the richest region was five times
per capita that of the poorest, and inequality was growing.) The capitalist
ethic of self-interest was triumphing over the socialist ethic of equality.
On top of this, Yugoslav leadership had additional concerns: student
unrest, rapid inflation, Tito's approaching death, and rivalry among
regions.

The early 1970s saw a substantial reassertion of central power. Cen-
sorship was tightened and dissidents were discharged or imprisoned. In
the economic sphere, the party's power was strengthened, plant autonomy was reduced, and measures of national planning (in the form of
"social compacts") were introduced to constrain unrestricted free market
competition. The shop Units, now renamed BOALs (Basic Organizations
of Associated Labor) were reorganized and in theory given more autonomy to plan their activities. The power and size of the enterprise-level
Workers Councils was cut back: now they were responsible chiefly for
coordination. Presumably BOALs' smaller size—ideally 300 workers or
so—would weaken the "technocracy" and permit direct democracy.
Finally, an effort was made to distinguish more sharply between the
executive responsibilities of management and the legislative responsibilities of the Workers Councils (Sachs, 1975). Overall, the net effect
was to weaken enterprise-level management (Wachtel, 1973, p. 95) and
to redirect participation to the shop level, where presumably it might be
more effective.

Reports to date (Sachs, 1975; Stephen, 1977; Miller, 1978) suggest that internal decisions are made faster under the new setup, but that coordination with other units is more complex and that the already existing paperwork and legalism has increased. Unfortunately, along with these changes, restrictions were placed on social scientists' freedom to operate in Yugoslav plants, thus stemming the flow of research.

Conclusion. Despite its problems, the Yugoslav experiment was fairly successful, at least up to 1972. It did much to transform a traditional, hierarchical society. GNP expanded rapidly. Growth was achieved with less stress than in most rapidly developing countries (Warner, 1975). Self-management acted as a safety valve, co-opting many potential dissenters and directing their energies toward safe plant-level issues. Further, self-management trained a whole generation of managers (Dunlop, 1958), a considerable accomplishment, even if homegrown managers become less needed as a college-trained generation takes over. Even if there was not "complete participative management," there was "managed participation" (Warner, 1975).

WPM may have given an opportunity to participate in a fairly meaningful way for most of those who wanted it. Perhaps we should be more impressed by the substantial numbers of rank-and-file workers who participated actively (or even learned silently) during workers council meetings—than by data suggesting these meetings were in fact controlled by small elites. Even for those with little desire to participate, WPM may have had an important symbolic meaning. Possibly "participation diminishes the meaninglessness of work, although it does not diminish the powerlessness of the worker" (Broekmeyer, 1977, p. 139)—this, despite findings of high alienation and dissatisfaction among these very workers.

Yet as of 1973, Yugoslav self-management still had some serious problems to solve: (1) The relationship between bottom-up participation and top-down management had yet to be resolved. All roles were diffuse and conflict ridden (though Rus, in press, calls this a strength). Councils still had not learned to develop an independent expertise. Workers still viewed managers as all powerful, even though managers themselves felt hamstrung by participative red tape. (2) There was little evidence of participation with regard to shop-level problems. (3) Communications between Workers Council members and their constituents remained poor. (4) Inadequate mechanisms had been developed for resolving the conflicting interests of individual workers, the enterprise, and society generally. (5) Yugoslav self-management seemed to work best in a stable environment where product mixes and prices changed infrequently. Under these circumstances, production efficiencies could accumulate. With a rapidly changing environment, the WPM system became overloaded.

(6) Finally, Yugoslavia may have been suffering from what OD people call "plateauing," a loss of initial enthusiasm after early problems are solved and more difficult ones emerge.

Producers Cooperatives

Producers Cooperatives (PCs) are worker-managed, worker-owned organizations (the terms "worker-managed" and "worker-owned" are both somewhat fuzzy and, as shown later, there are numerous cases that are only marginally PCs).

Israeli kibbutz are PCs and, in a way, so is Yugoslav self-management; but our concern here will be chiefly with PCs in the United States and Britain, plus two fairly unique PCs, Mondragon in Spain and Dynavac in Australia. PCs also exist in France and Italy (Oakeshott, 1978), and others were sponsored by revolutionary regimes in Peru (Berenbach, 1979), Chile (Espinosa and Zimbalist, 1978), Algeria (Clegg, 1971), and elsewhere.

American PCs date back to the early pioneers. Jones (1979) has identified 458 manufacturing PCs about which some data are available. Many were established as social or religious communes (with all property shared) whereas others had more purely economic ends. Most were short-lived, but some lasted 20 years or more.

Scholarly attention has been devoted to two sets of surviving "old" cooperatives: a group of plywood companies established in the Pacific Northwest during 1939–1955 (Bellas, 1972; Berman, 1967; Bennett, 1979) and a group of San Francisco scavenger companies (Perry, 1978; Russell, Hochner, and Perry, 1979). The PC approach also has been utilized to prevent plant shutdowns. These "plant rescue" cases have been intensively studied and will be discussed separately. Also, there is IGP (International Group Plans), an insurance company in which workers own half the shares, elect half the company board, help select managers and have extensive democratic rights regarding office-level problems (Zwerdling, 1979). Finally, there have been a number of generally short-lived "alternative institutions" or communes, such as food and farming cooperatives, legal collectives and craft communes. Generally these participant owned and managed organizations have been founded by counterculture members. They are highly equalitarian and antibureaucratic (Rothschild-Whitt, 1979; Berger, 1981).

PCs have an equally long history in Britain, and British scholars have found them of continuing interest (e.g., Jones, 1977; Oakeshott, 1978; Pateman, 1970). The early PC movement peaked around 1905, but one firm founded in 1874 still survives (Jones, 1977). Two of the better-known, more recent firms, the John Lewis Partnership (Flanders, Pomeranz, and Woodward, 1968) and the Scott Bader Commonwealth (Blum, 1968) were founded by paternalistic owners who transferred formal ownership to their workers. Under the recent Labour Government, three new PCs were established, as in the United States, to prevent depressed firms from being shut down (Oakeshott, 1978). Despite some government support, two of these have died and the third, Triumph Meriden, barely survives.

Mondragon is the great PC success story (Johnson and Whyte, 1977). Founded in 1956 under the guidance of a Basque priest, this PC federation is highly profitable and growing rapidly. It now has over 18,000 workers and is continually spawning new offshoots. Besides its success, three things make Mondragon unique. In the first place, it is a "pure" PC in that all employees (and only employees) are owners. Second, each new employee must make a significant investment (some of which may be borrowed) when hired; afterwards each employee's share of the profits is kept in a reserve fund until he leaves or retires. Finally, Mondragon is supported by a "shelter" organization (Vanek, 1975a) consisting of three affiliates: (1) a large, growing credit union that generates capital for investment, develops new PCs, and provides general technical assistance, (2) a school system to provide managerial and technical training, and (3) a League for Education and Culture, to provide ideological support.

Mondragon's governmental structure is less unique. The members annually elect a small Managing Board, which in turn selects the general manager and other key members of management. A somewhat larger elected but ineffective Social Council is supposed to advise the Management Board. Shop-level supervision is somewhat traditional, although there have been some experiments with autonomous work groups.

Finally, there is Dynavac, a 30-employee firm specializing in vacuum equipment (Cupper, 1980), with a highly unconventional government structure. There are no managers. Each member has a job description or "responsibility list." Within his area of responsibility, he is the boss. Anyone with a problem or suggestion that concerns the organization as a whole indicates this on a centrally posted "agenda" sheet. On Thursday, those who are interested in the week's supply of agenda items meet to discuss these. (Attendance varies from 0 to 20 employees.) The Group (as it is called) passes its recommendations on to a weekly General Meeting of all employees, which in turn makes the final decisions. Roughly, this procedure is applied to all organization decisions, including performance evaluation, salary setting, and discipline. The norm is that all members actively participate in the management process (not just sit through meetings). Those who fail to do their share receive a negative performance evaluation from their peers. Three individuals have been expelled for inability to work without close supervision and others have found self-management so distasteful that they have resigned. So this is a self-selected group, but it seems to work.

Purity and Degeneration. One could argue that in "pure" PCs (1) *all* workers should be owners, *only* workers should be owners, and ownership should be equally shared; (2) management should be democratically elected with each member having an equal vote, and (3) there should be a high level of participation in all decisions, big or little (Jones, 1980). Bernstein (1980) adds several additional requirements: (4) profit sharing among workers; (5) widespread dissemination of essential information; (6) guaranteed "basic political liberties"; (7) an independent appeals board to handle grievances; and (8) a "democratic consciousness." In practice, PCs vary greatly. Only Mondragon and some counterculture PCs appear to meet the first two criteria and none meet all eight.

Beginning with the Webbs (Webb and Webb, 1920), it has been widely argued (Bernstein, 1980; Vanek, 1975a; McGregor, 1977) that PCs have a tendency to "degenerate" over time, that is, to abandon the principle of worker ownership and control, and also to become economically less successful. These separate but related problems are discussed in the following sections.

Ownership. Many PCs have considerable nonworker ownership. Even where ownership is originally widely distributed among the work force, the percentage of nonowners in the work force tends to rise over time. Present owners are reluctant to share the profits with newcomers. As in the Israeli kibbutz, nonowners are hired, initially on a temporary basis but eventually permanently. Nonowners become second class citizens and eventually the spirit of cooperation is lost. This process may be accelerated by technological changes, which increase status differences within the work force. Thus, technological changes in San Francisco scavenging, such as centralized billing and containerized collection, contributed to the decision to retire stock, as owners left the business, rather than to sell it to newcomers who would work only on unskilled jobs.

On the other hand, the percentage of owners who are not workers may also increase. If PCs are successful, the value of their stock goes up, making it harder for new owners to buy in; eventually retiring owners may be allowed to sell their interests to outsiders. A partial solution to this problem is a requirement that only workers may own stock. Stock of retiring members can be bought out at a fixed price, and new workers may buy their stock on an installment plan. Alternatively, ownership may be held by some sort of trust (as in Dynavac, Scott Bader, and IGP), which eliminates individual ownership altogether. Ownership, of course, helps foster commitment. Beyond this, without selling some sort of stock, it may be difficult to obtain the capital to start the business or to permit growth. Retained profits may be insufficient (and at first are zero) and outside financing is often problematical.

Present Earnings Versus Investment. According to some observers, PCs tend to underinvest (Jones and Backus, 1977; Vanek, 1975b). Workers vote themselves high wages or take out their profits as dividends, rather than invest the substantial capital required for growth and modernization. In economic terms, capital is underrewarded and undersupplied; thus, labor is substituted for capital and the firm operates at a point of increasing returns to scale.

As a partial solution to this problem, the constitution of some British PCs requires that most profits be reinvested (Oakeshott, 1978). Another partial solution is not to rely so exclusively on owner investment and instead to obtain outside financing. Yet commercial banks are reluctant to invest in strange organizational forms. So "shelter organizations" that can provide financial (and also technical) support become important. Mondragon's success is due in part to its allied credit union, which generates the steady stream of capital its factories require. There are somewhat similar financial and advice-giving organizations in several European countries.

Governance. To what extent do worker–owners really run their companies? To what extent are they able to fend off Michel's iron law of oligarchy? The evidence we have is very limited (Abell, forthcoming). Dynavac suggests that town-meeting participation is possible in small, technologically advanced firms. In plywood PCs, all directors are worker–owners; these in turn appoint a manager who typically is not an owner. The fact that there is a high turnover of such managers suggests that the worker–owners retain control. All major decisions are made by a general membership meeting. Communications between directors and rank-and-file workers appear good and there is continuous shop-floor discussion of production problems (Greenberg, 1978; Bennett, 1979). In both Dynavac and the plywood PCs, workers take on substantial responsibility both for making difficult personnel decisions and for keeping themselves informed about organizational matters generally. By contrast, managerial level employees now dominate the boards in scavenger PCs, though elections may be hotly contested and worker–owners feel they have considerably more "say" than do comparable workers in other firms (Russell et al., 1979).

Scott Bader and John Lewis, the two well-known British PCs founded by benevolent owners, both provide an elaborate framework of committees, councils, and assemblies in which workers could take part (e.g., Scott Bader holds semiannual meetings for all members at which any subject of interest can be *discussed*). However, the power of these participatory bodies is so restricted that their role in primarily advisory. The Managing Director appoints a majority of the board in both cases. Limited and perhaps outdated evidence (Pateman, 1970), suggests that in neither case is there much worker participation in shop-floor or company-wide problem solving. In fact, white-collar workers and management seem to dominate the elaborate constitutional apparatus (Jones, 1977).

Similarly, Bradley (1980) concludes that worker directors had limited communications with the rank and file in two recent PCs established by the radical left: Manuest in France and *Scottish Daily News* in Britain. In both cases there was also "considerable doubt" whether even the directors controlled the firms' daily activities.

Communications between the rank and file and the Management Board in Mondragon's largest unit were reported as poor; the Social Council "serves mainly as a channel of communications from management to workers and does not provide a channel through which workers can influence management" (Johnson and Whyte, 1977, p. 25). But even the Management Board was powerless "because the managers have a near-monopoly of knowledge. . . . It is impossible for [the Management Board] which meets monthly to keep abreast . . . and provide any countervailing power" (Eaton, 1979, p. 36). So, in the largest Mondragon unit, "the ostensibly very democratic governing structure has become a sick joke" (Eaton, 1979, p. 34). But changes may be underway (Stern, private communication).

The situation at IGP, the insurance company, is somewhat different. Corporate-wide decisions regarding finance and marketing are made rather conventionally, but there are hot contests for the board of directors. Decisions regarding discipline and work procedures (e.g., installation of computers) are made democratically and somewhat chaotically (Zwerdling, 1979).

U.S. counterculture communes place high values on democracy, equality and decision-making by consensus. The typical commune spends countless hours discussing problems of governance (Rothschild-Whitt, 1979) yet few last long. Among their main problems (Gamson and Levin, 1980) are (1) inability to agree on common and appropriate decision-making norms, especially with regard to the legitimate use of authority, the handling of deviant behavior, and the productive use of meeting time, (2) lack of a common culture, and (3) lack of technical skills.

Evaluation. How successful have PCs been? The picture is somewhat mixed. Many of the more profitable ones have transformed into more conventional companies as ownership has fallen into the hands of non-workers and as higher management has eliminated democratic controls.

PCs remaining loyal to their principles have had problems of their own. Many have been slow to expand, either by investing new capital or by hiring new workers. On the other hand, Mondragon, spurred on by its credit union staff experts, has grown rapidly and even established a research lab.

How about technological change? Back in 1920 the Webbs argued that PCs were "perpetually tempted to maintain existing processes unchanged" (Webb and Webb, 1920, p. 68). The evidence (summarized in Jones, 1980) as to this is mixed. Certainly PCs tend to be small, many are in labor-intensive industries, and some utilize obsolete equipment and technology. On the other hand, the United States scavenger and plywood PCs have generally adjusted to technological changes in their industries. Still, Aldrich and Stern (1978) may be right: PCs may survive best in stable industries, with little technological change, where craftsmen predominate.

PCs' reluctance to accept either new members or new risks may contribute to "self-strangulation" (Jones, 1980). According to Jones (1979), the typical United States PC goes through a three-stage life cycle: first, both total employment and the number of worker–owners increases; second, the number of worker–owners declines, while total employment continues to grow; finally, employment also decreases and the firm dies. Some observers note a tendency to self-strangulate at age 20–30, though this has not been systematically demonstrated (Abell, forthcoming).

Nevertheless, comparisons between PCs and capitalist forms "do not seem to indicate a markedly different failure rate" (Abell, forthcoming). After all the mortality rate of small firms is always high. A number of cases (e.g., Bellas, 1972; Jones, 1980) suggest that at least in their earlier years PCs' labor productivity, profitability, and income per worker is higher than their capitalist counterparts; so is their owner–workers commitment to the organization (Russell et al., 1979; Greenberg, 1978).

Finally, there is fairly good evidence (Bellas, 1972; Jones, 1979, 1980) that, comparing PCs as a whole, those that come closest to the "pure" PC ideal tend to survive longer and to be more successful by a variety of economic criteria (but see Abel, forthcoming).

To conclude, PCs probably meet important noneconomic needs for *some* workers. Preserving worker ownership and control may be a more difficult problem than the maintenance of economic efficiency (Chaplin and Cowe, 1977). With some care, PCs may work, at least in some niches of the economy. But IGC, Dynavac, and the plywood PCs are among the few cases in which workers substantially contribute to management decision making.

Finally, I should emphasize that the data with regard to PCs is sketchy, noncomparable, and in some cases (e.g., with regard to Scott Bader, John Lewis, and perhaps Mondragon) out-of-date. Some of the findings (e.g., regarding PC life cycles) are based on historical data that are particularly sketchy. Only the plywood PCs have been studied in any real depth.

Ownership Without Control

PCs involve worker ownership *and* control. What is the relative significance of these two elements? We already have evidence as to the attitudinal and behavioral impacts of various forms of worker control. Here we examine the impacts of ownership, taken alone.

Theory suggests that even without control, worker ownership should lead to improved motivation, productivity, satisfaction, and labor relations. (1) Presumably the interests of the worker owners will be congruent with those of the organization itself. Thus, greater efforts will lead to greater economic rewards. (2) Ownership should lead to greater commitment, particularly if workers have voluntarily sunk some of their savings into the firm. Commitment should lead to greater efforts to prove the commitment decision was a right one and also to beliefs supportive of this commitment. (3) If other workers are owners, peer pressure should lead to harder work. (4) Resistance to change should be reduced. (5) Participation in decision making will be viewed as more legitimate by both workers and management. (6) Finally, because workers have a vested interest in company success, labor–management relations should improve.

Some data as to the impact of worker ownership is provided by six well-studied cases in which employees have helped buy plants that parent countries had threatened to shut down. Four are in the United States: Vermont Asbestos Group (Johannesen, 1979), a furniture factory (Stern, Wood, and Hammer, 1979; Hammer and Stern, 1980), a knitting mill (Zwerdling, 1979), and a lathe manufacturing company (Survey Research Center, 1977); the fifth, a trucking firm, is Canadian (Long, 1978a, 1978b, 1979); and the last, Hart, a solar heating firm, is Australian (Goldstein, 1978). (For summary articles, see Zwerdling, 1979 and Long, 1980.) Unfortunately, different variables were studied in these six plants, so detailed comparisons are difficult.

The six companies varied considerably as to the proportion of stock owned by blue-collar workers, white-collar workers, managers, and outside interests. Two firms were 100 percent *employee* owned, but much of this ownership was by managers. Of the five cases about which data are available, only at Vermont Asbestos was a majority of the stock *worker* owned, and there only 51 percent. In none of these cases did the money to buy the plant come primarily from workers. Most of it was loaned by banks and government agencies, subject to various restrictions, including specifically in one case that professional management keep control.

In none of the six cases were plans made for worker participation. In fact, the new arrangements were put together with such haste that little thought was given to internal governance. The motivation was to save jobs and radical new ideas might have scared off financial supports. Though workers were elected to three of the company boards, in no case were they in the majority. Even those who were elected were subject to co-optation. The seven hourly paid workers on the asbestos board kept its deliberations secret, despite some rank-and-file desire to know how each director voted (Johannesen, 1979). None of the reports suggest any special effort to involve rank-and-file workers in decision making.

Under these circumstances, these companies provide a fairly good test of the impact of ownership without control. But note that except for Hart, worker ownership had lasted for less than 2 years at the time of the studies. The initial results may be biased by worker euphoria: even though they may not have participated in management, they had participated in a successful effort to save their jobs. Interestingly, the study at Hart, conducted in the fourth year of worker ownership, when the plant was losing money, showed some signs of disillusionment.

What are the results of the various studies? Profits improved initially in all six cases, in some cases dramatically (Long, 1980; Goldstein, 1978; Survey Research Center, 1977; Johannesen, 1979). Worker productivity improved in four cases, turnover declined in two (Long, 1980; *Wall Street Journal,* May 31, 1978; Survey Research Center, 1977), with evidence as to the other plants not being available. Of course, part of the reported improvement may be explained by the fact that these plants had been neglected by the old management and the new managers had more independence. Yet, comparing three plants with varying degrees of employee ownership, Long (1980) concludes that improved economic performance is directly related to the degree of ownership.

Conte and Tannenbaum (1978; Survey Research Center, 1977) studied some 98 employee-owned firms. In 21 of these, workers owned half the equity; in 47, employees were on the Board of Directors. Profits, as a percentage of sales, in this group were 50 percent higher than for comparable firms in their respective industries. Further, the higher the proportion of equity owned by workers, the higher the profits. However, once employee ownership was controlled, there was a small, insignificant negative relationship between profitability and having employee directors.

Attitudes were reported to have improved in three firms (Long, 1980; Survey Research Center, 1977), but not in a fourth (Long, 1980). Most workers felt that conditions had become better under the new arrangements and that teamwork had increased. Managers were seen to communicate better and to be more considerate. Half the workers in one case perceived some increase in influence (Long, 1979); by contrast, 68 percent of the lathe company workers saw no changes in decision making (Survey Research Center, 1977, p. 54).

Two studies find that shareholders have more positive attitudes regarding such dimensions as involvement, integration (Long, 1980), challenge, and responsibility (Goldstein, 1978) than do nonshareholders. But in one company this difference in attitude depended largely on holding $100 or more of stock (Goldstein, 1978). The attitudes of small holders were much like those of nonshareholders.

Though workers generally believed that change in ownership had increased their influence, there was general agreement that management's influence remained higher than theirs (Long, 1979; Hammer and Stern, 1980). Managers were felt to "own" the plant more than did workers, with little correlation between worker sense of ownership and their actual ownership of stock (Hammer and Stern, 1980). There was little feeling of psychological partnership. Interestingly, management perceived greater change in the power relationship than did workers (Survey Research Center, 1977; Long, 1979).

Are workers satisfied with their relative lack of power? As do workers almost everywhere, the workers studied here would like some slight increase in their influence (Long, 1979); nevertheless, they felt that management should retain the greatest power regarding production and policy decisions while the union should be most powerful regarding wages (Hammer and Stern, 1980). Indeed the less alienated workers were, the more they wanted management to be powerful. Blue-collar workers preferred to exert their power through their union, not through a participative group; white-collar workers had greater interest in participation as such.

Why didn't blue-collar workers give higher priority to participation? One possible reason is that most of the workers were fairly skilled; perhaps they already had all the shop-floor autonomy they wanted (Hammer and Stern, 1980). A second reason is that there was little preparation for participation in higher level decision making. Neither management nor the institutional arrangements encouraged it. The workers had no available model of self-management. Nor had they any training in making the technical decisions self-management requires.

As mentioned earlier, the behavioral science research on the United States and Canadian cases was based on the first 2 years of workers ownership. Zwerdling (1979, p. 78), a journalist dedicated to self-management, reports recent signs of disillusionment in several of these cases. His (possibly unrepresentative) respondents are unhappy because the change in ownership has not led to greater change in worker–management relations. "People are happy their jobs were saved and the company is doing well . . . and there is no great drive for change. . . . On the other hand, insiders say, many workers *do* have a vague if inarticulated demand for greater involvement in participation—and they feel frustrated they've been denied it."

At the Vermont Asbestos Group, the Board of Directors ignored a negative stockholder vote and invested company money in a new subsidiary; whereupon a number of workers sold their stock to an outside investor. The outside investor became president and the workers earned a large profit. The lathe company suffered a 9-week strike in 1979. The union is suing the company to restore the workers' rights in a conventional pension plan, which they had surrendered in return for worker ownership. "Productivity in the plant has steadily declined during the last two years after a 25 percent spurt at first" (*Wall Street Journal*, December 8, 1980, p. 22).

To conclude, while there is some evidence that worker-owned companies can be more efficient than conventionally owned companies, at least in their first years, there are few signs that worker ownership generates an inevitable dynamic for greater participation. Indeed after the effect of the initial participative act of assuming ownership has been dissipated, plateauing and disillusionment may set in. Because many of the arguments for ownership assume participation, unless some special efforts are made to gain participation, the payoff from worker ownership may be limited. An effort is being made to avoid these problems at Rath, the packinghouse firm, now being launched into worker ownership. Here a variety of techniques are being utilized to increase participation at various organizational levels (Gunn, 1980).

WPM AND THE AFFECTED PARTIES

This section seeks to draw some generalizations from the four sets of case studies just discussed and also from the experience in other countries, especially Germany, Sweden, and Britain.

If representative participation is really to increase worker influence over managerial decisions, a whole series of new formal and informal relationships must be developed. A new organization is required, the joint worker–management participatory body (PB); and a new role must be created, that of worker representative on the participatory body. Older roles must change, too, particularly those of union and management.

What Participatory Bodies Do

Except for the smallest organizations, every WPM scheme has a participatory body, which includes worker representatives that are either directly elected by the workers themselves or appointed by the unions. Most of the participation in representative WPM occurs in PBs, yet most reports describe formal charters or attitudes toward WPM rather than what actually happens in PBs themselves. Often there is a wide gap between the PB's formal function and authority, as described in its charter, and what it does in practice. Some PBs are almost inert; others are in fact quite powerful.

PC boards and Yugoslav Workers Councils have been discussed already. Here we deal with three other PB forms: (1) Joint Consultative Committees (JCCs), whose function is primarily advice and consultation; (2) Works Councils—the best examples of which are in Germany—operating at the plant level, which have joint decision-making power (e.g., the power to block specific personnel actions); and (3) company boards containing worker directors selected to represent the rank-and-file workers. Each type varies in its effectiveness and each has unique problems.

Joint Consultative Committees. JCCs are common in a number of countries; (for British cites, see Jones, 1977; for a United States case, see Witte, 1980). Typically their mandate is open-ended: to deal with subjects of common interest to labor and management. Worker representatives may make suggestions whereas management is expected to keep the committee informed about important developments affecting the work force generally and sometimes to seek the committee's advice before taking action.

Some committees have broad formal jurisdictions but real power in only limited subsidiary areas. "Enterprise committees" in France have merely consultative and information-getting power over most topics but are solely responsible (with a budget) for certain welfare activities (e.g., canteens) and jointly responsible for company medical services (Sturmthal, 1964; Harrison, 1976). Scanlon Plan committees in the United States provide another example of successful limited-purpose committees. Their function is to process worker suggestions for increasing productivity, and their success results largely from the associated bonuses, which provide a strong economic incentive to make the Plan work.

By and large, general purpose JCCs have exerted little influence. In the first place, in unionized companies their jurisdiction is typically confined to non-"strategic" matters not subject to collective bargaining (but collective bargaining tends to be less all-encompassing in Europe than in the United States). By contrast, in nonunion companies, JCCs may perform some of the personnel-representative functions of a union (Witte, 1980).

Second, because JCCs lack the power to block management's actions, their influence may depend on management's faith and good will. Given management's interest in preserving its prerogatives, it often restricts the committee's scope to trivial matters of no great importance to either workers or management. (For a discussion of techniques management uses to downgrade committees, see Lammers, 1967, p. 210.)

A third reason for JCCs' limited success is that the parties fail to agree on their mission. Management expects them to help solve production, safety, housekeeping, and similar problems, whereas workers want them to deal with grievance and labor relations issues not subject to collective bargaining. Because neither side is interested in what the other is saying, not much gets done (de Bellecombe, 1968; Tabb and Galin, 1970; Legendre, 1969).

Thus, although committees are often established with high hopes, there is a tendency over time for fewer significant topics to be assigned to them, for attendance to drop, and for meetings to be convened less often until finally the committee becomes completely inactive. This was seen to occur in Israel. Much the same happened in India (Tanic, 1969). In England, committees flourished during the two world wars, but atrophied afterward as shop steward committees took over their functions (Clarke, Fatchett, and Roberts, 1972; Bullock Report, 1977). Production committees in the United States during World War II suffered the same fate, although there have been some efforts to revive these, especially in steel and autos (de Schweinitz, 1949; Gold, 1976). Kochan, Dyer, and Lipsky (1977) report that it is difficult to keep health and safety committees going in the United States.

These union–management constraints help explain United States and British studies finding "that the consultative machinery was of prime importance [only] where union organizations were weak and management was human-relations oriented" (Clarke et al., 1972, p. 80; see also Derber, 1955, p. 80). Indeed JCCs play a key role in several paternalistic examples of qualified industrial democracies, such as Glacier (Jaques, 1951; Kelley, 1968), Scott Bader, and John Lewis (previously discussed).

The implicit assumption behind most consultative systems is that the subjects with which they deal are those regarding which workers and management share common interests and that, therefore, committee deliberations will occur in a nonadversary atmosphere. Recently, however, as European unions have become more assertive, many have attempted to transform consultation into bargaining. Thus, in Sweden, purely advisory committees largely atrophied during the 1960s (Peterson, 1968), but now that they have been given some real power they work reasonably well. At Kockums and Fiskeby, for example, shop- and plant-level committees participate in such decisions as the introduction of new equipment and even in the selection of management (Gunzberg, 1978). To the extent such committees in fact exercise joint control, they transform themselves into what I call works councils.

Works Councils. The distinction I have drawn between JCCs and works councils is that the former are primarily advisory whereas the latter have significant power to block management's actions (i.e., management cannot go ahead without the PB's approval). Like many other WPM distinctions, this one may be more theoretical than practical because many PBs are advisory with regard to some subjects and have veto powers with regard to others. Further, we have the Swedish case where management is merely required to "negotiate" with the labor–management committees; presumably after negotiating it has the right to go ahead without committee approval, but it rarely does so.

Works councils in Germany have been studied more intensively than in other countries (for summaries, see Furstenberg, 1981; Wilpert, 1975). In Germany, the works council assent is required before management can make major changes in a wide variety of personnel areas: work and leave schedules, piece rates and other pay schemes, selection, training, safety, suggestion systems, and welfare services. Its approval is also required before management can introduce technological change affecting the "work place, work flow, or work environment" (Furstenberg, 1981). The jurisdiction of Swedish committees is even broader. It includes "any important change of the working or employment conditions."

Apparently some works councils are largely ineffective, but others, particularly those in larger plants and with better trained council members, tend to be quite powerful (Logue, 1978; Hartmann, 1979). In fact, they and management jointly make all decisions likely to affect workers' welfare. "As time passes, interaction between management and the works council seems to have gained in scope and depth" particularly with regard to managements' "drive toward advanced mechanization and attendant measures of personnel administration. Councillors are now drawn increasingly into functional committees established by management to cope with major problems" (Hartmann, 1979, p. 79). "The administration of social welfare services, supervision of working conditions . . . and, in particular, the selection of workers who have to be discharged in cases of lack of work are examples of works council's activities which management considers to be useful" (Furstenberg, 1981, p. 15).

Technically, at least in Germany, works council members are elected by the workers, not appointed by the unions. In practice, a majority of most works council members have close union ties. Nevertheless, as we shall see, the relationship between works councils and the union is not free from tension.

In powerful works councils, being a works council member in practically a full-time job and works council members have offices and even staffs of their own on company premises (Hartmann, 1979). To the United States observer, their function seems somewhat like that of the shop committeeman in the United States auto industry, who also has a full-time, company-paid position. Indeed, German works councils deal with matters that are subject to plant-level collective bargaining in the United States. The main difference is that United States plant-level labor relations are covered by company-wide and plant-wide contracts, usually negotiated at 3-year intervals. Because these contracts cover most major issues, in theory at least the parties merely interpret them. Works council labor relations tend to be more ad hoc, dealing with each problem on its merit as it comes up. Regardless, works councils may have more control over production rates than have United States unions (Herding, 1972).

Worker Directors. In seven European countries (Germany, France, Luxembourg, Austria, Norway, Sweden, and Denmark), the law requires some sort of worker representation on the boards of directors of at least some large companies (in most of these countries, the representatives sit on *supervisory boards;* these in turn elect *management boards* that run the company on a day-to-day basis). In all cases except the German iron and steel industry, the worker directors constitute only a minority of the board; in France, they are merely observers. In Britain, worker directors serve on the boards of several nationalized industries and in some private companies.

Worker directors have received a good deal of research attention (see particularly Batstone, 1976) with individual studies being done in Germany (Furstenberg, 1978), Norway (Engelstad and Quale, 1977), Sweden (National Swedish Industrial Board, 1976), Denmark (Westenholz, 1979), and Britain (Brannen, 1976; BSC Employee Directors, 1977; Chell and Cox, 1979).

How effective are worker directors? There is little agreement here, perhaps in part because the researchers begin with different expectations and value systems and in part because there may be in fact a wide difference in effectiveness among various companies and countries. Batstone (1976, p. 35) may take an extreme position: "Two conclusions can be easily reached: first, worker directors have generally had little effect on anything, and second and consequently, they certainly had no catastrophic effect on anything or anybody."

It is readily understandable why worker directors can be ineffective. With or without worker representation, many boards act merely to rubber stamp management decisions. They meet infrequently, sometimes for only a few hours a year. Management sets the agenda and controls the information flow. Even in those companies in which the board plays an important role, the discussion frequently relates to financial and other issues of little direct interest to workers. The addition of worker directors may do little to change this.

Once on the board, the new worker directors felt seriously handicapped. They lacked the background information to evaluate management's proposals. Even when this information was provided, they lacked the skills to evaluate it. Some were awed by management's wealth, experience, and status (Englestad and Quale, 1977; Adams and Rummel, 1977). They tended to discuss those issues about which they had some personal expertise and to keep silent when anything else was considered.

But worker directors may be less ineffective than such observers as Batstone have claimed. European unions themselves look upon the worker director scheme as an important, if sometimes only a symbolic, victory. Just as works councils institutionalize union power at the plant level, so worker directors ensure their role at the company level. But in many cases the impact of worker directors has extended well beyond the symbolic. They serve to provide unions with early warning as to management intentions. They constitute an alternate form of input into top management decision making. In some circumstances they have successfully delayed plant closings until appropriate plans have been developed to relocate or otherwise protect the displaced workers. They have affected investment decisions, for instance, holding up Volkswagen's decision to build plants in the United States. At Porsche, they successfully opposed the appointment of an allegedly autocratic managing director. In Norway, they have raised issues, such as health and safety, never before given board-level attention. Indeed, in Scandinavia, "changes in board composition have had a 'shock effect' on both corporate management and boards, tightening up board procedures, turning boards into real decision-making bodies rather than 'rubber stamp' institutions, and making management and labor more responsive to the needs of the other interest group" (Hammer and Stern, 1981, citing Engelstad and Quale, 1977).

Even though workers are typically in the minority, voting is rarely used to resolve differences. Instead, contested issues are often assigned to special study committees or resolved by off-board bargaining (Fogarty, 1964). The net result is that board representation results in delay, bargaining, and compromise but rarely complete stalemate (Wilpert, 1975, p. 61).

By a variety of measures, worker directors are relatively more effective in the German iron and steel industry, where workers and management have equal board membership, than they are in other situations (Furstenberg, 1981; Fogarty, 1964, p. 106). For example, in iron and steel (and in the British Steel Corporation), worker directors often sit on board subcommittees (Batstone, 1976; BSC Employee Directors, 1977); this occurs less commonly elsewhere. Where worker directors are relatively effective in other industries, they hold premeeting caucuses, prepare their own agenda, and often speak through a single spokesman.

In German iron and steel, workers nominate a full-time "labor director" who sits on the management board and is responsible for the industrial relations department. The consensus is that such labor directors become co-opted by management. They have done much to humanize personnel administration, but few act as workers representatives (Furstenburg, 1978).

To conclude, worker directors must have some (at least symbolic) significance because some companies try to restructure themselves to get around the law. Still German, Swedish, and some British unions view them more as a source of information than as a means of equalizing power. For power equalization these unions look to works councils or collective bargaining (Martin, 1977; Furstenberg, 1978; Chell and Cox, 1979, p. 27).

What Subjects Do PBs Handle? One of the assumptions behind the Human Relations–OB approach to WPM is that WPM permits workers to make greater inputs into how they do their jobs and the way the company is run. Outside of Yugoslavia there has been little analysis of the content of PB meetings (but see Witte, 1980). The evidence is largely anecdotal. As mentioned earlier, PBs deal with numerous personnel issues. But, beyond this, they touch on nonpersonnel issues (such as plant layout, manufacturing processes, new equipment, and investment policies) only when these affect job security, income distribution, and physical working conditions. An early British study (National Institute of Industrial Psychology, 1952) found that JCCs functioned more effectively when dealing with matters of joint interest, such as work rules and safety, than with purely managerial issues, such as training and quality. By and large, in Rus's (1979, p. 231) words, PBs have been "defensive and protective" rather than "offensive and active." They are reactive, not proactive in their relationships to management. Only in the Scanlon Plan and possibly in some Swedish consultative systems and a few German works councils have PBs been much concerned with how the work is done.

The Role of the PB Member

On the one hand, the PB member represents workers; on the other, he helps run his company. As a partner in management, he may be asked to assent to actions that, as a representative of the workers, he should oppose. "If he is effective, he may lose the confidence of his constituents by becoming too closely identified with management" (Bullock, 1977, p. 39). Thus the more power he accumulates, the more difficult his role becomes. The greater his opportunity to influence management, the more likely he will be co-opted himself. (For an excellent case, see Whyte, 1955. Batstone, 1976, reviews the literature, and BSC Employee Directors, 1977, is sheer good reading. See also Drenth, 1973; Jaques, 1951; Bullock, 1977, p. 39.)

Alternative Roles. In dealing with this dilemma of representation, PB members are likely to take a variety of roles (see also Westenholz, 1979).

1.   PB members may be *inactive,* possibly because they lack the skills, information, or initiative to take part in PB meetings or because they think being participative would be fruitless. This is the response of some worker directors and perhaps the majority response in "tea and toilet" JCCs.

2.   PB members may view themselves as primarily *adversaries:* they represent interests of workers regarding subjects about which there is a clear difference of interest and remain largely silent regarding others. To the extent that WPM's purpose is to provide workers immediate bread-and-butter economic interests, such behavior is functional. But in terms of larger objectives, such as increasing workers' involvement in work processes or improving the organization's long-range economic efficiency, the primarily adversary role is dysfunctional. Among other drawbacks, it induces management to take an equally adversary role and makes it harder for PB members to exert influence regarding noneconomic issues.

3.   By contrast, PB members may view themselves as *comanagers* and put the long-run interests of the organization as a whole above the immediate interests of their constituents. In so doing they agree to such unpopular actions as cutting pay rates, reducing employment, and raising individual production quotas. Having helped make these unpalatable decisions, they may also try to sell them to their constituents.

In several United States cases (Strauss and Rosenstein, 1970, n. 23), the union agreed to cooperate to raise productivity to save the company from bankruptcy. The union's cooperation consisted of (a) informing workers about changes introduced by management, and by implication rejecting in advance any grievance against them, (b) negotiating changes in contractual provisions that hindered production, and (c) pressing workers to work harder. Individual workers had little chance to make suggestions or to participate in the key decisions. Understandably these workers began to view their officers as management stooges and eventually voted them out of office.

4.   PB members may participate in joint decision making regarding subjects about which they possess *expert* knowledge but confine their

activities largely to the conference room, making little effort either to discern rank-and-file opinions or to communicate to them. Under these circumstances management uses the PB member to legitimate decisions and to obtain what it considers to be typical worker opinions (even, though, in fact these may not be representative). The worker director in one British company was viewed as one

> who would contribute to board business as one functional specialist among equals— his specialism being knowledge of shop values and opinions . . . his role was to contribute something new to management information resources rather than to make the shop floor aware of how the board works, or be responsible for putting forward or reporting back the progression of new or alternative plans derived from shop floor concerns (Chell and Cox, 1979, p. 29).

All four roles are dysfunctional when performed alone. Ideally, perhaps, the advocate, comanager, and expert roles should be somehow combined.

The Knowledge Gap. On the basis of experimental evidence, Mulder (1971) argues that when participants differ considerably in their expertise, participation accentuates rather than reduces differences in perceived power. This may well be the case with regard to much WPM. Management frequently fails to provide PB members with the information they need to make a meaningful contribution. Even when this information is provided, the members may lack the skills to evaluate it.

This knowledge gap is particularly serious for worker directors. After all, it is a big jump from work floor to boardroom. The role of worker director is very new and there are few role models to follow. The new director is unsure of how to handle himself at board meetings; more important, he typically lacks the skills to deal with legal, accounting, and marketing issues. Part of the blame for WPM failures in Peru (Berenbach, 1979) and Vermont Asbestos (Johannesen, 1979) is laid on the fact that the worker directors were insufficiently trained to perform their roles.

The knowledge gap helps explain the disillusionment and apathy reported in a number of cases, particularly in Yugoslavia. This apathy, in turn, leads to control of PBs by management, along with a small elite of PB members who are capable of bridging the gap.

To ease the bridging process, WPM rules in some countries (e.g., Sweden) specify the information PB members should receive. To help evaluate this information, training programs for PB members have been established in Britain, Germany, Yugoslavia, Sweden, and Norway. Even this is not enough. To match management at its own game and to avoid dependence on management's briefing, PB members must develop information sources of their own (BSC Employee Directors, 1977). All this takes time. To become really effective, many German works councillors converted their positions to full-time jobs.

But knowledge comes at a price. The more familiar PB members become with management problems and the more involved they become in dealing with them, the less sensitive they are likely to be to their constituents' needs and the more dependent they become on the management, which provides them their information. As Slichter (1941, p. 559) commented with regard to an early case of United States WPM, "Union–management cooperation turned out to be a process by which leaders gained such a thorough appreciation of the problems of the company that proposals that seemed unreasonable to the rank-and-file seemed reasonable to leaders." In some instances the co-optation process may be so effective that the workers' representative becomes little more than another member of management (Furstenberg, 1981, p. 14). Even where this does not happen, PB members "once elected and equipped with better access to information from 'the other' management) side begin to see 'both sides' and start to behave and/or appear as 'compromisers'" (Wilpert, 1975, p. 61).

Social Pressures. Social pressures, both within and without the PB, also foster co-optation. In the case of worker directors, there are strong, frequently explicitly stated expectations that they will represent the organization as a whole, not just their immediate constituents (Brannen, 1976; Thorsrud and Emery, 1970). "Existing board members" pressure them "to adopt an elite status and remove themselves socially, politically, and psychologically from a possible labor constituency" (Hammer and Stern, 1981).

> The company is seen in unitary terms. Worker directors in all [Western European] countries bear similar responsibilities to other directors. Their task is to look after the interests of the enterprise, although the responsibility for looking after workers' interests is often seen as one aspect of this general task. Accordingly there is little differentiation between the role of shareholder and worker representative; both are expected to defend the interest of the company as a whole. Court rulings in Germany have reinforced [this] view (Batstone, 1976, p. 14).

These expectations may be further reinforced by management-oriented training programs to which worker directors are sent; to counteract these, unions in a number of European countries offer training programs of their own.

Confidentiality. By custom or rule, company board members are expected to keep board deliberations confidential. This custom applies to worker directors as well. In theory, it could be a major block to communications. Certainly it provides an excuse for those who do not want to communicate. Thus, in the United States, the seven hourly paid workers serving on the Board of Directors of the partly worker-owned Vermont Asbestos Company kept the board's deliberations secret, despite rank-and-file workers desire to know how each director voted (Johannesen, 1979). Bradley (1980) argues that the perceived need to protect the company from outside competition will inevitably lead PB board members to withhold important information from the rank and file.

Nevertheless, most observers agree that confidentiality is not a serious problem in practice (BSC Employee Directors, 1977; Furstenberg, 1978; Batstone, 1976, p. 33; National Swedish Industrial Board, 1976), at least because PB members use discretion in what they reveal (Gunzburg, 1978). True secrets are generally respected, the few exceptions involving serious threats to workers well-being (Paul, 1979). Perhaps more of a problem is that PBs often deal with technical matters, at times in a somewhat legalistic manner. Even if the PB members understand what is happening, rank-and-file workers may not.

PBs Unrepresentative. Another block to communications is the fact that PB members often come from different occupations and reflect different values than the people they represent (Furstenberg, 1978; Batstone, 1976, p. 23–24; Berenbach, 1979). Better educated, skilled, male workers and union members tend to be overselected and "guestworkers" (in Germany) are underselected. White-collar workers hold more than their proportionate share of PB membership in Yugoslavia and Peru, but are underrepresented in Germany. A Norweigian study suggests that those who seek PB membership may be "management oriented" and suffer from blocked aspirations for upward mobility (Holter, 1965). Yugoslav workers council members have considerably greater interest in becoming managers than do nonmanagers (Obradovic, French, and Rodgers, 1970).

Professionalism and Elitism. As PB members develop expertise, they become more "professional" (Furstenberg, 1969). Indeed, in Germany (and perhaps elsewhere) a wholly new career path, that of full-time PB member, seems to be developing. In any case, the greater the influence PB members feel they have, the more anxious they are to be reelected (IDE, 1981: Table 8.6). Further, their superior knowledge and skills help them win reelection. Turnover in office is low, at least in Germany (Hartmann, 1979). In Yugoslavia and Israel, there are limits to tenure, but these can be evaded. The net result may be that the "representatives from an elite, and most members of the organization resign from actual participation" (Mulder, 1971, p. 36).

Breakdown in Communications. Whatever the cause, communications between PB members and the rank and file tend to break down. Council members fail to report what happens in PB meetings (Kolaja, 1966, p. 71; Sachs, 1975; Galin, 1980, p. 190; Gunzberg, 1978, p. 25; Adams and Rummel, 1977, p. 12; Johannesen, 1979). Even where PB members do hold meetings to report to constituents, such meetings are poorly attended (Adams and Rummel, 1977; Gunzberg, 1978). Perhaps PB members have good reasons for not making such reports; anyway, a German study (Hartmann, 1979) finds no relationship between works council "efficiency" (power) and the extent to which their members communicate with the rank and file.

Understandably, workers report that they know little about what happens in PBs and that PB members fail to represent their interests. Such attitudes are reported throughout Europe (Matejko, 1976, p. 921; Wilpert, 1975; Kolaja, 1966; IDE, 1981) and in United States Scanlon Plan companies (Driscoll, 1979). In turn, at least in Germany, workers are more likely to bring their problems to their supervisors and their colleagues than to their works councillors (Furstenberg, 1981, p. 9). As Wilpert (1975, p. 61) explains it, the "professionalization of representative functions could easily create an estrangement from the constituency. Representatives may now appear part of 'them,' the upper management. The cognitive dissonance of basic agreement with the idea of co-determination and dissatisfaction with its practice is then resolved by stating that 'the right people' were not available."

Obviously, this process can reinforce itself, as some PB members react to worker hostility by withdrawing into "safer" relationships with management, while, to alleviate suspicion, others behave less cooperatively than they might have otherwise (Goodman, 1979, p. 364).

How can PB member responsiveness be retained? Later I consider some of the suggestions that have been made for dealing with this difficult problem.

The Role of the Union

As we have seen, union attitudes toward WPM, as a *principle,* differ greatly. On one side we have French Communist and United States unions, who view WPM as weakening the adversary relationship and inviting cooptation. On the other side are German and Scandinavian unions, who see WPM as extending collective bargaining to the plant level. In between are schemes, such as the Scanlon Plan in the United States and works council control of welfare benefits in France, where WPM is the side show, concerned with integrative bargaining issues regarding which the parties have common interests; meanwhile, in the main tent, adversary distributive bargaining continues over economic conditions.

Related to the union's attitude toward WPM as a principle are questions concerned with the union's role once WPM has been introduced. Here we see a rough continuum.

No Union Role. Under self-management the union is either weak or absent. Although kibbutz members are nominally also union members, there is no independent union presence. Yugoslav unions are little more than welfare agencies. Mondragon had no union until apparently quite recently. In each case there was at least an implicit assumption that because the workers already managed themselves there was no need for separate union representation.

Unions and PBs are Rivals. The union may largely deny the PB's legitimacy as workers' representatives and treat management like any other management, and even strike against it (as it did in the worker-owned lathe company). This kind of relationship was a fairly common occurrence in Britain, where JCCs existed alongside increasingly militant stewards and where worker directors played an "expert" role, making no pretense of speaking for the workers as a whole (Chell and Cox, 1979).

Such a relationship appears viable chiefly when either the union or the PB is rather weak. If both are strong, rivalry is likely to develop between the two bodies, both claiming to represent workers interests. In Britain and Italy, the shop steward system existed alongside independent JCCs, just as long as the shop stewards were weak. Once the stewards gained strength, JCCs atrophied (Batstone, 1976). By contrast, German works councils quickly coopted and contained a union-sponsored movement for independent shop stewards (Hartmann, 1979).

Division of Labor. The union may accept WPM and the PB as legitimate, but keep collective bargaining and WPM distinctly separate. This separation may be required by law or occur because of management insistance or trade union preference. Often unionists fear that too close connection with WPM will result in the unions being coopted. To take an extreme example, union leaders were allowed to take only a limited role in Chilean self-management under Allende, purportedly because "if the union assumed management functions, then it would cease to lead the workers effectively in the class struggle" (Zimbalist, 1976: 50). From a very different perspective, Kochan et al., (1977: 83) argue that union and management contract negotiators should not sit on safety committees "because essentially different kinds of behaviors are required to make a problem-solving process work compared to the roles that must be played in contract negotiations." McGregor and Knickerbocker (1942) make a similar argument regarding the Scanlon Plan.

In some situations, as in German work councils, PB members are elected directly by the workers. In other cases they are appointed by the union, but the union makes sure that different people serve in each role. Worker directors in many British nationalized and private companies are expected to resign their union office once elected to the company board (Chell and Cox, 1979). Except for the union president, Scanlon Plan PB members in the United States may not hold positions in either the grievance or safety complaint mechanisms; neither may the PB discuss grievances or safety problems. A similar distinction exists in the Histadrut industries.

This separation occurs more frequently where collective bargaining occurs chiefly at the industry-wide level whereas works councils and co-determination are concerned chiefly with company- and plant-level personnel problems or where WPM covers the jurisdiction of several unions or both union and nonunion workers (BSC Employee Directors, 1977, p. 49).

In other instances active union officers may be appointed to PBs (particularly as worker directors) but abstain from discussion or absent themselves when collective bargaining issues are discussed. This is what President Fraser of the UAW announced he would do when he was elected to the Chrysler board. It occurs in Sweden, too (Batstone, 1976, p. 13).

The PB as a Union Instrument. The union may seek to use WPM as a form of plant-level bargaining and thus treat the PB as the rough equivalent of a United States plant-level grievance committee. This is what German unions intended works councils to become, though in fact the councils have maintained considerable independence. Swedish unions hope to do better in their new plant-level joint decision scheme.

The Union Runs Self-Management. At Kirby Manufacturing, a now-defunct British PC, the two trade union conveners (chief stewards) served also as the company's entire legal board of directors and as full-time company executives (Edelstein, 1979). In the state-owned Israel Electric Company, the union appointed three stewards to be full-time company officers (one as Personnel Director) while also serving as stewards. Eventually one steward was appointed general manager. (Galin and Tabb, 1978).

In a sense this last approach is like the first. Workers have no independent body to which to appeal. Indeed union, management, and the WPM scheme are rolled up into a single institution.

Tensions Among Roles. The third approach—that of separating the WPM and traditional bargaining roles—is probably the most common. Nevertheless the relationship between the adversary and collaborative functions is never easy. By fostering competitive power structures, such an approach makes conflict difficult to avoid (Peterson, 1968; Tanic, 1969; Hartmann, 1979; Galin, 1980). If nothing else, the leaders on the two sides may become political rivals. Driscoll (1979) observes that sometimes Scanlon Plan PB members may challenge incumbent union office holders. (But in plants where the Plan worked relatively successfully, PB members and union officers each tended to stay in their own "career paths," with the PB path often leading to a job as a supervisor.) On the other hand, in Germany, "works council election is generally the first step in a union career (Adams and Rummel, 1977, p. 19).

Beyond this, the two institutions represent different interests. From the union's point of view, PB members are too concerned with the economic success of their own firms. The union's focus is either narrower (*immediate* benefits for workers in the particular plant) or broader (the welfare of workers in the industry as a whole or of the working class generally). To take one example, union stewards in an Israeli plant fought for immediate wage increases while PB members argued for deferring these until the firm became more profitable (Rosenstein, 1977).

As unions "are organized on an industry-wide level they are much more interested in the progress within the whole industry than within a single factory"; so there are frequent complaints that PBs engage in "plant egotism," putting the interests of their own plant above those of the union movement generally (Furstenberg, 1978, p. 15; 1981). Indeed, in Germany, if there are separate union and works-council representatives on the company board of directors, the two sets of worker representatives may take conflicting positions (Batstone, 1976, p. 27).

To reduce this independence, German unions exert considerable influence to insure that the "right" persons win the works council elections (Furstenberg, 1978). Further, worker representatives on company boards are frequently key unionists (Batstone, 1976). It is partly to reduce possible union–PB conflict that British unions argued for "single channel" selection of worker directors (i.e., union appointment), a position supported by the Bullock Report (1977), and some British unions have reconsidered their opposition to having current union officers serve on company boards (BSC Employee Directors, 1977).

The Need for Union Support. Though unions are ambivalent toward WPM, union support seems quite important for WPM success. "In the last resort [the works council's] effectiveness is dependent on union power," even on the threat of strike (Adams and Rummel, 1977, p. 21).

Espinosa and Zimbalist (1978) found a significant (r = .37) relationship between union attitude toward WPM and WPM success. Without union support, the PB has little clout, a point that Kochan et al. (1977) demonstrate with regard to health and safety committees. With union opposition (or if the union or unions are divided by political rivalry) WPM will become a battleground, rendering cooperation difficult.

The Need for Checks and Balances. Much of the foregoing discussion assumes the existence of three competing power centers: the union, management, and the PB. But under workers self-management, the three parties may merge into one. Even where the parties maintain their institutional separation, the more cooperative they become, the less they check up on each other. The habit of working together leads the parties to assume that their interests are mutual.

The danger is that, to the extent this assumption of mutuality blocks consideration of problems where there is genuine conflict of interest, WPM may well increase discontent by preventing it from being brought out into the open. Unless discontent is adequately expressed through regular union or WPM channels, participation may lead workers to become alienated from their union as well as from management. It may also lead to strikes, as in Yugoslavia and Mondragon. As Whyte (1967, p. 25) puts it,

> Since conflicts are an inevitable part of organizational life, it is important that conflict-resolution procedures be built into the design of organizations. . . . [Cooperative relationships] do not arise when underlying conflicts of interest are ignored, but rather when the two parties have worked out procedures whereby the problems each faces are argued vigorously with each other.

Even under self-management there may be numerous instances where individual workers require separate representation.

1. Individual supervisors may be tyrannical, engage in favoritism, violate organizational policy, or just make stupid decisions.
2. The governing elite (top management, the PB, and the union, if present) may represent the long-run interests of the organization as a whole (as they tend to do in Yugoslavia); often these interests are inconsistent with the short-run interests of individual members. Quite often, for instance, the individual wants increased pay now, although the organization's long-run interest calls for investment; this conflict occurs particularly when, as in Yugoslavia, individual workers are not allowed to sell their share of the organizational assets.
3. Regardless of the organizational form, individuals and groups may compete for status or scarce resources, yet the "common good"

may not be clear. Under these circumstances vigorous argument may be required before a satisfactory solution can be reached.

If the union doesn't maintain its independence, then perhaps some independent institution is needed to expose inefficiency, to increase the range of solutions considered in decision making, to uncover new sources of leadership, to protect the rights of minorities, and generally to provide checks and balances. This point will be discussed later.

The Role of Management

Management support is critical to WPM success (for reviews, see Walker, 1974, p. 24; Espinosa and Zimbalist, 1978), yet it is easy to see why such support is difficult to achieve. WPM can be a bitter pill for top managers, who must now consult and negotiate before winning acceptance of the kinds of decisions that they once made entirely on their own. But it is even harder for middle managers and first-line supervisors who find that representative participation bypasses them completely.

There have been relatively few studies of how managers react to the *experience* of WPM (as opposed to their attitudes toward WPM in the abstract) and fewer still suggesting what the manager's role should be in a smoothly operating WPM system.

Top Management. According to the Webbs, "The relationship set up between a manager who has to give orders all day to his staff, and the members of the staff who, sitting as a committee of management, criticize his action in the evening, with the power of dismissing him if he fails to conform to their wishes, has been found by experience to be an impossible one" (Webb and Webb, 1920, p. 72).

Nevertheless, management tends to keep the upper hand, even in Yugoslavia. (Among the few exceptions to this rule: the kibbutz, where managers are rotated by design, and plywood PCs, where they are frequently fired.) With proper "handling," WPM may even increase management's effectiveness. Note, for example, how German management sometimes enlists works councils to handle difficult personnel chores and how Yugoslav workers councils help legitimate management decisions. Lammers (1967, p. 211) summarizes a common view when he says that WPM "can contribute toward employee motivation in the sense of heightened trust on the part of employees that their interests and views are well represented at top levels. Joint consultation can release relevant information to top executives, not primarily in the form of productivity suggestions, but rather in the form of insight into possible resistance to or alternatives for the managerial actions under consideration."

Still, WPM changes management's task and may lower its status. There is weak evidence (IDE, 1981, Tables 7.5 and 7.10) that WPM reduces top management's *absolute* influence and stronger evidence that it reduces it *relatively* (IDE, 1981, Figure 9.3; Tannenbaum et al., 1974; Nightingale, 1979). Managers of plywood PCs report lower job satisfaction than do capitalist plywood managers, even though PC managers are better paid (Bellas, 1972). Similarly Yugoslav and kibbutz top managers are less satisfied (and have more ulcers) than their United States, Italian, and Austrian capitalist counterparts. Further, workers in participative organizations are relatively less interested in being promoted to management than are workers in capitalist organizations (Tannenbaum et al., 1974, pp. 132, 83).

Supervisors and Middle Management. WPM threatens supervisors' power (Mako, 1978). In some cases their jobs are eliminated altogether, as in Dynavac, or substantially altered, as at Triumph Meriden (Edelstein, 1979) and Bolivar (Goodman, 1979). The power to discipline may be taken from them and handed to a workers' committee, as in Yugoslavia, Chile, and IGP (but in Yugoslavia supervisors are still the ones to initiate most disciplinary changes, Rus, in press).

WPM may also lead to the bypassing of lower levels of management. Workers belonging to PBs have contacts with higher management that are denied to their immediate bosses. German works councillors, for example, are more likely to communicate directly with higher management than with lower management (Furstenberg, 1978). The Scanlon Plan's suggestion system permits inefficiencies on the part of foremen, middle management, and staff to be brought directly to top management's attention, and many PB members do this with gusto (Driscoll, 1979; Strauss and Sayles, 1957)!

Not only do PB members bypass their bosses, but they become privy to information not available to them. (Somewhat the same problems occur when union members serve on plant-level or company-wide grievance committees. Sayles and Strauss, 1967.) As a British steel worker director put it, "Management below board level . . . became unsure of themselves, realizing that now I had access to levels of information they didn't have. . . . One day the department manager is my boss. . . . The next day I'm off to a board meeting, and its a meeting he'd love to go to" (BSC Employee Directors, 1977, p. 24).

Representing Managers' Interests. Middle and lower management participation may be especially important when WPM schemes are introduced. Enthusiastic top management support for WPM may not be enough, especially if this support inhibits frank expression of lower management concerns. Opposition from foremen at Rushton, whose power was reduced, and who were not sufficiently represented on the QWL steering committee, may have contributed to that QWL program being abandoned (Goodman, 1979). Schrank (1978) reports that management at Philips Eindoven in the Netherlands feared that extension of job enrichment would lead unionized foremen to strike. Ironically, Chilean evidence suggests that managerial policies that decentralize power to the supervisory level may actually inhibit WPM because supervisors may be reluctant to share their power with workers (Espinosa and Zimbalist, 1978, p. 52).

Managers need to participate, too. As organizational stakeholders, they have perspective and information to contribute. Further, beyond their links as links in the managerial chain, managers have personal and economic interests of their own. But how should their interests be represented? Trade unions, especially in Britain, have generally argued for "single channel" representation—through unions. If lower level managers want representation, they should join unions. Otherwise top management can speak for their interests. Essentially this was the position adopted by the Bullock Report (1977, p. 113) which said, "We do not think a special seat should be reserved for [professional and managerial employees]. . . . It would be unfortunate . . . to give the impression that certain employees had a special and presumably higher status in the law than other employees." By contrast, in some continental countries, works council members are elected on a "one man, one vote" principle, which gives managers representation equivalent to their number. Over strong union objection, the 1976 German Codetermination Act guarantees that senior executives will be given at least one of the seats on the "worker" side of the supervisory board. Norwegian middle managers, backed by their union, have shown much interest in serving on PBs (IDE, 1981).

In Yugoslavia, managers and staff not only serve on the workers council, they dominate it. On the other hand, PC boards typically exclude managers.

Foreman–Worker Relations. There is conflicting evidence as to whether WPM changes day-to-day managerial behavior. Insofar as there has been change, it has been toward making managers more participative. Nightingale (1979) compared managerial practices in ten participative and ten nonparticipative Canadian firms. In the more participative firms, workers perceived greater emphasis being placed on rules (as in Yugoslavia) and less on surveillance. Opportunities for initiative were greater and the hierarchy of authority was weaker. Communications were better and conflict was more often resolved by "problem solving" and less by "ignoring." (A caveat: Nightingale's sample included some forms engaged in direct participation only. In part, he may be measuring direct WPM itself, not the impact of representative participation.)

On the other hand, codetermination has done little to expand German workers' ability to influence what they do on the job. "On the job itself, management's discretion is hardly restricted" (Herding, 1972, p. 330). Many supervisors at Mondragon are autocratic and jobs are structured along traditional Tayloristic lines (Johnson and Whyte, 1977), though this may be changing. As we have seen, supervisors in union-controlled industries in Israel may be less participative than those in the private sector. Bellas (1972) found no significant difference in Initiating Structure and Consideration (Fleishman, 1957) between plywood PC managers and a small matched sample of their capitalist plywood counterparts. Further, Yugoslav and kibbutz industry managers may be less participative than their United States counterparts (Tannenbaum et al., 1974, p. 58), despite the Yugoslav and kibbutz participative superstructure.

The picture changes a bit when we look at quantitative studies. According to IDE (1981), influence of rank-and-file workers is positively correlated with both PB influence (Table 7.5) and perceived participative supervisory leadership (Table 7.22). Espinosa and Zimbalist (1978, p. 66) found a .70 correlation between shop- and plant-level extensiveness of WPM (though the two levels specialized in different subjects). Despite the limited efforts to formalize shop-floor WPM in Yugoslavia and Germany, the two countries with most extensive plant- and company-level participation, they ranked among the top five (of 12) countries in shop-floor *managerial* participative leadership (IDE, 1981, Table 8.8).

Few studies relate managerial behavior to WPM success. Ruh, Wallace, and Frost (1973) report that managers of plants that have discontinued Scanlon Plans tend to have less confidence in their employees and place lower value on participation than do managers in plants where the Scanlon Plan continues and is therefore presumably successful. Bellas (1972) looked at managers of plywood PCs ($n = 15$), finding a negative relationship between organizational performance and Initiating Structure but no significant relationship between performance and Consideration.

Aside from these studies, there has been almost no research as to how managers should behave under WPM. Conventional wisdom suggests that managers in WPM organizations should be patient, be good listeners and politicians, make decisions by consensus rather than by edict, and attend a lot of meetings. Beyond this, what should they do? Recall Adizes's (1971) two very different Yugoslav directors. Director XYZ acted chiefly as a facilitator of democratic decision making; decision making in XYZ was slow and cumbersome. By contrast, the more charismatic Director ABC took full advantage of his political power, social skills, and control over information to push through quick decisions.

Which form of management was more appropriate for WPM? This depends in part on the criteria one uses. Similar issues have been long debated in political science. Can government be run on a town-meeting basis? Or does effective democracy require strong leaders who initiate action and take responsibility for organizational success? Can the plant manager of a self-managed plant be a charismatic leader or should he be little more than a secretary to the works council? Or is there some viable compromise in between? Some argue that the most the electorate and the electorate's representatives can do is to react to initiatives, to criticize, reject, accept, or change them, and eventually to decide whether to retain the current leadership. Questions such as this have been barely raised by vestigial WPM theory.

TECHNOLOGY, VALUES, SKILLS, AND REWARDS

Having examined the role problems faced by people involved in WPM, I now turn to what might be called "contextual" variables that may affect WPM success: technology, values, skills, and rewards. As will be noted, many of these variables impact on WPM but are themselves changed by WPM. Each section begins with the relevant theories and then examines the somewhat scanty research that tests these theories.

Technology, Environment, and Size

Arguably, WPM will work best—in terms of increased employee influence—in small firms, with simple labor intensive technologies, where the work force is relatively homogeneous, where the work layout permits communications, and where the external environment is stable and predictable. This section considers some of these factors under three headings: size, production technology, and environmental turbulence.

Size. Theory suggests that WPM should be more successful in smaller organizations. In small organizations communications are easier, workers know more about the organization as a whole, and contacts between PB members and their constituents are more direct. The "knowledge gap" between management and workers should be less. Further, jobs are more likely to be homogeneous in terms of duties, salary, and status—thus making consensus easier. Finally, the smaller the group, the greater the social and economic incentive for the individual to work for the collective good (Olson, 1965).

Successful self-managing firms tend to be small (Bernstein, 1980). Kibbutzim and PCs rarely exceed 500 workers each. Mondragon, a decentralized organization, has over 15,000 members, but the participatory mechanism at Ulgor, its largest 3,000 member unit, seems to be largely ineffective (Johnson and Whyte, 1977). Yugoslavia shifted the emphasis of participatory mechanism to the shop level, justifying this as an attempt to strengthen participation. On the other hand, Scanlon Plan success appears unrelated to company size as long as the company has fewer than 600 employees (White, 1979).

Surprisingly, quantitative studies fail to support the hypothesized relationship between size and participation. Tannenbaum-type studies in Yugoslavia find no relationship between size and the slope of the influence gradient (Rus, 1970; Tannenbaum et al., 1974). IDE (1981) finds a nonsignificant but small positive relationship between size and two measures of direct and representative participation. Espinosa and Zimbalist (1978, p. 65) come to the same conclusion, using one composite measure. IDE (1981, p. 203) suggests that opposing forces may be at work here in small organizations "power sharing is achieved mainly through greater direct cooperation between workers and management"; in larger firms the PB acts as a counterbalance to management. An alternate explanation of the attitudinal data is that direct, face-to-face participation actually occurs in small organizations. Larger organizations, however, are more likely to establish formal participative schemes, at least on paper; once these are publicized, workers attribute to them greater influence for themselves. Relevant to this issue, works councils are more likely to be established in large German firms than in small ones (Wilpert, 1975, p. 60). Furthermore, works councillors in large firms tend to be better trained; and the better trained they are, the more "efficient" (in terms of accomplishment and "degree of participation") they become (Hartmann, 1979). On the other hand, voter turnout is proportionally higher in smaller firms (Furstenberg, 1981).

It may be that size places a restraint on self-managing organizations but not on forms of WPM that act chiefly to represent workers' interests with management.

Production Technology. Hypotheses abound here, but there is little firm evidence. Arguably, complex technology should widen the knowledge gap and reduce the homogeneity among workers, thus making participation more difficult (Walker, 1974). For example, as scavenging expanded from just garbage collecting to complex waste processing, control of the scavengers' PCs fell out of rank-and-file hands into those of technicians and managers (Russell et al., 1979). By contrast, Israeli agricultural kibbutzim do relatively little stoop or hard manual labor. They prefer growing crops which make use of mechanical equipment and their own technical skills.

On very simple work, workers may have very little to contribute. By contrast, craft work would seem suited for WPM because craftsmen are themselves a repository of critical production knowledge. Further, craftsmen are accustomed to exercising discretion and are less likely to be alienated from the entire system. Indeed, United States PCs have been especially common in industries involving the skilled crafts (Jones, 1979). Goldthorpe, Lockwood, Bechhofer, and Platt (1968, p. 108), found craftsmen to be the only occupational group to approve of WPM as a primary union goal. Finally, labor intensive production technology processes are more likely to be favorable to WPM (especially PCs; Aldrich and Stern, 1978), in part because in capital intensive processes workers' suggestions may be expensive to implement.

Espinosa and Zimbalist (1978) are among the few scholars to discover a statistical relationship between technology and WPM success. Their study of Allende-era Chilean self-management found artisan work was most favorable to the development of high levels of WPM, followed, in descending order by machine tending, continuous process, assembly, and assembly line work ($R^2 = .151$). Similar technological considerations moderated the relationship between intensity of participation and productivity. By contrast, Edlung (private conversation) found that in Sweden, process workers were most active in WPM, primarily because they had most time to talk. (The difference may be that Chilean WPM was driven by frustration, whereas Swedish workers responded to opportunity.)

Once more IDE data (1981, Tables 7.12, 7.13, 7.21, 7.22) are inconclusive, with different measures giving different results. Further White (1979) finds little relationship between technological factors and Scanlon Plan success. Two Yugoslav studies by Rus (1970, p. 154; 1979, p. 236) come to similar findings.

There has been little study of the impact of professionalism on WPM. I would hypothesize that professionalism would foster participation within a professional group but would legitimate efforts by such groups to protect their decision-making turf against the participative demands of nonprofessionals (Poole, 1975; Batstone, 1976).

Environmental Turbulence. Theory suggests that turbulence—rapid market changes, scientific advances, new laws—should inhibit WPM. WPM takes time, and turbulence requires both more and quicker decisions. Turbulence also increases the knowledge gap: The power of boundary spanners (many of whom are in management) is increased, whereas technological changes may make workers' traditional knowledge obsolete. Often, too, the effects of shop-floor decisions (e.g., those raising productivity) may be swamped by external changes over which workers have no control. Turbulence may even require PBs to keep decisions secret from the rank and file (Bradley, 1980).

Adizes (1971) describes how turbulence affected Yugoslav self-management. Prior to 1965, the twin objectives were to maximize productivity and participation. These goals were reasonably consistent, as participation mobilized workers' efforts toward clear productivity goals. After 1965, as the country switched to market economy, the emphasis changed from production to profits, and profits depended on selling the right goods for the right price. But with regard to sales and pricing, the workers could contribute little. Under the new system flexibility was all important, but "the democratic process, appropriately adhering to the system of maximum participation, made flexibility almost impossible" (p. 216). As in PCs (see previous discussion), self-management units were reluctant either to expand or contract employment. Even the United States Scanlon Plan may inhibit rapid technological change (Northrup and Young, 1968).

Zimbalist (1976, p. 53) reports that in Cuban farms and factories, "The uncertainty of the market is replaced by the clearness of the production plan. . . . Management at the farm and factory level thus is straightforward and largely demystified to the production worker. This facilitates a more equal distribution of power and more active participation by production labor in management." In other words, take the difficult questions out of workers' hands, and they can make a go of it.

Nevertheless self-management is not inconsistent with considerable technological change. Yugoslavia has enjoyed one of the world's highest rates of investment and economic growth (Batstone, 1976, p. 380). Mondragon has rapidly expanded into new technologies (but how efficiently will it abandon old ones?). In Chile, Espinosa and Zimbalist (1978, p. 165ff) found a positive relationship between extensiveness of WPM and various measures of technological change.

Once we move from self-management to codetermination, we find additional evidence that WPM *can* facilitate change. In Germany (Adams and Rummel, 1977; Batstone, 1976) and Sweden (Gunzburg, 1978, p. 22), WPM has been described as slowing down the decision-making process but making implementation much smoother. Indeed it may have increased adaptiveness and encouraged risk taking (for citations, see Batstone, 1976, p. 37). WPM is widely credited for Germany's peaceful run-down of employment in coal and steel.

Conclusion. The issues discussed here may more sharply constrain self-management than other forms of WPM. Self-management may be capable of handling only simple problems. Large size, complex technology, or environmental turbulence may easily swamp the fragile self-management vessel. However, to the extent that the function of forms of WPM other than self-management (e.g., codetermination) is not to run the organization but merely to represent workers' interests, the factors mentioned may be less constraining. Similarly I would hypothesize that technology would have less of an impact on representative WPM than on direct WPM.

Values and Skills

Logic suggests that if participation is to "work" (1) participants should want to participate, which requires that participation should be perceived to provide them with some rewards, whether economic or noneconomic, concrete or symbolic; (2) participants should have the knowledge and skills required to participate effectively; and (3) both management and workers should view participation as legitimate, a perception that itself is influenced by the parties' cultural and ideological values. Values and skills are discussed in this section, economic rewards in the next one.

Appropriate values and skills facilitate WPM's acceptance and sustenance. On the other hand, successful WPM helps develop values and skills.

The Impact of Values and Skills on WPM. Hypothetically, values and ideologies affect both the likelihood that (1) participative efforts will be perceived to pay off in terms of valued rewards and (2) WPM will be perceived as legitimate. The socialist ideologies in Yugoslavia, the kibbutz, and certain plants in Allende's Chile all taught that WPM would lead to a better world. Working for this world was socially legitimate. Further, participation made the organization "normative" and led to "moral" involvement (Etzioni, 1975) in working for superordinate organizational goals. In each case there was widespread initial acceptance of the values associated with participation, such as equality, a belief in the value of group decision making and responsibility, and organizational identification. In short, making participation work became an end in itself. Early religious communes had a similar involvement, although religiously rather than politically motivated. Professional organizations have an "ideology" of their own. WPM, as long as it is confined to professionals, is widely accepted as legitimate in universities, in many hospitals, and in scientific and welfare organizations.

Beyond this, WPM may be more easily accepted in societies where participation is valued generally. Johnson and Whyte (1977, p. 21) credit much of Mondragon's success to Basque society's equalitarian values, "associative spirit," and general atmosphere of trust. Similarly, the largely Scandinavian Pacific Northwest communities in which plywood PCs have developed are known for their support of consumer cooperatives. The kibbutz principles, with which children are indoctrinated—"voluntarism, cooperatism, and equalitarianism—aim at the complete identification of the individual with society" (Fine, 1973, p. 210). By contrast, we would expect strong hierarchical culture, such as in Peru (Whyte, 1969:chapter 32), to be somewhat less hospitable to WPM.

Finally, we should expect WPM to work better in situations where union–management relations were already harmonious.

Earlier sections stressed the importance of PB members developing at the least the minimum skills necessary to evaluate management's proposals. PB members need to learn management's language and management needs to learn to make reports intelligible to PB members. Thus, both parties need education. Even rank-and-file workers need education so they can evaluate PB members' effectiveness and prevent their co-optation.

Members of kibbutzim and counterculture communes in this country would argue that ability to evaluate PB effectiveness is not enough. Workers should be able to make basic decisions themselves. This means that knowledge should not be concentrated among a few high status experts. To help equalize knowledge and status, such organizations emphasize job rotation and continual training (Rothschild-Whitt, 1979).

The Impact on WPM of Values and Skills. Still, the importance of antecedent values and skills for successful WPM should not be exaggerated. German management ideology is supposedly autocratic; Yugoslav workers possessed few managerial skills in 1950. Yet WPM seems to have survived tolerably well in both seemingly unhospitable environments. Thus although it can be argued that appropriate ideologies and skills are required to make WPM work, just the reverse may be true. Participation (at least in its superficial forms) has been used in many developing countries to mobilize support for modernization, to legitimate change, and to manufacture consensus (Delacroix and Ragin, 1978). Numerous authors see, as one of WPM's main virtues, its enhancement of the values and skills necessary for a larger democratic (Pateman, 1970) or socialist (Vranicki, 1965) society. Yugoslav workers councils may be viewed as a massive management development scheme. The kibbutz trained a nation's leadership. At the very least, service on PBs helps develop management skills (Cupper, 1980). Experience in lower level PBs trains people for higher levels. Finally, motivation for participation "is learned; actual exertion of influence leads to a stronger motivation for further exertion of influence" (Mulder, 1971, p. 35). Experience with WPM may even change a worker's orientation from instrumental to expressive (Goldthorpe et al., 1968), thus in turn intensifying his interest in WPM.

This brings us to an old question bedeviling OD: Which should change *first,* structure or attitudes? Must attitudes change before structure can be altered, or will attitudinal change follow as an inevitable concomitant of change in structure? To be more specific: Could the Bullock Committee's recommendation—that British boards of directors be restructured to include equal representation of labor and management (plus some neutrals)—change Britain's disastrous labor relations? The Committee argued that the way to raise "the level of productivity and efficiency in British industry" was "not by recrimination or exhortation but by putting the relationship between capital and labour on a new basis which will involve not just management but the whole workforce in sharing responsibility for the success of the enterprise" (Bullock Report, 1977, p. 160). Would such a structural change transform years of bloody-minded, class-conscious, shop-level guerilla warfare into German-style harmony? Would British unions "accept a share of responsibility for the increased efficiency and prosperity of British companies" (p. 161) or would this structural change merely extend collective bargaining into the boardroom without substantially changing attitudes?

Social science research to date provides little ground for a firm answer. The IDE study (1981) suggests that formal participative schemes do indeed lead to perceptions of changed power and to greater satisfaction with the participative process. But we should note substantial differences between the German and British situations. German codetermination had widespread support during the late 1940s. Even management felt it was better than the total dismemberment of large plants. Both unions and management were weak, and the war-time experience gave everyone a desire to start anew. In contrast, British industrial democracy would have been crammed down management's throat; it would have had the support of only a few unions; and there was a long tradition of bitter, zero-sum gain bargaining. Further, even in Germany, unions have accepted very little "responsibility for . . . increased efficiency and prosperity."

Clearly this is not an either–or issue. Although favorable ideology and adequate skills facilitate WPM at first, it is the skills that workers develop and the economic and noneconomic rewards that they obtain that keep WPM going.

Economic Rewards

The role of rewards is rarely mentioned in the WPM literature (but see Wachtel, 1973; Bernstein, 1980). Yet for workers to exert the effort to keep WPM going they need to perceive that their efforts will be rewarded. Rewards can serve two purposes: they satisfy needs and, properly designed, they serve a form of feedback as to the participative effort's success. Rewards can be economic and/or noneconomic (moral). Economic rewards are discussed here. The role of rewards generally is considered in the concluding section.

Where participation is related to wages, fringes, or job security, successful WPM may carry its own reward (e.g., saving one's job). But where WPM is concerned with production decisions, workers in capitalist "utilitarian" (Etzioni, 1975) firms feel it only fair that if they produce more they should be paid more. Bernstein (1980) argues persuasively that such compensation should be (1) by right, (2) given everyone concerned, (3) apart from wages, (4) frequent, and (5) related to the success of the activities under workers control. Thus, if participation is at the shop level, then the bonus should depend on shop effectiveness.

The Scanlon Plan is among the few WPM schemes to meet most of Bernstein's requirements. It pays a bonus based on the previous month's production. Most United States job redesign programs (e.g., autonomous work groups) rely on moral rewards alone. This may be among their biggest weaknesses (Strauss, 1979b). In Hungary, as probably elsewhere, workers resist opportunities for more influence and independence unless this greater responsibility also leads to higher pay (Mako, 1978, p. 7).

In designing a WPM reward system, three questions are involved: (1) How equalitarian should the basic pay scale be; (2) How should the "profit" from increased efficiency be divided between present compensation and investment; and (3) how should the portion of the profits available for present compensation be divided among various claimants?

Pay Equality. Some PCs pay all workers alike, with some possible adjustment for need. Among these are the kibbutz, Triumph Meriden, the plywood PCs, and (for a while) the scavenger PCs (Edelstein, 1979). Other self-management schemes, such as Dynavac and Mondragon and those in Yugoslavia, provide for pay differentials, though there is some evidence that these have been narrowed by WPM (Cupper, 1980, p. 96; Oakeshott, 1978; Espinosa and Zimbalist, 1978). In Yugoslavia, the years 1956–1967 were associated with some decline in interskill differentials, perhaps due to WPM, and some increase in interfirm differentials, perhaps due to market factors (Wachtel, 1973). Arguably, pay differentials reflect power differentials, though the cause–effect relationship may be uncertain. Nevertheless, it may be no coincidence that some equal-pay PCs (kibbutz and plywood) have been among the most successful WPM schemes in terms of involving ordinary workers in WPM decisions.

Investments. The theory of investment under WPM has been heavily debated (Steinherr, 1978). The conventional view is that workers will prefer present consumption to some rather uncertain claim on future earnings, especially if present sacrifice is not directly related to future rewards. As we have seen, United States and British PCs provide some— not entirely consistent—support for this hypothesis (e.g., Jones, 1979, 1980). On the other hand, Scott Bader employees have voted for high investment levels (Bernstein, 1980), and Yugoslavia and Mondragon have enjoyed very high growth rates. Similarly Batstone (1976) concludes that codetermination has had no adverse effect on investment in Germany.

In Yugoslavia, total compensation (wages plus bonuses) tends to be set by labor market considerations; what is left is invested (Wachtel, 1973).

The Division of Rewards. The distribution of differential economic rewards is a prime cause of divisiveness in WPM systems. It has caused trouble in Yugoslavia, Dynavac, and in some United States union–management programs (Strauss, 1979b). Workers may resist creating divisions among themselves. In a Hungarian experiment, 14 work groups accepted management's offer to set their own wage scale but made it more equalitarian; the remaining five, who happened to be more cohesive, refused the offer altogether (Mako, 1978).

Conclusion. Economic rewards for greater efficiency may be necessary, at least in utilitarian organizations; and these rewards should be distributed in a manner that workers view as equitable. However, it should also be remembered that one presumed advantage of WPM is that it can also provide important moral rewards. A group bonus for high productivity can provide a concrete symbol of group success (Whyte, 1955) and thus serve intrinsic and extrinsic functions. But excess emphasis on monetary rewards alone may kill intrinsic motivation.

CONCLUSION

This concluding section seeks to pull together several themes which may help us evaluate WPM as a social intervention.

Outcomes

Is WPM a success? This depends on which of the many criteria one accepts. Productivity and satisfaction, the criteria mentioned by Locke and Schweiger (1979), are not the only relevant ones.

Survival. Those who say that WPM violates human or economic nature have been proven wrong. By the organization ecologists' test of survival a number of forms of WPM have taken root: German codetermination, Israeli kibbutz, Mondragon, plywood PCs, and Scanlon Plans have all survived for at least 25 years. Some of these successes have shown signs of degeneration or creeping bureaucratization; however, WPM as an institution has not yet been shown to be inherently unstable.

On the other hand, it is too early to predict the ecological niches in which WPM is most likely to be successful. Indeed WPM has survived in seemingly inhospitable cultures such as Germany and Yugoslavia.

Economic Variables. The evidence relating WPM to indices of economic success (e.g., productivity, profits, and worker earnings) is some-

what spotty. Because WPM is often accompanied by other forms of
change, the impact of WPM alone is difficult to decipher. A few studies
suggest that more participative firms function better than do their less
participative counterparts (Rus, 1970; Melman, 1971; Bellas, 1972; Espinosa and Zimbalist, 1978; Svejnar, 1981); others find no significant
impact (e.g., Batstone, 1976). Aside from a few PCs approaching "de-
generacy" (Jones, 1980), there is almost no evidence that WPM firms
do less well. In some instances, workers in PCs and in Yugoslavia have
worked so hard as to engage in "self-exploitation" (Rus, in press; Eaton,
1979).

In theory, one would not expect representative WPM to have a substantial impact on productivity, especially because (except in the Scanlon
Plan) effective PBs rarely discuss production questions or, if they do
discuss them (as in Yugoslavia), management dominates the discussion.
The main impact of representative WPM on productivity may be through
reducing resistance to change and facilitating the handling of personnel
grievances.

Job Satisfaction. Most studies of participation, formal or informal,
show a positive relationship between extent of participation and overall
job satisfaction (Locke and Schweiger, 1979). WPM research confirms
this for direct, shop-level participation and personal participation on
participative bodies. But there is little evidence that job satisfaction is
higher in organizations enjoying representative WPM. The latter finding
is a bit surprising, as one might expect positive relationships because
of response biases and attribution effects.

IDE (1981, Table 8.18) found a positive correlation between job satisfaction (three measures: correlations .25, .23, .27; $n = 134$ companies)
and extent of direct WPM but no relationship between satisfaction and
various measures of representative participation. Rubenowitz, Norgren,
and Tannenbaum (unpublished) report somewhat similar findings in a
study of ten Swedish companies. Similarly, job satisfaction was no higher
in worker-owned scavenger companies than in their capitalist or public-
sector counterparts (Russell et al., 1979). By contrast, Nightingale (1979)
does find that satisfaction is higher in participative than in matched
nonparticipative firms, but his measure confounds direct and indirect
measures of participation.

Industrialization and Management Development. As previously mentioned, self-management in the kibbutz, Yugoslav industry, and Mondragon has trained management and facilitated industrialization.

Management and Change. As we have seen, there is some evidence
that workers' self-management may inhibit the organization's ability to
adjust to change. Arguably, self-management works better when the goal

is efficiency (making optimum use of current technology) than when it is effectiveness (successful adjustment to external stress). By contrast, codetermination, at least in Sweden and Germany, may facilitate rapid technological change. Nevertheless there is the prospect that, if our society becomes ever more turbulent, more and more decisions will be made externally by forces over which plant- or company-level WPM may have little impact. Employees may gain "more and more freedom for participation within a less and less free system" (Rus, 1979, p. 240).

WPM, whether self-management or codetermination, requires the development of some sort of consensus, at least with regard to major decisions. Commitment may take the place of control as the primary management tool (at least at the levels where WPM occurs). Responsibility may be shared, diffused, and blurred. Hypothetically, political skills may become more important for the manager than analytic ones. Nevertheless, Adams and Rummel (1977, p. 17) conclude, "There is general consensus that, due to codetermination, management has become more rational, more professional, and more efficient." (In fact, the requirements of successful management under WPM have been scarcely studied.)

Labor Relations. Codetermination has been part of the strategy of European unions to increase their power at the plant and company levels and to extend collective bargaining's coverage beyond wages. In part, codetermination merely brought United States-style labor relations to Western Europe. But European unions have gone beyond this: They can now significantly influence company investment decisions. They have been able to block layoffs, at least temporarily. Although they have not prevented plant shutdowns altogether, most observers agree they have significantly slowed the process down (Batstone, 1976, p. 34 summarizes the literature).

WPM is designed to change the predominantly adversary character of labor relations. To some extent it has been successful. This does not mean that differences have been obliterated, but their mode of expression is less ritualized. Though more research is necessary, it seems that PB members (and PB membership somewhat overlaps union leadership) have accepted considerable responsibility for overall organizational success. All this may have contributed to Germany's good postwar record of labor peace, especially in iron and steel (Batstone, 1976, p. 36). Strikes have not been eliminated in Yugoslavia, but all parties seem to accept the responsibility to keep them short.

Co-optation. It is widely charged that PB members will inevitably be co-opted. Co-optation is, of course, a standard technique by which the organization gains resources and neutralizes opposition (Pfeffer and Salancik, 1978). Hammer and Stern (1981) suggest that PBs serve three functions for management: (1) as an information *conduit*, upward and downward, between workers and management; (2) as a means of winning *support* for (or legitimating) management's decisions; and (3) as *appeasement*, that is, to control labor–management conflict. However,

> the success of cooptation as a strategy . . . depends on the ease with which targets can be coopted. . . . An offer to share power through board representation does not mean that an actual trade takes place. For cooptation strategies to work, it is necessary that a formal action like board representation . . . *not* evolve into real power whereby the worker representatives take full advantage of their positions to actually control board decisions. This means that the worker representatives have to be controlled informally (Hammer and Stern, 1981, p. 5).

The record suggests that a considerable amount of co-optation occurs, but that in many cases PB members also exert "real power" and influence, if not "actually control board decisions." Instead of being fully co-opted, they develop into a quasi-independent interest group that has interests (or at least perspectives) of its own. They are less interested in immedite profits or efficiency than is management and more concerned with the general welfare of the organization whole than are specific groups of subordinates.

Conflict. Earlier it was suggested that WPM—especially workers' self-management—might squash and hide interest group differences. Though this may occur in some cases, there is some evidence that on balance WPM helps bring such conflict out into the open. According to IDE (1981, Table 7.8), "frequency of conflicts" is positively correlated ($r = .26$) with PB power but negatively correlated with supervisors' power. The difference may be in the way conflicts are settled. Nightingale (1979) reports that, compared to nonparticipative organizations, participative organizations are more likely to use problem-solving as a conflict resolution technique and less likely to use ignoring or forcing. Rus (1982) concludes that diffuse social relations plus the "higher order" ideology prevailing in Yugoslavia combine to permit conflicts to be more easily surfaced and resolved.

Power Distribution. For some of its proponents, WPM's major objective is to equalize power. Clearly, in such countries as Germany, WPM has increased the power of unions at the company and plant levels, even though the power has to be expressed through the union's membership on PBs. Indeed unions have become the partner of management (albeit junior partner) in the operation of the economic sphere. PB members have gained power of their own, to some degree independent of that of the union. The impact of WPM on management is less clear. If we view total power as a fixed amount, as some socialists do, then management's relative power has been reduced. But Tannenbaum and others (see especially Lammers, 1967) argue that effective participation increases total power. By this standard WPM has increased management's power in many instances.

Reaction of Workers to WPM. Whether WPM in fact increases the power of lower participants, workers enjoying WPM *report* having more power than do workers not enjoying WPM (Nightingale, 1979; Russell et al., 1979; Tannenbaum et al., 1974).

Attitudes toward WPM as such have been extensively studied (IDE, 1981; Furstenberg, 1981; DIO, 1979; Adams and Rummel, 1977). The findings are a bit hard to interpret. By and large, they suggest that most workers support WPM as an institution, even though few report receiving direct benefit from it. Support tends to be positively correlated with both direct involvement with participation and with the PB's power, both formal (de jure) and actual (IDE, 1981, chapter 8). Satisfaction with participation is highest in Yugoslavia and Germany, the two countries with the strongest PBs in the IDE sample. Satisfaction with participation is also correlated with various demographic characteristics, although not consistently across countries. Insofar as there are negative reactions to WPM, they are directed either toward WPM in practice or toward individual PB members.

> A major difficulty with German participation is that it seems to provide the individual worker with little sense of involvement . . . the worker, although satisfied with the representation scheme, feels that he has little ability to affect his own destiny. Decisions are taken mostly at distant places and, although the worker may benefit from them, he has little perceived capacity to notably influence them (Adams and Rummel, 1977, p. 22).

Support for WPM as a concept is always stronger than desire to participate personally (Holter, 1965). In capitalist countries, the percentage of workers willing to serve on PBs ranges from 14 to 28 (IDE, 1981, Table 8.6) though it may be higher in Communist countries (Jacob and Jacob, 1979). Interviews suggest that the reasons for not participating in WPM are much the same as those for not participating in unions or democracy generally. According to a Hungarian report, participation is time consuming as well as a "new and hazardous affair . . . a worker . . . risks making himself ridiculous or even provoking social conflict. . . . [It] entails passing judgment, intentional or unintentional, on the work of others" (Hethy and Mako, 1977, p. 16).

This lack of involvement is readily understandable. Apathy is common in unions, governmental politics, and even in universities. A few people

participate actively because they feel a responsibility for the larger organization and/or because they get their kicks from participative activity.
But most people participate only with regard to subjects important to
them and about which they feel some competence to affect the final
result.

Desire to participate personally often consists of little more than the
wish to be informed or to have the opportunity to discuss matters (Rus,
1979; IDE, 1981). Even in Yugoslavia, only 31 percent of the workers
wish to "decide" the criteria for income distribution, and with regard
to other issues desire to participate is less (Rus, 1979, pp. 232–233).

Even aside from personal participation, most studies indicate a greater
desire for "influence" or "say" with regard to shop floor rather than
higher level problems (Wall and Lisheron, 1977; Holter, 1965; Hethy and
Mako, 1977; Ramsay, 1976). On the other hand, Yugoslav workers show
equal desire to participate at shop and plant levels, perhaps because they
are already familiar with plant-level participation (Rus, 1979).

What do workers want to have influence about? Generally, desire for
WPM at the plant or organization level is with regard to topics directly
affecting their pocketbooks: pay, bonuses, and layoffs. Concerns for
participation at the shop level are broader: worker assignments, holiday
schedules, personal equipment, safety and physical working conditions
(Rus, 1970, 1979; IDE, 1981; Ramsay, 1976; Wall and Lisheron, 1977;
Heller, Wilders, Abell, and Warner, 1979; Witte, 1980). There is some
suggestive evidence that workers who have already enjoyed some WPM,
as in Yugoslavia and Hungary, have different sets of preferences than
do United States workers who have had none (compare Rus, 1979, with
Witte, 1980 and Quinn and Staines, 1978, p. 178). The limited research
suggests that United States workers appear to be more interested in
participating in such subjects as work procedures than do their Yugoslav
counterparts but much less interested in selecting co-workers or managers.

Pateman (1970), Mulder (1971), and Rus (1979) all argue that participation is addictive: the more one has, the more one wants. There is
some evidence that perceived and desired participation are positively
correlated (IDE, 1981; Rus, 1979). Nevertheless, just the opposite is
possible: if experience with participation is disillusioning, desire for further participation may decline.

Impact on Shop-Floor Activities. As we have seen, there is some
evidence that supervisors tend to be more participative in dealing with
their subordinates in plants with strong PBs (IDE, 1981). On the other
hand, except for a few cases in Scandinavia, there has been little reported
effort to link plant-level representative WPM with shop-level job redesign
efforts, such as autonomous work groups. (Indeed, Furstenberg, personal

communication, tells how one German works council opposed the development of autonomous work groups, fearing that they would lead to the development of rival power centers, some of which might be dominated by guestworkers.) Except in United States plywood PCs (Bennett, 1979), there are few reports of shop-level discussions of production problems.

Similarly, only a few examples can be given of WPM involving more than one level with regard to the same topic. Among the exceptions, the Scanlon Plan deals with suggestions generated by individual workers, which are discussed by shop and plant committees successively. Here participation typically starts at the bottom (though occasionally management may use Plan channels to obtain advance reactions to proposed technological changes). In contrast, important initiatives start at the top in Yugoslavia but normally are at least cleared through shop meetings. Shop-level meetings are frequently asked to deal with plant-wide problems in plywood PCs (Bennett, 1979).

Aside from these perhaps significant exceptions, representative WPM seems to have had little impact on the shop. Indeed, German "codetermination has been least effective in providing shop-floor control" and "in humanizing immediate shop conditions" (Adams and Rummel, 1977, pp. 14–15, citing Herding, 1972). Given workers' propensity to participate only with regard to matters salient to their interests and about which they have some expertise, WPM is unlikely to involve large numbers of workers or to affect how they feel about their jobs unless it is extended to the shop-floor and job-design levels.

Requirements for Effective WPM

Knowledge of expectancy theory may be helpful in preparing a summary of the conditions under which WPM is most likely to be "successful." If workers are to invest effort into participation, they must expect (a) that these efforts will not be wasted and will in fact affect decisions (valence), which in turn depends on their ability (skills and power) to make their voices heard, and (b) that the decisions so made will lead to valued rewards (instrumentality).

Power. If workers are to exert the effort to participate, they must believe that their efforts will have some impact on managerial decisions. In short, that they must have power (see especially Poole, 1975). With so-called "managerial participation," management listens to workers' suggestions but retains the right to make final decisions. Or it may even grant workers the right to make final decisions, but only with regard to topics it feels are unimportant (even if some such topics, e.g., vacation schedules, happen to be important to workers). But management is un-likely voluntarily to give workers extensive powers over subjects im-portant to it. Even the paternalistic ex-owners of John Lewis and Scott Bader retained a large measure of final say for themselves. Joint con-sultative committees in various countries have had little impact largely because management has had the right to ignore their input.

For power to be securely in workers' hands, they must be able to have the final say themselves (or at least to block management's action) with regard to some significant topics. One source of such power is a formal charter or law. But charters are not self-enforcing. Workers need in-dependent sources of power to enforce their legal rights, for example, a strong non-co-opted union or the credible threat of going on strike. Power can also be drawn from status and control over resources, the most important of which may be knowledge and having a key position in the communications channel.

The major dilemma with regard to power is that one must have power to exercise it. Union power is often controlled by its leadership. Experts and other resource controllers have power. But how will WPM help the powerless? Too often WPM is confined to a small elite.

Knowledge. As Mulder (1971) dramatically pointed out, putting people with unequal knowledge together in a formally participative structure actually increases the power differential between them and leads to frustration.

Two kinds of knowledge are required: first, the organizational skills to function well in meetings or a bureaucracy, and second, content skills necessary to contribute to problem solving. The second is obvious, but inability to function as a board member has been a problem in numerous contexts.

It is hardly surprising that the totally untrained workers in Peru and Algeria proved unequal to the demands of WPM or that the knowledge-elite dominated Yugoslav workers councils. German PB members have positioned themselves to gather knowledge; indeed their quasi monopoly of it has increased strains with the rank and file.

Yet, as with power, there are limits as to the extent to which knowledge may be equalized. As organizations become more complex, specialists may increasingly outsmart generalists (at best, PB members are gener-alists). Indeed, by weakening top management's power, WPM may strengthen that of the experts. "The end result of attempts at democ-ratization could therefore be an extension of the autonomy and power of experts whose perspectives and skills run counter to the interests of workers, and this may be legitimized by apparently democratic struc-tures" (Batstone, 1979, p. 256; see also Bradley, 1980).

Rewards. The outcomes or rewards of WPM take many forms: saving one's job, protecting oneself against tyrannical supervision, demonstrating one's political or technical problem-solving ability, reducing class differences. Rewards may derive either from the *results* or the *process* of participation (because participation will right a grievance in one's favor or because one just enjoys talking). Rewards may also be extrinsic (economic) and/or intrinsic (moral). Though there has been considerable analysis of the relative roles of extrinsic and intrinsic motivation among both psychologists (Staw, 1976) and socialist economists (e.g., Bernardo, 1971), little of this analysis has been applied to WPM.

Ideologically oriented WPM, as in the kibbutz and in the early days in Yugoslavia, can make organizational (or even national) welfare a superordinate goal. Unfortunately, the strength of such superordinate goals is likely to decay. The provision of other superordinate goals that will be of interest to more than a small, politically oriented group of activists is among the most difficult of WPM's problems.

Whatever the reward—intrinsic or extrinsic—it should be significant for the workers involved, and it should satisfy *their* needs (not the needs that liberal-minded consultants think they should have).

Introducing and Sustaining WPM

Not enough attention has been given to viewing WPM as an OD intervention, a form of planned change. WPM has been introduced for a variety of idealistic and materialistic reasons. Similarly it has been introduced in a variety of ways: by starting from the bottom up, as when individual San Francisco scavengers joined together to form their PC; from the top down, as in Yugoslavia, and in PCs formed by paternalistic owners; or through the instigation of intellectuals, as in some recent British PCs. None of these factors seem to have made much difference for eventual WPM viability. Only one firm conclusion seems justified: it helps to have a "shelter organization" (as at Mondragon), namely, an institution (or institutions) that can provide financing, technical advice, and ideological support. Such organizations now exist in several European countries.

Among the major findings of the IDE (1981) group is that the existence of formal (de jure) rules for WPM has a strong influence on workers' influence and involvement: in other words, that laws requiring participation in fact increase participatory behavior (at least perceived participatory behavior). But, as just discussed, laws are not enough; power and knowledge are also important. Beyond this, it seems to help if workers have a psychological sense of "owning" WPM (Gunzburg, 1978). (This is different from actual ownership of the firm, although clearly actual ownership encourages psychological ownership.) For psychological ownership to be felt, it may be necessary that the workers (or at least their representatives) make a substantial psychological investment to introduce WPM in the first place. This facilitates commitment. For example, the German and Swedish labor movements committed a considerable proportion of their political clout in the campaign to get WPM introduced. This heavy investment may have helped codetermination succeed. WPM success in Chile was closely related ($r = .50$) with whether plant nationalization was preceded by a struggle (Espinosa and Zimbalist, 1978, p. 103).

Theory would suggest that for WPM to be truly accepted, it needs some initial success. Once such success is achieved, WPM begins to develop the kinds of participative skills and ideologies that help sustain it. Participation may become addictive, at least for a while.

Plateauing. But early success cannot maintain WPM indefinitely. Even if early efforts richly pay off, without adequate reinforcement—continued triumphs—initially favorable ideology may decay. The first problems to be solved may be the easiest ones; later problems may be more difficult. Further, if expectations are too high, they become easily dashed. The state of perpetual mobilization for collective goals may become exhausting; the relative values of collective, superordinate, noneconomic rewards may decline and that of economic goods may increase. If the real reward system diverges too far from that proscribed by the participative ideal, faith in the ideal may erode. Along with this, the actual practice of WPM may increasingly be restricted to a small elite, and management may take over. All of this may have occurred in Yugoslavia. Finally, a new generation that lacks even their parents' initial commitment may emerge.

If plateauing is so likely a danger, how can WPM's initial verve be sustained? Hypothetically, a continuing effort might be made to widen WPM to cover more issues and levels. For example, if WPM begins at the plant level, it might be extended to the shop (e.g., autonomous work groups). If it initially deals primarily with personnel issues, it might be extended to production problems or investment. To the extent that more and more people gain success experiences for personally making participative decisions, the participative momentum may continue, at least for a while.

However, workers' willingness to participate directly in workplace decisions is limited. Except perhaps for short periods, the responsibility for daily decisions is likely to be delegated to a small elite (either by plan or by practice). Usually the elite is concentrated on the PB. The trick, therefore, is to keep the PB responsive.

Maintaining PB Responsiveness. The PB role is a new one and its incumbents are still learning to play it. Nevertheless, the members' role problems, arising largely from the conflicting requirements of expertise and responsiveness, are not that different from those of union leaders and congressmen. In each case they must deal with technical issues about which they know less than does management and more than does the rank and file. They frequently must make decisions to which some of their constituents greatly object; they must compromise when their constituents think they should hold fast.

Some members thrive under their conflicting role as part-worker, part-manager. "Being twin-hatted isn't a problem for me," one British worker director explained. "If you can't ride two horses at once, you don't belong in the circus" (BSC Employee Directors, 1977, p. 47). It takes courage, but it is not impossible to be adversary, comanager, and even partly expert, all at once. Essentially all this requires is that one agrees with management, when one thinks its proposals are in the workers' best long-run interests—and disagree when they are not. As do experienced legislators, wise PB members know how to keep experts "on tap, not on top." (Some of the more effective worker directors in Britain had prior service on elected local legislative bodies. Handling management experts, they said, was not much different from handling civil service experts. BSC Employee Directors, 1977.)

To be effective, communications with the rank and file should be two way. PB members need to listen carefully to their constituents but also to educate them (Whyte, 1955). Face-to-face communication may be supplemented by news bulletins of various sorts (Bernstein, 1980). Attendance at shop meetings may improve if the PB member uses this opportunity to seek workers opinions rather than merely to make a speech (Bennett, 1979). Above all, the PB member needs to function like Lawrence and Lorsch's (1967) "integrator," sensitive to the values of both workers and management.

As in democracy generally, the PB member's responsiveness may increase when there is competition for his job. Furstenberg (conversation) reports that some of the most effective German workers councils exist in plants where there is an organized communist opposition. Perhaps WPM requires contested elections and even a party system. If this happens, will WPM be immobilized by pressure group politics? Does it need a strong executive?

But even a two-party system may leave the question of responsiveness unresolved. The United States political system has not been particularly successful in developing courageous political leaders who act only in the best interests of the country as a whole and who fearlessly educate their constituents to sacrifice their own special interests. For the most part, the rank-and-file member, whether voter or worker, tends to ignore the governmental process except when his own ox is being gored. Further, the task of industrial democracy may be even more difficult than that of political democracy. The political government may pass new laws that bother us *personally* only several times a year. Industrial democracy (whether self-management or joint decision making) involves the supervision of our daily activities. Being closer to us, it affects us more directly. Democratic determination of our daily behavior may be more difficult than democratic determination of general codes of social conduct.

Protection of Minority Interests. Democratic elections alone may not protect the interests of individual workers. The bulk of the membership may be apathetic; even with contested elections, the majority may tyrannize the minority; and both PB and union may be co-opted by management.

Bernstein (1980) argues that an enforceable bill of rights may help protect individual opportunities to dissent. But this is not enough unless there is some formal institution through which individuals *and* groups may express their viewpoints when the primary participatory channel becomes blocked. Without such an institution, self-managing organizations may be prone to oligarchy.

Even under worker ownership, United States workers prefer the union to preserve its separate role (Hammer and Stern, 1980). But if the union won't fulfill this function, perhaps some other agency, at least an ombudsman or appeals system, should. Mondragon's separate Social Council is supposed to represent workers' interests but does so with only moderate effectiveness (Johnson and Whyte, 1977). The John Lewis Partnership has a grievance committee, a separate appeals body, and a newspaper in which individual employees may publish anonymous complaints, which management must answer. Triumph Meriden has a grievance committee, Scott Bader an appeals board, and IGP a "community relations board", all of which serve as independent power centers outside the main WPM hierarchy (Bernstein, 1980; Edelstein, 1979; Zwerdling, 1979). Yugoslav firms (Adizes, 1971) and plywood PCs (Bennett, 1979) have disciplinary committees to protect individual workers against unfair discipline.

Considerably more attention is needed with regard to these essentially political questions of responsiveness and protecting workers' rights.

A Last Word

In terms of some of its proponents' objectives, representative WPM has had only limited success. It has involved top leadership more than the rank and file, and it has almost ignored middle and lower levels of management. It has not brought substantial power or influence to the ordinary worker; nor has it unleashed workers' creativity or even actively involved them in making production decisions. The division of labor between decision-makers and those who carry out decisions has not been abolished. Workers are not more involved in their work than before. WPM has not created a juster, more equal society.

WPM (or organizational democracy) has many of the strengths and weaknesses of political democracy. Despite the dreams of eighteenth century philosophers, it is difficult to show that political democracy has made our citizenry any more happy, law abiding, patriotic, or considerate of others. Similarly, there is little evidence that WPM has reduced workplace discontent, increased productivity, or created self-actualized workers. Perhaps all that either political or organizational democracy provides are orderly procedures for effecting compromises, developing consensus, and legitimating decisions. But this alone may make democracy of either sort worthwhile.

APPENDIX

A Research Agenda

For my taste, studies investigating such issues as desire for participation have reached the point of declining returns. Perhaps, too, some time should be spent digesting the results of recent international comparative large-sample, cross-section studies before undertaking a new wave. For the moment, researchers are long on data but short on explanatory hypotheses. Without further hypotheses as to the dynamics of WPM, further data gathering may be undirected.

Case studies may prove little, but they do suggest hypotheses. So my first priority would be for a series of carefully monitored longitudinal case studies that would follow the evolution of WPM in specific organizations from (or before) the date of its initial implementation for at least 5 years. Nonparticipant observation (as practiced, for example, by Adizes) would be the heart of each study. The observer would be concerned chiefly with how WPM (especially the PB) affects decision making, politics, and industrial relations within each affected organization. These observations might be supplemented by several waves of questionnaires (or interviews) designed to examine the changing perceptions of the principle parties (rank-and-file workers, union officers, PB members, supervisors, top managers, etc.) as to how participation is affecting their own behavior and the behavior of others.

Five years should be long enough to permit researchers to observe the dynamics of co-optation and plateauing. Aside from time and cost, the major danger with research of this sort is that the intensity of observation may affect the behavior being studied.

A second priority would be for cross-section, probably cross-national, studies examining how decisions are made regarding each of a small number of specific topics (e.g., layoffs, new investment, or discipline) under various forms of WPM. For example, researchers might compare a set number of (and reasonably equivalent) new investment decisions in 20 companies in 5 countries. Each study would examine the decision-making process in detail (as did the DIO group). It should report anecdotal material and not merely answers to questions such as, "How much say do you have with regard to. . . ." The emphasis in this research should be on WPM as a decision-making (or conflict resolution) process occurring over time, not on its psychological meaning.

A third priority would be to learn more about workers' attitudes toward engaging in WPM *themselves*. Years ago Sayles (1954) used projective tests to discover that though most union members supported their union as an institution, they evidenced a generalized hostility toward their leaders and a deep-seated reluctance to cause trouble by filing grievances. Are workers equally reluctant today to take part in shop-floor participative efforts or to initiate action through their PB member? Do workers ever gain a vicarious sense of participation through identification with their representatives' actions? Strikes provide an opportunity for active, physical participation. Are there psychological equivalents of the strike in WPM?

Projective techniques might also help researchers explore the differences in the meaning of various forms of participation across cultures. It might be fascinating to study the different meaning given to various forms of consultative actions by Japanese, United States, Yugoslav, and German workers.

REFERENCES

Abell, Peter. An evaluation of industrial co-operatives, the successes and failures. *International Yearbook of Organizational Democracy*, (forthcoming) *1*.

Adams, R. J., & Rummel, C. H. Workers participation in management in West Germany. *Industrial Relations Journal*, 1977, *8*, 4–22.

Adizes, Ichak. *Industrial democracy: Yugoslav style*. New York: Free Press, 1971.

Agassi, Judith. The Israeli experience in democratization of work life. *Sociology of Work and Occupations*, 1974, *1*, 82–109.

Albeda, Wil. Changing industrial relations in the Netherlands. *Industrial Relations*, 1977, *16*, 133–145.

Aldrich, Howard, & Stern, Robert. Social structure and the creation of producers' co-operatives. Paper presented to the IX World Congress of Sociology, Uppsala, Sweden, August 14–19, 1978.

Alutto, Joseph A., & Belasco, James A. A typology for participation in organizational decision making. *Administrative Science Quarterly,* 1972, *17,* 117–125.

Arzensek, Vladimir. Managerial legitimacy and organizational conflict. In Josip Obradovic & William N. Dunn (Eds.), *Workers' self-management and organizational power in Yugoslavia.* Pittsburg, PA: University Center for International Studies, University of Pittsburg, 1978.

Batstone, Eric. Industrial democracy and worker representation at board level: A review of the European experience. In Eric Batstone & P. L. Davies (Eds.), *Industrial democracy.* London: Her Majesty's Stationery Office, 1976.

Batstone, Eric. Systems of domination, accommodation and industrial power. In T. R. Burns, L. E. Karlsson, & V. Rus (Eds.), *Work and power.* London: Sage, 1979.

Baumgartner, Tom, Burns, Tom R., & Sekulic, Dusko. Self-management, market, and political institutions in conflict: Yugoslav development patterns and dialectics. In T. R. Burns, L. E. Karlsson, & V. Rus (Eds.), *Work and power.* London: Sage, 1979.

Bellas, Carl J. *Industrial democracy and the worker owned firm: A study of twenty-one plywood companies in the Pacific Northwest.* New York: Praeger, 1972.

Bennett, Leamon. When employees run the company. *Harvard Business Review,* 1979, *57,* 75–90.

Ben-Porat, A. Political parties and democracy in the Histadrut. *Industrial Relations,* 1979, *18,* 237–243.

Berenbach, Shari. Peru's social property: Limits to participation. *Industrial Relations,* 1979, *18,* 370–375.

Berger, Bennett. *The Survival of a Counterculture.* Berkeley: University of California Press, 1981.

Berman, K. F. *Worker-owned plywood companies: An economic analysis.* Washington: Pullman, 1967.

Bernardo, Robert M. *The theory of moral incentives in Cuba.* University, AL: University of Alabama Press, 1971.

Bernstein, Paul. *Workplace democratization, its internal dynamics.* New Brunswick, NJ: Transaction Books, 1980.

Bertsch, Gary K., & Obradovic, Josip. Participation and influence in Yugoslav self-management. *Industrial Relations,* 1979, *18,* 322–329.

Blum, Fred H. *Work and community: The Scott Bader Commonwealth and the quest for a new social order.* London: Routledge and Kegan Paul, 1968.

Bornstein, Stephen, & Fine, Keitha. Worker control in France: Recent political developments. In G. David Garson (Ed.), *Worker self-management in industry: The West European experience.* New York: Praeger, 1977.

Bradley, Keith. A comparative analysis of producer cooperatives: Some theoretical and empirical implications. *British Journal of Industrial Relations,* 1980, *18,* 155–168.

Brannen, P. *The worker directors: A sociology of participation.* London: Hutchinson, 1976.

BSC (British Steel Corporation) Employee Directors. *Worker directors speak.* Westmead, England: Gower Press, 1977.

Broekmeyer, Marius. Self-management in Yugoslavia. *Annals of the American Academy of Political and Social Science,* 1977, *431,* 133–140.

Bull, P. E., & Barton, G. A. Attitudes towards worker participation. *Journal of Industrial Relations,* 1978, *20,* 303–310.

Bullock, Lord Alan. *Report of the Committee of Inquiry on Industrial Democracy.* London: Her Majesty's Stationery Office, 1977.

Burt, W. J. Workers participation in management in Yugoslavia. *International Institute for Labour Studies Bulletin,* 1972, *9,* 129–172.

Chamberlain, Neil W. *Forces of Change in Western Europe.* London: McGraw-Hill, 1980.

Chaplin, P., & Cowe, R. A survey of contemporary British worker cooperatives, Manchester Business School Working Papers, 1977.

Chell, Elizabeth, & Cox, Derek. Worker directors and collective bargaining. *Industrial Relations Journal,* 1979, *10,* 25–31.

Clarke, R. O., Fatchett, D. J., & Roberts, Ben C. *Workers participation in management in Britain.* London: Heinemann, 1979.

Clegg, Hugh A. *A new approach to industrial democracy.* Oxford: Basil Blackwell, 1960.

Clegg, Ian. *Workers' self-management in Algeria.* London: Allen Lane, 1971.

Coates, Ken, & Topham, Anthony (Eds.), Industrial democracy in Great Britain. London: MacGibbon and Kee, 1968.

Conte, Michael, & Tannenbaum, Arnold. Employee owned companies: Is the difference measureable? *Monthly Labor Review,* 1978, *101,* 23–28.

Cupper, Les. Self-management: The Dynavac experiment. In Russell Lansbury (Ed.), *Democracy in the work place.* Melbourne: Longman Cheshire, 1980.

Dachler, H. Peter, & Wilpert, Bernhard. Conceptual dimensions and boundaries of participation in organizations: A critical evaluation. *Administrative Science Quarterly,* 1978, *23,* 1–39.

Daniel, W. W. Understanding employee behaviour in its context. In J. Child (Ed.), *Man and organization.* New York: Wiley, 1973.

de Bellecombe, L. Greyfie. Workers participation in management in Poland. *International Institute of Labour Studies Bulletin,* 1968, *5,* 188–220.

Delacroix, Jacques, & Ragin, Charles. Modernizing institutions, mobilization, and third world countries: A cross-national study. *American Journal of Sociology,* 1978, *84,* 123–150.

Derber, Milton. *Labor-management relations at the plant level under industry-wide bargaining.* Urbana, IL: University of Illinois Press, 1955.

Derber, Milton. Advancing Australian union democracy. *Industrial Relations,* 1978, *17,* 112–116.

de Schweinitz, Dorothy, *Labor and management in a common enterprise.* Cambridge, MA: Harvard University Press, 1949.

DIO (Decisions in Organizations). Participative decision making: A comparative study. *Industrial Relations,* 1979, *18,* 295–309.

Drenth, P. The works council in the Netherlands. In Eugene Pusic (Ed.), *Participation and self-management.* Zagreb: 1973.

Driscoll, James W. Working creatively with the union: Lessons from the Scanlon Plan. *Organizational Dynamics,* 1979, *8,* 61–80.

Dunlop, John T. *Industrial relations systems.* New York: Holt, Rinehart, and Winston, 1958.

Eaton, Jack. The Basque workers' cooperative. *Industrial Relations Journal,* 1979, *10,* 32–40.

Edelstein, J. David. Trade unions in British producers' cooperatives. *Industrial Relations,* 1979, *18,* 358–363.

Elliott, John. *Conflict or cooperation: the growth of industrial democracy.* London: Kogan Page, 1978.

Engelstad, Per, & Quale, Thoralf. *Innsyn og innflytelse i styre og bedritsforsamling* (Understanding and influence in boards of directors). Oslo: Tiden, 1977.

Espinosa, Juan G., & Zimbalist, Andrew S. *Economic democracy: Workers' participation in Chilean industry, 1970–73.* New York: Academic Press, 1978.

Etzioni, Amitai. *A comparative analysis of complex organizations.* New York: Free Press, 1975.

Fine, Keitha. Workers participation in Israel. In Gerry Hunnius, G. David Garson, & John Case (Eds.), *Workers control*. New York: Vintage Books, 1973.

Flanders, Allan, Pomeranz, Ruth, & Woodward, Joan. *Experiment in industrial democracy*. London: Faber & Faber, 1968.

Fleishman, E. A. A leader behavior description for industry. In R. M. Stogdill & A. E. Coons (Eds.), *Leader behavior: Its description and measurement*. Columbus, OH: Bureau of Business Research, 1957.

Fogarty, M. Co-determination and company structure in Germany. *British Journal of Industrial Relations*, 1964, *2*, 79–113.

Furstenburg, Fredrick. Workers' participation in management in the Federal Republic of Germany. *International Institute for Labour Studies Bulletin*, 1968, *6*, 94–148.

Furstenberg, Fredrick. *Workers' participation in management in the Federal Republic of Germany*. Geneva: International Institute for Labour Studies, Research Series No. 32, 1978.

Furstenberg, Fredrick. Co-determination and its contribution to industrial democracy. *Proceedings of the thirty-third annual meeting of the Industrial Relations Research Association*, 1981, 185–190.

Galin, Amira. An evaluation of industrial democracy schemes in Israel. In Russell Lansbury (Ed.), *Democracy in the workplace*. Melbourne: Longman Chesire, 1980.

Galin, Amira, & Tabb, Jay. *Workers participation in management in Israel, successes and failures*. Geneva: International Institute for Labour Studies, Research Series No. 29, 1978.

Gamson, Zelda, & Levin, Henry. *Obstacles to the Survival of Democratic Workplaces*. Unpublished manuscript, 1980.

Garson, G. David. *Workers self-management in industry: The West European experience*. New York: Praeger, 1977.

Globerson, Arie. Spheres and levels of employee participation in organizations: Elements of a conceptual model. *British Journal of Industrial Relations*, 1970, *8*, 252–262.

Gold, Charlotte. *Employer-employee committees and worker participation*. Ithaca: New York State School of Industrial and Labor Relations, Cornell University, 1976.

Goldstein, S. G. Employee share ownership and motivation. *Journal of Industrial Relations*, 1978, *20*, 311–330.

Goldthorpe, J. H., Lockwood, D., Bechhofer, F., & Platt, J. *The affluent worker: Industrial attitudes and behavior*. Cambridge: Cambridge University Press, 1968.

Goodman, Paul, *Assessing organizational change: The Rushton quality of work experiment*. New York: Wiley, 1979.

Greenberg, Edward S. *Producer cooperatives and democratic theory: the case of the plywood firms*. Unpublished manuscript, 1978.

Gunn, Christopher. Towards workers' control. *Working Papers for a New Society*, 1980, *7*, 4–7.

Gunzburg, Doron. *Industrial democracy approaches in Sweden: An Australian view*. Melbourne: Productivity Promotion Council of Australia, 1978.

Haire, Mason, Ghiselli, Edwin E., & Porter, Lyman W. *Managerial thinking: An international study*. New York: Wiley, 1966.

Hammer, Tove, & Stern, Robert. Employee ownership: Implications for the organizational distribution of power. *Academy of Management Journal*, 1980, *23*, 78–100.

Hammer, Tove, & Stern, Robert. *Worker members on company boards of directors*, unpublished manuscript, Cornell University, 1981.

Harrison, Roger, *Workers' participation in Western Europe, 1976*. London: Institute of Personnel Management, 1976.

Hartmann, Heinz. Codetermination in West Germany. *Industrial Relations*, 1970, *9*, 137–147.

Hartmann, Heinz. Works councils and the iron law of oligarchy. *British Journal of Industrial Relations*, 1979, *17*, 70–82.

Heller, Frank, Wilders, Malcolm, Abell, Peter, & Warner, Malcolm. *What do the British want from participation and industrial democracy?* London: Anglo-German Foundation for the Study of Industrial Society, 1979.

Herding, Richard. *Job control and union structure*. Rotterdam: Rotterdam University Press, 1972.

Hethy, L., & Mako, C. Workers direct participation in decisions in Hungarian factories. *International Labour Review*, 1977, *116*, 9–21.

Holter, Harriet. Attitudes towards employee participation in company decision-making processes. *Human Relations*, 1965, *18*, 297–321.

Hunnius, Gerry, Garson, G. David, & Case, John (Eds.). *Workers' control: A reader on labor and social change*. New York: Random House, 1973.

IDE, Industrial Democracy in Europe International Research Group. Participation: Formal rules, influence and involvement. *Industrial Relations*, 1979, *18*, 273–294.

IDE, Industrial Democracy in Europe International Research Group. *Industrial democracy in Europe*. London: Oxford, 1981.

Jacob, Betty M. The effective trade union. In *Automation and industrial workers*, 2. Oxford: Pergamon, 1978.

Jacob, Betty M., & Jacob, Philip E. *Automation and humanization*. Honolulu: Research Corporation of the University of Hawaii, 1979.

Jacob, Philip, & Ahn, Chungsi. Around the world on the automated line. *The Wharton Magazine*, 1979, 64–67.

Jacob, Philip, Jez, V., Koval, B., Margulies, F., Rantalaiho, L., Rehak, J., & Wieser, G. (Eds.). *Automation and industrial workers: International comparisons*. Oxford: Pergamon, (in press).

Jain, H., Vanachter, O., & Gevers, P. Success and problems with participative schemes—the case of Belgium. In Hem C. Jain (Ed.), *Worker participation: Success and problems*. New York: Praeger, 1980.

Jaques, Eliot. *The changing culture of the factory*. London: Tavistock, 1951.

Johannesen, Janette Eadon. VAG: A need for education. *Industrial Relations*, 1979, *18*, 364–369.

Johnson, Ana G., & Whyte, William F. The Mondragon system of worker production cooperatives. *Industrial and Labor Relations Review*, 1977, *31*, 18–30.

Jones, Derek C. Worker participation in management in Britain. In G. David Garson (Ed.), *Worker self-management in industry*. New York: Praeger, 1977.

Jones, Derek C. U.S. producer cooperatives: The record to date. *Industrial Relations*, 1979, *18*, 342–357.

Jones, Derek C. Producer cooperatives in industrialized Western economies. *British Journal of Industrial Relations*, 1980, *18*, 141–154.

Jones, Derek C., & Backus, David K. British producer cooperatives in the footwear industry: An empirical evaluation of the theory of financing. *Economic Journal*, 1977, *87*, 488–510.

Jovanov, Neca. Strikes and self-management. In Josip Obradovic & William Dunn (Eds.), *Workers' self-management and organizational power in Yugoslavia*. Pittsburgh, PA: University of Pittsburgh, 1978.

Kelley, Joe. *Is scientific management possible? A critical examination of Glacier's theory of organization*. London: Faber & Faber, 1968.

Kester, Gerard. *Transition to workers' self-management: Its dynamics in the decolonizing economy of Malta.* The Hague: Institute for Social Studies, 1980.

Kochan, Thomas A., Dyer, Lee, & Lipsky, David. *The Effectiveness of union-management safety and health committees.* Kalamazoo, MI: Upjohn, 1977.

Kolaja, Jiri. *A Polish factory: A case study of workers' participation in decision making.* Lexington, KY: University of Kentucky Press, 1960.

Kolaja, Jiri. *Workers' councils: The Yugoslav experience.* New York: Praeger, 1966.

Koziara, Edward C. Workers' participation in Malta. *Industrial Relations,* 1979, *18,* 381–384.

Lammers, Cornelius J. Power and participation in decision-making in formal organizations. *American Journal of Sociology,* 1967, *73,* 201–216.

Lane, David, & O'Dell, Felicity. *The soviet worker: Social class, education, and control.* New York: St. Martin's Press, 1978.

Lansbury, Russell (Ed.), *Democracy in the work place.* Melbourne: Longman, 1980.

Lawrence, Paul R., & Lorsch, Jay W. *Organization and environment: Managing differentiation and integration.* Boston: Division of Research, Harvard Business School, 1967

Legendre, M. *Quelques aspects des relations professionnelles.* Paris: Service d'Etudes pour le Developpement, 1969.

Leviaton, Uri. Organizational effects of management turnover in kibbutz production branches. *Human Relations,* 1978, *31,* 1001–1018.

Little, D. Richard. *Political participation and the soviet system. Problems of communism,* 1980, *29,* 62–67.

Locke, Edwin, & Schweiger, David M. Participation in decision-making: One more look. In Barry Staw and L. L. Cummings (Ed.), *Research in organizational behavior,* 1. Greenwich, Conn.: JAI Press.

Lockett, M. Organizational democracy and politics in China. *International Yearbook of Organizational Democracy,* (in progress) *1.*

Logue, John. On the road toward worker-run companies? The employee participation act in practice. *Working Life in Sweden,* 1978, *9.*

Long, Richard. The effects of employee ownership on organizational identification, employee job attitudes, and organizational performance. *Human Relations,* 1978a, *31,* 29–48.

Long, Richard. The relative effects of share ownership vs. control on job attitudes in an employee owned company. *Human Relations,* 1978b, *31,* 753–764.

Long, Richard. Desires for and patterns of worker participation in decision-making after conversion to employee ownership. *Academy of Management Journal,* 1979, *22,* 611–617.

Long, Richard. Job attitudes and organizational performance under employee ownership. *Academy of Management Journal,* 1980, *23,* 726–737.

Lowin, Aaron. Participative decision making: A model, literature critique, and prescriptions for research. *Organizational Behavior and Human Performance,* 1968, *3,* 68–106.

Mako, Csaba. *Shopfloor democracy and the socialist enterprise.* University of Turko, Sociological Studies Series A:3, 1978.

Maley, Brian, Dunphy, Dexter, & Ford, Bill. *Industrial democracy and worker participation.* Adelaide, South Australia: Unit for Industrial Democracy, 1979.

Marclay, Annette. *Workers participation in management—a selected bibliography, 1950–1970.* Geneva: International Labor Organization, 1971.

Martin, Andrew. Sweden: Industrial democracy and social democratic strategy. In G. David Garson (Ed.), *Worker self-management in industry: The West European experience.* New York: Praeger, 1977.

Matejko, Alexander. Work and management in Poland. In Robert Dubin (Ed.), *Handbook of work, sociology, and society*. Chicago: Rand McNally, 1976.

McGregor, Andrew. Rent extraction and the survival of agricultural production cooperatives. *American Journal of Agricultural Economics*, 1977, *59*, 478–488.

McGregor, Douglas, & Knickerbocker, Irving R. Union-management cooperation: A psychological analysis," *Personnel*, 1942, *19*.

Melman, S. Managerial vs. cooperative decision making in Israel. *Studies in Comparative International Development*, 1970–71, *6*, 47–58.

Michael, Avraham, & Bar-El, Rafael. *Strikes in Israel: 1960–69: A quantitative approach.* Ramat-Gan: Bar-Ilan University, 1977.

Miller, Richard F. Worker self-management in Yugoslavia. *Journal of Industrial Relations*, 1978, *20*, 264–285.

Mulder, Mark. Power equalization through participation. *Administrative Science Quarterly*, 1971, *16*, 31–38.

National Institute of Industrial Psychology. *Joint consultation in British industry*. London: The Institute, 1952.

National Swedish Industrial Board. *Board representation of employees in Sweden*. Stockholm: LiberForlag, 1976.

Nightingale, Donald V. The formally participative organization. *Industrial Relations*, 1979, *18*, 310–321.

Northrup, Herbert R., & Young, Harvey A. The causes of industrial peace revisited. *Industrial and Labor Relations Review*, 1968, *22*, 31–47.

Oakeshott, Robert. *The case for workers' co-ops*. London: Routledge & Kegan Paul, 1978.

Obradovic, Josip. Participation and work attitudes in Yugoslavia. *Industrial Relations*, 1970, *9*, 161–169.

Obradovic, J. Workers' participation: Who participates? *Industrial Relations*, 1975, *14*, 32–44.

Obradovic, Josip. Participation in enterprise decision-making. In Josip Obradovic & William N. Dunn, *Workers' self-management and organizational power in Yugoslavia*. Pittsburgh, PA: University Center for International Studies, University of Pittsburgh, 1978.

Obradovic, Josip, French, R. P. John, & Rodgers, Willard L. Workers' councils in Yugoslavia: Effects on perceived participation and satisfaction of workers, *Human Relations*, 1970, *23*, 459–471.

Olson, Mancur. *The logic of collective action*. Cambridge: Harvard University Press, 1965.

Pateman, Carole. *Participation and democratic theory*. London: Cambridge University Press, 1970.

Paul, Bill. Germany's requiring of workers on boards causes many problems. *Wall Street Journal*, 1979, December 10, p. 1.

Perry, Stewart. *San Francisco scavengers: Dirty Work and the pride of ownership*. Berkely, CA: University of California Press, 1978.

Peterson, Richard B. The Swedish experience with industrial democracy. *British Journal of Industrial Relations*, 1968, *6*, 185–203.

Pfeffer, Jeffrey, & Salancik, Gerald R. *The external control of organizations*. New York: Harper & Row, 1978.

Poole, Michael. *Workers participation in industry*. Boston, MA: Routledge & Kegan Paul, 1975.

Pugh, D. S., Hickson, D. J., Hinings, C. R., & Turner, C. Dimensions of organizational structure. *Administrative Science Quarterly*, 1968, *13*, 65–105.

Quinn, Robert P., & Staines, Graham. *1977 quality of employment survey*. Ann Arbor, MI: University of Michigan, Institute for Social Research, 1978.

Ramondt, Joop. Workers self-management and its constraints: The Yugoslav experience. *British Journal of Industrial Relations*, 1979, *17*, 83–94.

Ramsay, Harvie. Participation: The shop floor view. *British Journal of Industrial Relations*, 1976, *14*, 128–141.

Riddell, D. S. Social self-government: The background and theory in Yugoslavian socialism. *British Journal of Sociology*, 1968, *19*, 47–75.

Rosenberg, Richard, & Rosenstein, Eliezar. Participation and productivity: An empirical study. *Industrial and Labor Relations Review*, 1980, *33*, 355–367.

Rosenstein, Eliezar. Worker participation in Israel: Experience and lessons. *Annals of the American Academy of Political and Social Science*, 1977, *431*, 113–122.

Rosner, Menachem. Political and organizational democracy in the Israeli kibbutz. *International Yearbook of Organizational Democracy*, (forthcoming) *1*.

Rothschild-Whitt, Joyce. The Collectivist Organization: An Alternative to Rational-Bureaucratic Models. *American Sociological Review*, 1979, *44*, 509–527.

Rubenowitz, S., Norgren, F., & Tannenbaum, A. S. Some social psychological effects of direct and indirect participation in ten Swedish companies. Unpublished manuscript, 1980.

Ruh, Robert A., Wallace, Roger L., & Frost, Carl F. Management attitudes and the Scanlon Plan. *Industrial Relations*, 1973, *12*, 282–288.

Rus, Veljko. Influence structure in Yugoslav enterprise. *Industrial Relations*, 1970, *9*, 148–160.

Rus, Veljko. Limited effects of worker participation and political counter-power. In Tom Burns, Lars E. Karlsson, & V. Rus (Eds.), *Work and power*. London: Safe, 1979.

Rus, Veljko. Conflict regulation in self-managed Yugoslav enterprises. In Richard Peterson & Gerard Bommers (Eds.), *Conflict management and industrial relations*. Boston: Kluwer-Nijhoff, 1982.

Russell, Raymond, Hochner, Arthur, & Perry, Stewart E. Participation, influence, and worker-ownership. *Industrial Relations*, 1979, *18*, 330–341.

Sachs, Stephen M. *Implications of recent developments in Yugoslav self-management*. Unpublished manuscript, 1975.

Salancik, Gerald R., & Pfeffer, Jeffrey. An examination of need-satisfaction models of job attitudes. *Administrative Science Quarterly*, 1977, *22*, 427–456.

Sayles, Leonard R. Field use of projective techniques. *Sociology and Social Research*, 1954, *38*, 169–173.

Sayles, Leonard R., & Strauss, George. *The local union*, rev. ed. New York: Harcourt, Brace, & World, 1967.

Schrank, Robert. *Ten thousand working days*. Cambridge, MA: MIT Press, 1978.

Slichter, Sumner. *Union policies and industrial management*. Washington, D.C.: The Brookings Institution, 1941.

Smith, W. R. Attitudes toward workers control in France. *Sociological Review*, 1977, *25*, 877–885.

Staw, Barry M. *Intrinsic and extrinsic motivation*. Morristown, NJ: General Learning Press, 1976.

Steinherr, Alfred. The labor managed economy: A survey of the economics literature. *Annals of Public and Cooperative Economy*, 1978, *49*, 129–148.

Stephen, Frank H. Yugoslav self-management 1945–74. *Industrial Relations Journal*, 1977, *7*, 56–65.

Stephens, Evelyne. *The politics of workers' participation: The Peruvian approach in comparative perspective*. New York: Academic Press, 1980.

Strauss, George. Managerial practices. In J. R. Hackman & Lloyd Suttle (Eds.), *Improving life at work*. Santa Monica, CA: Goodyear, 1977.

Strauss, George. Can social psychology contribute to industrial relations? In Geoffrey Stephenson & Christopher Brotherton (Eds.), *Industrial relations: A social psychological approach*. New York: Wiley, 1979a.

Strauss, George. Quality of worklife and participation as bargaining issues. In Hervey Juris & Myron Roomkin (Eds.), *The Shrinking Perimeter*. Lexington, MA: Lexington Books, 1979b.

Strauss, George, & Rosenstein, Eliezer. Workers participation: A critical view. *Industrial Relations*, 1970, *9*, 197–214.

Strauss, George, & Sayles, Leonard R. The Scanlon Plan: Some organizational problems. *Human Organization*, 1957, *16*, 15–22.

Stern, Robert, Wood, K. Haydn, & Hammer, Tove. *Employee ownership in plant shutdowns*. Kalamazoo, MI: Upjohn, 1979.

Sturmthal, Adolf. *Workers' councils*. Cambridge, MA: Harvard University Press, 1964.

Survey Research Center, University of Michigan. *Employee Ownership*. Unpublished manuscript, 1977.

Svejnar, Jan. Relative wage effects of unions, dictatorship and codetermination: Economic evidence from Germany. *Review of Economics and Statistics*, 1981, *43*, 188–197.

Tabb, Jay, & Galin, Amira. *Workers participation in management*. Oxford: Pergamon, 1970.

Tanic, Zivan. *Workers participation in management*. New Delhi: Siri Ram, 1969.

Tannenbaum, Arnold S., Kovcic, Bogdan, Rosner, Menachem, Vianello, Mino, & Wieser, Georg. *Hierarchy in organizations*. San Francisco, CA: Jossey-Bass, 1974.

Thorsrud, E., & Emery, F. E. Industrial democracy in Norway. *Industrial Relations*, 1970, *9*, 187–196.

Vanek, Jaroslav (Ed.). *Self-management: Economic liberation of man*. Baltimore, MD: Penguin, 1975a.

Vanek, Jaroslav. The basic theory of financing of participatory firms. In Jaroslav Vanek (Ed.), *Self-management*. Baltimore, MD: Penguin, 1975b.

Vanek, Jaroslav. *The labor-managed economy*. Ithaca, NY: Cornell University Press, 1977.

Vardi, Yoav, Shirom, Arie, & Jacobson, Dan. A Study of the leadership beliefs of Israeli managers. *Academy of Management Journal*, 1980, *23*, 367–374.

Vranicki, Predrag. Socialism and the problem of alienation. *Praxis*, 1965, *1*, 307–317.

Wachtel, Howard M. *Workers' management and workers' wages in Yugoslavia: The theory and practice of participatory democracy*. Ithaca: Cornell University Press, 1973.

Walder, Andrew. Participative management and worker control in China. *Sociology of Work and Occupation*, 1981, *8*, 224–251.

Walker, Kenneth F. Workers' participation in management: Problems, practice, and prospect. *International Institute for Labour Studies Bulletin*, 1974, *12*, 3–35.

Wall, Toby, & Lisheron, Joseph. *Worker participation: A critique of the literature and some fresh evidence*. London: McGraw-Hill, 1977.

Walton, R. D., & McKersie, R. B. *A behavioral theory of labor negotiations*. New York: McGraw-Hill, 1965.

Warner, Malcolm. Whither Yugoslav self-management? *Industrial Relations Journal*, 1975, *6*, 65–72.

Webb, Sidney, & Webb, Beatrice. *A constitution for the socialist commonwealth of Great Britain*. London: Longmans, 1920.

Westenholz, Ann. Workers' participation in Denmark. *Industrial Relations*, 1979, *18*, 376–380.

White, J. Kenneth. The Scanlon Plan: Causes and correlates of success. *Academy of Management Journal*, 1979, *22*, 292–312.

Whyte, William F. *Money and motivation*. New York: Harper, 1955.

Whyte, William F. Models for building and changing organizations. *Human Organizations*, 1967, *26*, 22–31.

Whyte, William Foote. *Organizational behavior: Theory and application*. Homewood, IL: Irwin, 1969.

Williams, Carol. *Workers' participation: A bibliography*. Kingston, Ont.: Industrial Relations Centre, Queens University, 1976.

Wilpert, Bernhard. Research on industrial democracy: The German case. *Industrial Relations Journal*, 1975, *6*, 65–72.

Windmuller, John (Ed.). Industrial democracy in international perspective. *Annals of the American Academy of Political and Social Science*, 1977, *431*.

Witte, John F. *Democracy, authority, and alienation in work*. Chicago, IL: University of Chicago Press, 1980.

Young, F. John. Workers participation in management in New Zealand: A survey. (mimeographed), 1979.

Zimbalist, Andrew. The dynamic of worker participation. In G. David Garson & Smith, Michael P. (Eds.), *Organizational democracy*. London: Sage, 1976.

Zupanov, Josip. Two patterns of conflict management in industry. *Industrial Relations*, 1973, *12*, 213–223.

Zwerdling, Daniel. Employee ownership: How well is it working? *Working Papers for a New Society*, 1979, *7*, 15–27.

UNIDIMENSIONAL MEASUREMENT, SECOND ORDER FACTOR ANALYSIS, AND CAUSAL MODELS

John E. Hunter and David W. Gerbing

ABSTRACT

The research process is conceptualized as the analysis of (1) relations between constructs and (2) the measurement of constructs. The formalization of this process is the construction of two interrelated models, causal and measurement models, which are analyzed with path analysis and confirmatory factor analysis, respectively. This article departs from previous work in this area in two ways: First, we draw a sharp distinction between causal processes versus regression equations and path coefficients. Causal processes are events that occur either between people or inside people's heads and are only indirectly reflected in changes in the values of the variables that we invent to summarize our observations of these processes. Many contemporary authors have reified beta weights as if there were actually causal relations between variables. Second, we draw out the implications of confirmatory factor analysis for measurement models at the level of second-order factor analysis as well as at the level of item analysis. These points are illustrated in a reanalysis of data drawn from the organizational behavior literature.

Research in Organizational Behavior, Vol. 4, pages 267–320
Copyright © 1982 by JAI Press Inc.
All rights of reproduction in any form reserved.
ISBN: 0-89232-147-4

OVERVIEW

The goal of most scientific research is the investigation of the relations among variables, which are constructs such as abilities, attitudes, desires, policies, or perceptions. For example, the causal relations among the variables may be shown in the correlations among the variables. An explicit network of causal relations among the variables is called a "causal model" or a "structural equation model." In pictorial form the model is called a "path diagram." The parameters of the model represent the causal impact that variables have on one another. Once a causal model has been constructed, the parameters can be estimated and the model can be tested and revised using path analysis (e.g., Kenny, 1979).

The researcher must first measure the variables of interest before the relations between them can be analyzed. The problem is that observed measurements are never perfect; they are only indirect estimates of the intended constructs. Thus observed values should not be used as measurements unless there has first been an accounting of the nature and degree of error in the observations (e.g., Cochran, 1968; Wiley, 1973; Issac, 1970; Schwab, 1980). The formal operationalization of the constructs in terms of observables is called a "measurement model." The measurement model is defined by the specification of each construct in the model as a causal antecedent to a set of indicator variables. Most current measurement models can be cast in the language of "cluster analysis" (Tryon, 1939; Tryon and Bailey, 1970) or "Spearman factor analysis" (Spearman, 1904) or "confirmatory factor analysis of congeneric tests" (Joreskog, 1971, 1978), which are all statements of the same basic model.

The subject of this article is the construction and analysis of the measurement and causal models, which together form an integrated approach to data analysis and theory construction. A complete research project can be conceptualized as the construction and analysis of the two models: a measurement model using confirmatory factor analysis and a causal model using path analysis. The researcher builds causal models among variables. The variables of interest must first be measured according to the measurement model and their indicator variables.

The causal and measurement models share several conceptual and statistical similarities in their analysis. In either case the researcher must (1) construct the model, (2) estimate the values of the parameters of the model from the data, the observed correlations among the variables in the model, and (3) test the fit of the model to the data by comparing the observed correlations with the correlations among the variables predicted by the model. The substantive and statistical similarities of the measurement and causal models are so great that the models may even be analyzed simultaneously, as with Joreskog's program LISREL (Joreskog and Sorbom, 1978), although arguments have been presented against this simultaneous procedure (Gerbing and Hunter).[1]

The interplay between the measurement and causal models can also be expressed in the language of construct validity and substantive validity. In the definitions provided by Schwab (1980), "Construct validity is defined as representing the correspondence between a construct (conceptual definition of a variable) and the operational procedure to measure or manipulate that construct. . . . Substantive validity . . . [is concerned with] the relationship between constructs" (pp. 6 and 33). The construct validation of a variable operationalized with multiple indicators is accomplished by the analysis of the measurement model. The substantive validation of a causal network relating the constructs can be accomplished by the analysis of a causal model.

The preceding discussion of the measurement model adopts the traditional view that the primary problem in measurement is random error, that is, randomness in the basic response process of the person surveyed. However, from the beginning there has also been a concern about a different source of error, the "specific" error. Specific error is nonrandom variation that occurs in the person's response and that is produced by processes irrelevant to the purposes of the researcher. If the causes of specific error vary from one item to the next, then specific error cannot be distinguished from random error in cross-sectional studies. However, it can be distinguished in longitudinal studies because specific error causes the test–retest correlations to be larger than would be predicted from classical reliability theory or confirmatory factor analysis.

The crucial problem posed by specific error emerges when the same determinant of specific error enters into a whole set of items. If one source of specific error is present in one set of items and another source of specific error is present in another set of items, then the two sets of items will act as if they measure two different constructs (as is indeed the case). However, if the two sources of specific error are conceptually trivial (say, idiosyncratic meanings given to particular words), then primary factor analysis and classical confirmatory factor analysis will falsely suggest to the researcher that two different constructs are measured with random error when in fact one construct is being measured with two kinds of specific error. That is, specific error can create false distinctions between *scales* comparable to the random error distinguishing between items.

Consider Hackman and Oldham's (1975) dimensions of Autonomy and Task Variety in job perception. At the level of items, these dimensions appear to be separate factors, though highly correlated. (Corrected for attenuation, they are correlated .73 in the study by Pierce (1979), which is reviewed later.) Could these factors differ from one another by only trivial specific factors? The answer is found by treating the scale scores as if they were items and performing a "second-order" factor analysis. This process will be handled separately from the main treatment of measurement models presented in the following section.

THE MEASUREMENT MODEL

The measurement model specifies the causal relations between the theoretically defined variables of interest and the responses to the observed variables, which are presumed to be determined by the theoretical variables (e.g., Schwab, 1980). Measurement theories are needed because the relationship between the observed and theoretical variables is usually imperfect; the observed responses are generated or caused by both the underlying construct *and* measurement error. The sources of measurement error, which are examined in detail by Thorndike (1951), include (1) random error—the randomness inherent in the response process of the person surveyed—and (2) specific error—the invalidity inherent in a given observed variable.

As noted in the overview, specific error is a source of variation that enters a measure and contributes to its true score but that is actually irrelevant to the purposes of the investigator. For example, Spearman (1904) originally identified "specific factors" in achievement tests as the main source of error in measuring intelligence. His theory was that idiosyncratic experiences caused learning in specific areas to differ from that which would be determined from intelligence alone and hence rendered specific achievement tests to be only indirect estimators of ability.

Given the presence of random and specific error, the central problem of measurement focuses on the distinction between observed variables and latent or theoretical variables. Other common words for latent variables are "traits," "true scores," "domain scores," "universe scores," "unobserved variables," "underlying variables," "factors," "constructs," and "molar variables." Observed variables are also referred to as "items," "tests," "scales," "indicators," "overt variables," "fallible measures," and "molecular variables."

The standard answer to the problem of the error in the observed variables is multiple observations. The key idea is this: If several items measure the same construct, then the influence of construct on response is common to all the responses whereas the processes that create errors vary randomly from one item to the next. Thus the common thread running through the set of responses should be much more indicative of the construct than is any single response.

The usual method of finding the common thread through several responses is to add or average them. The observed variables, for example, the items on a questionnaire, are organized into clusters or tests or scales such that each cluster of observed variables corresponds to a single underlying latent variable. The average score across the items that define the cluster, the "cluster score," provides a level of analysis that is intermediate to the molar and molecular. If the items satisfy the empirical procedures of construct validation, then the composite is potentially a more reliable and valid estimate of the latent variable of interest than any of the component single item responses. However, the composite is still only an imperfect estimate of the corresponding latent variable.

Mathematically, any set of items can be defined as a cluster. And for any cluster, a score can be formed by summing over the responses to these items. However, *if* each of the items in the cluster are to be alternate indicators of a single underlying trait or construct, then the corresponding cluster score is interpretable only if the cluster is unidimensional. That is, *if* there is a measurement model that specifies that only a single latent variable or construct (and error) is causally antecedent to each of the component items on a scale, then the corresponding cluster score is an estimate of an underlying construct only if the component items form a unidimensional scale (or homogeneous scale or unifactor scale or congeneric test). A measurement model that specifies a set of unidimensional scales is called a *multiple groups* or sometimes a *multiple indicator measurement model*. The statistical evaluation of a multiple groups measurement model, historically called "Spearman factor analysis," is a specific example of a "confirmatory factor analysis" after Joreskog (1966, 1969). The complete analysis of a measurement model, an example of construct validation (Cronbach and Meehl, 1955; Jackson, 1980; Schwab, 1980), involves (1) model construction, (2) parameter estimation, and (3) model evaluation, followed by (4) an analysis of the reliability of the cluster scores for multiple groups models. These are the subjects of the remainder of this section.

Construction of the Model

The first step in the analysis is the writing and partitioning of the items into distinct scales, that is, each item is placed in only one cluster. The initial set of clusters may be defined in two ways: on the basis of an a priori analysis of item content or on the basis of statistical summaries of relationships such as the inter-item correlations. Purely statistical procedures for generating clusters are called either "exploratory" or "blind" analyses. For simplicity in the following discussion, the general issues are phrased in the language of questionnaire data: "items" and "traits" are used for "observed variables" and "latent variables", respectively.

Analysis of Content. During all phases of the analysis, the researcher should have a theory of how a set of items can be written for each trait, that is, a theory relating item responses to traits by a clustering of the items. The most important criterion for clustering at each phase of the analysis is item content or the meaning of the items.

The initial measurement model should be rationally constructed *before* the data is collected. That is, there should be a rationally constructed a priori set of clusters or scales of items that is ready for parameter estimation and evaluation before the first computer run. At this point, the *only* basis for the writing and partitioning of the items is item content. Usually, there is an indefinitely large set of items that can be used as alternate indicators or measures of each trait. Writing items can be thought of as generating a sample from that item domain (Tryon, 1959) or universe of content (Guttman, 1944). Each item should be concise and unambiguous, and the meaning of all the items in a cluster should be similar. The items should be worded so that they will discriminate between the individuals in the sample. If everyone agrees or everyone disagrees with an item, the item would have no variance and thus would not correlate with anything else. An excellent treatment of problems in item writing is given in Ebel (1972).

Items should not be mixed together in the same cluster unless the items share a specific and common meaning. A frequent mistake is to lump together items that are only superficially related. After a tentative cluster is written, a careful reading of the items may reveal that further subclustering is possible. Simply on the basis of meaning alone, a purification of the scales at this stage often forces the investigator to be very explicit regarding the exact nature of the variables of interest. The result is that the theory relating the variables is often refined and sharpened before data collection begins. Moreover, if a cluster or scale is further partitioned into sets of smaller scales, then more items can be written for these scales with three or fewer items *before* the data have been collected.

"Blind" Analysis. An alternate technique for defining cluster membership is to let a "blind" set of computational procedures define the clusters *after* the data have been collected. Instead of specifying a measurement model in advance, the investigator lets a computational algorithm uncover a structure purely on the basis of the correlational structure of the items.

One popular blind algorithm for generating clusters is an exploratory factor analysis of the inter-item correlation matrix—usually a principal axis factor analysis with communalities followed by a varimax rotation. For each factor, a corresponding cluster is defined. The items are assigned to the clusters on the basis of their factor loadings, that is, the correlations of the items with the factors. Each cluster is made up of those items whose highest loadings are on the corresponding varimax factor. In fact, many researchers stop at this point. They define a set of scales based on an exploratory factor analysis but never formally evaluate the scales for unidimensionality with a confirmatory factor analysis as they should.

Many other clustering algorithms, such as other forms of exploratory factor analysis, ordering procedures (Tryon, 1939; Hunter, 1973), multidimensional scaling (Nunnally, 1978), and explicit clustering procedures based on similarity measures other than correlations (Hunter, 1973; Everitt, 1974), have been programmed. Any of these blind techniques may be used to construct a multiple groups measurement model. The restriction is that the chosen clustering method should group the items into mutually exclusive clusters.

Our experience with exploratory factor analysis has shown it to be a poor ending point for the construction of unidimensional scales. Typically, exploratory factor analysis "underfactors", that is, it produces fewer factors than there are underlying variables in the data. This is particularly true for causally oriented studies because causal models deliberately include variables that are hypothesized to be highly correlated. Factor analysis tends to throw all highly correlated variables into the same factor. Thus factor analytic clusters usually must be subclustered. A second problem is that exploratory factor analysis has no "residual cluster," that is, no "garbage can" for bad items. Because every item must ultimately have its highest loading on some factor, the unwary user may include bad items in the clusters. For the worst cases, the varimax factors may bear little resemblance to the natural cluster in the data. For example, the presence of a central cluster highly correlated with the remaining clusters causes the rotation to place factors far away from the correlated centroids.

Parameter Estimation and Factor Analysis

The parameters of a measurement model are estimated by a "confirmatory factor analysis" or "cluster analysis" of the correlations among the observed variables. The most basic parameters of a measurement model are the "factor pattern coefficients" and the "factor–factor correlations." The factor pattern coefficients are the regression weights of the observed variables on the corresponding latent variables as specified by the measurement model. Because in a multiple groups model each observed variable is generated by only a single factor, there is only one number in the factor pattern of each item, namely, the correlation between the item and the factor that it measures.

A second parameter associated with each item is its "communality." As shown later, the communality of an item is the hypothetical correlation of an item with another item of the same reliability, that is, the variance of an item attributable to only the underlying factor with error variance removed. If the multiple groups model fits the data, then the communality is the square of the factor pattern coefficient. Also shown later is that (1) the correlations of an item with factors other than the factor that generated the item and (2) the communalities can be calculated from the factor pattern and factor–factor correlations.

Other parameters of the model are the "factor loadings": a matrix of the correlations of each observed variable with all of the factors. The factor loadings are used primarily in the analysis of the measurement model, that is, in testing the fit of the measurement model to the data.

Once the fit of the measurement model has been established, the correlations among the factors are critical because it is the factor correlations that are the data for subsequent causal analyses and/or second-order factor analyses. Indeed, if the measurement model fits, then only the factor–factor correlations have any substantive interest. The relevance of the item data is primarily restricted to the construction of the measurement model.

Communalities. Once a set of clusters has been tentatively stated, the conceptual nature of the factors is determined. However there are still two sets of "factors" which might be of interest. For each cluster, the factor of interest might be the trait score or *latent* variable underlying the cluster; or the "factor" might be the *observed* scale score that is the empirical estimate of the underlying trait. The technical terms for these alternatives are the use of "communalities" or "ones" in the diagonal. Most factor analytic computations can be done either on the given correlation matrix with ones in the diagonal or with the diagonal ones replaced by the smaller numbers called "communalities."

If ones are placed in the diagonal, then the item–factor correlations are the correlations between the items and the *observed* scale score rather than its underlying trait. Each scale or cluster is defined by a set of items. An individual's observed score on that cluster is simply the average or sum of the individual's score on each of the relevant items. The correlation of an item with its own cluster score is the item–total correlation, which is greatly *inflated* by a spurious common error term. The error in a component item may contribute substantially to the error in the entire scale that the component item partially defines. The factor–factor correlations are the correlations between observed scales and are attenuated or reduced by the measurement error inherent in each scale.

If communalities are placed in the diagonal of the original correlation matrix, then the parameters of the model are based on cluster *true* scores (the psychometric term for the score on the underlying traits). The cluster true score is that score which would be obtained if the construct were measured without error. The item–factor correlations are the *estimated* correlations between items and cluster true scores, and the factor–factor correlations are the *estimated* correlations between cluster true scores. This option is generally preferred because correlations of items and true scores are corrected for the error involved in (1) measuring the variables with only a small number of items, and (2) the correlation of an item with an entity of which it is a substantial part, as is the case with an item–total correlation. The error inherent in each item is not shared by the cluster true score, so the correlation of item and cluster true score is not biased upward by a shared common error component.

The cluster true score is the average score of the entire indefinitely large domain of items instead of only the few items that are sampled from this domain and that appear on the questionnaire. The use of communalities implicitly corrects for attenuation and hence eliminates the effect of error of measurement from the estimated correlations between items and factors or between factors and factors. However, correction for attenuation does not eliminate sampling error. In fact, the sampling error in these corrected correlations is larger than would be predicted by conventional formulas (Hunter).[1] And the accuracy of these correlation estimates depends on the fit of the model. If a cluster is not unidimensional, then the correlations for the corresponding cluster true score are suspect.

Estimation Procedures. There are currently two statistical procedures available for computing the parameter estimates of a multiple groups measurement model. As reviewed by Gerbing and Hunter,[2] the basis of the classical technique (Spearman factor analysis or centroid oblique multiple groups analysis) was developed by Spearman (1904) and Burt (1917) and later refined by Tryon (1939), Holzinger (1944), and Guttman (1952). A program for the computations (PACKAGE; Hunter and Cohen, 1969) is provided by Hunter, Gerbing, Cohen, and Nicol.[3] The more recent technique (full information maximum likelihood analysis) was implemented by Joreskog (1966) and is available in the two related programs LISREL (Joreskog and Sorbom, 1978) and COFAMM (Sorbom and Joreskog, 1976).

Although both LISREL and centroid multiple groups can be used for a multiple groups confirmatory factor analysis, LISREL is currently the most frequently recommended procedure (e.g., Mulaik, 1972; Kenny, 1979). However, Burt (1976) has pointed out some problems with LIS-REL and Gerbing and Hunter[1] have argued that the centroid multiple groups analysis is most often the *preferred* analysis. LISREL uniquely provides several purported features: multiple factor analysis, significance testing, correlated measurement errors, respecification with first derivatives, full information estimation, and a simultaneous analysis of measurement and causal models. Gerbing and Hunter[1] argue that these advantages are either misleading or redundant with information provided by a centroid analysis. An example supporting some of these arguments is given by Kotsch, Gerbing, and Schwartz (in press), who performed several confirmatory factor analyses using both centroid multiple groups and LISREL.

Evaluation of the Model

Any measurement model should be evaluated in terms of content and statistics. From the substantive viewpoint of theory building, the most important criterion is content. However, the procedures of construct validity go beyond content validity in requiring empirical evaluation by statistical analysis. A measurement model is evaluated by comparing the observed correlations between the variables with the correlations predicted by the model. That is, the patterning of the item correlations—or the "covariance structure" in Joreskog's (1978) terminology—is the key idea underlying statistical evaluation of a model. For multiple groups measurement models, not only must the items in each cluster share a common meaning, the observed correlations must conform to the product rules of internal and external consistency.

A First Statistical Test for Unidimensionality: Internal Consistency. The causal relations between the items of a unidimensional cluster are determined by their causal relationship to the underlying trait. This relationship can be shown in its most general form in a causal diagram such as that shown in Figure 1, where T is the score on the trait, X_i is the response to item i, and e_i is the net effect of extraneous causal factors for item response X_i.

If the relationship between each item and the trait is linear, then this diagram can be translated into linear regression equations; for example,

$$X_1 = a_1 T + e_1$$

$$X_2 = a_2 T + e_2$$

$$X_3 = a_3 T + e_3$$

or, in general,

$$X_i = a_i T + e_i$$

where a_i is the slope of the item response X_i onto T, and e_i is the error in the regression of X_i on T. By definition, the errors of regression are uncorrelated with T. However, the extent of the correlation between errors for different items constitutes the crux of the assumption of uni-dimensionality. If the only significant causal factor determining each item response is the given underlying trait, then the errors e_i should be un-correlated with each other. In a linear model, this is the definition of uni-dimensionality.

If all the items in a cluster measure the same factor, then the corre-lations between the items will satisfy a "product rule for internal con-sistency." If X_i and X_j are two items in the same unidimensional cluster and T is the cluster true score, then the correlation between the items should satisfy the product rule:

$$r_{X_i X_j} = r_{X_i T} \, r_{X_j T}$$

That is, the correlation between two items in the same cluster should be the product of their correlations with the underlying trait. There are then two steps to test for internal consistency: (1) Estimate the param-eters $r_{X_i T}$ from the data, and (2) see if the product rule reproduces the inter-item correlations to within sampling error.

Figure 1. A One Factor Measurement Model

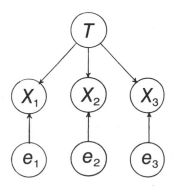

The reference to two items implies that i does not equal j in the product rule above. What happens if the product rule is used with i equal j?

$$r_{X_iX_i} = r_{X_iT} \, r_{X_iT} = (r_{x_iT})^2$$

The number "$r_{X_iX_i}$" is *not* the correlation between X_i and itself, which would be 1.00, but is called instead the "reliability" or the "communality" of X_i. However, because of this product rule the notation "$r_{X_iX_i}$" is the traditional notation for the reliability even though it is ambiguous with the regular correlation notation of $r_{X_iX_i} = 1.00$. Because the communality "$r_{X_iX_i}$" equals $(r_{X_iT})^2$, the computation of communalities is tantamount to computation of the factor loadings r_{X_iT} and is often treated as such in factor analysis texts.

A useful guide for the evaluation of the fit of the observed correlations among the items on a scale with the product rule for internal consistency is an inspection of the correlation matrix. There are two basic patterns for unidimensional matrices. First, if all the items have equal quality, that is, if all the items have the same correlation with the cluster true score, then any two items will have the same correlation (to within sampling error). In this case, the correlation matrix is said to be "flat."

Second, if the items do not have uniform quality, then the correlation matrix can be reordered so as to show a "strong–weak gradient" or "hierarchical ordering" (Spearman, 1904) to within-sampling error. If the items are ordered in terms of their true score correlation (or communality) from strong to weak, then the high correlations will be in the upper left-hand corner and the lowest correlations will be in the lower right-hand corner of the correlation matrix.

A more rigorous test of the product rule for internal consistency is to partial out the trait variable. The formula for a partial correlation between X_i and X_j with T held constant is

$$r_{X_iX_j} = \frac{r_{X_iX_j} - r_{X_iT} \, r_{X_jT}}{[1 - (r_{X_iT})^2]^{1/2}[1 - (r_{X_jT})^2]^{1/2}}$$

The numerator of the above expression is the "residual" form of the product rule, that is, the difference between the obtained and reproduced correlations. This "residual" is therefore predicted to be zero. If the cluster is unidimensional, each such partial correlation should be zero to within sampling error.

A Second Test for Unidimensionality: Parallelism. The second statistical criterion for the covariance structure of unidimensional scales is parallelism. The criterion of internal consistency specifies how the items composing a unidimensional cluster should correlate with one another. The criterion of external consistency or parallelism specifies how these items should correlate with variables outside of the cluster. The general statement of parallelism is that the items in a unidimensional cluster have similar patterns of correlations with (1) items in other clusters or (2) other traits. In fact, the correlations for items of the same quality should be equal (to within-sampling error) across all other variables. Differences in the correlations for two items in the same cluster should be directly proportional to differences in the reliability of those items.

Consider three items X_1, X_2, and X_3, which are indicators of T, and let U be some other latent variable or trait. If U and T are correlated, then each X_i is also correlated with U. These relationships can be illustrated by the path diagram in Figure 2. The curved double-headed arrow in Figure 2 represents correlation with no specification of direction of causality. The crucial fact in this diagram is that each X_i is correlated with U because T is correlated with U, and the size of $r_{X,U}$ depends directly on the size of r_{TU}. The formal statement of parallelism (called "the product rule for external consistency") follows from the relationships specified in the diagram. This product rule is

$$r_{XU} = r_{XT} r_{TU}$$

which is a generalization of the product rule for internal consistency.

If this product rule for external consistency is applied to two items

Figure 2. The Relation between a Cluster of Items and Another Group Factor

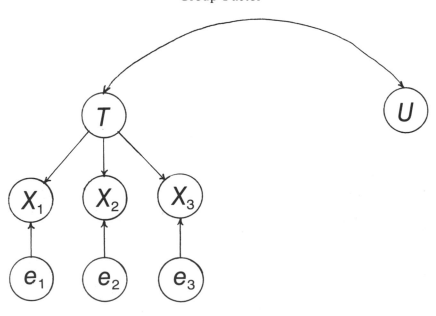

in a unidimensional cluster, X_i and X_j, then it follows from this product rule, according to Hunter (1973) and Tryon and Bailey (1970), that

$$\frac{r_{X_iU}}{r_{X_jU}} = \frac{r_{X_iT}}{r_{X_jT}} = \lambda_{ij}$$

where λ_{ij} is the constant of proportionality for X_i and X_j. For a unidimensional cluster, the ratio of the correlations between two items and a trait is equal to the ratio of their own respective true score correlations. Moreover, U could be any trait, so this same proportionality is maintained across all other variables.

A second version of the product rule for external consistency reproduces the correlation between two items in different clusters. This relation is illustrated in Figure 3, in which X_1, X_2, and X_3 are indicators of the trait T, and Y_1, Y_2, and Y_3 are indicators of the trait U. This model specifies that the correlation between items in different clusters is, for items X_i and Y_k

$$r_{X_iY_k} = r_{X_iT}\, r_{TU}\, r_{UY_k}$$

This formula expresses the predicted correlations or covariance structure of indicators of different factors.

If this version of the product rule for external consistency is applied to two items in a unidimensional cluster, X_i and X_j, then the same constant of proportionality results:

$$\frac{r_{X_iY_k}}{r_{X_jY_k}} = \frac{r_{X_iT}}{r_{X_jT}} = \lambda_{ij}$$

Figure 3.   A Two Factor Multiple Groups Measurement Model

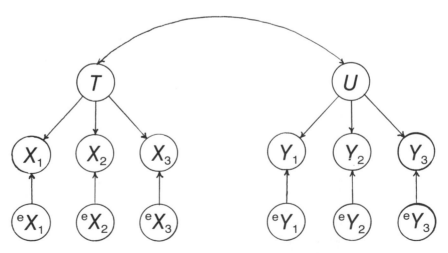

Thus, the parallelism product rule is applicable to items as well as to traits but is usually applied to traits because the reliability of an item is lower than the trait it measures.

A summary index is also available for specifying the parallelism of two items. Adaptation of the following formula, originally used as a measure of the similarities of two factors, is advocated by Tryon (1939), Tryon and Bailey (1970), and Hunter (1973).

$$\phi_{X_i X_j} = \frac{\sum\limits_{k=1}^{n} r_{X_i Y_k} r_{X_j Y_k}}{\left[\sum\limits_{k=1}^{n} (r_{X_i Y_k})^2\right]^{1/2} \left[\sum\limits_{k=1}^{n} (r_{X_j Y_k})^2\right]^{1/2}}$$

Tryon and Bailey call the square of this index the "index of proportionality," whereas Hunter refers to the index as a "similarity coefficient." If communalities are placed in the diagonal of the correlation matrix, the value of ϕ ranges from -1 to 1 with ϕ equaling 1 or -1 if the two items X_i and X_j are perfectly proportional, that is, perfectly parallel.

Reliability

If a cluster is unidimensional, then all the items measure the same trait. However, the amount of error of measurement in those items might be great or small. If the items are summed to form a cluster score, then the errors tend to cancel out so there is less error in a cluster score than in an item. However, if the individual items are very noisy and if the number of items in the cluster is small, then the amount of error in the cluster score could still be large. Thus, it is important to assess the quality of the cluster score in terms of the amount of error of measurement as well as in terms of unidimensionality. The measure of lack of error in a score is its "reliability."

Although the issues have often been confused in the literature, the dimensionality of the scale and the reliability of the cluster score are independent concepts (Hunter[2]; Green, Lissitz and Mulaik, 1977). One index of measurement error in a cluster score is coefficient alpha. The closer the value of coefficient alpha is to 1.00, the more reliable the measurement of the underlying variable. However, coefficient alpha provides an unbiased estimate of the reliability of the cluster score only if the scale is unidimensional. For multidimensional scales, alpha is an underestimate of the reliability of the composite score (Novick and Lewis, 1967). Thus the value of alpha should be interpreted only after the cluster has been demonstrated to satisfy the three criteria of unidimensionality.

There is a version of coefficient alpha for multidimensional scales (Tryon, 1959; Rajaratnam, Cronbach, and Gleser, 1965), but Moiser's (1943) theoretical formula for the reliability of a composite score is both more accurate and more appropriate conceptually. Heise and Bohrnstedt (1970) use Moiser's formula with communalities as item reliabilities and call their estimate of composite reliability coefficient omega. However, Smith (1974) shows that omega also underestimates the reliability of a multidimensional composite, though not as much as alpha.

THE CAUSAL MODEL

Once variables have been properly measured by a successful confirmatory factor analysis of the measurement model (and hence all correlations are corrected for measurement error), the next task is to explain the correlations among the variables. Ideally, the explanation comes before the data in the form of a theory that guides the design of the study. In practice, often only part of a theory is specified in advance and other parts are left to be filled in during the data analysis.

The most common form of explanation is to postulate a set of "causal relations among the variables." The classic question in elementary statistics is, "If X and Y are correlated, then (1) does X cause Y, (2) does Y cause X, or (3) are X and Y correlated because both are the causal consequents of yet another variable Z?" When answers to such questions are integrated into a theory of relations among all the variables in a study (or some important subset of them), then the resulting theory can be stated in the form of a "path diagram." If the relations among the variables are all linear, then that path diagram can be interpreted in a series of equations called a "path model" or "structural equation model." This section presents the main ideas in path analysis; extended treatments of this topic can be found in Asher (1976), Wright (1921), Blalock (1971), Lewis-Beck (1974), Duncan (1975), Heise (1975), Kenny (1979), Billings and Wroten (1978), and Bentler (1980).

Causal Relations Versus Statistical Summaries

The phrase "causal relations between variables" can be very misleading. A variable is a procedure for assigning numbers (or other labels) to persons. Causal relations exist among processes and events—not among numbers. Thus it is impossible in the sense of ordinary English for one variable to "cause" another. Rather the phrase "X exerts a causal influence or impact on Y" is a shorthand expression for a much more complicated idea. The values of Y represent differences among people. These differences arise from differences in the causal processes that determine the value of Y for each particular person. To say that X has an impact on Y is to say that differences in the value of X are associated with differences in the causal processes that determine the value of Y.

One kind of causal impact occurs when differences in the value of X are associated with differences in the parameter value of a causal process that governs the impact of some environmental event on the person. For example, suppose that X is a measure of family reaction to social institutions. The variable X varies from deference at one end to cynicism and hostility at the other. Suppose that Y is the person's feeling of organizational commitment at the end of an entry-level management training program. There is considerable ambiguity in the actions taken by trainers toward the persons in the program. A person who enters with a positive outlook toward institutions in general is likely to start with positive expectations toward the organization and hence positive interpretations of the various ambiguous actions of the organization. These positive interpretations will tend to press the person toward organizational commitment. A person who enters with a negative attitude will interpret the same ambiguous events negatively and hence be pressed toward lack of trust and lack of commitment toward the organization. Thus differences on X lead to differences in response to the same environmental events and hence to differences on Y.

Another kind of causal impact occurs when differences in the antecedent variable X are associated with differences in the environment to which the person will be exposed. For example, let Y be the organizational commitment of a cohort of persons who have all been with the organization for 10 years, and let X be a composite measure of the entry-level cognitive abilities that in part determine job performance. A person with low ability will usually do poorly at the job, will receive constant hassling from the supervisor, will therefore develop a negative attitude toward the job, and hence will tend to have a low level of organizational commitment after 10 years on the job. A person with high ability will usually avoid hassle, may be rewarded by special incentive programs or by promotion, and will ultimately tend to have a high degree of organizational commitment. Thus people with high and low levels of X are exposed to different environments and hence come to have different values on Y.

We believe that the construction of a path model should begin not with a list of the variables but with a list of the important causal processes that take place in the setting under consideration. If an arrow representing causal impact is drawn from one variable to another, then that arrow represents the net impact of all those causal processes that carry differences in the value of the first variable into differences in the value of the second. On the other hand, the same causal process may influence several variables and may thus be represented within several arrows. There is no one-to-one relationship between causal arrows and underlying causal processes.

Thus the distinction should be maintained between the underlying causal processes specified by the theory and the effect these processes have on the corresponding variables. A path model represents a set of predicted relationships within the data, which is *derived from* a theory and is *not* the theory itself. Thus path analysis per se should be regarded as a data summary technique like factor analysis and not as a procedure for specifying a theory. The theory is a specification of the underlying causal processes, not a description of the correlations between the variables. The theory is explanation rather than description.

Multiple Causation

To specify X as a causal antecedent of Y is not to assert that it is the only causal antecedent. Perfect prediction of Y from X is not expected unless the model contains all other causal antecedents as well. The scope of the path model is increased and improved to the extent that other relevant causal antecedents are added.

For example, suppose that we believe that quality of supervision has a causal impact on the quality of work done by subordinates. We might believe that a good supervisor (1) stands as a positive role model for the subordinate and (2) is perceived as fair and objective so that criticism is taken as advice on how to improve rather than as a statement of low esteem. These two causal processes would each contribute to an arrow from quality of supervision to quality of performance on the job as shown in Figure 4a. However, quality of supervision would certainly not be the only determinant of quality of performance. In fact it might not even be the most important determinant. Consider the subordinates' ability to do the work. Talent or lack of talent might have much more impact on job performance than does quality of supervision. Adding this variable results in the model in Figure 4b.

The curved, double-headed arrow linking quality of supervision and ability represents an unstated or unknown causal relationship between those two variables. For example, if people are randomly assigned to supervisors, then quality of supervision and ability of worker would be independent and the curved arrow would be replaced by no arrow at all. On the other hand, if good workers can transfer to good supervisors and poor workers can transfer away from them, then the curved arrow would be replaced by an arrow from ability to quality of supervisor. Alternately, if good supervisors are rewarded by the assignment of good workers

Figure 4.   Single and Multiple Causation

Figure 4a.   Quality of supervision specified as the sole causal antecedent to quality of job performance

Figure 4b.   Quality of supervision and ability specified as multiple
causal antecedents of quality of job performance

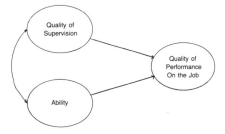

while poor supervisors are sent the problem personnel, then the curved
arrow would be replaced by an arrow from quality of supervision to
ability of worker.

The identification of additional causal antecedents can greatly increase
the quality of estimation within the path model. For example, suppose
that the population correlation between quality of supervision and quality
of performance is .10, that sample size is 100, and that ability is not
observed in the study. Then by conventional practice, the detection of
the causal arrow from quality of supervision to quality of performance
requires that the observed correlation between them be statistically significant at $p < .05$. But for a sample size of 100, a correlation must be
.20 or higher in order to be significant. Given a population correlation
of .10, the probability that the observed sample correlation will be significant is only 16 percent. Thus the investigator would have an 84 percent
chance of incorrectly rejecting his hypothesis. Furthermore, if the sample
correlation is significant, then it must be at least .20, which is much
higher than the actual population correlation. Thus the investigator pays
a price not only in terms of probability of false conclusions but in terms
of bias in parameter estimates as well.

On the other hand, suppose that ability was included in the study, that
workers are randomly assigned to supervisors, and that the population

correlation between ability and performance is .70. With two causal
antecedents, the statistical test for the hypothesis about quality of supervision changes from a test of a simple correlation to a test for a
significant beta weight in the multiple regression of quality of performance
onto quality of supervision and ability. If we denote quality of supervision
by X_1, ability by X_2, and quality of performance by Y, then the appropriate F test is

$$F = (N - 2) \frac{R^2_{Y \cdot X_1 X_2} - r^2_{YX_2}}{1 - r^2_{YX_2}}$$

Because ability and quality of supervision have been assumed uncorrelated in this example, the increment in squared correlation in the numerator is $(r_{X_1 Y})^2 = .01$, as for the test of a simple correlation. However,
the denominator is not 1.00, but .51, which doubles the value of F over
the univariate test. That is, the expected value of F for the multiple
regression test is 1.94, and hence the probability of significance is about
50 percent. The test using multiple regression has about three times the
probability of reaching the correct conclusion as does the test for quality
of supervision considered alone. Moreover, there will be correspondingly
less bias in the beta weights accepted as significant.

If the model is expanded to include other relevant causal antecedents
of any variable, then the model is not only improved conceptually but
will also be greatly improved in terms of statistical estimation as well.
To the extent that all relevant predictors are included in the model, there
can be very good estimation of parameters even with modest sample
size.

Causal Chains

Reasoning about causal processes often proceeds from chains of
events. For example, if A always causes B and B always causes C, then
A always results in C. Similar reasoning can be applied to causal relations
among variables, except that the statistical nature of those relations must
be taken into account. One would expect that the strength of the relationship between variables at the ends of a long chain would be less than
the strengths of the relationships within the chain. In fact, path analysis
assumes that the correlation between variables at the ends of a chain
as in Figure 5 is the product of the correlations for each link.

Figure 5.   A Causal Chain

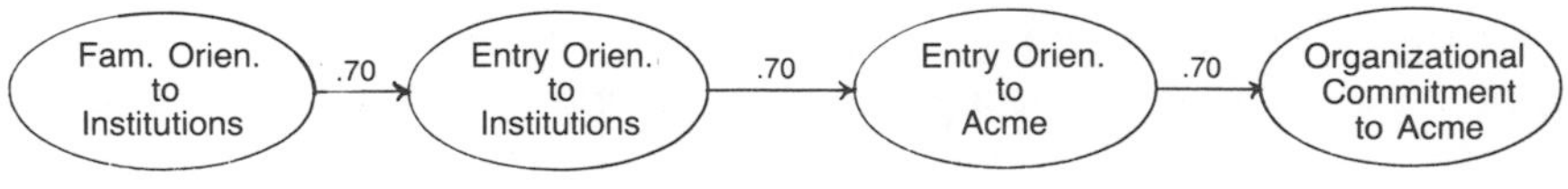

The causal chain in Figure 5 is an expanded version of the earlier example relating organizational commitment at the end of training to early exposure to different family attitudes toward institutions. This model assumes that family orientation toward institutions is one of the determinants of the person's own attitude toward institutions at the time of graduation from college, which is then one of the determinants of the person's attitude toward Acme Corporation in particular at the time of entry. Attitude at the time of entry is then one of the determinants of attitude at the end of training. In each case, it is assumed that the correlation between measures is less than perfect (though the value of .70 is arbitrarily chosen for purposes of illustration). For example, even though a child is raised in a home that is very hostile to social institutions, his initial attitude might be reversed by positive experiences in school, in church, in athletics, etc. The correlation matrix implied by the preceding model is given in Table 1. Because all the adjacent correlations were set to the same value of .70, the correlation between two variables separated by one mediating variable is (.70)(.70) = .49, and the correlation between the variables at the end of the chain is (.70)(.70)(.70) = .34.

The product rule for causal chains is the basis of mathematical path analysis, though it is not always so simple. If there is multiple causation, then the path coefficients will be beta weights rather than simple correlations. Also, two variables may be linked by more than one causal chain. However, there is always a decay in prediction as the length of the linking chain increases.

Recursive and Nonrecursive Models

The great divide in causal models is the distinction between those models that are "recursive" or "hierarchical" or "unidirectional" and those that are "nonrecursive." A *nonrecursive* model contains one or more *circular* causal chains. For example, Figure 6a illustrates a model in which "*X* has an impact on *Y,* which has an impact on *X*." A more general causal cycle is illustrated in Figure 6b in which "*X* has an impact

Table 1. Correlation Matrix Implied by the Causal Chain in Figure 5

Variables	Variables			
	FOI	*EOI*	*EOA*	*OCT*
Family orientation to institution	100	70	49	34
Entry orientation to institution	70	100	70	49
Entry orientation to Acme	49	70	100	70
Organizational commitment after training	34	49	70	100

Figure 6. Nonrecursive Models

Figure 6a. Direct mutual causal influence

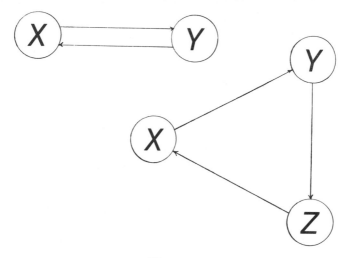

Figure 6b. A causal cycle

on *Y*, which has an impact on *Z*, which has an impact on *X*." A model without causal cycles, that is, a model in which the causal diagram can be arranged so that all the causal arrows point in the same direction, is recursive.

The Conversion of Nonrecursive Systems into Recursive Systems

Consider the two variable nonrecursive system in Figure 6a in which each variable is thought to exert a causal influence on the other. For example, *X* might be how Sam feels toward his boss and *Y* might be how Sam's boss feels toward him. To the extent that Sam likes his boss, he will smile warmly, express genuine concern and so on. This is likely to have a positive influence on the boss whose attitude toward Sam will become more positive. Thus *X* has a causal influence on *Y*. But identical logic applies in the opposite direction, to the extent that Sam's boss dislikes him, he will frown and show little concern and so on. Thus *Y* has a direct causal impact on *X*.

The problem that nonrecursive relations pose in cross-sectional models can be seen by considering the implication that a two-way arrow has for indirect effects. If *X* and *Y* have an effect on each other, then *X* has an impact on *Y*, which has an impact on *X*, which has an impact on *Y*. That is, by the traditional recursive system rules, *X* not only has a direct effect on *Y* but has an indirect effect (through itself!) on *Y* as well. Furthermore this cycling can go on as many steps as can be imagined.

Figure 7. A longitudinal recursive model of mutual direct causation

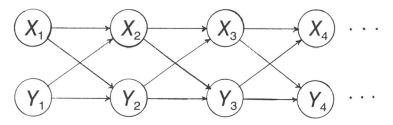

In reality, there is no such instantaneous cycling process. If Sam acts nicely to his boss and the boss acts nicely in return, then the return act follows later in time than the original act. Thus, even though some estimation procedures such as are contained in LISREL permit the estimation of causal parameters in nonrecursive models with cross-sectional data, nonrecursive models are fundamentally not suitable for treatment in a cross-sectional model. On the other hand, if a nonrecursive system is analyzed in a longitudinal context, then it becomes a recursive model. For example, the two-variable model described above can be represented by the model in Figure 7 where X and Y are subscripted by time.

Exogenous and Endogenous Variables

In a recursive system, there must be certain variables that are used to explain other variables but that are not themselves explained. These "starter" variables, whose causal antecedents are regarded as outside the scope of the given system, are called "exogenous" variables. All other variables are called "endogenous" variables, that is, the endogenous variables are those that are explained inside the system. Exogenous variables are often inscribed in a box instead of a circle, as with variables X and Y in Figure 8a. If the exogenous variables are not independent

Figure 8. Exogenous Variables

Figure 8a. A causal model with two uncorrelated exogenous variables

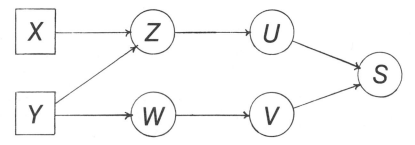

Figure 8b.   A causal model with two correlated exogenous variables

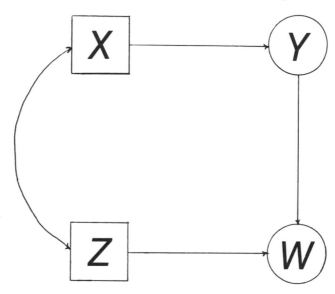

of one another, then they are connected with a *curved* two-way arrow as shown in Figure 8b. The curvature of the arrow indicates that the causal nature of the correlation is unknown.

PATH ANALYSIS

If a model is recursive, and if all the relations between variables in the model are linear; then each arrow in the model can be associated with a number called a "path coefficient." Every correlation between variables in the path diagram can then be predicted from a set of path coefficients. This set of predicted correlations can then be compared to the obtained correlations in order to generate a test of the path model. The process of (1) constructing the model, (2) estimating the path coefficients from the data, and (3) testing the path model is called "path analysis" or "structural model construction" and is described below for recursive models.

Path analysis is a procedure for systematically combining the use of partial and multiple correlation to study the causal relations among a set of variables. Within a path analysis, any variable may be both an independent variable and a dependent variable. A variable will act as an independent variable if it is used to explain some other variable. However, that "independent variable" may in turn be explained in terms of other variables to which it is related as a dependent variable. The set of all variables in a discourse is called a system.

Types of Variable Linkages

In path analysis, two kinds of diagrams can be drawn: a qualitative causal diagram and a quantitative causal diagram. The qualitative diagram uses arrows pointing from one variable to another to indicate causal influence. The quantitative diagram has numbers on each link that represent the strength of the causal impact. Within a path diagram there are three different ways that two variables can be linked: by a direct causal relation, by indirect causal linkages, or by a "spurious" relationship to a common causal antecedent variable.

Direct Link. The variable X has a direct link to variable Y if and only if X exerts a direct causal impact on Y. If X exerts a direct influence on Y, then the causal diagram shows an arrow from X to Y.

Indirect Causal Impact. The variable X is said to have an indirect causal impact on variable Y if and only if there is a set of intermediate variables $Z_1, Z_2, Z_3, \ldots, Z_n$ (which may have as few as one member) such that X exerts a direct influence on Z_1, and Z_1 exerts a direct influence on Z_2, and $\ldots$, and Z_n exerts a direct influence on Y. An example appears in Figure 9a.

Spurious Relation. Variable X is said to have a spurious relation to variable Y if they have a common antecedent cause. In Figure 9b and 9c, there is some variable Z, which exerts a direct or indirect causal impact on both X and Y.

Multiple Linkages. The definitions presented above are not mutually exclusive. A variable X can simultaneously (1) exert a direct influence on variable Y, (2) exert an indirect influence along several paths, and (3) be spuriously related to Y by one or more common antecedent variables. An example of this is shown in Figure 9d in which X exerts (1) (1) direct and (2) indirect causal influences on Y and (3) Z is a common antecedent to both X and Y.

One of the major contributions of path analysis is that it provides for a decomposition of the correlation coefficient into numerical components measuring the net effect of each type of relationship separately (Lewis-Beck, 1974; Wright, 1934). This decomposition will be considered later in the article.

Missing Links

In a strict mathematical sense, the logical content of a qualitative path diagram lies in the links that are *in* the model. In fact, in order to dervive any of the quantitative relations below, we must make very strong assumptions about the missing links. In a nutshell, these assumptions define a sort of "completeness" definition for the model given. The assumptions amount to the assertion that any other causal determinants of the en-

Figure 9.   Types of Variable Linkages in Causal Models

Figure 9a.   The indirect causal influence of X on Y

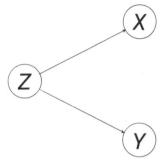

Figure 9b.   The spurious relation of X and Y due to the direct effects
of Z on X and Y

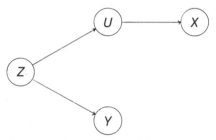

Figure 9c.   The spurious relation of X and Y due to the indirect effect
of Z on X and the direct effect of Z on Y

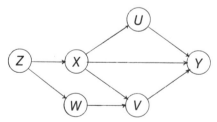

Figure 9d.   Multiple linkages of X and Y

dogenous variables are completely independent of those shown. Suppose
that the two variables X and Y are shown without a link in the model.
Then the model is correct only if

(1)   There is no direct causal impact of X on Y or of Y on X.
(2)   There is no missing variable through which X has an indirect

impact on Y or through which Y has an indirect impact on X. (There could be an exception to this rule if there were *two* missing variables such that the indirect effects were equal in magnitude and opposite in sign. The net effect of the two missing variables would then be zero.

(3) There is no missing variable that acts as a common causal antecedent to X and Y and that does not act indirectly through the exogenous variables.

Estimation of Parameters

Given the causal model, the parameters of the causal system are estimated from the estimated sample correlation matrix of the corresponding latent variables derived from the confirmatory factor analysis. If a model is recursive and complete, the parameters can be estimated using simple correlations or multiple regression; path coefficients are equivalent to regression weights.

Links between exogenous variables are numerically translated into path coefficients by simply inserting the corresponding correlation coefficient. Path coefficients for all other links are generated by considering the endogenous variables one at a time. Let Y be an endogenous variable. The key question is how many variables are direct causal antecedents of Y. If only one variable X has a direct causal impact on Y, then the corresponding path coefficient p_{XY} is estimated to be the simple correlation between X and Y. That is, if X is the only causal antecedent of Y, then

$$p_{XY} = r_{XY}$$

If Y has two causal antecedents X_1 and X_2, then the path coefficients for X_1 and X_2 are beta weights in the regression of Y onto X_1 and X_2. That is, let

$$Y = a_1 X_1 + a_2 X_2$$

be the multiple regression of Y onto X_1 and X_2. Then $p_{X_1 Y} = a_1$ and $p_{X_2 Y} = a_2$.

If three or more variables each have a direct causal impact on Y, then each of the path coefficients is estimated to be the corresponding beta weight in the regression of Y onto its antecedents. Note that the rule for a single causal antecedent is a special case of this rule. In the multiple regression of Y onto the single variable X, the regression weight of X is simply the correlation between X and Y.

These estimation procedures are illustrated in Figure 10, given the model of Figure 8b and the correlations in Table 2. The two exogenous variables X and Z are correlated .20, so

$$p_{XZ} = p_{ZX} = r_{XZ} = .20$$

Figure 10. The Quantitative Path Diagram Derived from the Qualitative Diagram of Figure 8b and the Correlations in Table 2

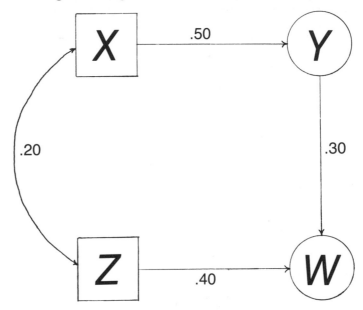

X is the sole antecedent of the endogenous variable Y so

$$p_{YX} = r_{YX} = .50$$

W has two antecedents, Y and Z, so the values for p_{WY} and p_{XZ} are estimated from the regression equation

$$W = .30Y + .40Z$$

Any multiple regression program can be used for parameter estimation of recursive models, though a more specialized program such as the path analysis program contained in PACKAGE (Hunter, Gerbing, Cohen, and Nicol)[3] is recommended. A specialized path analysis program provides statistics that are for evaluating the fit of the model and that are not provided by a program designed only for regression analyses.

Table 2. Correlation Matrix for the Parameter Estimates in Figure 10

	Variables			
Variables	X	Y	Z	W
X	100	50	20	21
Y	50	100	10	34
Z	20	10	100	43
W	21	34	43	100

For nonrecursive models, the estimation of causal parameters is relatively complex. Algorithms such as "two-stage least squares" (Heise, 1975; Duncan, 1975; James and Singh, 1978; Fox, 1979) or "full information maximum likelihood" (e.g., LISREL) should be used.

Reproducing the Correlation Matrix

Independent Exogenous Variables. If the system has only one exogenous variable, or if the exogenous variables are independent of each other, then the reproduced correlations between the variables can be expressed as the sum of three terms: one representing the direct effect of one variable on the other (if any), one representing the indirect effects of one variable on the other (if any), and a third term representing the "spurious" effect of common antecedent variables. If X has a direct causal impact on Y, then the direct effect of X on Y is measured by the path coefficient of X on Y. If X has indirect effects on Y through one or more intermediate variables, then the indirect effect of X on Y is the sum of the indirect impact determined for each path from X to Y. The impact of a path from X to Y is the product of the path coefficients along that path. For each common antecedent to X and Y, there will be one or more paths leading from the antecedent to X and one or more paths leading from the antecedent to Y. Each combination of paths to X and to Y generates a contribution to the spurious effect, which is the product of the path coefficients on *both* paths. The net effect for that common antecedent is the sum of the products across all combinations of paths to X and Y. The total spurious effect for X and Y is the sum of the net effects for all common antecedents.

An example is given in Figure 11. In Figure 9d, we provided a model in which X and Y are related in terms of direct, indirect, and spurious effects. In Figure 11, this model is presented as a quantitative path diagram with arbitrary path coefficients chosen for ease of calculation. Given these coefficients, the correlation between X and Y can be quantitatively decomposed.

The direct effect of X on Y is simply

$$p_{YX} = .40$$

X indirectly impacts on Y through the mediating variables U and V. The indirect effect through U is $p_{UX}p_{YU}$, and through V the indirect effect is $p_{VX}p_{YV}$. Thus the complete indirect effect of X on Y is

$$p_{UX}p_{YU} + p_{UX}p_{YV} = (.2)(.3) + (.5)(.6) = .36$$

The only common antecedent of X and Y is Z. The spurious effect of Z on X and Y is

$$[p_{XZ}][p_{WZ}p_{VW}p_{YV}] = [.1][(.7)(.8)(.6)] = .03$$

Figure 11. A Quantitative Version of the Path Diagram in Figure 9d

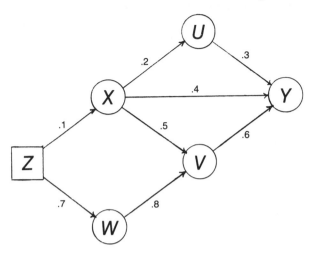

The correlation of X and Y accounted for or reproduced by the model in Figure 11 is the sum of the direct, indirect, and spurious effects, or

$$r_{XY} = .40 + .36 + .03 = .79$$

Correlated Exogenous Variables. If two or more exogenous variables are correlated, then the correlation between exogenous variables can make a contribution to the correlation between endogenous variables. However, because the nature of the correlation between the exogenous variables is taken to be unknown, then the contribution of such links may be of unknown nature. There are two cases.

First, consider the correlation between an exogenous variable X and an endogenous variable Y. If X is linked to Y through another exogenous variable Z, then that path may be a path from X to Z to Y or a path from Z to X to Y or it may be two paths from Z acting as a common antecedent to X and Y. Thus we must create a fourth component of the reproduced correlation: an *unexplained effect* (to go with the direct, indirect, and spurious effect as defined in the previous section).

Second, consider the correlation between two endogenous variables. Any contribution made to these variables involving a link between two exogenous variables must necessarily consider one of the exogenous variables to be a common antecedent to the endogenous variables under consideration. Thus any such contribution can be added to the spurious effect.

One computational process is the following. Convert the model to one with only one exogenous variable by assuming some set of links that permits errorless reproduction of the correlations between the exogenous variables. For example, if there are only two exogenous variables, simply replace the curved arrow between them by a one-way arrow in either direction. If there are three exogenous variables X, Y, Z; then generate path coefficients assuming that X has direct effects on Y and Z and that Y has a direct effect on Z (where the order of X, Y, and Z is immaterial). Once the model has been converted to a model with only one exogenous variable, proceed to compute direct, indirect, and spurious effects for the converted model. However, the contribution for any product with one or more links between exogenous variables may go into a different category. For the reproduction of the correlation between two endogenous variables, such terms should always go into the spurious effect. For the reproduction of the correlation between an exogenous with an endogenous variable, such terms should be added to the unexplained effect.

A Multiple Regression Algorithm. For purposes of assessing the fit of the model, only the reproduced correlations are needed. The decomposition of the correlations into effects is irrelevant. If the decomposition of the reproduced correlation is not needed, than there is a much simpler procedure for generating reproduced correlations based on multiple regression, such as the algorithm used in PACKAGE (Hunter, Gerbing, Cohen, and Nicol).[3]

In a recursive model, the variables can be listed in a causal order so that each variable comes after all those variables that have a direct impact on it. To find such a list, first list the exogenous variables (in any order) and then list the endogenous variables so that no variable is listed before its antecedent variables (there are usually at least several alternative orders all of which are equivalent for our purposes). Because each variable depends only on those that precede it in the list, the multiple regression of each variable onto the others can be written

$$X_{n+1} = \sum_{k=1}^{n} \beta_k X_k + e_{n+1}$$

where the error term e_{n+1} is uncorrelated with any variable listed before X_{n+1}. That is, e_{n+1} is uncorrelated with variables $X_1, \ldots, X_n$. Multiplying each side by X_j and taking expectations gives

$$r_{X_{n+1},X_j} = \sum_{k=1}^{n} \beta_k r_{X_k X_j} \quad \text{for } j = 1, \ldots, n$$

where $r_{X_k X_j}$ is the reproduced correlation between X_k and X_j. To use this formula, the reproduced correlation matrix is generated one variable at a time. First, the correlations between the exogenous variables are simply entered as is. Second, the first endogenous variable is entered into the matrix using the equation above, which contains the path coefficients (i.e., the beta weights) for that endogenous variable and the already entered correlations between the exogenous variables. Third, the next endogenous variable is entered using the equation above, which contains the path coefficients for that endogenous variable and the correlations between exogenous variables and between the exogenous variables and the first endogenous variables. The formula is sequentially applied to each successive variable in the path model.

SPECIFIC ERROR AND SECOND ORDER FACTOR ANALYSIS

If the confirmatory factor analysis was done with communalities or if the scale correlations have been corrected for attenuation, then the estimated correlations between factors cannot contain measurement error attributable to the random response component of the observed responses. That is, the correlation matrix is free of the effect of randomness in the response process. However, there may still be specific errors that can only be eliminated by a second-order factor analysis.

An Example

Consider again our model of the process of formation of organizational commitment to Acme Corporation during entry-level management training; family orientation is one determinant of entry orientation, which is one determinant of posttraining commitment as shown in Figure 12. However suppose that entry orientation is not measured globally but is defined by two related scales: (1) a scale of items assessing the trainee's expectations concerning fairness of compensation at Acme and (2) a scale assessing the trainee's expectations concerning challenge in the job at Acme. The four-variable matrix of observed correlations resulting from the confirmatory factor analysis might appear as in Table 3.

Figure 12. A Version of the Model of Formation of Organizational Commitment from Figure 8

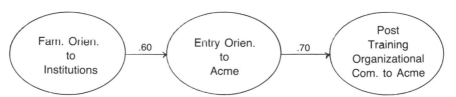

Table 3. Correlations Among the Variables in Figure 12 with Two
Measures of Entry Orientation

	Variables			
Variables	*FAM*	*FAI*	*CHL*	*COM*
	Observed Correlations			
Family orientation	100	48	48	42
Expected fairness	48	100	64	56
Expected challenge	48	64	100	56
Organizational commitment	42	56	56	100
	Reproduced Correlations			
Family orientation	100	48	31	17
Expected fairness	48	100	64	36
Expected challenge	31	64	100	56
Organizational commitment	17	36	56	100
	Reproduced Correlations with Expected Challenge Deleted			
Family orientation	100	48		27
Expected fairness	48	100		56
Expected challenge				
Organizational commitment	27	56		100

No path model that correctly reflects the assumed causal structure will
fit this data. If the model is Orientation to Fairness to Challenge to
Commitment, then all reproduced correlations between nonadjacent variables will be much too small, as shown in Table 3: If the chain has
Challenge ahead of Fairness, the predictions are the same with Fairness
and Challenge reversed in the matrix. If Challenge were deleted, the
resulting three-variable chain model would still fail as shown in Table
3. The observed correlation between Family Orientation and Commitment would be much larger than that predicted by the model.

On the other hand, if a second-order factor analysis is used with the
two expectation variables defining a cluster, then the resulting three-
variable, second-order factor matrix is defined by the correlations among
the Family Orientation and Organizational Commitment variable and the
new variable corresponding to the expectation variables. The resulting
three-variable correlation matrix computed by the *second* confirmatory
factor analysis is exactly that predicted by the original model with Orientation to Acme as the underlying variable or factor for the expectation
variables. The factor loadings for the two expectation variables will each

be .80 (i.e., the square root of the correlation between them is .64). The difference between each expectation score and the score predicted by the Entry Orientation factor is defined to be the *specific factor* for that expectation factor. These two specific factors are uncorrelated with each other and with the other two variables in the model. Because the specific factors are not related to other variables of interest, they can be regarded as "error" terms, though they are not the random response error as defined in reliability theory or conventional one-stage confirmatory factor analysis.

Note that, in this example, second-order factor analysis is not an option for reducing the complexity of the model. Second-order factor analysis is a *necessary* step to obtaining the correct causal model.

Primary and Specific Factors

The mathematics of second-order factor analysis are identical to that for first-order factor analysis; the factor analysis is simply applied to a correlation matrix at a different level. The primary factors of the first-order confirmatory factor analysis play the role of items and the second-order factors play the role of traits. The interpretation of the error terms depends on whether or not the confirmatory factor analysis was done with communalities or not. If uncorrected scale correlations are used in the second-order factor analysis, then the error terms are a composite of random and specific error. The random error term is obtained by subtracting the reliability of the scale (i.e., coefficient alpha or the like) from 1.00. Subtracting the communality of the scale from the reliability yields the variance of the specific factor for that scale.

The identification of second-order factors follows from the path diagram in Figure 13 in which F_1 and F_2 are the primary factors defining the general factor G, S_1 and S_2 are the specific factors for F_1 and F_2, respectively, and Y is any other variable of interest. Figure 13 is very similar to Figure 2, which was used to introduce the concept of parallelism between items. The similarity of these figures implies the following fact: If two first-order factors are to be measures of the same underlying second-order factor, then their correlations with all other variables must be parallel. In particular, if two variables have identical correlations (to within sampling error) with all other variables, then they can be regarded as measures of the same underlying second-order factor.

There is a directionality to this theorem and this directionality is crucial. If primary factors are measures of the same entity, then they must be parallel. However, variables that are parallel are *not* necessarily equivalent. The crucial question has to do with the correlation between them. Assume the correlations have been corrected for attenuation. Let variable Y be parallel to variable X with the correlations between Y and

Figure 13.   The Relation Between First and Second Order Factors and
Another Variable of Interest

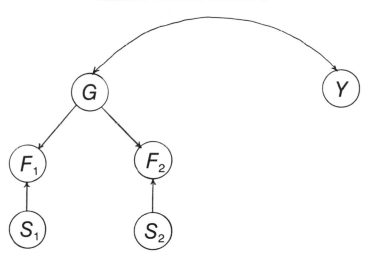

other variables all exactly half the size of those for variable X. If the
correlation between X and Y is also .50, then the data will fit a path
model in which Y is linked to the other variables in the model through
X. Thus there can be cases in which two variables are parallel but can
be maintained separately.

The one case in which combination is always required is the case in
which the first-order factors are parallel and equal in strength. If the
correlations for X and Y with other variables are identical (to within
sampling error), then no recursive path model will fit the data with X
and Y as separate entities.

AN ILLUSTRATION: REANALYSIS OF A STUDY
BY PIERCE

Review of Pierce (1979)

Pierce (1979) conceived of organizational development in terms of
three separate systems of variables:

(1)   Structural characteristics—work unit design;
(2)   Structural characteristics—job design;
(3)   Employee affective responses

Without specifying the postulated mediating causal processes, Pierce
(1979) argued that work unit design determines job design, which in turn

determines affective response to the job. To test this hypothesis, he collected data that contained variables at all three levels. He then did one canonical regression to demonstrate that there is some correlation between work unit design and job design, a second canonical regression to demonstrate that there is some relation between job design and employee affective response. He then partialled out all the job design variables from the matrix and did a third canonical regression between the work unit variables and the affective variables in hopes of finding no relation (as was the case in the data). In the end, his approach is theoretically rather vague and analytically cumbersome.

An Alternative Analysis

Examination of the actual variables revealed that there is a potentially much simpler conceptualization of the data. The three work unit variables that are correlated with job design variables are level, stratification, and centralization. Level is the number of steps from the work unit supervisor to the chief executive. If reverse scored, level is a measure of how high the person is in the organization. Stratification is the size of salary differentials within the work unit. But salary differentials are much higher at higher levels of the organization than at lower levels. Centralization is a measure of degree of decision-making participation, which also increases with level of the organization. Thus all three measures of "work unit design" may be interpreted as measures of job status.

The measures of "job design" were taken from Hackman and Oldham's (1975) job diagnostic survey (JDS) with the variety and significance scales amalgamated. Autonomy on the job might be used by employees as a measure of how bright they think the organization thinks that they are and is thus a measure of perceived job status. The same is true for job variety and clearly for job significance. The feedback scale is also a measure of perceived status though it does not distinguish at the higher levels as well as the others. Thus it may be that all the JDS variables can be regarded as measures of one underlying variable: perceived job status.

The measures of "employee affective response" are general satisfaction, intrinsic satisfaction, and kind of work satisfaction. It seems plausible that these may differ only trivially from one global affective job satisfaction response.

Thus careful examination reveals that Pierce's analysis at three levels of abstraction in the organization may actually be an analysis of three variables. This hypothesis is shown in Figure 14. Figure 14a shows the measurement model with three underlying factors: status, perceived status, and satisfaction. Figure 14b shows the causal model: actual status tends to determine perceived status, which tends to determine satisfaction with the job.

Figure 14.   An Alternate Conceptual Analysis of the Variables in the
Pierce (1979) Study

Figure 14a.   The measurement model for the reanalysis of the Pierce
(1979) study

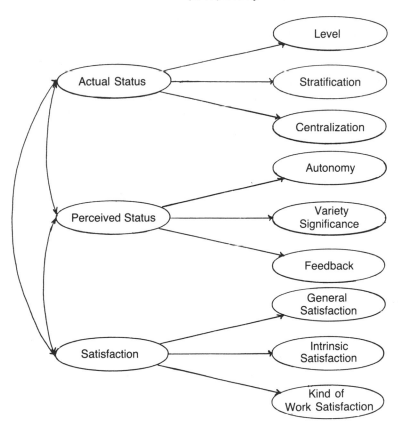

Figure 14b.   The causal model for the reanalysis of the Pierce (1979)
study

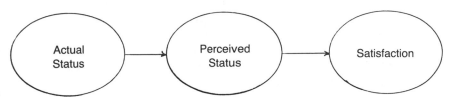

Reanalysis

The correlations among the nine variables in the Pierce analysis that are part of the measurement model of Figure 14a are shown in Table 4, listed by clusters. Correlations within each cluster are high and more or less uniform. There is an indication that the feedback scale is a poorer measure of perceived status than the other scales, and that kind of work is a poorer measure of satisfaction than the others. The correlations between clusters satisfy the expectations of parallelism: the correlations for all three status measures are uniform, the correlations for feedback are similar to but smaller than the correlations for autonomy and variety, which are equal to each other, and the correlations for kind of work are similar to but smaller than the correlations for general and intrinsic satisfaction, which are equal to each other. Thus the data fit the multiple groups measurement model, that is, the data are consistent with the hypothesis that these nine variables from the Pierce data are actually measuring only three variables.

The second-order confirmatory factor analysis implied by the measurement model of Figure 14a is shown as a set of appended variables to the matrix of Table 4. The analysis was done with communalities, and hence the factors are assumed to be perfectly measured. The part–whole correlations bear out the relative weakness of the feedback and kind of work scales.

The causal model of Figure 14b is too simple to warrant tabular presentation. The sole prediction of the model is that the correlation between status and satisfaction will equal the product of the correlation between status and perceived status and the correlation between perceived status and satisfaction. The product is $(.57)(.85) = .48$ whereas the actual correlation is only .33. Thus the model actually overpredicts the correlation between status and satisfaction. That is, whereas the partial correlation between status and satisfaction was expected to drop from .33 to .00, it actually drops from .33 to $-.37$.

The explanation for this lack of fit is probably contaminated measurement. The correlations between intrinsic satisfaction and autonomy and variety are higher than would be predicted by the correlation between intrinsic satisfaction and general satisfaction. It is likely that the intrinsic satisfaction scale contains items that unintentionally assess perceived status directly rather than the person's affective response *to* the perceived status. If the removal of such contaminated items reduced the correlation between perceived status and satisfaction from .85 to .70, then the predicted correlation would drop to .40 and the partial correlation would be only $-.12$, which is not significantly different from .00. If the removal of contaminated items dropped the correlation to .58, there would be no discrepancy at all.

Table 4. Confirmatory Factor Analysis of Correlations from Pierce (1979)[a,b]

Variables	Variables											
	LEV	STR	CNT	AUT	VAR	FDB	GST	IST	KWS	ACT	PER	SAT
Level[c]	79											
Stratification	74	76										
Centralization	83	79	83									
Autonomy	48	53	52	59								
Variety	35	46	33	59	59							
Feedback	12	14	14	34	44	27						
General satisfaction	32	31	24	54	55	41	93	93	75			
Intrinsic satisfaction	31	30	26	61	61	42	93	93	77			
Kind of work satisfaction	24	25	18	50	62	40	75	77	62			
Actual status	89	87	91	57	43	15	33	33	25	100		
Perceived status	47	56	49	77	77	52	74	91	75	57	100	
Satisfaction	32	32	25	56	66	45	96	96	79	33	85	100

[a] Decimals omitted.
[b] Communalities in the diagonal.
[c] Reverse scored.

305

Why was the Hackman–Oldham factor labeled "perceived status" instead of "job complexity," which is closer to the content of the scale items? First, a variable is actually defined by the individual difference dimension that determines differences in response. This dimension may differ from the investigator's perception if the investigator has an incorrect theory of the instrument. That is, content as perceived by the investigator need not match the content as measured by the subject's response. Second, the choice made here did not stem from an idiosyncratic assessment of item content, but from the pattern of correlations in the data. The Hackman–Oldham general factor was named "perceived job status" because it mediates actual status and job satisfaction.

Suppose that the Hackman–Oldham factor is actually job complexity and that there is a separate perceived job status variable that was not measured. Then the implied causal structure of the full data set in which perceived status were measured would be that shown in Figure 15.

Figure 15.   A Hypothetical Model in Which There Are Two Different
Variables for Perceived Job Status and Job Complexity

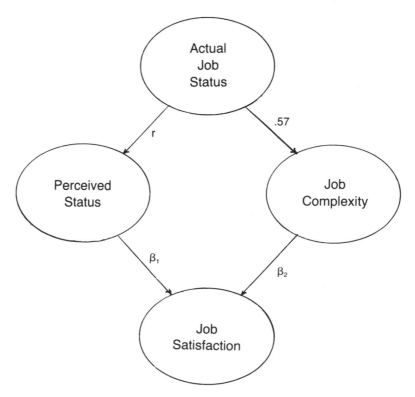

Without further information, the numbers r and β_1 cannot be separately estimated. However, the product $r\beta_1$ must be equal to the beta weight for actual status in the prediction of job satisfaction from actual status and job complexity. This beta weight depends on the value of the correlation between job complexity and job satisfaction. We have considered three values for this: the potentially contaminated observed value of .85 or two reduced values of .70 and .58. All three values can be used to generate an estimate of the product $r\beta_1$:

$$\text{If } r_{JC,JS} = .85, \text{ then } r\beta_1 = \frac{.33 - (.57)(.85)}{1 - .57^2} = -.23$$

$$\text{If } r_{JC,JS} = .70, \text{ then } r\beta_1 = \frac{.33 - (.57)(.70)}{1 - .57^2} = -.10$$

$$\text{If } r_{JC,JS} = .58, \text{ then } r\beta_1 = \frac{.33 - (.57)(.58)}{1 - .57^2} = .00$$

The first two values are negative. If a product is negative, then the two factors are of opposite sign. Thus either the correlation between actual status and perceived status would have to be negative or the causal impact of perceived status onto job satisfaction would have to be negative. The other possible value for the product is .00. But if a product is 0, then at least one of the factors must be 0. This would imply that either the correlation between actual and perceived status is 0 or that the impact of perceived status on job satisfaction is 0.

Thus the data do not fit Figure 15 with theoretically permissible values. Therefore, it can be concluded that job complexity has not been measured separately from perceived job status but is coordinate to it. That is, it can be concluded that the variable measured by the job complexity items is in fact perceived job status.

AN ILLUSTRATION: REANALYSIS OF A STUDY BY JERMIER AND BERKES

Review of Jermier and Berkes (1979)

Jermier and Berkes (1979) studied effective leadership in an urban police department. They defined effective leadership in terms of either job satisfaction or organizational commitment. They chose predictors to contrast the quasi-military model with the human relations model. The authoritarian indicators were essentially uncorrelated with either measure of leadership effectiveness, whereas the human relations indicators made large contributions to the multiple regression equations. Reanalysis of their data will not only simplify the data but will show that there is a fundamental ambiguity in their data of which they were unaware. Their data fit several models which are quite at variance from their interpretations. However, some of this ambiguity can be removed by reference to other data, including that of Pierce (1979) reanalyzed above.

Reanalysis of Jermier and Berkes

Table 5 shows the Jermier and Berkes correlations with the indicators of authoritarian leadership style deleted. The diagonal entries are the reliabilities. The data are blocked to show the human relations leadership cluster and the job complexity cluster. In both cases, the correlations within the cluster are still well below 1.00 (even when corrected for attenuation), but the scale correlations are parallel and hence indicate equivalence at the seond-order factor level. Therefore a confirmatory factor analysis was done with four factors. The first factor was defined by the human relations leadership scales: instrumental leader behavior (role clarification), supportive leader behavior, and participatory leader behavior. The second factor was defined by the job complexity scales: task variety and task interdependence. The third factor was defined by job satisfaction alone, though the diagonal entry for its communality was its reliability. Thus the job satisfaction factor was corrected for measurement error. The fourth factor was defined by organizational commitment alone, but it too was corrected for attenuation by using the reliability as its communality. Thus the four-factor correlation matrix is completely corrected for measurement error.

Table 6 shows the correlations between the four factors underlying the Jermier and Berkes (1979) data. The pattern in these correlations is stark: human relations leadership, job complexity, and organizational commitment all have their highest correlations with job satisfaction and have much lower correlations with each other. In fact, if job satisfaction is held constant, then the other three variables are virtually uncorrelated. Thus the data fit a model in which job satisfaction is causally *prior* to perceived human relations leadership, perceived job complexity, and organizational commitment.

Figure 16 shows four path models that fit the data quite well. Figure 16a is that suggested in the previous paragraph and assumes that job satisfaction is causally prior to all three of the other variables. The error analysis for the model in Figure 16a is shown in Table 7. The three nonconstrained errors are all trivial in magnitude and well below the level of statistical significance; that is, the data show perfect fit for the model in Figure 16a. This model directly reverses the major reasoning expressed by Jermier and Berkes (1979). Jermier and Berkes assumed that high use of human relations leadership style by bosses and high job

Table 5. The Correlation Matrix from Jermier and Berkes (1979)

Variables	Variables						
	ILB	*SLB*	*PLB*	*TV*	*TI*	*OC*	*JS*
Instrumental leader behavior	94	68	40				
Supportive leader behavior	68	94	47				
Participative leader behavior	40	47	80				
Task variety	23	14	20	86	39		
Task interdependence	23	10	20	39	82		
Organizational commitment	29	29	33	35	20	91	
Job satisfaction	54	54	49	44	23	68	92

Table 6.   The Correlations Among the Second-order Factors in the
Jermier and Berkes Study Obtained by Applying Confirmatory
Factor Analysis to the Correlation Matrix

	Variables			
Variables	*HRL*	*JC*	*OC*	*JS*
Human relations leadership	100	40	44	75
Job complexity	40	100	46	56
Organizational commitment	44	46	100	74
Job satisfaction	75	56	74	100

complexity cause high job satisfaction. This model asserts just the reverse: that a high level of job satisfaction causes people to perceive their
leaders' behavior as participatory and causes people to perceive their
jobs as complex.

The model in Figure 16b is even worse. In this model, organizational
commitment is causally prior to job satisfaction and job satisfaction is
causally prior to perceived human relations leadership and perceived job
complexity. This exactly reverses every causal assumption made by
Jermier and Berkes. The predictions made by the model of Figure 16b

Figure 16.   Four Models Which Fit the Jermier and Berkes (1979)
Data

Figure 16a.

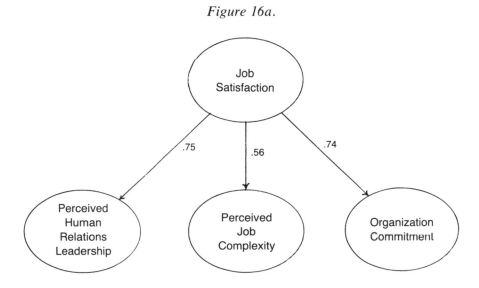

Figure 16b.

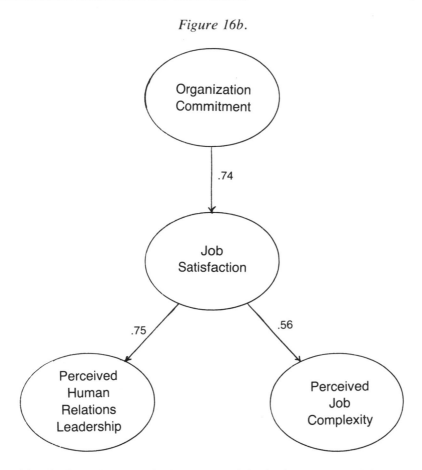

are identical to those made by the model of Figure 16a and hence the error analysis is that of Table 7. Thus the model of Figure 16b, which exactly reverses the beliefs of Jermier and Berkes, fits the data perfectly.

The models of Figure 16c and d make the same predictions as does the model of Figure 16a and hence have the error analysis in Table 7. They also fit the data perfectly.

Does the Jermier and Berkes model in Figure 17 fit their data? Table 8 presents the error analysis. The two unconstrained errors are trivial in magnitude and are far from statistical significance. Hence the model fits the data perfectly.

By the mechanical principles of purely mathematical criteria for path analysis, the Jermier and Berkes model would be rejected in favor of the models in Figure 16. This is because the models of Figure 16 are more parsimonious than the Jermier and Berkes model. The models of

Figure 16c.

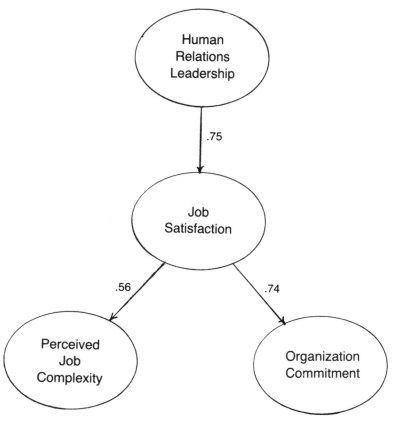

Figure 16 fit the data using only three path coefficients whereas the Jermier and Berkes model uses four. The models of Figure 16 fit the data with three unconstrained errors whereas the Jermier and Berkes model has only two. In substantive terms, the models of Figure 16 each have an explanation of the correlation between human relations leadership and job complexity whereas the Jermier and Berkes model treats this correlation as an unexplained exogenous effect. This is why the principle of parsimony is rejected by many researchers.

Linking Jermier and Berkes (1979) to Pierce (1979)

At the level of primary measurement, there is not a single instrument that overlaps between the studies of Jermier and Berkes (1979) and Pierce (1979). Yet at the level of second-order factor analysis, there are two

Figure 16d.

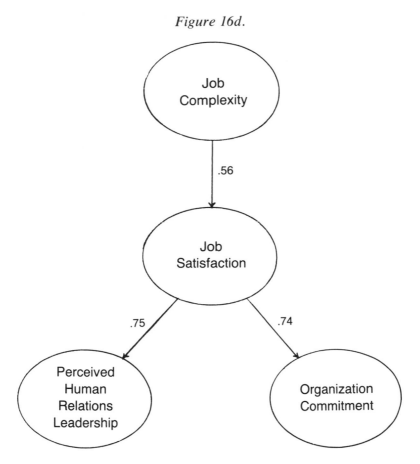

overlapping factors: job complexity and job satisfaction. Moreover, in the Jermier and Berkes study, the job satisfaction scale did not contain job complexity items and hence their correlation between factors should be uncontaminated. The Jermier and Berkes correlations between job complexity and job satisfaction was .56, which almost exactly matches the estimate of .58 required in the Pierce study to produce perfect fit of the model to the data.

Linking the two studies provides strong evidence that job complexity in the Jermier and Berkes study is causally prior to job satisfaction. This would eliminate the models of Figure 16a, b, and c from further consideration. This assumes that perceived human relations leadership is causally antecedent to job satisfaction. However this, too, is counter to the many experiments showing the positive impact of training in interpersonal skills.

Table 7. Error Analysis for the Models in Figure 16

Variables	Variables			
	HRC	CMP	COM	SAT
	Observed Correlations			
Human relations leadership	100	40	44	75
Job complexity	40	100	46	56
Organizational commitment	44	46	100	75
Job satisfaction	75	56	74	100
	Reproduced Correlations			
Human relations leadership	100	42	56	75
Job complexity	42	100	41	56
Organizational commitment	56	41	100	75
Job satisfaction	75	56	74	100
	Errors			
Human relations leadership		−02	−12	00
Job complexity	−02		05	00
Organizational commitment	−12	05		00
Job satisfaction	00[a]	00[a]	00[a]	

[a] Errors constrained to be zero by the estimation process.

Linking the two studies also suggests an explanation for the correlations between human relations leadership and job complexity. This explanation is illustrated in the model in Figure 18a, which shows actual job status as a common antecedent to both job complexity and human relations leadership. The assumption here is that supervisors at higher levels are more likely to make heavy use of interpersonal skills. The problem with the model in Figure 18a is that it implies that the correlation between actual job status and job satisfaction be .62 whereas the observed value in the Pierce study is only .33.

Figure 18b shows a model that fits all the data in the Jermier and Berkes study along with an implied correlation between actual job status and human relations leadership of .24, and job complexity of .57 (as observed in Pierce), and job satisfaction of .33 (as observed in Pierce), and occupational commitment of .24. Thus the model in Figure 18b fits all the data in both studies except the contaminated correlation of .85 between job complexity and job satisfaction in the Pierce study. The difference between the models is that Figure 18b assumes that human relations leadership has an impact on job complexity. This does not fit

Figure 17.   The Jermier and Berkes (1979) Model for Their Own Data
              (as Implicitly Stated in Their Discussion)

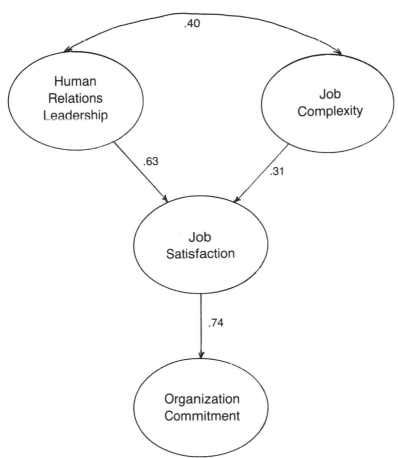

the usual content of job complexity, but it does fit our earlier conclusion
that job complexity is actually a measure of perceived job status.

Conclusion

The Pierce (1979) and Jermier and Berkes (1979) study were not selected a priori because they complement each other. We were just randomly looking for recent studies that published their entire correlation
matrix. Yet our findings here are probably typical of what we have
observed in other studies. Analyzing studies at the level of second-order
factor analysis not only greatly simplifies single studies but also reveals

Table 8.   Error Analysis of the Jermier and Berkes Model in Figure 17

Variables	Variables			
	HRC	CMP	COM	SAT
	Observed Correlations			
Human relations leadership	100	42	56	75
Job complexity	42	100	41	56
Organizational commitment	56	41	100	74
Job satisfaction	75	56	74	100
	Reproduced Correlations			
Human relations leadership	100	40	56	75
Job complexity	40	100	41	56
Organizational commitment	56	41	100	74
Job satisfaction	75	56	74	100
	Errors			
Human relations leadership		00[a]	-12	00
Job complexity	00[a]		05	00
Organizational commitment	-12	05		00
Job satisfaction	00[a]	00[a]	00[a]	

[a] Errors constrained to be zero by the estimation process.

the overlap between different studies. It has also been our experience that the combination of equivalent variables in second-order factor analysis eliminates "anomalies" that might otherwise lead to nonrecursive models.

SUMMARY

With illustrations from the organizational literature, this article presented an integrated research paradigm defined by the construction and analysis of two interrelated models. According to this paradigm, the researcher first constructs a theory of the causal processes among a set of variables. The theory of causal processes generates predictions of the relationships among the variables. These predictions are stated in the form of a causal model and tested with a path analysis.

The variables in the causal model are constructs that must first be measured before the relations among them may be analyzed. The presence of specific and random measurement error in any single indicator of a construct is accounted for by the operationalization of the constructs in terms of multiple indicator variables. The relation between indicators

Figure 18. Two Models Which Seek to Integrate Findings from Jermier and Berkes (1979) and Pierce (1979); One Which Does Not Fit and One Which Does Fit

Figure 18a.   *Figure 18b.*

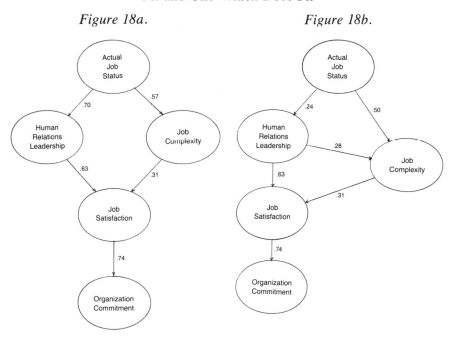

and constructs is specified by the measurement model and is tested with a confirmatory factor analysis. The estimated correlations among the constructs computed by the confirmatory factor analysis become the data for the path analysis.

There may, however, be an intermediate step between the confirmatory factor analysis of the measurement model and the path analysis of the causal model. The confirmatory factor analysis of cross-sectional data accounts for random response error and specific error unique to a single indicator variable. However, two or more clusters of indicator variables may define the same true score *except* for a shared specific component unique to the indicators within each cluster. Within a cluster this shared specific component contributes to the underlying factor, but between clusters measuring similar true scores it acts like random measurement error. The accounting of this within-cluster shared specific component is accomplished by the construction of a second-order measurement model and analyzed with a second-order confirmatory factor analysis. The resultant second-order factors define the constructs of the path analysis, and the correlations among the factors computed by the second-order factor analysis are the data for the subsequent path analysis.

NOTES

1. Hunter, J. E. *Cluster analysis: reliability, construct validity, and the multiple indicators approach to measurement.* Paper presented at a workshop titled "Advanced Statistics" given at the U.S. Civil Commission on March 21, 1977.

2. Gerbing, D. W., and Hunter, J. E. *The return to multiple groups: Analysis and critique of confirmatory factor analysis with LISREL.* Paper submitted for publication, 1980.

3. Hunter, J. E., Gerbing, D. W., Cohen, S. H., and Nicol, T. *PACKAGE 1980: A system of Fortran routines for the analysis of correlational data.* User's manual prepared by Academic Computing Services, Baylor University, Waco, Texas, 1980. (Manual and program available from the second author.)

REFERENCES

Asher, H. B. *Causal modeling.* Sage University Paper series on Quantitative Applications in the Social Sciences, No. 07-003. Beverly Hills and London: Sage Publications, 1976.

Bentler, P. M. Multivariate analysis with latent variables: Causal modeling. In M. R. Rosenzweig and L. W. Porter (Eds.), *Annual Review of Psychology.* Palo Alto, Ca.: Annual Reviews Inc., 1980, *31,* 419–456.

Billings, R. S., & Wroten, S. P. Use of path analysis in industrial/organizational psychology; Criticisms and suggestions. *Journal of Applied Psychology,* 1978, *63,* 677–688.

Blalock, H. M., Jr. (Ed.). *Causal models in the social sciences.* Chicago: Aldine Publishing Company, 1971.

Burt, C. *The distribution and relations of educational abilities.* London: P. S. King and Son, 1917.

Burt, R. S. Interpretational confounding of unobserved variables in structural equation models. *Sociological Methods and Research,* 1976, *5,* 3–52.

Cochran, W. G. Errors of measurement in statistics. *Technometrics,* 1968, *10,* 637–646.

Cronbach, L. J., & Meehl, P. E. Construct validity in psychological tests. *Psychological Bulletin,* 1955, *52,* 281–302.

Duncan, O. D. *Introduction to structural equation models.* New York: Academic Press, Inc., 1975.

Ebel, R. L. *Essentials of educational measurement.* Englewood Cliffs, N.J.: Prentice-Hall, Inc., 1972.

Everitt, B. *Cluster Analysis.* London: Heinemann Educational Books, 1974.

Fox, J. Simultaneous equation models and two-stage least squares. In K. F. Schuesster (Ed.), *Sociological methodology,* San Francisco: Jossey-Bass, 1979.

Green, S. B., Lissitz, R. W., & Mulaik, S. A. Limitations of coefficient alpha as an index of test unidimensionality. *Educational and Psychological Measurement,* 1977, *37,* 827–838.

Guttman, L. A basis for scaling qualitative data. *American Sociological Review,* 1944, *9,* 139–150.

Guttman, L. Multiple group methods for common-factor analysis: Their basis, computation, and interpretation. *Psychometrika,* 1952, *17,* 209–222.

Hackman, J. R., & Oldham, G. R. Development of the Job Diagnostic Survey. *Journal of Applied Psychology,* 1975, *60,* 159–170.

Heise, D. R. *Causal analysis.* New York: John Wiley and Sons, 1975.

Heise, D. R., & Bohrnstedt, G. W. Validity, invalidity and reliability. In E. F. Borgatta and G. W. Bohrnstedt (Eds.), *Sociological Methodology.* New York: Jossey-Bass, Inc., 1970.

Holzinger, K. J. A simple method of factor analysis. *Psychometrika,* 1944, 257–262.

Hunter, J. E. Methods of recording the correlation matrix to facilitate visual inspection and preliminory cluster analysis. *Journal of Educational Measurement,* 1973, *10,* 51–61.

Hunter, J. E., & Cohen, S. H. PACKAGE: A system of computer routines for the analysis of correlational data. *Educational and Psychological Measurement,* 1969, *29,* 697–700.

Issac, P. D. Linear regression, structural equations, and measurement error. *Psychological Bulletin,* 1970, *74,* 213–218.

Jackson, D. N. Construct validity in personality assessment. In *Construct validity in psychological measurement,* Princeton, New Jersey: Educational Testing Service, 1980.

James, L. R., & Singh, B. K. An introduction to the logic, assumptions, and basic analytic procedures of two-stage least squares. *Psychological Bulletin,* 1978, *85,* 1104–1122.

Jermier, J. M., & Berkes, L. J. Leader behavior in a police command bureaucracy: A closer look at the quasi-military model. *Administrative Science Quarterly,* 1979, *24,* 1–23.

Joreskog, K. G. Testing a simple structure hypothesis in factor analysis. *Psychometrika,* 1966, *31,* 165–190.

Joreskog, K. G. A general approach to confirmatory maximum likelihood factor analysis. *Psychometrika,* 1969, *34,* 183–202.

Joreskog, K. G. Statistical analysis of sets of congeneric tests. *Psychometrika,* 1971, *36,* 109–133.

Joreskog, K. G. Structural analysis of covariance and correlation matrices. *Psychometrika,* 1978, *43,* 443–477.

Joreskog, K. G., & Sorbom, D. *LISREL IV: Analysis of linear structural relationships by the method of maximum likelihood.* Chicago: National Educational Resources, Inc., 1978.

Kenny, D. A. *Correlation and causation.* New York: John Wiley and Sons, 1979.

Kotsch, W. E., Gerbing, D. W., & Schwartz, L. E. The construct validity of the differential emotions scale for children and adolescents. In C. E. Izard (Ed.), *The measuring of emotions in infants and children.* Cambridge University Press, in press.

Lewis-Beck, M. S. Determining the importance of an independent variable: A path analytic solution. *Social Science Research,* 1974, *3,* 95–107.

Moiser, C. I. On the reliability of a weighted composite. *Psychometrika,* 1943, *8,* 161–168.

Mulaik, S. A. *The foundations of factor analysis.* New York: McGraw-Hill Book Co., 1972.

Novick, M. R., & Lewis, C. Coefficient alpha and the reliability of composite measurements. *Psychometrika,* 1967, *32,* 1–13.

Nunnally, J. *Psychometric methods.* New York: McGraw-Hill Book Co., 1978.

Pierce, J. L. Employee affective responses to work unit structure and job design: a test of an intervening variable. *Journal of Management,* 1979, *5,* 193–211.

Rajaratnam, N., Cronbach, L. J., & Gleser, G. C. Generalizability of stratified-parallel tests. *Psychometrika,* 1965, *30,* 39–56.

Schwab, D. P. Construct validity in organizational behavior. In B. M. Staw and L. L. Cummings (Eds.), *Research in Organizational Behavior,* Volume II, Greenwich, Conn.: JAI Press Inc., 1980.

Smith, K. W. On estimating the reliability of composite indexes through factor analysis. *Sociological Methods and Research,* 1974, *2,* 485–511.

Sorbom, D., & Joreskog, K. G. *COFAMM: Confirmatory factor analysis with model modification.* Chicago: National Educational Resources, 1976.

Spearman, C. "General intelligence" objectively determined and measured. *American Journal of Psychology,* 1904, *15,* 201–293.

Thorndike, R. L. Reliability. In E. F. Lindquist (Ed.), *Educational measurement*. Washington: American Council on Education, 1951.

Tryon, R. C. *Cluster analysis*. Ann Arbor, Michigan: Edwards Brothers, Inc., 1939.

Tryon, R. C. Domain sampling formulation of cluster and factor analysis. *Psychometrika*, 1959, 113–135.

Tryon, R. C., & Bailey, D. E. *Cluster analysis*. New York: McGraw-Hill Book Co., 1970.

Wiley, D. E. The identification problem for structural equation models with unmeasured variables. In A. S. Goldberger & O. D. Duncan (Eds.), *Structural equation models in the social sciences*. New York: Academic Press, Inc., 1973.

Wright, S. Correlation and causation. *Journal of Agricultural Research*, 1921, *20*, 557–585.

Wright, S. The method of path coefficients. *Annals of Mathematical Statistics*, 1934, *5*, 161–215.

A MATRIX APPROACH TO LITERATURE REVIEWS

Paul Salipante, William Notz and John Bigelow

ABSTRACT

Literature reviews provide one of the principal means by which knowledge is extracted from accumulated studies. These reviews are important in helping social scientists keep abreast of literature beyond the boundaries of their own speciality. However, in contrast to the well-developed literature on the methodology for designing single studies, little has been written about the methodology of performing reviews. This article is an initial effort toward the development of a general model of review methods. Methods are discussed which allow more sophisticated analysis of entire sets of studies for the purpose of determining review findings and assessing their validity. New approaches to dealing with validity threats are emphasized. The article presents methods from a major literature review performed by the authors on job satisfaction and productivity and from a number of other large-scale reviews. The applicability of the model and methods to reviews with various goals and types of literature is also considered.

Research in Organizational Behavior, Vol. 4, pages 321–348
Copyright © 1982 by JAI Press Inc.
All rights of reproduction in any form reserved.
ISBN: 0-89232-147-4

This article considers methods that can improve the validity of conclusions derived from literature reviews. The embryonic literature on review methods has been insightful but sparse. Therefore, this article presents a general model of review methods and, within the framework of the model, considers specific methods developed by ourselves and others.

The methods presented offer distinct advantages over currently prevalent review procedures. In particular, the methods draw reviewers' attention to assessment of the validity of their review findings, a problem either largely neglected or inadequately addressed in almost all reviews. The method illustrated enables reviewers on the one hand to draw the most knowledge possible from a set of studies and on the other to specify exactly which alternative explanations threaten the findings. For example, applying the methods to a review of work redesign experiments led to the conclusion that several very plausible alternative explanations existed for the findings produced by the entire set of studies. That is, despite the overwhelmingly positive nature of the results from these field experiments, advocates of various types of job redesign are not justified in citing these results as convincing support for the innovations. In contrast, a preliminary, post hoc application of the methods described here to a review of the effects of school desegregation (Bradley and Bradley, 1978) led to the conclusion that this review may have quite seriously underestimated the faith that could be placed in the efficacy of desegregation.

Clearly, errors of either type—over- or understatement of the validity of findings from a set of studies—can seriously impede the accumulation of knowledge in the social sciences. What is required is a methodology to guide reviewers in deriving review findings while accurately assessing their validity and indicating explicitly what flaws must be overcome in future research.

THE CURRENT STATE OF REVIEW METHODS

Current social science reviews are based on a variety of methods, ranging from a highly subjective, literary process of evaluation and summarization (the most frequent) to a number of more formal and intensive methods of extracting the meaning from a set of studies. Jackson's (1980) methodological analysis of 36 randomly selected reviews clearly demonstrated the lack of concern for methodology and, particularly, for validity in recent reviews. The variability and lack of rigor in review methods can create a corresponding variability in review findings. The debate on the effects of school desegregation, for which the Bradley and Bradley review cited above provides the most recent arguments, is a good illustration. Armor (1972) concluded on the basis of his review that "four out of five premises of the integration policy model are not supported by the data . . ." (p. 109). This conclusion was roundly attacked by Pettigrew, Useem, Normand, and Smith (1973). Citing unrealistically high standards, bias in selecting studies, and methodological problems in Armor's own busing study, they concluded, "Armor's sweeping policy conclusion against 'mandatory busing' is neither substantiated nor warranted" (p. 90). Here it seems that the vagaries of current review methods provided both parties with enough slack to extract their own conclusions from the data. A similar example is provided by reviews of studies on Herzberg's two-factor theory: Whitsett and Winslow (1967) concluding the theory was supported, and House and Wigdor (1967) finding that most of the studies they reviewed contradicted the theory. In a later review, King (1970) found five different versions of the two-factor theory and concluded that the findings that supported these could all be explained by methodological artifacts. As a final example, the recent controversy over the validity and value of need satisfaction theories of job attitudes between Salancik and Pfeffer (1977) and Alderfer (1977) was partially stimulated by their differing assessments of the empirical literature in the area.

Although a more formal review methodology would not remove all such differences of opinion, it would certainly help in distinguishing opinion from review conclusion. A number of social scientists have made important contributions that can be incorporated into a formalized methodology. Jackson (1980) has presented an excellent discussion of numerous aspects of review methodology, the only general treatment of review methods known to us. Concerning particular review issues, Rosenthal (1969, 1978, 1979) has improved our ability to summarize bodies of research with respect to significance levels and their vulnerability to nonsignificant results unknown to the reviewer; Cook (1974) and Cook and Gruder (1978) have suggested several models of meta evaluation (review of evaluation research); Light and Smith (1977) and Light (1979) have considered methods for resolving conflicting results among a set of studies and, similarly, Schmidt, Hunter, Pearlman, and Shane (1979), Hunter (Note 1), Schmidt (Note 2), and Schwab, Olian-Gottlieb, and Heneman (1979) have analyzed sources of variance in results across studies; Glass (1976) and Smith and Glass (1977) have introduced procedures for deriving review findings by treating each study as the unit of analysis and applying multivariate analysis; and Yin and Heald (1975) have developed methods for reviewing case studies. However, lacking any general model of review methods, this literature has remained somewhat disconnected, undeveloped, and underutilized across different domains of research; for example, most social science research continues to be reviewed in a literary fashion.

The general model of review methods presented in this article makes no attempt at complete integration of this growing literature, though it is intended to contribute to such a development. This article seeks to develop and support two basic contentions stemming from our perception of the shortcomings of many reviews. The first contention is that reviews should utilize methods that create and assess *sets* of studies, deriving the most information possible from these sets. The second contention is an application of the first to the assessment of a review finding's validity, specifically, that this assessment should be based on the *distribution* of threats to validity across the set of studies.

Our approach to review methodology, then, is similar (and owes much) to Campbell and Stanley's (1966) approach to research methods. However, whereas their concern was with the validity of individual studies, ours is with the validity of sets of findings. Somewhat surprisingly, most literature on review methods has covered the development of review findings, with little explicit discussion of most issues of validity. As in individual studies, researchers have been concerned largely with statistical conclusion validity to the exclusion of the numerous other threats to the validity of a review finding.

A GENERAL MODEL OF REVIEW METHODS

The reviewer's task may be divided into two steps. The first is an arraying of information from a number of studies into a form allowing integration of findings whereas the second is an assessment of the validity of findings emerging from the array. The array may be conceived of as a matrix having three dimensions as presented in Figure 1. One dimension identifies the studies, each of which may contain several findings. The second dimension categorizes the findings themselves. By a "finding" we simply mean the relationship between two or more variables. The findings dimension includes contingencies, that is, variables identified as moderating a relationship. The third dimension of the matrix contains threats to the validity of each finding. In following a modified version of Cook and Campbell (1976), there are four kinds of validity: internal, external, construct validity of causes (independent variables), and construct validity of effects (dependent variables).[1] Ideally, the validity dimension of the matrix should display information on the extent to which the various threats (e.g., a selection artifact) to each type of validity can be ruled out. In practice, the type(s) of validity of greatest import will vary with the review's goals, as discussed later. For many reviews, internal validity will be the primary concern, as it is in the examples used in this article.

The process of assembling the information needed for the review matrix may be termed "matrix creation." The steps needed for matrix creation are

1. *Defining the review's goals,* in terms of areas and types of con-clusions to be drawn.
2. *Selecting and obtaining literature,* guided by the review's goals.
3. *Identifying the substantive findings* in each piece of literature, including contingencies. Each study produces a row on the front face of the matrix in Figure 1.
4. *Grouping of like findings* (i.e., grouping the columns along the front face of the matrix). The reviewer must decide which findings are sufficiently similar in terms of variables involved to be con-sidered as one group.
5. *Assessing the threats to validity* to each finding (e.g., a row along the end face of the Figure 1 matrix). For each type of validity (internal, external, construct) there will be a number of threats to be assessed, with those to internal validity (e.g., history, selection) usually being primary.

Following matrix creation, the reviewer assesses the matrix infor-mation to generate review findings and estimates of their validity, a process we term "matrix assessment." The matrix information may be analyzed in two primary ways during matrix assessment. Analyzing a finding across a set of studies (a column on the front face of the matrix) is necessary to derive a tentative review finding (e.g., X is related to Y in the presence of Z). A slice arraying the validity threats to the set of studies that produced this finding (the slice depicted in Figure 1) may

Figure 1. Matrix of Review Information

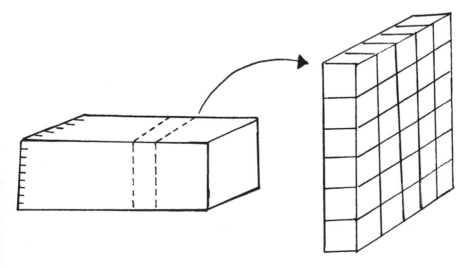

then be analyzed to estimate the validity of the review finding. Hereafter we will refer to this slice of the matrix as the "validity threat array."

There are two steps, then, in matrix assessment.

1. *Determining review findings.* The reviewer must generate his own findings by integrating the findings across the studies (within each finding's group) into a review finding. For example, the reviewer may identify a contingency by comparing sample characteristics across studies having conflicting findings.
2. *Assessing the validity of each review finding,* by analyzing the threats to validity across the studies (i.e., the validity threat array).

Analyzing Sets of Studies

This general model reflects our contention that entire sets of studies must be analyzed to derive the most information possible from a literature, both in terms of the review findings themselves and the assessment of their validities. The model puts a premium on the literature search process. If reviewers create matrices that largely exhaust the relevant empirical literature, interreviewer differences in findings due to differences in selection criteria will be reduced.

A close parallel may be drawn between reviewing a set of studies and analyzing a set of observations in a single study. Review methods are proceeding in exactly this direction: treating each study within a findings group as one (or more) observation(s). In both single studies and reviews, one is interested in deriving findings from the entire set of observations. The researcher is very hesitant to discard individual observations; so too should be the reviewer. The researcher utilizes analytical methods that operate on the entire body of data; so should the reviewer. Our later discussion will present specific review methods of exactly this sort, both for deriving findings and for assessing their validity.

Heterogeneity of Contexts and Threats

The more unique characteristics of our methods depend on our second contention, which concerns the distribution of validity threats to a set of findings. Although the contention is a relatively simple one, it calls into serious question the appropriateness of all methods (except that of Light and Smith, 1977) that are currently being used to assess the validity of review findings. For example, a few of the strongest reviews to date have included in their analyses single variable measures of each study's internal validity, yet our contention implies that even this approach is inadequate.

Our contention is that a review's matrix assessment methods must address the variation across studies (1) in contextual variables and (2) in the threats to validity that are not controlled. The greater the variation in these, the greater the confidence in the review finding. If the reviewer discovers that a particular relationship has been consistently found across a wide range of settings and populations, the possibility that the relationship is highly contingent on some unidentified variable is lessened. Similarly, if individual studies in a set vary in the validity threats that they do not control, the possibility that one or two of those threats account for the observed relationship (making the relationship spurious) is reduced. To state the same argument conversely: among studies reporting similar findings, the reviewer should seek to identify uncontrolled validity threats that run through many of the studies, thereby offering plausible alternative explanations to the findings. The fewer that are found, the greater the validity that can be assigned to the relationship. In other words, the more heterogeneous the distribution of uncontrolled validity threats in a set of similar findings, the greater the validity of the findings from the set.

Of course, important contingencies that did not vary across the set of studies might exist. Because the number of possible contingencies is virtually limitless, this argument can never entirely be dismissed. Nevertheless, its plausibility (as well as the importance of the unidentified contingencies) diminishes as the number and variety of studies considered increases. With regard to assessing validity threats, the reviewer's conclusions may be more assured because the important validity threats are all potentially identifiable. If all the internal validity threats not controlled in each study are listed in the assessment matrix, analysis of the distribution of threats in the set of studies will reveal whether any threats run through most of the studies. If not, and if the studies produce the same finding, the resulting review finding can be accepted as having strong internal validity.

The preceding argument implies that *reviewers cannot assess the validity of a review finding as a simple and sole function of the validity of individual studies*. To elaborate, it is quite possible to have a set of individually strong studies that is much weaker in aggregate than an alternative set composed of individually flawed studies. This apparent paradox follows from the fact that the confidence that can be placed in a finding is determined less by the number of alternative explanations than it is by their plausibility; and for a finding from a set of studies, the plausibility of rival explanations is largely determined by their distribution within the set. Thus the confidence that could be placed in a finding would generally be less if it were based on a set, the individual studies of which all suffered from the same *single* flaw, than on a comparable set within which threats to validity were more numerous but heterogeneously distributed.

Combining our two contentions yields a very direct and basic implication: that reviewers should not confuse matrix creation with matrix assessment. Because an entire validity threat array must be analyzed to determine the validity of a review finding, reviewers are not justified in rejecting individual studies that are individually weak. Hunter and Schmidt (1978) point out the large Type I bias in review findings that can result from exclusion of studies. Similarly, a bias in the assessment of validity can result from exclusion of studies. Jackson (1980) found that most reviewers handled methodological weaknesses in studies either by simply saying the review findings were unreliable or by discarding the inadequate studies. Worse, some reviewers attacked on methodological grounds studies supporting one point of view without applying the same standards to studies supporting an opposing view. Clearly, review findings themselves and estimates of their validities could be improved by removing from reviewers' discretion the ability to exclude or greatly discount individual studies on methodological grounds.

We will now turn to specific methods that are congruent with the preceding contentions. The primary example used to illustrate these methods is a large-scale review of literature on job satisfaction and productivity. We will consider matrix assessment methods for two different types of empirical studies: quasi-experimental and correlational. Methods for reviewing experimental studies would closely parallel those for quasi experiments.

MATRIX ANALYSIS

Matrix Creation for Quasi Experiments

Our review yielded 58 field experiments of varying validity. After identifying the variables investigated in each, we grouped them into 14 broadly defined independent and dependent variables. Table 1 (adapted from Cummings, Molloy, and Glen, 1977) presents findings information on a few of the 58 field experiments reviewed. The table represents a part of the front face of the matrix in Figure 1. The left side of the table indicates which of the nine broadly defined independent variables were manipulated by the innovation whereas the right side indicates which dependent variables were measured by the study and the impact on each.

The next task is to organize the studies' findings into homogeneous groups. This task would be straightforward for quasi experiments that manipulate only a single variable, such as job variety, and control all

Table 1. Job Restructuring: Contextual, Independent, and Dependent Variables

Author(s)	Treatment Took Effect	Pay/Reward Systems	Autonomy/ Discretion	Support	Training	Organization Structure	Technical/ Physical	Task Variety	Information/ Feedback	Interpersonal/ Group Process	Costs	Productivity	Quality	Withdrawal	Attitudes
		INDEPENDENT VARIABLES									DEPENDENT VARIABLES				
Alderfer, C.	?				X			X							+
Conant, E. and Kilbridge, N.	Yes	X	X				X	X			−	+	+		+
Cox, D. and Sharp, K.	?						X	X				+	+		
Davis, L. and Valfer, E.	Yes		X		X						+ 0	0 0	+ +		+ +
Davis, L. and Werling, R. (a)	No		X		X	X	X	X							−
Davis, L. and Werling, R. (b)	Yes		X	X	X	X		X			−	+			+
Ford, R. (a)	Yes		X					X	X			+	+	−	+
Ford, R. (b)	Yes		X					X	X			+	+		+
Ford, R. and Sheaffer, H.	?		X					X	X		−	0	+	−	
Foulkes, F.	?		X				X					+	+	−	+

CODE: Blank, not relevant; X, variable manipulated; ?, insufficient data; +, variable increased; −, variable decreased; 0, variable static.

others. Such quasi experiments would closely resemble true experiments and could be grouped by the single independent variable manipulated (and subgrouped by dependent variable). Single variable manipulation, however, is not likely to be the case in field situations, where the usual aim is to do whatever is necessary to meet the field project's goals. A treatment in which several variables are manipulated is the typical approach. The result for the reviewer is a "multiple treatment" problem, illustrated by the independent variables in Table 1. The left side of the table indicates that two to five variables were manipulated per study. What can be done in such a case is to increase by one level of abstraction what is meant by a "treatment." A more abstract classification of treatments is justified if these classifications satisfy two conditions: (1) strong similarities in the variables manipulated by all studies grouped under one treatment (low within-group variance) and (2) strong differences across these abstracted treatments (high between-group variance) in terms of the variables manipulated. Our review found that grouping into four commonly recognized change orientations met these conditions. Table 2 shows the similarities within and the differences across classifications in variables manipulated. Collapsing treatments into coarser groupings is desirable not only when the multiple treatment problem is encountered but also when the number of differing treatments is large relative to the number of studies. For example, the Smith and Glass (1977) review of psychotherapy studies grouped ten types of therapy into four classes by applying multidimensional scaling methods to judges' ratings.

For the completion of the matrix creation phase, information on the validity threats to each study must be collected and assembled. In the examination of the threats to internal and external validity, some time can be saved by determining the study's design because the design implies which threats are controlled. The work of Campbell and Stanley (1966) and Cook and Campbell (1976) may be used to categorize the design of each field experiment and to estimate which validity threats are not controlled or are only poorly controlled by the design.[2] Some studies were found to use different designs for different dependent variables, and in these instances each research design was critiqued separately. To assess threats not controlled by the design, information should be sought from the study itself. For instance, if the design did not control selection as a threat to internal validity, information in the report of the study might indicate that control and experimental groups did not differ on several variables, thereby reducing the plausibility of the selection threat. Therefore a study whose design did not control selection could still be coded as adequately dealing with that threat.

Table 3 (see later) displays the validity threat array (the slice in Figure 1) for a number of the sociotechnical field experiments in our review.

Table 2. Grouping Quasi Experiments[a]

	INDEPENDENT VARIABLES: A Summary of the Percentages of Field Experimental Studies that Manipulated a Particular Variable									DEPENDENT VARIABLES: A Summary of the Percentage of Field Experimental Studies that Produced Totally Positive Results[b]				
	Pay/ Reward Systems	Autonomy/ Discretion	Support	Training	Organization Structure	Technical/ Physical	Task Variety	Information/ Feedback	Interpersonal/ Group Processes	Costs	Productivity	Quality	Withdrawal	Attitudes
Sociotechnical Systems (n = 16)	56 (16)[c]	88 (16)	31 (16)	44 (16)	19 (16)	63 (16)	63 (16)	63 (16)	75 (16)	88 (8)	93 (15)	86 (7)	(73) (7)	70 (10)
Job Restructuring (n = 27)	14 (27)	92 (27)	22 (27)	33 (27)	14 (27)	22 (27)	79 (27)	45 (27)	4 (27)	90 (10)	75 (20)	100 (17)	86 (7)	76 (21)
Participative Management (n = 7)		100 (7)		14 (7)	14 (7)					100 (1)	57 (7)	100 (1)	80 (5)	80 (5)
Organization Change (n = 7)	29 (7)	43 (7)	43 (7)	43 (7)	100 (7)	29 (7)	14 (7)	71 (7)	43 (7)	50 (2)	100 (4)	100 (2)	67 (3)	50 (6)

[a] From Srivastva, Salipante, Cummings, Notz, Bigelow, & Waters, 1977.
[b] The percentages represent those studies that reported no negative, mixed, or zero-change findings for the dependent variable in that column.
[c] Numbers in parentheses indicate the base number of studies on which the percentage is based, that is, the denominator.

Each cell in the array gives an assessment of the degree to which the validity threat in that column was controlled by the study in that row.

Matrix Assessment for Quasi Experiments

At this point matrix creation has been completed in a manner consistent with our first contention. Few if any studies have been excluded because of weak methodology, and the reviewer can now analyze the studies in sets. The matrix assessment phase begins by determining the tentative review findings. Consider in our review the criterion variables on the right side of Table 2. Of the studies in a particular category (e.g., job restructuring) that used a given criterion variable, the percentage reporting positive results on that criterion is presented. In general, the average magnitude of the effect and the percentage of null and negative results should also be reported. The percentages on the criterion variables are useful in two ways. First, questions of validity temporarily put aside, the percentages indicate whether a particular treatment had a positive effect on a certain criterion. For the work redesign field experiments, the indication is of a positive effect on each criterion for each treatment category. Second, the criterion percentages may be compared across treatments to estimate their relative efficacy. For instance, a higher percentage of job restructuring studies produced positive withdrawal findings than did the other treatments. With some hazard, these comparisons can be extended to implications concerning the possible effects of particular independent variables. For example, Table 2 indicates that autonomy alone may be sufficient to produce positive attitudinal results because the participative management studies manipulated only autonomy yet produced either about the same or a higher percentage of positive attitudinal results as compared to the treatments that manipulated several independent variables. This approach to analyzing findings does succeed in analyzing the studies as sets, as each row in Table 2 represents one set of studies all investigating the same general treatment. However, the analysis itself is quite crude and does not treat contingencies. It will only suffice when there is broad agreement in findings across a set of studies.

Meta Analysis

When the number of studies is relatively large, a more sophisticated approach to determining review findings is to perform multivariate analysis on the set of studies, using each study as one observation. As another method of dealing with the multiple treatment problem, we utilized regression analysis in such a manner, regressing the nine treatment variables in Table 1 on one of the criterion variables (productivity) across the 46 studies that reported productivity results. For each study, a score of 1 was assigned to each treatment variable actually manipulated and 0 was assigned to all other variables. Scores of $+1$, 0, and -1 were assigned to the criterion, indicating positive, null, or negative changes, respectively. With the exception of one variable, the variables chosen by a stepwise regression procedure were those judged to be important by the alternative analysis described earlier. The variable that was the exception (autonomy) did not enter the equation because it had little variance across the field experiments. Hence this procedure is not without pitfalls. As with any multivariate analysis, the distributions of the independent and dependent variables must not be seriously skewed.

A number of reviews have used multivariate analysis in a more comprehensive fashion. Among others, Smith and Glass (1977) and Kulik, Kulik, and Cohen (1979) have applied this approach, terming it *meta analysis*. These reviewers alleviated the potential problem of lack of variance in the criterion variable by using as the criterion the effect size in each study: the difference in means between the treated and control groups divided by the standard deviation (of the control group or pooled from both groups). For both Smith and Glass and Kulik et al., meta analysis produced a rich set of review findings. Both reviews were able to investigate the effect size produced by differing treatments given particular contextual variables. Similarly, Schwab, Olian-Gottlieb, and Heneman (1979) were able to relate variance across expectancy theory studies in effort–performance correlations to different constructs of the independent and dependent variables. Thus meta analysis appears to be a new and powerful approach to determining review findings, including contingencies. It succeeds in meeting our ideal of treating studies as a set and deriving as much information as possible from the set. Meta analysis will be most appropriate when the number of studies is large (about 400 for Smith and Glass, 75 for Kulik et al.) and when conceptually similar criteria have been used by the various studies.

Having generated the review findings, the next step for the reviewer is to assess the findings' validity. For the set of quasi-experiments categorized as sociotechnical in our review, Table 3 shows the validity threat array (the type of slice indicated earlier in Figure 1) for the set of quasi experiments categorized as sociotechnical. Each cell in the array gives an assessment of the degree to which the validity threat in that column was controlled by the study in that row. This matrix permits an evaluation of the heterogeneity of validity threats across the entire set, in keeping with our second contentions. As argued earlier, if one or more of the threats to internal validity were controlled by only a small fraction of the studies in the set, the threat(s) would provide a highly plausible alternative explanation to the findings of the set. On the other hand, if the internal validity threats were heterogeneously distributed across the

Table 3. Assessment of Validity Threats[A]

Reference	Time Lapse (months)	Research Design	THREATS TO INTERNAL VALIDITY								THREATS TO EXTERNAL VALIDITY			Representative Variable
			History	Instability	Testing	Instrumentation	Statistical Regression	Selection	Mortality	Selection–Interaction	Testing/Treatment	Selection/Treatment	Experimental Treatment Arrangements	
Bregard et al.	6	000X000	-	?		?	?	+	?	+			?	Costs
Cummings (a)	12	$\frac{X0}{0}$	+	+		+		-	-	-		-	?	Productivity
Cummings (b)	18	$\frac{0X0}{0\ 0}$	+	+	+	+		-	?	-	-	?	?	Quality
Emery et al.	3	$\frac{000X_000X_000}{000X_000X_000}$	+	?	+	+	+	+	?	+		-	?	Productivity
Englestad	24	0X000	-	?		?	?	+	?	+		?	?	Quality
Gorman and Molloy	4	0X0	-	?	-	-		+	?	+		?	?	Productivity
Prestat	24	0X0	-	?	-	-	?	+	?	+		?	?	Productivity
Rice (a)	3	000X000	-	?		?	+	+	?	+		-	?	Productivity
Rice (b)	11	$\frac{X000}{000}$	+	?		+		-	-	-		-	?	Productivity
Trist et al. (a)	?	$\frac{X0}{0}$	+	?		+		-	-	-		-	?	Productivity
Trist et al. (b)	20	$\frac{X000}{000}$	+	?		+		-	-	-		-	?	Productivity

Code: Blank, threat not relevant; +, threat controlled; -, threat not controlled; ?, threat questionable.
[A] Adapted from Cummings, Molloy, and Glen (1977).

studies, the validity of the set of studies would be high, even though no single study controlled all validity threats. That is, the most parsimonious explanation would be to attribute the results to the treatment (common to all studies in the set) rather than to different threats in different studies.[3]

Table 3 shows several threats to internal validity common to almost all the studies in the set. The cell values showing a strong threat to validity are coded " − " and "?", indicating, respectively, that the threat was not controlled or that information on the threat was not available in the study. A " + " indicates that the threat was controlled, and a blank indicates that the threat did not arise because of the study's design. Table 3 shows that the likely alternative explanations of the results were instability and mortality. Treating these studies as a set when estimating validity reduced the plausibility of the other validity threats explaining the results. (Note that the same approach can be followed to assess the threats to external validity on the right side of Table 3.)

In this case, the value of matrix assessment (i.e., of applying our second contention regarding heterogeneity of threats) was to reveal that despite the overwhelmingly positive impacts of sociotechnical innovations on the outcome variables (see the sociotechnical studies row in Table 2), two strong threats existed to the validity of this finding. Identifying the particular threats is useful to readers, who may draw their own conclusion as to whether the impacts are more plausibly attributed to the threats or to the treatment. Further, identifying the threats is valuable as a guide to secondary analysis of existing studies (e.g., analysis of instability and mortality in specific studies) and to the design of future studies.

This validity assessment process may be usefully supplemented by meta analysis. For example, Smith and Glass (1977) and Kulik et al. (1979) included a few design variables in their analyses of findings. We suggest that the reviewer initially perform a separate meta analysis of the relationship of all measured internal validity threats (i.e., the entire validity threat array) to the criterion of effect size. In a manner similar to the determination of review findings, such an analysis would indicate the extent to which particular validity threats explain the results. This must only be a supplement to the main analysis of the validity threat matrix because a threat running through almost all the studies will not have sufficient variance to be identified by this analysis. On the other hand, meta analysis of validity threats is more conservative than the main analysis above because it can identify a combination of threats that explain the review findings.

If an overall meta analysis of validity threats did indicate particular threats to be plausible explanations of studies' effects, the reviewer could then determine if these threats removed or substantially modified the observed effect of a particular treatment. It is possible that the validity threats acted against the hypothesized relationship rather than for it; a simultaneous analysis of treatment variables and validity threats would shed light on this issue. For example, Rosenthal (1976) performed a meta analysis indicating that the effects of experimenter expectancy (the treatment variable) were greater in studies having more carefully controlled designs. Subject to the caveats attending any cross-sectional, multivariate analysis, meta analysis seems to have strong potential, as yet largely ignored, for analyzing the validity of review findings.

The key point is that analysis of the validity threat array, through meta analysis and the visual matrix analysis described earlier, enables a reviewer to assess the validity of the studies as a set, rather than simply relying upon the adequacy of the validity of individual studies. By analyzing the distribution of validity threats, the reviewer can better assess a review finding's validity and also identify which threats should be attended to in future research.

Reviewing Correlation Studies

Because studies with correlational designs suffer inherently from several threats to internal validity (history, maturation, selection, and mortality) and because each might occur prior to observations of the units being compared, any relationship observed between variables (e.g., X and Y) across the units will be subject to alternative explanation by innumerable third variables. On the other hand, correlational studies on a given topic typically outnumber (quasi-) experimental studies (in our review, by a ratio of nine to one), thereby offering a potentially rich source of information to the reviewer. In particular, knowledge can be gained on whether a specific relationship holds up across a number of different settings and populations (i.e., external validity) and even across different measures of the same construct (i.e., construct validity). Even a single correlational study can give important insight into contextual or population contingencies through explicit tests for interaction effects. Because of their frequency, correlational studies may also contribute to a review by permitting examination of a larger number of independent variables than would be possible with experimental studies alone. Further, multivariate analyses may attempt to establish the independent contributions made by several variables, information not commonly available from field experiments.

Reviewers should play on these strengths when reviewing correlational studies. In particular, a reviewer may use correlational studies in three ways: (1) to investigate external validity and contingencies by analyzing similarities and differences in findings across studies performed in a wide range of contexts; (2) to investigate construct validity by examining the findings resulting from use of differing measures thought to represent one underlying construct; and (3) to eliminate certain third variables as plausible threats to internal validity. The choice of review procedures depends on which of these uses the reviewer wishes to emphasize. In keeping with our focus on issues of validity, especially internal validity, we will discuss here procedures for the third and most difficult use.

Despite the internal validity flaws inherent in their design, the reviewer will usually find a number of correlational studies that reduce the plausibility of particular validity threats. The reviewer should determine for each study in a findings group which potential third variables (i.e., threats) have been controlled. The third variables may be controlled through a study's sampling procedure (or, similarly, through showing no important differences in population characteristics across the units of observation) or through explicit inclusion of third variables in a multivariate analysis. Once the reviewer has determined which third variables have been controlled, these variables can be arrayed by studies and by the threats to which they are relevant. The information may then be formed into a validity threat array and analyzed using the procedures covered in the preceding section.

Often it will not be necessary for the reviewer to analyze and array validity information for all the correlational studies in one findings group. Consider a case where the reviewer has located and analyzed a set of (quasi-) experimental studies bearing on the finding in question and analysis reveals one or more validity threats running through this set. Here the reviewer may limit the validity analysis of correlational studies to those studies that have investigated variables related to the threats identified in the analysis of experimental studies. The validity information from these particular correlational studies can be added to the validity threat array. The reviewer can then make an overall assessment of which threats have been adequately ruled out in the entire set of experimental and correlational studies and which specific variables have been ruled out in the remaining threats.[4] Disconfirming findings from particular correlational studies (i.e., that X and Y are not related when Z is controlled) will increase the reviewer's confidence that a particular threat, which was found to run through many of the experimental studies (and with which Z is associated), was indeed an adequate explanation of the findings.

A similar approach for using correlational studies to supplement the assessment of validity threats may be illustrated by our review. Analysis of quasi experiments studying the effect of participative management innovations on job attitudes revealed mortality as a significant threat to the set of studies. Our associated review of correlational studies shed some light on this threat because it found that withdrawal behavior (turnover and absenteeism) was negatively related to a number of job attitudes. This finding increased the plausibility of mortality as an alternative explanation for the quasi-experimental effects of participative management. Similarly, where selection is revealed to be a prominent threat to a set of quasi experiments, correlational studies that test for individual differences in the effect of the relationship can be particularly helpful in identifying which selection factors are plausible alternative explanations.

The preceding discussion makes clear that our contention concerning heterogeneity in the validity threat array can be usefully applied to correlational studies, especially when the reviewer is able to draw on both (quasi-) experimental and correlational studies.

Conflicting Results and Secondary Analysis

Most of the foregoing discussion has concerned methods for increasing confidence in findings that converge. Many of the most important reviews, however, have analyzed findings that conflict across studies, leading the reviewers to develop new hypotheses. For example, Hulin and Blood's (1968) review of job enrichment studies disclosed an urban–rural difference in employees' response to job enrichment. Their hypothesis that the underlying contingency variable was alienation to middle class norms stimulated further research into the operative contingencies. Most reviews encountering conflicting findings, however, handle the variations in a totally inadequate manner. Jackson (1980) found that only 7 of 36 reviews analyzed study characteristics for possible relations to variations in results.

Results that conflict across studies can be the result of one or more of the following: (1) chance variation (i.e., statistical conclusion validity); (2) weak internal validity in at least some of the studies; (3) differences across studies in operationalizing the variables (construct validity); (4) the operation of important contingency variables (external validity). These causes summarize the major categories of validity threats. The analysis of conflicting results is thus an analysis of validity. That is, validity issues become of primary importance in reviews that find conflicting findings.

Regarding chance variation, Mosteller and Bush's (1954) procedure for finding the combined z score for a set of studies also provides a means of estimating the probability that conflicting results could have occurred by chance alone. Their formula indicates that the z score (Z_s) of a set of n studies and the collective z scores of the individual studies are related as follows:

$$Z_s = \frac{Z_i}{n}$$

Using a standard normal table, the probability of random occurrence of a set of studies can be determined from Z_s. However, this procedure pools data from divergent studies and ignores the other possible causes of conflicting findings. Light and Smith (1977) have argued convincingly that one must determine that studies do not differ in important ways before pooling their data. Thus, use of the formula for the combined z score should only be the final step in investigating conflicting findings.

The differences across studies that Light and Smith address primarily concern causes (1) and (2) above. Their approach to resolving contradictory findings relies on secondary analysis of data from the divergent studies. The unit of analysis, which must be common to all the studies, is termed a "cluster" and the overall approach "cluster analysis." A cluster could thus be an individual, a work unit, or an entire organization. The reviewer must search for five types of differences across the clusters: (1) in variable means; (2) in variable variances; (3) in the relationship between a dependent variable and a covariate (an independent variable other than the focal independent variable); (4) in subject-by-treatment interactions; and (5) in contextual effects. Finding a difference of any one of these types will give the reviewer insight into the causes of the conflicting findings. For example, a difference in subject-by-treatment interactions would indicate differences in what might have otherwise been considered similar treatments. If no important difference of the above types is found across clusters, probably a rare occurrence, the data from the clusters can be combined into one large sample and analyzed, or the Mosteller and Bush equation can be applied. If some differences are found across the clusters, appropriate adjustments can be made before the data are combined.

Because cluster analysis does not explicitly investigate internal validity threats as a possible source of conflicting findings, a procedure that compares the internal validities of sets of conflicting studies can be a useful precursor to cluster analysis. The reviewer should first divide the conflicting studies into pro and con sets, then compare the distribution of threats in the validity threat arrays (as described in the preceding sections) for the two sets of studies. The comparison may reveal severe validity threats to one or both sets. A good example is Bradley and Bradley's (1978) comprehensive review of studies on the effects of desegregation on achievement of black students. As noted earlier in this article, previous reviews of this literature had lead to divergent conclusions. Bradley and Bradley presented an excellent analysis of the validity threats to 29 individual studies. Their basic findings were that many of the studies not dismissed as having totally inadequate designs found a positive effect (16 studies) but that each suffered from some methodological deficiencies. Five studies found disconfirming evidence. Restricting the studies to those with the best designs revealed that five reported a positive effect and one found no effect. The reviewers concluded that "the data collected since 1959 regarding school desegregation has been inconsistent and inadequate" (p. 688).

One must question whether the research on desegregation will ever be substantially improved over its current level. Given the number of studies and the reasonable strength of many of them, it would have been possible to reach more specific conclusions by considering the validity of the sets of studies. Applying the procedure recommended for quasi experiments, the confirming and disconfirming studies could have been usefully grouped into two sets to permit analysis of the distribution of validity threats to each set. A limited analysis of this type, using Bradley and Bradley's methodological information, shows that the distribution of threats to the set of confirming studies is largely heterogeneous, with only the selection threat running through most of the studies (14 of 16). However, selection, history, and mortality are all threats to the smaller set of disconfirming studies. This approach leads to a more definitive review conclusion and clarifies for future researchers the major methodological threat to be overcome. It also indicates that differences in populations should be the major focus of a cluster analysis of these studies. Such an analysis is clearly justified by the importance of the desegregation issue and the methodological quality of many of the studies.

Meta analysis may also be applied to conflicting results. However, to alleviate the problem of pooling data from studies that differ in important ways (Light and Smith, 1977), adequate specification must be made of the treatment variables and especially of the contextual variables. Most meta analyses to date have done so. The advantage of using meta analysis for analyzing conflicting results is that one can test for interactions between the treatment(s), contextual variables, and validity threats as explanations for differences in the direction and magnitude of effects. Meta analysis is therefore preferable to cluster analysis in including internal validity threats in the analysis. It is potentially weaker in losing information by using the study, rather than the cluster, as the unit of analysis.

Another approach to conflicting results is the work of Schmidt, Hunter, and their associates. In a manner similar to Light and Smith (1977), they call for corrections to individual studies' findings before the findings are aggregated. In particular, their method applies corrections for sample size, variable reliability, and restriction in variable range. This approach has yielded important results concerning selection test validities, showing that apparently conflicting results across studies can be attributed to statistical artifacts. The method is quite powerful in correcting for the instability and instrumentation threats to internal validity, but it has not, to date, been applied to other validity threats. Only if the impact of other validity threats on a study's findings could be statistically estimated could the Hunter and Schmidt approach be considered a general solution to the problems of cumulating studies and handling threats to validity. Ideally, a reviewer would want to correct for all plausible and important study differences before cumulating their findings. Because this typically cannot be done, reviewers should apply the Hunter and Schmidt corrections to the findings of individual studies before deriving review findings, then use the techniques outlined above to treat the other plausible validity threats.

The discovery of conflicting results has important implications for the reviewer. One is that issues of validity will become paramount in the review and extra effort will be required. Although the procedures described in earlier sections of this paper require only marginal effort (primarily in the analytical techniques used for matrix assessment) over that found in most current reviews, these procedures will only be the first steps in the case of conflicting results. Typically, secondary analysis of the existing studies, such as cluster analysis, will be required to discover the source of the conflict. More than balancing the extra effort will be the prospect for the reviewer to make a major contribution by explaining anomalous results (Kuhn, 1970), possibly developing new theory. However, much greater awareness among reviewers of the importance of validity assessment procedures is needed to make this prospect a reality.

DISCUSSION

The various approaches described in the preceding sections illustrate how our two contentions can be operationalized. Clearly, no rigid set of procedures will be suitable to all reviews. However, we believe that any procedures that reviewers adopt should be compatible with both our contentions.

These contentions stem from our view that past reviews have overly emphasized summarizing individual studies and reporting the degree of agreement among them. Reviewers should strive to derive richer review findings by applying better analytical techniques. They should also attend to the validity of their findings. In the past, issues of validity have been seriously addressed only by a few reviews that investigated conflicting findings. However, the discovery of serious threats to validity in the review of sociotechnical studies discussed earlier illustrates the importance of assessing validity even when findings are in strong agreement.

With regard to determining findings, reviews could be strengthened by giving more attention to the search for contingencies and by utilizing analytical procedures, such as meta and cluster analysis, more powerful than merely counting the number of findings. In comparison with the quite powerful analytical techniques that are commonly employed in individual studies, the techniques used by most reviews have been rudimentary. We may expect to see continuing progress in reviews in the use of analytical procedures that treat the individual study, or cluster within a study, as the unit of analysis.

Even the most methodologically advanced reviews seem to have been remiss in evaluating the validity of review findings. Only a very few have treated validity threats across an entire set of studies, and these have only measured a few validity threats and have not analyzed and discussed their impact on the review findings. Such analysis is clearly within the methodological capabilities of reviews. It seems clear that validity assessment of review findings could be greatly improved in future reviews, as through the use of the two procedures presented in this article: visual evaluation of the validity threat matrix and application of meta analysis with the Hunter and Schmidt corrections. Although reviewers have made important progress in "counting" studies (i.e., cumulating findings), they must pay greatly increased attention to the danger pointed out by Light and Smith of cumulating findings from dissimilar studies. Even the Hunter and Schmidt corrections only control two sources of dissimilarity. Creation and assessment of the validity threat matrix, which take advantage of dissimilarity in threats to validity, appear to be the most feasible way of handling the problem.

General Applicability of Review Procedures

This article has attempted to develop the contention that reviewers should use procedures that permit analysis of entire sets of studies for deriving findings and, especially, for assessing their validity. To support this view, we have found it useful to enumerate the basic tasks required for such analysis (our general model) and to categorize the two basic tasks as matrix creation (essentially, data collection) and matrix assessment (data analysis). The procedures presented to illustrate how our model and contention could be applied were drawn from our own and several other reviews, with the emphasis on reviews in which internal validity issues were central. A question that remains is whether the model and contentions are applicable to a wider range of reviews.

In general, we believe that reviewers will be able to follow the model we have outlined, although there will be varying emphasis on the two components of matrix creation and matrix assessment and on the types of validity assessed. In particular, a review's objectives in terms of formulation of concepts versus testing and of theory versus practice will strongly influence the relative importance of the differing threats to validity, the types of studies selected for review, and the cost/benefit ratio of obtaining data on the relevant threats to validity from the individual studies.

In order to elaborate these points, it is necessary to examine how the importance of the different types of validity will tend to vary with the reviewer's purpose. Following the modified version of Cook and Campbell (1976) noted earlier, there are four kinds of validity: internal, external, construct validity of causes, and construct validity of effects. The relationships between the different classes of validity are such that studies high on one kind of validity tend to be low on another. And just as the priority ordering of the types of validity varies with the goals of a single study, so will their relative importance vary with the objectives of different reviews.

Consider first the formulation versus testing dimension of review goals. Much of our prior discussion has been oriented toward the testing of hypotheses. However, if the review is considering a topic that is new, fragmented, and only poorly conceptualized, the reviewer will probably wish to emphasize the formulating function of the review: raising hypotheses and tentative constructs rather than testing or screening them. Such a review might therefore look at case studies and perhaps correlational studies. Given this kind of research literature and concern with the development of practical or theoretical constructs, attention should be focused on the threats to the construct validity of the review findings. Each of the review findings should be evaluated against the eight threats to construct validity identified by Cook and Campbell (1976), with the reviewer's confidence in any given finding again being determined by the distribution of threats within the set of studies.

The theoretical versus practical dimension of review goals and the differing types of literature will likely influence both the effort required to assess internal validity and the priority ordering of the other types of validity. A theoretically oriented review will generally focus on true experimental studies, usually the product of controlled, laboratory situations wherein the threats to internal validity have been ruled out through randomization. (Randomization distributes the threats to internal validity across comparison groups within an experiment such that a single study is the logical equivalent of a set of quasi-experiments within which the threats to internal validity are heterogeneously distributed across studies.) Even with true experiments, of course, the reviewer must be alert to the possible existence of any factor common to a large proportion of the studies that could function as an alternative explanation of the findings. Thus Chapanis and Chapanis (1964) criticized dissonance research because many of the studies they reviewed, although true experiments, suffered from the same flaw: mortality or a variation thereof. More generally, however, reviewers of experiments will find that there are few, if any, threats to internal validity, so that the validity dimension of the review matrix will contain primarily threats to construct and external validity. Within these latter types of validity, theoretical reviews will generally be most concerned with threats to construct validity of causes. For example, in the area of organizational behavior, Goodman and Friedman's (1971) review of the research on Adams' (1963) theory of inequity was primarily, though not exclusively, concerned with whether the manipulated variable adequately represented inequity or whether it had been confounded with devalued self-esteem, increased job insecurity, etc. These are clearly issues of construct validity of causes; for example, which of these alternative meanings were most approximate to the empirical operations (experimental induction)? The critical question was not whether the several studies in the review had demonstrated a causal relationship between X, as manipulated, and Y, as measured, but rather with the appropriate labeling of those variables. As observed by Cook and Campbell (1976), it will never be sufficient for those persons whose focus is on theoretical issues to merely show that something causes something (e.g., to merely demonstrate internal validity).

In opposition to the theoretical review, the reviewer who is concerned with applied questions is very unlikely to have research literature of the type that will permit issues of internal validity to be easily dismissed. Because of the importance of external validity, applied research is usually field research; and the intransigencies of field settings are such that randomization and therefore true experimentation are less likely. The first task of a reviewer with an applied orientation will therefore be an intense examination of all threats to internal validity such as was used in our quasi-experimental review. Moreover, because selection and regression are such ubiquitous problems in quasi-experimental studies, the analytical techniques recommended by Kenny (1975) for more accurately estimating the effects of these biases would be a valuable addition to this process. In this sense, Kenny's work is a valuable elaboration of the taxonomy of threats originally developed by Campbell (1957) and could be profitably employed by reviewers of applied research.

Making the Most of the Data

The preceding discussion has focused on the interaction between review purpose and type of literature in order to illustrate some of the effects of that interaction on the general review model and how it is operationalized. In doing so, it might appear that we have been advocating a rigid and narrow relationship between review purpose and the relevant type of literature (e.g., laboratory studies for theoretical reviews and field studies for applied reviews). In fact, we would encourage the opposite. Because studies high on one kind of validity tend to be low on another, a reviewer with several different types of studies will obviously be able to make much stronger evaluations of the overall validity of his findings than would be possible from only a single type of study. For example, a more recent review of the equity literature by Carrell and Dittrich (1978) included both laboratory and field studies. Unfortunately, the review was literary in nature and much of the potential benefit of a combined laboratory–field research review was not realized. Because the majority of the research had been conducted in the laboratory, the authors concluded their review by simply stating that there was a great need for additional field research. Although such a general conclusion was probably accurate, a systematic effort at matrix evaluation probably would have indicated the *specific* threats to external and construct validity that were important because of the way in which they were distributed across the combined set of laboratory and field studies. Review conclusions that were based on such information would help to more sharply focus the efforts of future researchers, both laboratory and field, on those specific issues of validity that were the most important to the further development of equity theory. The point, as with Bradley and Bradley's (1978) review critiqued earlier, is that the reviewer should strive to use methods that will extract the most information possible from the studies at hand and provide the best guide to future research.

One qualification must be added to this point. The reviewer, in deriving findings and assessing their validity, is inevitably bound by the studies available. The reviewer, and consumers of reviews, must recall that another level of threats exist to entire sets of studies. For example, there will often be a reporting bias in terms of the types of studies that are published (Waters, Salipante, and Notz, 1978), with studies having nonsignificant results most likely to be underreported.[5] Similarly, there is often bias in the choice of results that are reported within a single study, and their level of significance may be inflated by data massaging.

Such threats notwithstanding, reviewers must seek to make the most of the studies at hand. Elaborate description of individual studies' findings and validity are not an adequate substitute for integration and analysis, no matter what the review goal is. Literature reviews provide one of the principle means by which sets of findings can be integrated and evaluated and are one of the few ways by which social scientists can keep informed of the enormous literature beyond the boundaries of their own specialty. We feel that widespread adoption of formal review methods (in particular, the more powerful analytical methods for determining review findings and assessing their validity) would greatly contribute to the development of the social sciences, and we anticipate further discussion of review methods in the literature.

ACKNOWLEDGMENTS

Requests for reprints should be sent to any of the authors. We would like to thank Dave Brown, Paul Buchanan, Tom Cook, Larry Cummings, Greg and Karen Gaertner, Les Roos, and Barry Staw for their helpful comments on various drafts of this paper.

REFERENCE NOTES

1.   Hunter, J. E. Cumulating results across studies: Correction for sampling error, a proposed moratorium on the significance test, and a critique of current multivariate reporting practice. Paper based on an invited address at the *American Psychological Association,* September 1979.

2.   Schmidt, F. L. The research tasks of the 1980's: Integrating research findings across studies to produce cumulative knowledge. Paper based on an invited address at the *American Psychological Association,* September, 1980.

NOTES

1.   Cook and Campbell distinguished another kind of validity, statistical conclusion validity. We have chosen to treat this source of error as one of the threats to internal validity in the same manner as did Campbell (1969) in an earlier presentation.

2.   The correspondence between a study's design and the degree to which it controlled a particular validity threat was not one-to-one, a fact that must be recalled when attempting to design the most valid field experiment possible in a particular situation. Given the limited information available on most of the studies, however, utilizing the designs in the above manner is appropriate for purposes of a review.

3.   Jackson (1980) notes that congruent findings can result from different validity threats in different studies producing about the same net bias, but also notes that this is not particularly likely.

4.   Because no correlational study can control all possible third variables, correlational studies can never entirely rule out a history, maturation, selection, or mortality threat. However, a group of correlational studies may well control the most plausible third variables constituting a particular threat.

5.   The magnitude of this particular threat, which Rosenthal has called the "file drawer problem," can usually be estimated by using Rosenthal's (1978, 1979) procedures.

REFERENCES

Adams, J. S. Toward an understanding of inequity. *Journal of Abnormal and Social Psychology*, 1963, *67*, 422–436.

Alderfer, Clayton P. A critique of Salancik and Pfeffer's examination of need satisfaction theories. *Administrative Science Quarterly*, 1977, *22*, 658–669.

Armor, D. The evidence of busing. *Public Interest*, 1972, *28*, 90–126.

Bradley, Laurence A., & Bradley, Gifford W. The academic achievement of Black students in desegregated schools: A critical review. In Howard E. Freeman (Ed.), *Policy Studies Review Annual* (Vol. II). Beverly Hills: Sage Publications, 1978.

Campbell, D. T. Factors relevant to the validity of experiments in social settings. *Psychological Bulletin*, 1957, *54*, 297–312.

Campbell, Donald T. Reforms as experiments. *American Psychologist*, 1969, *24*, 409–429.

Campbell, Donald T., & Stanley, Julian C. Experimental and Quasi-Experimental Designs for Research. Chicago: Rand McNally & Co., 1966.

Carrell, Michael R., & Dittrich, John E. Equity theory: The recent literature, methodological considerations, and new directions. *The Academy of Management Review*, 1978, *35*, 202–210.

Chapanis, N. P., & Chapanis, A. Cognitive dissonance: Five years later. *Psychological Bulletin*, 1964, *61*, 1–22.

Cook, Thomas D. The potential and limitations of secondary evaluations. In M. W. Apple, M. J. Subkoviak, & H. S. Lufler, Jr. (Eds.), Educational Evaluation: Analysis and Responsibility. Berkeley, California: McCutchan, 1974.

Cook, T. D., & Campbell, D. T. The design and conduct of quasi-experiments and true experiments in field settings. In M. C. Dunnette (Ed.), Handbook of Industrial and Organizational Psychology. Chicago: Rand McNally, 1976.

Cook, Thomas D., & Gruder, Charles. Metaevaluation research. *Evaluation Quarterly*, 1978, *2*, 5–51.

Cummings, T. G., Molloy, E., & Glen, R. A methodological critique of 58 selected work experiments. *Human Relations*, 1977, *30*, 675–708.

Glass, G. V. Primary, secondary, and meta-analysis of research. Paper presented at the meeting of the American Educational Research Association, San Francisco, 1976.

Goodman, P. S., & Friedman, A. Adam's theory of inequity. *Administrative Science Quarterly*, 1971, *16*, 271–288.

House, R. J., & Wigdor, L. A. Herzberg's dual factor theory of job satisfaction and motivation: A review of the evidence and a criticism. *Personnel Psychology*, 1967, *20*(4): 369–389.

Hulin, C. L., & Blood, M. R. Job enlargement, individual differences and worker responses. *Psychological Bulletin*, 1968, *69*, 41–55.

Hunter, J. E., & Schmidt, F. L. Differential and single group validity of employment tests by race: A critical analysis of three recent studies. *Journal of Applied Psychology*, 1978, *63*, 1–11.

Jackson, G. B. Methods for integrative reviews. *Review of Educational Research*, 1980, *50*, 438–460.

Kenny, D. A. A quasi-experimental approach to assessing treatment effects in the nonequivalent control group design. *Psychological Bulletin*, 1975, *85*, 345–362.

King, N. Clarification and evaluation of the two-factor theory of job satisfaction. *Psychological Bulletin*, 1970, *74*(1): 18–31.

Kuhn, Thomas S. The Structure of Scientific Revolutions, 2nd edition, Chicago: University of Chicago Press, 1970.

Kulik, James A., Kulik, Chen-Lin C., & Cohen, Peter A. A meta-analysis of outcome studies of Keller's personalized system of instruction. *American Psychologist*, 1979, *34*, 307–318.

Light, R. J. Capitalizing on variation: How conflicting research findings can be helpful for policy. *Educational Researcher*, 1979, *8*(9): 7–14.

Light, R. J., & Smith, P. V. Accumulating evidence: Procedures for resolving contradictions among different research studies. In M. Guttentag and S. Saar (Eds.), Evaluation Studies: Review Annual (Vol. II). Beverly Hills: Sage Publications, 1977.

Mosteller, F., & Bush, R. R. Selected quantitative techniques. In G. Lindzey (Ed.), Handbook of Social Psychology (Vol. I). Cambridge, Mass.: Addison-Wesley, 1954.

Pettigrew, T., Useem, E., Normand, C., & Smith, M. Busing: A review of 'the evidence.' *Public Interest*, 1973, *30*, 88–118.

Rosenthal, Robert. Interpersonal expectations. In Robert Rosenthal & Ross L. Rosnow (Eds.), Artifact in Behavioral Research. New York: Academic Press, 1969.

Rosenthal, Robert. Experimenter Effects in Behavioral Research (enlarged ed.). New York: Irvington, 1976.

Rosenthal, Robert. Combining results of independent studies. *Psychological Bulletin*, 1978, *85*, 185–193.

Rosenthal, Robert. The "file drawer problem" and tolerance for null results. *Psychological Bulletin*, 1979, *86*, 638–641.

Salancik, Gerald R., & Pfeffer, Jeffrey. An examination of need-satisfaction models of job attitudes. *Administrative Science Quarterly*, 1977, *22*, 427–456.

Schmidt, F. L., Hunter, J. E., Pearlman, K., & Shane, G. S. Further tests of the Schmidt-Hunter Bayesian Validity generalization procedure. *Personnel Psychology*, 1979, *32*, 257–281.

Schwab, D. P., Olian-Gottlieb, J. D., & Heneman, H. G., III. Between subjects expectancy theory research: A statistical review of studies predicting effort and performance. *Psychological Bulletin*, 1979, *86*, 139–147.

Smith, M. L., & Glass, G. V. Meta-analysis of psychotherapy outcome studies. *American Psychologist*, 1977, *32*, 752–760.

Srivastva, S., Salipante, P., Cummings, T., Notz, W., Bigelow, J., & Waters, J. Job satisfaction and productivity: An evaluation of policy-related research. Kent, Ohio: Kent State University Press, 1977.

Waters, J. A., Salipante, P. F., Jr., & Notz, W. W. The experimenting organization: Using the results of behavioral science research. *Academy of Management Review*, 1978, *3*, 483–492.

Whitsett, D. A., & Winslow, E. K. An analysis of studies critical of the motivator-hygiene theory. *Personnel Psychology*, 1967, *20*, 391–415.

Yin, R. K., & Heald, K. A. Using the case survey method to analyze policy studies. *Administrative Science Quarterly*, September, 1975, 371–381.

Research in Organizational Behavior

An Annual Series of Analytical Essays and Critical Reviews

Edited by **Barry M. Staw**
School of Business Administration, University of California, Berkeley
and **L.L. Cummings**
J.L. Kellogg Graduate School of Management, Northwestern University

REVIEWS: . . . "A new approach for the area of organizational behavior . . . The nine intermediate length essays presented here provide a valuable new facet . . . quality is variable — in this case from good to excellent . . . The text is highly recommended for acquisition but with the caveat that series acquisition will be required to maximize utility . . . " —*Choice*

" . . . this collection is a well-written, scholarly contribution to other texts because of its integration of new theoretical considerations and critical literature review. It is very well organized and may be consulted frequently by those of us teaching management and administration in schools of social work." —*Administration in Social Work*

Volume 1, 1979, 478 pp.
ISBN 0-89232-045-1

Edited by **Barry M. Staw,** *Graduate School of Management, Northwestern University*

Volume 2, 1980, 368 pp.
ISBN 0-89232-099-0

Edited by **Barry M. Staw,** *Graduate School of Management, Northwestern University and* **L.L. Cummings,** *Graduate School of Business, University of Wisconsin*

Volume 3, 1981, 356 pp.
ISBN 0-89232-151-2

Edited by **L.L. Cummings,** *Graduate School of Business, University of Wisconsin and* **Barry M. Staw,** *School of Business Administration, University of California, Berkeley*

Volume 5, Winter 1983, Ca. 350 pp.
ISBN 0-89232-271-3

 **JAI PRESS INC., 36 Sherwood Place, P.O. Box 1678**
Greenwich, Connecticut 06836
Telephone: 203-661-7602   Cable Address: JAIPUBL

Administrative Science Quarterly

Articles for December 1981 issue:

"Threat-Rigidity Effects in Organizational Behavior:
A Multilevel Analysis"
Barry M. Staw, Lance E. Sandelands, and Jane E. Dutton

"Perceptions of Organizational Effectiveness over
Organizational Life Cycles"
Kim S. Cameron and David A. Whetten

"Interpersonal Attraction and Organizational Outcomes:
A Field Examination"
Jerry Ross and Kenneth R. Ferris

Each issue also contains review essays based on new books in organizational behavior, and news and notes about the field.

Subscription Rates:

	1 year	2 years	3 years
Individuals	20.00	37.50	56.00
Institutions	40.00	75.00	112.00
Students	18.50	37.50	56.00

Back issues from Vol. 1, No. 1 (June 1956) through Vol. 13, No. 3 (December 1968) are available at $6.00 per copy prepaid. All later issues are available at $8.00 per copy prepaid. (Vol. 22, No. 3 (September 1977) is no longer available.)

For more information, write *Administrative Science Quarterly*, Malott Hall, Cornell University, Ithaca, NY 14853.

Administrative Science Quarterly

*Dedicated to advancing the understanding of
administration through empirical investigation
and theoretical analysis.*

Research in Corporate Social Performance and Policy

Edited by **Lee E. Preston**

Center for Business and Public Policy, University of Maryland, College Park

Volume 1, 1978, 291 pp.
ISBN 0-89232-069-9

Volume 2, 1980, 352 pp.
ISBN 0-89232-133-4

Volume 3, 1981, 250 pp.
ISBN 0-89232-184-9